Rethinking Modern European Intellectual History

Rethinking

Modern European

Intellectual History

Edited by

DARRIN M. McMAHON AND SAMUEL MOYN

OXFORD
UNIVERSITY PRESS

OXFORD
UNIVERSITY PRESS

Oxford University Press is a department of the University of Oxford.
It furthers the University's objective of excellence in research,
scholarship, and education by publishing worldwide.

Oxford   New York
Auckland   Cape Town   Dar es Salaam   Hong Kong   Karachi
Kuala Lumpur   Madrid   Melbourne   Mexico City   Nairobi
New Delhi   Shanghai   Taipei   Toronto

With offices in
Argentina   Austria   Brazil   Chile   Czech Republic   France   Greece
Guatemala   Hungary   Italy   Japan   Poland   Portugal   Singapore
South Korea   Switzerland   Thailand   Turkey   Ukraine   Vietnam

Oxford is a registered trade mark of Oxford University Press
in the UK and certain other countries.

Published in the United States of America by
Oxford University Press
198 Madison Avenue, New York, NY 10016

© Oxford University Press 2014

Library of Congress Cataloging-in-Publication Data
Rethinking modern European intellectual history / edited by Darrin M. McMahon
and Samuel Moyn.
pages cm
ISBN 978-0-19-976923-0 (alk. paper)—ISBN 978-0-19-976924-7 (pbk. : alk. paper)
1. Europe—Intellectual life. 2. Learning and scholarship—Europe. 3. Europe—Civilization.
I. McMahon, Darrin M. II. Moyn, Samuel.
D1055.R436   2014
940.2—dc23   2013019914

Contents

Acknowledgments

The editors are grateful to the Radcliffe Institute for Advanced Study for supporting the conference at which initial versions of the chapters of this book were presented. In addition to contributing essays, David Armitage, Peter Gordon, and Judith Surkis selflessly collaborated in our venture to secure the Radcliffe venue; and Allyson Black-Foley and Phyllis Strimling of the Radcliffe staff were perfect hosts at the event itself. At a later stage, readers who will remain nameless—but who deserve to be warmly acknowledged—offered generous and incisive criticism of the book. Gwen Colvin shepherded the book through the press, and Dave Prout made the index. Finally, from the inception of the volume to its completion, Susan Ferber of Oxford University Press provided expert guidance and support.

Contributors

David Armitage is Lloyd C. Blankfein Professor of History at Harvard University. He is author of *The Ideological Origins of the British Empire* (Cambridge University Press, 2000), which won the Longman/*History Today* Book of the Year Award, *The Declaration of Independence: A Global History* (Harvard University Press, 2007), which was chosen as a *TLS* Book of the Year, and *Foundations of Modern International Thought* (Cambridge University Press, 2013). He is coeditor of the Cambridge University Press series *Ideas in Context*.

Warren Breckman is professor of history at the University of Pennsylvania. He is the author of *Marx, the Young Hegelians, and the Origins of Radical Social Theory* (Cambridge University Press, 1999) and *Adventures of the Symbolic: Postmarxism and Radical Democracy* (Columbia University Press, 2013). He is the executive coeditor of *Journal of the History of Ideas* and a founding editorial board member of *Zeitschrift für Ideengeschichte*.

Peter E. Gordon is Amabel B. James Professor of History at Harvard University. He is the author of *Rosenzweig and Heidegger: Between Judaism and German Philosophy* (University of California Press, 2003), which won several awards, and *Continental Divide: Heidegger, Cassirer, Davos* (Harvard University Press, 2010), which received the Jacques Barzun Prize of the American Philosophical Society. He has also coedited several collections, including *The Cambridge Companion to Modern Jewish Philosophy* (Cambridge University Press, 2007) and *Weimar Thought: A Contested Legacy* (Princeton University Press, 2013). His newest book, *Adorno and Existence*, is forthcoming from Harvard University Press.

Shruti Kapila lectures in the Faculty of History at the University of Cambridge and is Fellow and Director of Studies at Corpus Christi College. She is a historian of modern India, and her primary interests and publications lie in intellectual history, political thought, and the history of science. She is author of the forthcoming book *Formations of the Political: Violence, Nonviolence and the Indian Twentieth Century* and editor of *An Intellectual History for India* (Cambridge University Press, 2010) and coeditor of *Political Thought in Action: The Bhagavad Gita and Modern India* (Cambridge University Press, 2013).

Antoine Lilti is directeur d'études at the Ecole des hautes études en sciences sociales and former editor of the journal *Annales*. He has published numerous studies on the social, intellectual, and cultural history of the Enlightenment, including *Le monde des salons: Sociabilité et mondanité à Paris au XVIIIe siècle* (Fayard, 2005).

Suzanne Marchand is professor of history at Louisiana State University. She has published *Down from Olympus: Archaeology and Philhellenism in Germany* (Princeton University Press, 1996) and *German Orientalism in the Age of Empire: Religion, Race and Scholarship* (Cambridge University Press, 2009), which won the American Historical Association's George Mosse Prize.

Tracie Matysik is associate professor of history at the University of Texas at Austin. She is the author of *Reforming the Moral Subject: Ethics and Sexuality in Central Europe, 1890–1930* (Cornell University Press, 2008) and is writing a book on modern Spinozism, pantheism, and materialism in modern Germany.

Darrin M. McMahon is the Ben Weider Professor of History at Florida State University. He is the author of *Enemies of the Enlightenment: The French Counter-Enlightenment and the Making of Modernity* (Oxford University Press, 2001), *Happiness: A History* (Atlantic Monthly Press, 2006), and *Divine Fury: A History of Genius* (Basic Books, 2013).

Samuel Moyn is James Bryce Professor of European Legal History at Columbia University. His publications include *Origins of the Other: Emmanuel Levinas between Revelation and Ethics* (Cornell University Press, 2005) and *The Last Utopia: Human Rights in History* (Harvard University Press, 2010). Most recently he has coedited *Global Intellectual History* (Columbia University Press, 2013). He is also a coeditor of the journal *Modern Intellectual History*.

Jan-Werner Müller is professor of politics at Princeton University, where he directs the Project in the History of Political Thought, University Center for Human Values. His most recent books are *Constitutional Patriotism* (Princeton University Press, 2007) and *Contesting Democracy: Political Ideas in Twentieth-Century Europe* (Yale University Press, 2011).

John Randolph is associate professor of history and Conrad Humanities Scholar at the University of Illinois at Urbana-Champaign. He is the author of *The House in the Garden: The Bakunin Family and the Romance of Russian Idealism* (Cornell University Press, 2007). His current book project, *When I Served the Post as a Coachman*, studies the system of obligations undergirding communication in early modern Russia, and how they affected the empire's political, social, and cultural geography.

Marci Shore is associate professor of history at Yale University. She is the author of *Caviar and Ashes: A Warsaw Generation's Life and Death in Marxism, 1918–1968* (Yale University Press, 2006) and *The Taste of Ashes: The Afterlife of Totalitarianism in Eastern Europe* (Crown, 2013). Currently she is working on a book about phenomenology in East-Central Europe.

Judith Surkis is associate professor of history at Rutgers University. She focuses on modern French cultural and intellectual history; gender, sexuality, and empire; and interdisciplinarity. Her first book was *Sexing the Citizen: Morality and Masculinity in France, 1870–1920* (Cornell University Press, 2006). She is currently writing a book about gender and law in colonial Algeria.

John Tresch is associate professor of history and sociology of science at the University of Pennsylvania. He is author of *The Romantic Machine: Utopian Science and Technology after Napoleon* (University of Chicago Press, 2012), awarded the 2013 Pfizer Prize for outstanding book in history of science. He is currently writing a book on intersections between romanticism and industrialization in antebellum America, focusing on the scientific writing of Edgar Allan Poe.

Rethinking Modern European Intellectual History

Introduction: Interim Intellectual History

Darrin M. McMahon and Samuel Moyn

It is difficult to remember a time when intellectual history figured so centrally in the larger historical enterprise as well as in the humanities as a whole. The field remains only one of a number of competing disciplinary approaches, of course. And lingering accusations of elitism and irrelevance may never subside. Still, in relative terms, intellectual history is currently enjoying a moment of prominence and self-confidence greater than it has known in decades. Yet surprisingly for a field whose practitioners pride themselves on intellectual self-awareness, its star may have risen along with a decline in self-reflection.

Few recent theoretical statements have attempted to "justify" intellectual history, to explain what makes its practice worthwhile and methodologically sound. This situation is ironic. The time of bitter and divisive disputes about the place of intellectual history in the humanities may be a living memory, but it is an improbably distant one. Everyone seems to be getting along these days: intellectual historians with other kinds of historians, and intellectual historians with one another. Yet only a generation ago, the field was faced with marginalization—if not extinction—by powerful external forces, which imposed a kind of exile, prompting a period of intense theoretical self-examination and contention. Now intellectual history is ascendant in the profession, and a kind of mutual admiration, almost to the point of complacency, flourishes where bitter polemics once festered. There is "no king in Israel, and every man [does] that which is right in his own eyes," is the tagline from the book of Judges

(21:25) that Peter Novick once used to describe current historiographical practice.[1] Only now, hopes for a common regime are gone too. Everyone cultivates his or her private garden as if writing history were a largely personal task.

To reflect on this extraordinary reversal and to chart future directions in the field are the purposes of this collection of essays. They appear at an "interim" moment because the field of European intellectual history stands at a critical juncture. Despite recent successes, intellectual historians can claim today no widespread agreement about how to conduct their work, and they often seem to lack the will to argue out the alternatives. The situation is comfortable. Yet the absence of self-reflection and theoretical contest—which were once compulsory, and arguably taken to excess—risks devolving into a celebration of eclecticism under a large and cozy tent.

If eclecticism is a risk, it is also an opportunity, which offers to intellectual historians the prospect of enriching their own field and the broader practice of history through novel openings and exchange. A wider disciplinary world beckons, as does a frequently elusive interdisciplinary (and international) space. Intellectual historians have an important role to play in fostering such spaces, and European intellectual historians, in particular, have an interest in doing so at a moment when the study of "Europe" seems increasingly parochial to many when not connected to the faraway lands Europeans once ruled and where their ideas have long traveled. In this global and globalizing age, at this juncture for the field, it is appropriate to step back from practice to engage in a bout of theoretical reflection. The time is right to take stock of where European intellectual history has been, to assess where it is now, and to reflect on future possibilities.[2]

The Revival of Intellectual History

"A malaise is spreading among intellectual historians," Robert Darnton reported in an oft-cited essay first published in 1980. "Twenty years ago, they saw their discipline as the queen of the historical sciences. Today she seems humbled."[3] Darnton conceded that the dethronement was neither sudden nor complete. Nor was it ever strictly true that intellectual history had ascended to the regal stature he implied. Yet the essay captured well how the prestige enjoyed by intellectual historians for much of the twentieth century had been called into question since the 1960s and steadily eroded over the following two decades.

The main impetus was the spectacular rise of social history, a methodological breakthrough often linked to quantitative approaches that channeled the widespread sentiment that to focus on political and intellectual elites was to overlook the widest swathes of humanity. Social historians charged, frequently with good reason, that intellectual history had lost itself in flights of idealist abstraction, underestimated the importance of material factors in shaping the human past, and ignored the plight of ordinary people. They made every effort, accordingly, to include the excluded in the historical record. Before long the vogue of social history entered its own period of self-examination and "crisis," as some of its most able practitioners began to feel that a relentless focus on quantification slighted the meaningful dimension of even the humblest people's lives. Whereas the French tradition of the *histoire des mentalités* had long sought to reproduce the mental habits of ordinary people, the "new cultural history" that surged in the 1980s aimed to interpret meaning through a novel recourse to anthropological and other theories that understood "culture" as a pervasive semiotic web. The consequences for traditional intellectual history were similar to the previous assault. Just as the social history of the 1970s treated past intellectual formations as largely irrelevant when not stained by their elitism, the new cultural history focused on meaning in a guise that privileged the thick description of the mental worlds of ordinary men and women, tending to push what it regarded as old-fashioned intellectual history to the side.[4]

It may seem surprising that the return to meaning after the crisis of social history did not favor intellectual history, especially since some votaries of the new cultural history, following those of the related movement in literary scholarship known as "new historicism," were ultimately most interested in using the anthropological reconstruction of meaning to cast light on the documents of high culture. Yet just at this moment intellectual historians themselves began to insist on the relevance and centrality of theories that precluded any obvious role for their own discipline in the rise of cultural history. Increasing attention to Western Marxism, poststructuralism, and psychoanalysis suggested that historians of the past had carried out their work based on rather simpleminded understandings of meaning and textuality that now needed to be rethought. It was precisely this newfound complexity that bred arcane and internecine debates tending to marginalize intellectual historians from the discipline of history as a whole.

The displacement of intellectual history from the privileged center of historical inquiry thus coincided with a period of intense self-reflection and critical investigation among intellectual historians themselves. Already in the 1970s intellectual historians were speaking of a "crisis" in their discipline. Largely in response to that self-diagnosed malaise Dominick LaCapra and Steven L. Kaplan organized a major conference at Cornell University in 1980.

The resulting volume, *Modern European Intellectual History: Reappraisals and New Perspectives*, made no claim to comprehensiveness, yet it did serve as a barometer of change. Should intellectual history take a linguistic turn and, if so, in what direction? What were the different ways available to theorize meaning and language? Might the tools and critical perspectives opened up by poststructuralist literary theory offer intellectual historians a new methodology for the reading of texts? Roger Chartier, speaking on behalf of the *Annales* school as its latest scion, suggested that there were ways for intellectual historians to write the social history of culture or a sociocultural history that attended much more to issues of intellectual diffusion, reception, production, and consumption. The volume's contributors broached all these issues and more, providing searching answers still relevant today.[5]

Kaplan and LaCapra's venture brought European intellectual history to a high point of acuity and an unprecedented level of self-reflexive interrogation. At the same time, the enterprise seemed to divorce intellectual historians from other branches of the discipline whose members did not always share the same sense of urgency regarding the need for theoretical articulation and reflection. Indeed, the self-reflexivity of intellectual historians seemed to some practically demobilizing. In a classic review essay, John Toews worried that the attention to the linguistic dimension of thought and the consequent profusion of contending directives for historiographical practice were leading some to throw up their hands in despair: "One begins to wonder," he wrote of the experience of reading theoretically rigorous intellectual history, "if it is possible to avoid the pitfalls of [defective] theory at all without ceasing to 'do' history and restricting oneself to thinking about it."[6]

Though some contributors to this volume continue to feel the imperatives of that moment of self-reflexivity a quarter-century ago, or long to recover some of its lost features, it may have been worth transcending. Brought on by a reaction to crisis and marginalization, the pioneering self-scrutiny of intellectual historians engendered not just internecine dispute but also the field's isolation, as the bar to entry—or even friendly understanding by interested outsiders—became forbidding. To some, the preoccupation with methodological and theoretical self-scrutiny ran the risk of converting intellectual history into historiographical criticism, forgoing a more productive relationship with the larger historical discipline.

Viewed from the vantage point of the present generation, the scholarly horizon looks altogether different. No longer are hostile forces present at the gates, and the field seems far removed from a period of crisis. The so-called cultural turn has been renounced by some of its most influential partisans, and the politics of historiography have proceeded in ways that have helped to free intellectual history of its stigma and even made it popular once again.[7] The appointment of chairs in intellectual history at some of the country's leading universities, the revitalization of older publications like the *Journal of the History of Ideas* or the founding of new journals like *Modern Intellectual History*, along with renewed interest and excitement among students, publishers, and readers all attest to a palpable sense that something has changed. Yet this very success has provided new cause for self-questioning. What unites intellectual historians today? And how can they answer the persisting imperative to work out both a rationale for defining the approaches and methods of the field in relation to those of the larger historical enterprise?

A Range of Proposals

The essays gathered here represent an attempt by a new generation of European intellectual historians to wrestle with these questions. The essays reflect their authors' profound debts to the earlier generations of historians who trained them and who provided crucial methodological orientations. They also attest to a new confidence and to new pathways and departures.

   The opening set of essays looks back at some of the major schools of intellectual history in the twentieth century and seeks to show what endures, and what may be exhausted, from their theoretical and methodological interventions. Darrin McMahon begins by examining the marginalization—and perhaps the return—of the history of ideas, arguing that although the discipline's founding father, Arthur Lovejoy, is more often dismissed than read today, he deserves better than the condescension of posterity and may still serve as a fruitful source for current reflection. Peter Gordon interrogates the zeal with which Quentin Skinner, the paladin who famously slew the dragon of a noncontextual "history of ideas," approached exhaustive contextual explanation. Combined, the two essays suggest a spirit that—while still profoundly historicist—is committed to what would have been denounced as idealism a few short years ago. For McMahon, ideas can share enough unity over time to merit explanation across the *longue durée*. For Gordon, the critical process in which historians are engaged requires them to attend to the context-transcendent as well as the context-bound features of the ideas they study.

   Both McMahon and Gordon's engagement with the writings of Quentin Skinner calls attention to the fact that there is no essay in this volume that deals exclusively with the method of intellectual history associated with the so-called Cambridge School founded by Skinner and colleagues such as J. G. A. Pocock and John Dunn. The exclusion was neither purposeful nor premeditated.

Indeed a number of the contributors to this volume (most notably David Armitage) were trained directly in that tradition, whereas a good number of the essays themselves, beginning with those of McMahon and Gordon and continuing in those of Jan-Werner Müller and Samuel Moyn, are clearly intended as respectful, if at times critical, assessments, as well as invitations to further conversation. If Cambridge, England, is more often invoked here as a subject of reflection and target of criticism than as a germinating source for the intellectual history of tomorrow, the reason may also reflect simple geography: the conference at which these essays were workshopped was held in Cambridge, Massachusetts. The American provenance of the volume and the majority of its contributors along with its temporal focus on modern intellectual history undoubtedly have much to do with its constitution. For reasons that no one has adequately explained, the impact of the Cambridge School has remained largely restricted to early modern studies, reaching modernists in the United States only selectively, while the distinctly American discipline of "intellectual history" has offered its own exciting theoretical proposals, as well as its own indigenous traditions. They receive more attention here than they might elsewhere, but this volume leaves very much open the possibility of further dialogue with the British tradition of the "history of political thought."

Turning to the European continent, Müller and Antoine Lilti investigate schools of intellectual history and historiography that have evolved in important ways in recent years. Former editor in chief of the *Annales*, Lilti explores why intellectual history has had a hard time finding a disciplinary niche in France until now, while also reviewing how the French tradition of sociocultural history continues to provide a novel fund of approaches for outsiders to consider and adapt. Müller offers a state-of-the-art consideration of German *Begriffsgeschichte*, which was never fully domesticated in the Anglo-American sphere, despite heroic efforts by Melvin Richter and some international dialogue.

The next set of essays explores modern European intellectual history in relation to several cognate fields. Judith Surkis offers a provocative reminder of how best to understand the sometimes-divisive alternative of cultural history in relation to intellectual history in the recent past. She proposes that a muddy and supplementary relationship between the two areas is preferable to standoff and mutual disdain. Samuel Moyn takes up the long-term phobia of intellectual history toward not only the cultural domain but the social domain of practices, contending similarly that it no longer makes sense to maintain relations of suspicion and avoidance. Relying on the history of social theory and the now much-discussed category of the "social imaginary," he contends that the social history that ascended so explosively as to leave intellectual history in ruins needs the field it temporarily vanquished—and vice versa. Next, Suzanne Marchand examines the rise and fall of the "history of disciplines," which provided an exciting way to link intellectual history to the sociology of knowledge, if not by connecting ideas to their larger life-world, then at least by showing how the politics of erecting and sustaining academic domains critically determined the character of thought pursued within them. Finally, John Tresch reviews the fission that led to the independence of the history of science, recently one of the most methodologically exciting fields in the humanities, precisely because it came to emphasize social practices like observations and experiments in novel ways. Tresch finds the pronounced current distinction between the history of ideas and the history of science unfortunate. Where Marchand is more pessimistic about the continuing fecundity of the history of the disciplines (which not infrequently intersected science studies), Tresch parallels McMahon in finding in Lovejoy a fruitful source of future harmonization.

A third group of interventions offers more thematic reflections, frequently dwelling on topics that earlier generations of intellectual historians tended to slight: gender and subjectivity, most prominently. Each contribution here shows that rectification of past omissions is no longer as interesting as discovering how selfhood (as well as its embodied and affective dimensions) might prompt future revisions to the theory and method of intellectual history. Tracie Matysik shows how the continuing uses of Sigmund Freud and Michel Foucault point beyond the history of gender that has tended to be the most significant beneficiary of their influence. And Marci Shore draws on current work on European phenomenology to craft a case for the biographical contextualization of ideas. Both essays attest to a "subjective turn" currently under way in the field, though there is no clear agreement about what it means to connect thought to selfhood. Indeed Matysik's and Shore's proposals point in opposite directions, one forcing engagement with ongoing theoretical ventures for the sake of a more astute and engaged approach to the ideational realm, the other calling for a less officious empathy, almost as if intellectual history is sometimes too learned to grasp what is personally at stake for past actors.

Traditional homeland of the field of intellectual history and the topic of this volume, the European continent today finds itself increasingly decentered and "provincialized." At the same time, it sometimes seems to return to even greater indispensability in new proposals for an enlarged or even global intellectual history. To broach these topics, a final section of the volume takes up European intellectual history in relation to its more distant borders and frontiers, whether these be disciplinary in the broadest sense or geographical, encompassing the entire world.[8] John Randolph offers a pioneering survey of theories of humanistic space, which have commanded much attention in recent years and which he applies to the realm of ideas. David Armitage makes the case for a geographically extended intellectual history that transcends spatial constraints, much as Lovejoy transcended chronological ones, registering just how far and how fast the move beyond national or even continental accounts of ideas has gone. The days when Europe served as the sole terrain of European intellectual history are clearly over. An intellectual historian of modern India in its global context, Shruti Kapila, considers how this move in European intellectual history might be regarded—and corrected—by those whose expertise lies outside of Europe in places where "European" ideas are often presented as descending upon and traveling within. In the volume's final essay, Warren Breckman provides a subtle account of intellectual history's relations to a whole panoply of disciplines, enlarging the scope of the case for complementarity mounted by other essays in this volume to the humanities as a whole.

A Space in Common and Alternatives in Contention

In returning to the question of what unites intellectual history in its present moment, it should be clear even from this brief synopsis that a number of cohesive tendencies emerge from these essays beyond common enthusiasm and mutual excitement. An embrace of intellectual history's role as a field that crosses disciplinary frontiers; a reinvigorated interest in intellectual biography and the self; a willingness to scale outward beyond the immediate contextual confines of time or space; an unapologetic interest in the study of ideas for their own sake; and a desire to overcome tired dichotomies (intellectual history versus social or cultural history, high versus low, science versus the arts) that no longer seem fruitful or sustainable—all are evident here. Readers will detect a certain presentism in the present moment, as well—a healthy and self-conscious desire to treat the past not simply as a world unto itself, but as a place of revelation and response to questions that concern us in the here and now. Perhaps this reflects the weight of an uncomfortable question that presses on all who work in the humanities today: what is the value of what we do? Or perhaps it represents a more subtle questioning of the contextual imperative that has dominated the historical profession for some time. In any case, to make the past relevant to our own time seems an end that many of the contributors to this volume share.

If common tendencies are apparent in the groupings of these essays, equally interesting are the tensions that emerge in their interstices and that might become even clearer through more vigorous confrontation. The editors of this volume suggest in their respective essays that a history of ideas and a history of the social might be compatible on some level through the broader interrogation of the imaginary horizons of cultures. But is this really the case? Does the study of the history of ideas as conceived, say, by Peter Gordon not remain fundamentally at odds with the social history of culture presented, say, by Antoine Lilti? A similar tension is apparent in the turn inward toward the lives and selves of intellectuals: to what degree can a focus on subjectivity be reconciled with the wider social life that shapes it? Finally, although the move to push European intellectual history beyond the boundaries of the nation, and indeed beyond Europe itself, represents an undeniably fertile means to maintain the relevance of what might otherwise seem a parochial discipline in a global age, how much does it really tell us about how to practice intellectual history in those vast spaces it opens up? If *Rethinking Modern European Intellectual History* can serve as a stimulus for the future, it would succeed mainly in catalyzing more intense scrutiny around such questions, forcing intellectual historians to confront where their practices came from for the sake of a more serious debate about what those should become.

For the time being, intellectual historians seem reluctant to fight about these matters. That may represent a belief that eclecticism is a good in its own right, and that intellectual history is an inherently eclectic field. Different problems, after all, require different methods, and posing different questions will always yield different answers. The danger, however, is a complacent version of eclecticism that refuses to acknowledge the fact that different approaches simply are not compatible in their basic premises. If differing methods rest on conflicting assumptions, the result may not be happy eclecticism so much as contradiction and confusion. What Horace once said of the *ars poetica* may well be true of the *ars historica*. "'Painters and poets,' someone objects, 'have always had an equal right to dare to do whatever they wanted.' We know it and we both seek this indulgence and grant it in turn. But not to the degree that the savage mate with the gentle, nor that snakes be paired with birds, nor lambs with tigers."[9] Then again, this is an interim moment, and perhaps a time for such crossbreeding and fertilization. At the very least, these essays are intended to clarify the alternatives for the future, indicating the trajectories of the present of modern European intellectual history in relation to the past.

Notes

1. Peter Novick, *That Noble Dream: The "Objectivity Question" and the American Historical Profession* (Cambridge: Cambridge University Press, 1988).

2. Intellectual historians have of course attended to such stocktaking before, perhaps none as regularly and assiduously as Donald R. Kelley. See, among his many

writings on the subject, "Horizons of Intellectual History: Retrospect, Circumspect, Prospect," *Journal of the History of Ideas* 48, no. 1 (1987): 143–69.

3. Robert Darnton, "Intellectual and Cultural History," in his *The Kiss of Lamourette: Reflections in Cultural History* (New York: Norton, 1990), 191.

4. For a helpful autobiographical guide to these "turns," see William H. Sewell, Jr., *Logics of History: Social History and Social Transformation* (Chicago: University of Chicago Press, 2005), chap. 2. See also Lynn Hunt, ed., *The New Cultural History* (Berkeley: University of California Press, 1986).

5. Dominick LaCapra and Steven L. Kaplan, eds., *Modern European Intellectual History: Reappraisals and New Perspectives* (Ithaca, NY: Cornell University Press, 1982).

6. John E. Toews, "Intellectual History after the Linguistic Turn: The Autonomy of Meaning and the Irreducibility of Experience," *American Historical Review* 92, no. 4 (October 1987): 886.

7. Victoria E. Bonnell and Lynn Hunt, eds., *Beyond the Cultural Turn: New Directions in the Study of Society and Culture* (Berkeley: University of California Press, 1999).

8. See also Samuel Moyn and Andrew Sartori, eds., *Global Intellectual History* (New York: Columbia University Press, 2013).

9. Horace, "Ars Poetica," 9–13, trans. Leon Golden, in O. B. Hardison, Jr. and Leon Golden, *Horace for Students of Literature: The "Ars Poetica" and Its Tradition* (Gainesville: University Press of Florida, 1995), 7.

I

The Return of the History of Ideas?

Darrin M. McMahon

One of the safest (and most useful) generalizations resulting
from a study of the history of ideas is that every age tends to
exaggerate the scope or finality of its own discoveries, or
re-discoveries, to be so dazzled with them that it fails to
discern clearly their limitations and forgets aspects of truth
against prior exaggerations of which it has revolted.
—Arthur Lovejoy, "Reflections on the History of
Ideas" (1940)

When it comes to the state of their discipline, historians are often
curiously obsessed with the future—as interested, it would seem, in
what stands ahead as in what lies behind. Our metaphors are
revealing: We speak of outstanding colleagues as "pioneers," "blazing
new trails," "breaking new ground," and "mapping uncharted terrain."
Even as we look over our shoulders toward the other country of the
past, we are forever pushing forward toward new methods and
understanding, seeking out undiscovered questions and tracking
down unrevealed answers. It may be that the quest to find novelty in
what is dead and gone is inherently paradoxical. But as historians
themselves are well placed to know, our interest in what lies in the
future is itself a product of the past, the consequence of a great
temporal reorientation that dates to the eighteenth century, a period
when the future opened up as an unexplored horizon.[1] In this age,
the notions of progress, originality, and the need to be new asserted
themselves in the arts and letters no less than industry and commerce.

Demanding constant innovation, the field of history is no different in this respect from the many other *champs intellectuels* that developed alongside it in the natural and human sciences, requiring those who would assume its *habitus* to distance themselves in just the right measure from all that smelled of old.

Given these rules of the game, it may seem perverse to suggest the revival of a form of history that has been described as "old-fashioned" so often over the last forty years as to render the phrase an "old-fashioned history of ideas" positively redundant. Yet it remains the case that a number of intellectual historians, working discretely and at various stages of their careers, have begun publishing of late what are, in effect, histories of ideas. Few openly embrace that label, and the studies themselves draw on different methods and critical orientations. But whether their subjects are "experience" or "creativity," "democracy" or the "self," "common sense," "civil war," "happiness," "genius," or "equality," these works share a willingness to widen the temporal horizon, pursuing the continuities and departures of ideas over vast tracts of time in multiple discourses and domains.[2] To do so is to run up against dominant orthodoxies. As the historian John Hope Mason has observed in introducing his own rich history of the idea of creativity:

> In recent years it has become common to assert that this kind of
> history is no longer valid; that assumptions of continuity are wrong
> (and discontinuity should be the norm); that the broad view ignores
> (or distorts or suppresses) individual qualities; that there are no
> essential, persistent, or universal human attributes; that past texts
> can be understood only within the terms of a specific and limited
> context.

And yet, after weighing advantages and disadvantages, Mason concluded that "the subject was too interesting to be abandoned," and carried on regardless.[3] Might interest of this kind, and the interesting studies it has begun to produce, signal a certain restlessness among intellectual historians, a dissatisfaction with the reigning "parameters and stringencies" Mason describes? Might such work possibly herald the "return" of the history of ideas?

Admittedly, the notion of a "turn" or "re-turn" is inherently fraught.[4] And in any case, such deviations are always deceptive. "*Returns* to past styles," Pierre Bourdieu cautions, "are never 'the same thing' since they are separated from what they return to by negative reference to something which was itself the negation of it (or the negation of the negation, etc.)."[5] Put positively, and perhaps a little more clearly, a new history of ideas would inevitably look different from what came before. But that observation begs the question of just what a re-fashioned history of ideas might look like.[6] While there can be no single prescriptive answer to the question, one way of addressing it is to ask what led to the history of ideas' initial fall from fashion. By revisiting how the history of ideas was rendered old, it may be possible to imagine it anew.[7]

The Unfashioning of the History of Ideas

Viewed in hindsight, it seems more than a little ironic that "ideas" should have become a term of opprobrium in Western universities, and that historians, beginning roughly in the late 1960s, should have seen fit to dismiss their study as an antiquated, if not altogether reactionary, undertaking. This was clearly a transatlantic phenomenon. Although the "history of ideas" as conceived as a discrete discipline by its founder, Arthur Lovejoy, was in many respects a distinctly American enterprise, it had analogues and important predecessors in Europe. In his exhaustive studies of the history of intellectual history, Donald Kelley traces efforts to chronicle the history of ideas all the way back to the ancient world. Self-conscious attempts to write what Jacob Brucker and Giambattista Vico were already calling in the eighteenth century the "history of the doctrine of ideas" or the "history of human ideas" have been in place since the Enlightenment, morphing in the nineteenth and early twentieth centuries into a range of approaches to historical inquiry, including French eclecticism and the *histoire des idées*, German *Geistesgeschichte* and *Ideengeschichte*, the history of philosophy, and Italian *storia delle idee*.[8] It would certainly be interesting to trace opposition to these various undertakings in their different national settings, with an eye to how that opposition informed later criticism, but the goal here is more modest. Confined largely to the Anglo-American discussion, this essay focuses on specific opposition to the "history of ideas" as theorized and practiced by Lovejoy himself. In doing so, it will pay closest attention to two traditions that have articulated that opposition in a particularly forceful and influential manner: the "social history of ideas," as conceived by (among others) Robert Darnton, and the study of "ideas in context," as advocated by (among others) Quentin Skinner, J. G. A. Pocock, and the "Cambridge School."[9] Although the main lines of their respective criticisms were laid out some time ago, both traditions continue to exert an important influence on the reception of the history of ideas.

Neither of these two traditions, of course, conducted their criticism in a vacuum. The specific fate of the subdiscipline of the history of ideas was bound up with the broader "crisis" of intellectual history that critics and apologists alike were beginning to acknowledge in the early 1970s.[10] The advent of social history, with its laudable attempts to reconstruct the experience of ordinary people, its objection to the privileging of the cultural production of elites, its distrust of any form of idealism, and its often Marxian-inspired tendency to treat ideas as ideology, provided, as it were, the frontal assault. But attacks came from many other quarters as well, including from within the broad family of cultural and intellectual historians. Developments in twentieth-century language philosophy, in both its Continental and Anglo-American varieties, were an important driver, fostering the charge that a traditional history of ideas was naive or insensitive to the constitutive role of language. Students at Princeton University's famously analytical philosophy department allegedly affixed a banner in the halls that declared, "Just say No to the History of Ideas."[11] On the Continent, Hans-Georg Gadamer gave a hermeneutical inflection to that sentiment, taking aim at the German tradition of the history of ideas in his influential *Truth and Method*. And Michel Foucault mounted a direct attack on the *histoire des idées* in *The Order of Things* and the *Archaeology of Knowledge*, where he declared categorically that "I cannot be satisfied until I have cut myself off from 'the history of ideas.'"[12] Foucault's curiously obsessive worry—"Perhaps I am a historian of ideas after all"—left room to wonder whether he himself had fully achieved the desired separation.[13] But there can be little doubt that his efforts played an important role in de-legitimating the practice in the minds of others. By 1980, such developments, when combined with trends in literary theory, cultural anthropology, and the new cultural history, helped ensure that a stodgy old history of ideas, as Darnton put it in an insightful essay published that year, was "surrounded by rude new varieties of sociocultural history and bewildering language—*mentalité*, episteme, paradigm, hermeneutics, semiotics, hegemony, deconstruction, and thick description."[14] By 1980, the history of ideas was already passé.

Both Skinner and Darnton helped to make it so, grounding and constituting their own historiographical interventions in the larger debate over the fate of intellectual history largely through an explicit rejection of the history of ideas as conceived and practiced by Lovejoy. Skinner, in his landmark essay of 1969, "Meaning and Understanding in the History of Ideas," took pains to emphasize his departure from the methods of Lovejoy, observing that "my concern here is not empirical but conceptual: not to insist that such histories can sometimes go wrong, but that they can never go right."[15] A number of other important methodological essays of the 1970s were written, as Skinner stresses elsewhere, with the express purpose of questioning "the assumption influentially propagated by Arthur Lovejoy and his disciples about the proper task of the historian of ideas."[16] Similarly, Darnton, beginning in the early 1970s, distinguished his own work from what he described as the "summit view" of intellectual history, which he criticized as "overly highbrow, overly metaphysical," and prone to lose itself in "clouds of vaporous generalizations."[17] The social history of ideas, he later explained, was born from a sense "of dissatisfaction with the conventional history of ideas."[18] To this day it continues to represent what another scholar describes as "a standing rebuke to Lovejoy's approach (as commonly read—or misread) to the history of ideas."[19]

The main thrust of these criticisms—considerably elaborated, refined, and debated since their initial formulations—is by now familiar to anyone who follows methodological developments in the humanities. Skinner and Pocock—whose methods and approaches are by no means identical, though closely allied—set out to apply the insights of Wittgenstein and Anglophone analytical philosophy to understand political language as speech acts. To understand texts historically, they argued, involved situating them in relation to broader discursive contexts that would highlight their particularities and illustrate their reliance on conventions. Whereas Lovejoy, in Skinner's account, "had argued that, beneath the surface of ideological debate, there will always be a range of perennial and unchanging 'unit ideas,'" Skinner sought to "speak up for a more radical contingency in the history of thought," illustrating the particular uses "to which [ideas] had been put by different agents at different times." "There is nothing," Skinner affirmed, "lying beneath or behind such uses; their history is the only history of ideas to be written."[20]

Darnton, too, sought to broaden the scope of inquiry around ideas, expressing admiration early on for the efforts of Skinner, Pocock, John Dunn, and their like-minded colleagues to understand ideas contextually, though his own work aimed to situate ideas "more precisely in a social context."[21] Claiming that the "summit view" of intellectual history had been told "so often and so well," Darnton aimed to "get to the bottom" of his chosen field of study, the Enlightenment, by "grubbing in archives instead of contemplating philosophical treatises," examining eighteenth-century intellectual life "from below." Moving down, Darnton also proposed moving "out"—tracing the dissemination of ideas through quantitative methods and meticulous attention to publishing history modeled on the pioneering work of the French scholar Daniel Mornet, the *Annales* school, and early efforts to write the history of the book. By focusing on conditions of production and transmission, Darnton hoped to answer such questions as "How did great intellectual movements like the Enlightenment spread through society? How far did they reach, how deeply did they penetrate? What form did the thought of the *philosophes* acquire when it materialized into books, and what did the process reveal about the transmission of ideas?"[22]

The last line is worth highlighting, as it suggests a point that is at once obvious and easy to overlook. Although both the study of ideas in context and the social history of ideas constituted themselves through an explicit opposition to Lovejoy's history of ideas, they at the same time retained certain of its features, or at least made more concessions to an older history of ideas than they readily acknowledged. On one level this continuity is straightforward. Both practices invoke the term "ideas" in their self-descriptions, with Skinner occasionally referring to himself still as "a historian of ideas," albeit with a full appreciation of the "confusing variety of ways in which this seemingly inescapable phrase has been used."[23] The word itself is complex and multivalent, with a long technical history in ancient, scholastic, early modern, and modern thought, a subject that would itself make for an interesting history, a history, as it were, of the idea of idea. Nonetheless, whatever the extent of their break with older methods, both practices set out to study, after a fashion, the history of ideas, a continuity that makes for a certain tension of the sort also found in Foucault.

This is perhaps most surprising in the case of Darnton, who has not always resisted the temptation to resort to a certain populist rhetoric in decrying "high ideas" as "highbrow." To follow ideas downward was allegedly to get "down to earth" and closer to the people. It was also, it seemed, to get more radical. That this was a slightly ironic position to be taken by a Harvard-educated, Oxford-trained Rhodes scholar who made his career at Princeton need not concern us here. Nor need we dwell on the related ironies of what Dominick LaCapra famously described as Darnton's "archival fetishism," with its rhetorical efforts to associate the methods of social history ("grubbing in archives") with manual labor, and so to cast aspersion, by implication, on the apparently lazy methods of "armchair" intellectual historians.[24] Darnton captured perfectly in these and similar asides a certain ethos of the 1960s and 1970s, with its attendant suspicion of "ideas" and those who studied them. But despite the rhetoric, ideas have continued to play an important role in Darnton's work. This can be seen most clearly in his relation to Mornet, who in his landmark *Les Origines intellectuels de la révolution française* (1933) had proposed to study "the purely intellectual origins" of the French Revolution, but to do so through an assiduous study of the diffusion of ideas, asking what, precisely, eighteenth-century men and women read. By working through publication figures, canvassing private libraries, and seeking to follow the precise diffusion of the works of the leading *philosophes* of the Old Regime, Mornet hoped to give more specificity to the old claim that "*la Révolution c'est la faute à Voltaire.*" He undoubtedly did so, and those scholars who took up his "diffusionist" methods in subsequent years greatly enriched the history of the eighteenth-century world of letters. Yet, as Darnton himself observes, there was a problem. "The Mornet model operated like a French filter coffee machine: it assumed that ideas trickled down from an intellectual elite to the general public, and that once they became absorbed in the body politic, they stimulated a revolutionary spirit."[25] In the end, trickle-down intellectual history was no more appealing to social historians than trickle-down economics, and a number of the best practitioners who had originally cultivated book history and diffusionist methods—Daniel Roche and Roger Chartier, most notably—essentially abandoned the study of ideas qua ideas in favor of models that privileged the study of institutions, forms of sociability, cultural practices, or the social history of culture more broadly as factors determining the origins of the Revolution. Darnton, however, retained a certain allegiance to studying the diffusion and circulation of ideas in the tradition of Mornet, even though he was more concerned to show how ideas percolated up, as opposed to trickling down.

Few would deny that this effort has proved tremendously fruitful.[26] Yet from the point of view of its criticism of the history of ideas, there are problems. The distinction between low and high breaks down upon closer inspection. As a number of critics have pointed out, and as Darnton's own most recent work makes abundantly clear, many of the radical pamphlets and libels that allegedly bubbled up from below in the eighteenth century were instigated and financed from on high, commissioned by courtiers and even ministers who hoped to discredit rivals. Social standing, in any event, is rarely an accurate index of "radicalness," as Robespierre's famous claim in the Year II that "atheism is aristocratic" underscores. It is also clear from Darnton's own careful studies of eighteenth-century "best sellers" that canonical authors sold in great volume, and so presumably merit the attention they have long received. Unquestionably, Darnton has recovered scores of previously unknown or little known works that were avidly read in their time. Yet the fact remains that in his own list of the most popular forbidden works of eighteenth-century France (measured by number of books ordered), five of the top ten authors are High Enlightenment figures (Voltaire, Holbach, Raynal, Rousseau, Helvétius).[27] Darnton's early claim that "the summit view of eighteenth-century intellectual history has been described so often and so well"—with its attendant implication that there are few surprises left to be found in the High Enlightenment—has also proven on closer inspection to be far from true. Skinner and Pocock, among others, have produced continuing revelations and steady surprises, and, in the French context, Keith Baker has shown repeatedly that there is much still to be discovered at the peak, the summit, and in the surrounding foothills. The study of the High Enlightenment and high intellectual history is even now hardly exhausted. When Jonathan Israel insists, however polemically, that the High Enlightenment "continues to be very inadequately understood and described," he has a point.[28] Finally, although Darnton has displaced the study of ideas downward, the ideas themselves are fairly crude, working, as Darnton himself acknowledges, on the principle of "radical simplification," which "closed off debate" and "polarized views," forcing the public "to take sides and see issues as absolutes: either/or, black or white, them or us."[29] Granted, complexity is hardly an indication of influence, and Darnton may well be right to affirm that literature of this type played an important role in bringing down the Old Regime. But after four decades of careful exploration, it might be time to put a little more emphasis on ideas that can sustain the scrutiny.

As for Skinner and Pocock, the claim has been made that despite Skinner's overt criticism of Lovejoy in his early work, his real antagonist was less Lovejoy than historians of political thought, and that it was primarily from the work of the latter that Skinner assembled the "formidable syllabus of errors" that makes his landmark essay, "Meaning and Understanding in the History of Ideas," such a delicious read.[30] The criticism that Skinner does level directly at Lovejoy was arguably somewhat off target, even unfair. In turn Lovejoy himself would likely have been sympathetic to a good deal of Skinner and Pocock's project, particularly their emphasis on context. Lovejoy, after all, was implacably opposed to the internalist formalism of the New Criticism. He scoffed at the notion that, as Skinner describes it, "the source of a text's intelligibility lies within itself and its understanding does not require the commentator to consider its context," or, in Lovejoy's own words, that "it makes no difference . . . who wrote it, or when, or what sort of person he was, or from what motive he wrote it, or even what he meant to convey by it."[31] A proper reading of a text, on the contrary, Lovejoy insisted, required "going beyond the work itself," for a good reading was "dependent upon a knowledge—or an assumption—about what [the author] was trying to do, which can by no means always be safely or fully inferred from the obvious content of the work."[32] To be sure, Lovejoy was opposed to any crude attempt to reduce an individual's ideas to the mere reflection of social position, personal biography, economic interest, or the like. But he was also explicit about how far one would have to go outside the text in order to properly reconstruct its meanings. In a well known reflection in his essay "The Historiography of Ideas," Lovejoy explained how "the quest of a historical understanding even of single passages in literature often drives the student into fields which at first seem remote enough from his original topic of investigation."[33] He used the example of Milton's *Paradise Lost*, stressing how a full engagement with the text would lead one out into the history of philosophy, science, theology, religious poetry, aesthetic doctrines, and numerous others domains, while insisting that "even to recognize what is distinctive of either [Milton's] style or his thought as distinctive, it is necessary to have both an extensive and fairly intimate acquaintance with manifestations of the same ideas elsewhere."[34] This was a plea for attending to multiple intellectual contexts with a vengeance.

Like all polemical constructions, then, Skinner and Pocock's depiction of Lovejoy is less than a perfect rendering; in truth their programs are more similar than they have acknowledged. Pocock seems to have sensed this similarity on occasion, noting for example in the 2002 afterword appended to the *Machiavellian Moment* that "some would describe this as doing the 'history of ideas,' but I find neither this term nor its connotations satisfactory as an account of what I have been and am doing."[35] No doubt Pocock would insist that he is engaged in writing the history of the *uses* of ideas, not the history of the ideas themselves, and so, as he puts it elsewhere, "The 'history of ideas' thus gives way before a history of languages, vocabularies, ideologies, paradigms."[36] Fair enough, but it is still possible to argue, as the late John Patrick Diggins did, that some of Pocock's discourses rather closely resemble Lovejoy's "unit ideas," what the latter regarded as the basic and essentially unchanging (though constantly re-described and re-expressed) elements that make up broader "idea complexes" like the "Great Chain of Being."[37] Conversely, if the "Great Chain of Being" were re-described as a discourse like classical republicanism, rather than a composite of unit ideas, and slightly more attention were paid to its strategic deployments, then Lovejoy's magnum opus might not appear so foreign in Cambridge. In any case, a man who once identified sixty-six different meanings and uses of the term "nature" in antiquity alone cannot be readily dismissed for having treated ideas simply as abstractions, or for having neglected entirely the different ways in which ideas are put to use.[38]

Refashioning the History of Ideas

To revisit the process by which the history of ideas became last year's mode is to catch sight of the wisdom evoked in the epigraph to this chapter: every age tends "to exaggerate the scope or finality of its own discoveries," distorting what it rejects in the rage to be new. Like other trends, the history of ideas was rendered passé for reasons that were not confined exclusively to its own deficiencies or to the intellectual superiority of its rivals. In part, it simply got old.

This is not to say that the demise of the history of ideas was all style and no substance. Skinner and Pocock's trenchant criticism of Lovejoy's "unit ideas," in particular, which he compared to eternal substances that could somehow be combined and re-combined like the elements of the periodic table, was entirely justified and added powerfully to earlier criticisms of the notion. It might be said, in Lovejoy's defense, that his theoretical statements about unit ideas were less subtle than his actual historical practice, which rarely treated the complex interactions of thought as simple chemical reactions. Still, Skinner and Pocock's pointed reminder that ideas do not somehow magically exist outside of the languages in which they are embedded and the uses to which they are put is an insight that few practicing intellectual historians would choose now to discount. Their repeated insistence on the need to remain sensitive to the particularities of intention, the dangers of reification, the nuances of reception, and the distinctions of rhetorical performance are not to be gainsaid. Similarly, Darnton's general call to abandon the "summit view" of intellectual history to study ideas closer to the ground and in their wide diffusion rested on an apt survey of the lay of the scholarly land. Lovejoy himself registered a similar plea, pointing out that the history of ideas as "I would wish to define it" is especially concerned with the "collective thought of large groups of persons," "not merely . . . the doctrines or opinions of a small number of profound thinkers or eminent writers. . . . It is, in short, interested in ideas which attain a wide diffusion, which become a part of the stock of many minds." A "minor writer," he insisted, was often "more important" than "the authors of what are now regarded as masterpieces."[39] Notwithstanding that often-overlooked contention, Lovejoy and his acolytes remained closer to the summit than this citation would suggest. Trained as a philosopher, Lovejoy was frank in describing philosophy as the "common seed-plot, the *locus* of initial manifestation in writing, of the greater number of the more fundamental and pervasive ideas."[40] Insofar as the social history of ideas forced practitioners to consider other methods of diffusion besides descent, and other points of origin beyond the philosopher's head, its mapping of the past and the profession alike are only to be welcomed. The terrain of history is vast and expansive.

Yet that very fact suggests that the history of ideas might still claim a place on the scholarly horizon. Surely the days when historians fought over their dominions and parcels of turf like colonizing generals are behind us. To imagine a "return" of the history of ideas is no more to seek its imperial "triumph" over other methods than to regret its original "defeat," or to yearn for the rebirth of a lofty idealism that will move all before it by the power of spirit alone. It is simply to ask for a place on the map, free from the prejudice that what it might have to say is inherently out of date, and hence entirely irrelevant.

One way of seeking that indulgence is to consider those forgotten "aspects of truth" invoked in the second part of Lovejoy's epigraph and to ask how a new history of ideas might be able to recall them, while correcting for certain "limitations" induced by the amnesia of current historical practice. To my mind there are four principal areas that the recent spate of monographs in the history of ideas suggests are particularly amenable to this kind of recollection.

The first has to do with temporal ambition and scope. One of the strengths of Lovejoy's approach was its goal of tracing the "life histories" or "total life history" of particular ideas.[41] The analogy to life, with its intimations of birth, maturity, decline, and death, implies a metanarrative that will not always suit and may frequently distort. But there are other framing devices at hand, from genealogy to what Martin Jay, in following the fortunes of "experience," has likened to the "theme and variations" of a song-cycle in an attempt to avoid the dangers of a "totalizing account."[42] David Armitage has described his own efforts to follow the idea of "civil war" from the ancients to the modern as "serial contextualization," a sort of synchronic crosscutting in which the historian slices deeply at particularly strategic points in an idea's diachronic line of development, marking off its unique particularities, contextual uses, and play. The point is less the particular narrative (or non-narrative) strategy that is put in place than the effort to write what Armitage calls "trans-temporal history," history pursued over broad tracts of time. Another way of putting it would be the "intellectual *longue durée*," and indeed it is rarely noted that Fernand Braudel's landmark essay, "Histoire et sciences sociales: La longue durée," which first introduced the concept in the *Annales ESC* in 1958, took pains to observe that the "same element of permanence or survival" evident in social structures applied to "the vast domain of cultural affairs" as well. In making this point, Braudel cited Ernst Robert Curtius's *Europäische Literatur und lateinisches Mittelalter*—a high intellectual history, written by a literary scholar—to emphasize that "right up to 13th and 14th centuries . . . the intellectual elite fed on the same subjects, the same comparisons, the same commonplaces and catchwords." He even stressed something that Lovejoy (adding Plato) was concerned to show, "that the Aristotelian concept of the universe persisted unchallenged, or virtually unchallenged, right up to the time of Galileo, Descartes, and Newton."[43] Historians of science would likely want to qualify the claim, although as John Tresch points out in his essay in this volume, Lovejoy was not a bad historian of science. In part for that reason, Tresch as well as other innovative practitioners like Simon Schaffer are currently rethinking aspects of Lovejoy's contribution, particularly his innovative work on "series" and "seriality."[44] The broader point is that ideas, too, can have a *longue durée*, and that tracing them has the potential to open up sight lines and reveal connections that are potentially obscured by a more intense focus on immediate context.

To mention context is to draw attention to a second area in which a reinvigorated history of ideas might be able to correct for current limitations and call forth aspects of a forgotten truth. It was precisely against the trans-temporal dimension of Lovejoy's enterprise—its efforts to "trace the morphology of some given doctrine 'through all the provinces of history in which it appears'"—that Skinner originally called for a more precise focus on local context to correct for the abuses he so well identified: the "mythology of doctrines," the endless search for "influence," the assumption of timeless universals, and the tendency toward reification.[45] For Skinner, as for Darnton and many others, to take ideas out of the clouds of such abstractions was to root them in a specific time and place, with all its local inflection and color. If one lingered there long enough, one could learn the language and get the jokes, developing an ear for the *patois*, the intentions with which ideas were employed, and the uses to which they were put. Yet if one lingered too long, or focused too closely on the particulars of a given place, one might forget how people spoke beyond the next hill. The danger of provincialism, in short, was the counterpart to a misplaced universalism. Indeed, as Peter Gordon argues in his essay in this volume, an underlying premise of the many varieties of contextualism that serve as the default philosophy of much of current historical practice is the "premise of the monad," the assumption that contexts are self-contained and windowless worlds unto themselves. On this reckoning, a certain provincialism is guaranteed: If the past is another country, each contextual monad is a separate land with sealed borders.

Yet clearly no single context can ever hope to police the borders of meaning fully, to prevent news and information from slipping in from another village or across the high grass of another age. Skinner and Pocock recognize this, acknowledging that "the problems to which writers see themselves responding *may have been posed in a remote period, even in a wholly different culture*," and hence that there is "no implication that the relevant context be an immediate one."[46] Indeed, they have both written exemplary works that transcend time and place, including the history of the state embedded in Skinner's *Foundations of Modern Political Thought*, and the free-ranging *Liberty before Liberalism*, to say nothing of Pocock's magisterial *Machiavellian Moment* or John Dunn's sweeping *Democracy: A History*. But if Skinner has never denied "that there are long continuities in Western moral, social and political philosophy, and that these have been reflected in the stable employment of a number of key concepts," it is fair to say that his work (and even more so, that of his acolytes) has tended to emphasize the opposite.[47] Despite Skinner's own recent and cautiously favorable comments with respect to the more sweeping *Begriffsgeschichte* advocated by Reinhart Koselleck, Skinner concedes that "this kind of long-term shift in the *fortuna* of concepts has not remained one of my primary interests," nor that of the great majority of his followers, who have similarly resisted "broader chronologies" in favor of the "pointillist study of sudden conceptual shifts."[48] Given that the merits and beauties of pointillism have been amply demonstrated, perhaps it is time again for some to try to paint with a broader brush, and to do so in the recognition that if the past is another country, it needn't always be conceived as a particular hamlet locked away in time. To follow ideas across temporal frontiers, paying due attention to the key moments at which they shift their shapes and change their colors in different local settings, while still retaining a recognizable form, is to allow for the prospect of a landscape on which we might situate ourselves. If contextualism, as Gordon notes, is the talisman erected to guard against the historical sin of presentism, then a new history of ideas should help preserve us from the exception of the moment. To see how "experience" has been impoverished and enriched through the ages; how "common sense" in political discourse is seldom just that; how "creativity" was created as amongst the highest human attributes; or how "civil war" has been defined historically in ways that bear directly on the momentous decisions of policy makers in the here and now are just some of the many ways in which a new history of ideas, in dialogue with current problems and contemporary concerns, may help remind us that not all ideas are the prisoners of context, trapped in time, long ago defeated and dead. A certain historical presentism need not be a dirty word, and in fact at a time when humanists are continually being challenged to justify their "relevance," presentism may be a useful strategy of survival. The larger point is that a new history of ideas—or a history in ideas, as Armitage prefers, to avoid confusing the old and the new—that bears on contemporary concerns is well placed to do self-consciously what the best historical writing often does anyway: use the past to illuminate the present. Needless to say, historians of good conscience must always seek to avoid imposing their present problems on other ages. But perhaps they might try to listen in different time zones to ideas that have something to tell us about how we live (or don't live) now. Ideas get around, and not just in time, but in space. As Lovejoy stated emphatically, "Ideas are the most migratory things in the world."[49]

To invoke travel and migration is to suggest a third area in which a reconstituted history of ideas might benefit from a re-examination of the past. Migration, in Lovejoy's conception, occurred not only across borders and geographical frontiers—the history of ideas, in this respect, was comparative and international from the start—but also through provinces of conceptual "space," whether these be the kingdoms of philosophy, literature, art, religion, politics, folklore, economics, the natural sciences, or some other realm. The effort to follow an idea wherever it might roam rendered Lovejoy, as John Randolph notes in his contribution to this volume, an early "mental geographer," while also distinguishing him, as Warren Breckman observes, as an early and outspoken champion of the interdisciplinary ideal. Granted, Lovejoy's conquest of space was imperialistic—he conceived of the history of ideas as a "meta-discipline," uniting and reconciling all others, and he understood philosophy as the indispensable jewel in the crown. A revived history of ideas need not follow him in this respect, but rather should take even more seriously than Lovejoy himself the enjoinder to investigate the "collective thought of large groups of persons," by focusing on ideas "which attain a wide diffusion." In this way, a renewed history of ideas might push into territory largely ignored by the Cambridge School, which has focused overwhelmingly on the moral and political thought of elites. It might also break down the distinction between low, middle, and high, which has unnecessarily restricted the purview of the social history of ideas. An almanac or a newspaper article is as good a source for tracing the fortunes of many ideas as a philosophical treatise, sermon, or play. While the work of professional philosophers will likely always remain an important touchstone for intellectual historians, the greatest gains for a revived history of ideas are likely to be made by creative migrations into other pastures. There is no reason why historians of ideas can't be social, following ideas outward wherever they were lived, investigating how they took shape institutionally, and how they were disseminated, diffused, and produced. It may even be that to follow the migration of ideas across multiple domains—if only within the provinces of high culture alone—will provide valuable clues to the broader "social imaginary" discussed in Samuel Moyn's essay. In any case, Lovejoy's insistence that "there is a great deal more that is common to . . . these provinces than is usually recognized" is a useful reminder today, when disciplines and discourses are most often configured as distinct, and when historians are trained to go in search of alterity, discontinuity, and difference rather than to seek common ground.[50] A revitalized history of ideas ought at the very least to be eclectic, reveling in the interdisciplinary ideal that first defined it, counting itself a citizen, though hardly a king, of infinite space.

Of course, there are limits to what any one person can do—limits, as Lovejoy put it, to what "the historian's resources permit."[51] Yet the development of search engines, databases, n-grams, and tools in the digital humanities now offers possibilities to the historian of ideas beyond anything that Arthur Lovejoy could have dreamed. And these are only in the early stages of development. Still, to write history over the *longue durée*, in multiple contexts, and in different "provinces" is necessarily to abandon the noble dream of exhaustive inquiry in the hope that we may gain in broad perspective what is lost in fine-grain detail. To do this well involves narrative plotting and mapping—the structuring of the whole in ways that require far greater attention than is customarily given to the average historical monograph.

This points to a fourth area in which a new history of ideas might be able to correct for current limitations and recall something that is too often neglected: writerly craft. Intellectual historians have spent a good deal of time and effort over the last several decades thinking intently about the constraints imposed by their medium (language). But I would argue that this kind of reflexivity has offered diminishing returns. Intellectual historians pride themselves, rightfully, on their methodological awareness and self-awareness; they are not likely to dispense with that, nor should they. Nor can they simply revert to a more innocent, precritical age, a point that Donald Kelley insists on with his use of the metaphor of the "descent of ideas" to describe their long historical and methodological fall from a once lofty Platonic *alter mundus* to earth and sea, where "language is the ocean in which we all swim." "Ideas won't keep," in this world, he insists, quoting Whitehead, for "the return of skepticism, or criticism" in the wake of the linguistic turn, "forbids a reversion to an innocent faith in ideas except as unexamined shorthand for deeper questions of language, discourse, interpretation, and communication imposed on historians."[52] Risking innocence, let me confess a bit of nostalgia, as well, for a time when intellectual historians not only thought about language and its (de-)constructive relationship to thought, but when they used it with art to conjure works of enchantment and beauty, works that were put together with the same care that too often now is used to pull them apart, works that inspired, that filled one with the sense that even if ideas cannot grow wings and take flight, there is surely such a thing as intellectual ascent. Readers, at least, can soar.

Lovejoy would not be my model here—and beauty of course is in the eye of the beholder—but I felt something of this uplift in my youth in first reading Isaiah Berlin. I am sympathetic to Noel Annan's remarks to the effect that "nobody in our time has invested ideas with such personality, given them a corporeal shape and breathed life into them more than Isaiah Berlin." Berlin succeeds in doing so, Annan continues, "because ideas for him are not mere abstractions. They live . . . in the minds of men and women, inspiring them, shaping their lives, influencing their actions and changing the course of history."[53] More recently, Tony Judt felt, wrote, and thought with a similarly vital elegance. As his wife, Jennifer Homans, tellingly observes, "For Tony, ideas were a kind of emotion, something he felt and cared about in the way most people do about feelings like sadness and love."[54] To invest ideas with passion and life, and to clothe them in elegance and grace, may seem a tad old-fashioned. Yet good writing is timeless, and too many intellectual historians, for all their professed interest in language, have done considerable disservice to their own native tongues. When someone like Pocock says of the "complex and discursive style" of his own work, that it "has not been easy reading," I remind myself that not all reading should be so.[55] But for all my tremendous admiration for Pocock's scholarship, his immense erudition and analytical skill, I long at the same time for works less discursive and more lyrical, works that might restore a little of the passion and personality that ideas, those chimera, were said once to have inspired. Perhaps a revivified history of ideas might give us some of that.

Notes

The author thanks David Armitage, David A. Bell, Samuel Moyn, Sophia Rosenfeld, Jacob Soll, and the two anonymous reviewers of this volume for their helpful thoughts and considerations.

1. See, for example, Reinhart Koselleck, *Futures Past: On the Semantics of Historical Time*, trans. Keith Tribe (New York: Columbia University Press, 2004), and Marcel Gauchet, *The Disenchantment of the World: A Political History of Religion*, trans. Oscar Burge (Princeton, NJ: Princeton University Press, 1997), esp. 176–93.

2. Martin Jay, *Songs of Experience: Modern American and European Variations on a Universal Theme* (Berkeley: University of California Press, 2005); John Hope Mason, *The Value of Creativity: The Origins and Emergence of a Modern Belief* (Burlington, VT: Ashgate, 2003); James Kloppenberg, *Tragic Irony: Democracy in European and American Thought* (New York: Oxford University Press, forthcoming); Jerrold Siegel, *The Idea of the Self: Thought and Experience in Western Europe since the Seventeenth Century* (Cambridge: Cambridge University Press, 2005); Sophia Rosenfeld, *Common Sense: A Political History* (Cambridge, MA: Harvard University Press, 2011); David Armitage, *Civil War: A History in Ideas* (New York: Knopf, forthcoming); Darrin M. McMahon, *Happiness: A History* (New York: Atlantic Monthly Press, 2006; and McMahon, *Divine Fury: A History of Genius* (New York: Basic Books, 2013). On equality, see Siep Stuurman, *De Uitvinding van de Mensheid* (Amsterdam: Prometheus, 2010), the rationale of which is provided in English in Stuurman's "How to Write the History of Equality," *Leidschrift* 19, no. 3 (December 2004): 23–38. One might also draw attention to the work of scholars like Mark Lilla and Charles Taylor, who—though not historians professionally speaking—produce what are in practice varieties of the history of ideas.

3. Mason, *Value of Creativity*, vi, 10.

4. See the AHR Forum "Historiographic 'Turns' in Critical Perspective," *American Historical Review* 117, no. 3 (June 2012): 698–813.

5. Pierre Bourdieu, "The Field of Cultural Production; or, The Economic World Reversed," in *The Field of Cultural Production: Essays on Art and Literature*, ed. and intro. Randal Johnson (New York: Columbia University Press, 1993), 60.

6. David Armitage has posed a similar question and rehearsed a provocative response in his "What's the Big Idea?," *Times Literary Supplement*, September 20, 2012, a fuller version of which appears in "What's the Big Idea? Intellectual History and the *Longue Durée*," *History of European Ideas* 38, no. 4 (December 2012): 493–507. Given that we were in constant contact in the writing of our respective essays and organized together with Sophia Rosenfeld and James Kloppenberg a roundtable on the subject at the 2012 annual meeting of the American Historical Association in Chicago ("What Is the Big Idea? Challenges and Perspectives for Long-Range Intellectual History"), there is necessarily a good deal of overlap in our arguments, which complements a more general meeting of minds.

7. In addition to the thoughtful reassessments of Arthur Lovejoy and the history of ideas by Anthony Grafton and John Patrick Diggins cited below, one should see William F. Bynum, "The Great Chain of Being after Forty Years: An Appraisal," *History*

of Science 13 (1975): 1–28; Frank Manuel, "Lovejoy Revisited," *Daedalus* 116, no. 2 (Spring 1987): 125–47; and the many fine articles devoted to Lovejoy in the fiftieth-anniversary edition of the publication of the *Great Chain of Being* in the *Journal of the History of Ideas* 48, no. 2 (1987).

8. See Donald R. Kelley, *The Descent of Ideas: The History of Intellectual History* (Burlington, VT: Ashgate, 2002).

9. These are both traditions, I hasten to add, that I greatly admire, and that have informed my own work to a considerable extent, even if in what follows I focus predominately on what I see as a number of their current limitations.

10. See, for example, Gene Wise, "The Contemporary Crisis of Intellectual History Studies," *Clio* 5 (1975): 55–71.

11. Anthony Grafton, "The History of Ideas: Precept and Practice, 1950–2000 and Beyond," *Journal of the History of Ideas* 67, no. 1 (2006): 18.

12. Michael Foucault, *The Archaeology of Knowledge and the Discourse on Language*, trans. A. M. Sheridan Smith (New York: Vintage, 1982), 136.

13. Ibid. For an insightful case that Foucault did in fact remain a historian of ideas, see François Azouvi, "Pour une histoire philosophique des idées," *Le Débat* 72 (November–December 1992): 17–28.

14. Robert Darnton, "Intellectual and Cultural History," in his *The Kiss of Lamourette: Reflections in Cultural History* (New York: Norton, 1990), 191. This essay was first published in 1980.

15. Quentin Skinner, "Meaning and Understanding in the History of Ideas," *History and Theory* 8, no. 1 (1969): 35. All subsequent citations will refer to the slightly revised version of this essay published in Skinner, *Visions of Politics*, vol. 1, *Regarding Method* (Cambridge: Cambridge University Press, 2002).

16. See Skinner, "Epilogue," *Visions of Politics*, 1:176. The essays in question were "Some Problems in the Analysis of Political Thought and Action," *Political Theory* 2 (1974), and "The Idea of a Cultural Lexicon," *Essays in Criticism* 29 (1979).

17. See Robert Darnton, "High Enlightenment and the Low-Life of Literature in Pre-Revolutionary France," *Past and Present* 51 (May 1971): 81–115, and Darnton, "In Search of Enlightenment: Recent Attempts to Create a Social History of Ideas," *Journal of Modern History* 43, no. 1 (1971): 113–32.

18. Robert Darnton, *The Forbidden Bestsellers of Pre-Revolutionary France* (New York: Norton, 1996), 1.

19. Donald R. Kelley, "Horizons of Intellectual History: Retrospect, Circumspect, Prospect," *Journal of the History of Ideas* 48, no. 1 (January–March 1987): 143–69 (citation on p. 164).

20. Skinner, "Retrospect: Studying Rhetoric and Conceptual Change," in *Visions of Politics*, 1:176.

21. Darnton, "The Social History of Ideas," in *The Kiss of Lamourette*, 219, and "Intellectual and Cultural History," 210.

22. Robert Darnton, *The Business of Enlightenment: A Publishing History of the Encyclopedia 1775–1800* (Cambridge, MA: Harvard University Press, 1979), 1.

23. The line may be found in the first footnote to Skinner, "Meaning and Understanding," in *Visions of Politics*, 1:57.

24. Dominick LaCapra, "Is Everyone a Mentalité Case? Transference and the 'Culture' Concept," *History and Theory* 23, no. 3 (October 1984): 296–311.

25. Darnton, *Forbidden Bestsellers*, 171.

26. For a current assessment of the place of Darnton's work in the reconfigured intellectual history of the Enlightenment, see John Robertson, *The Case for the Enlightenment: Scotland and Naples 1680–1760* (Cambridge: Cambridge University Press, 2005), esp. 5–6, 16–18.

27. See table 2.6 in Darnton, *Forbidden Bestsellers*, 65.

28. Jonathan Israel, *Enlightenment Contested: Philosophy, Modernity, and the Emancipation of Man, 1670–1752* (New York: Oxford University Press, 2006), v.

29. Darnton, *Forbidden Bestsellers*, 246.

30. See Francis Oakley, *Omnipotence, Covenant, and Order: An Excursion in the History of Ideas from Abelard to Leibniz* (Ithaca, NY: Cornell University Press, 1984), 30.

31. Quentin Skinner, "Some Problems in the Analysis of Political Thought and Action," *Political Theory* 2, no. 3 (1974): 279, and Arthur Lovejoy, "Reflections on the History of Ideas," *Journal of the History of Ideas* 1, no. 1 (January 1940): 3–23 (citation on p. 9). Skinner is here citing what he takes to be the accurate characterization of his own position by two critics.

32. Lovejoy, "Reflections," 13–14.

33. Arthur Lovejoy, "The Historiography of Ideas," in *Essays in the History of Ideas* (New York: Capricorn Books, 196), 6. Lovejoy later repeated the claim for emphasis in his "Reflections," 5.

34. Lovejoy, "Historiography of Ideas," 4. As Darnton saw fit to acknowledge, "In fact, Lovejoy had shown great sensitivity to philosophical contexts in his masterpiece, *The Great Chain of Being*" (*Forbidden Bestsellers*, 174).

35. J. G. A. Pocock, *The Machiavellian Moment: Florentine Political Thought and the Atlantic Republican Tradition*, rev. ed. (Princeton, NJ: Princeton University Press, 2003), 554.

36. J. G. A. Pocock, "The Machiavellian Moment Revisited: A Study in History and Ideology," *Journal of Modern History* 53, no. 1 (March 1981): 49–72 (citation on p. 51).

37. John Patrick Diggins, "Arthur O. Lovejoy and the Challenge of Intellectual History," *Journal of the History of Ideas* 67, no. 1 (January 2006): 181–208 (esp. 185–86). Pocock develops his own theoretical orientation most thoroughly in "The Concept of a Language and the Métier d'historien: Some Considerations on Practice," in *The Languages of Political Theory in Early-Modern Europe*, ed. Anthony Pagden (Cambridge: Cambridge University Press, 1987), 19–41, and in "Introduction: The State of the Art," in *Virtue, Commerce, and History: Essays on Political Thought and History, Chiefly in the Eighteenth Century* (Cambridge: Cambridge University Press, 1985), 1–34.

38. Lovejoy pursued the subject of the many meanings of "nature" in various writings, but with regard to antiquity, see his "Some Meanings of Nature," the appendix to Arthur Lovejoy and George Boas, *Primitivism and Related Ideas in Antiquity* (Baltimore: John Hopkins University Press, 1935).

39. Arthur Lovejoy, *The Great Chain of Being: A Study of the History of an Idea* (1936; Cambridge, MA: Harvard University Press, 1978), 19–20. This is from the opening chapter, "The Study of the History of Ideas."

40. Lovejoy, "Historiography of Ideas," 8.

41. Ibid., 9.

42. See Jay, *Songs of Experience*, 4–6.

43. Fernand Braudel, "Histoire et sciences sociales: La longue durée," in *Histories: French Constructions of the Postwar French Thought*, ed. Jacques Revel and Lynn Hunt, trans. Arthur Goldhammer et al. (New York: New Press, 1998), 122–23.

44. See the many articles in the special double issue of the *History of Science* 48, nos. 3–4 (September–December 2010), particularly Simon Schaffer's "Lovejoy's Series," which is also insightful on the topic of the interesting relations between Foucault and Lovejoy.

45. Skinner, "Meaning and Understanding," in *Visions of Politics*, 1:62–63.

46. Skinner, "Interpretation and the Understanding of Speech Acts," in *Visions of Politics*, 1:116 (my emphasis). Pocock, to an even greater degree, has insisted on this point, and *The Machiavellian Moment* illustrates it well, ranging freely from antiquity to the end of the eighteenth century. See, for example, his "Political Ideas as Historical Events: Political Philosophers as Historical Actors," in *Political Theory and Political Action*, ed. Melvin Richter (Princeton, NJ: Princeton University Press, 1980), 139–58.

47. Skinner, "Meaning and Understanding," in *Visions of Politics*, 1:85.

48. Skinner, "Retrospect," in *Visions of Politics*, 1:180. See, as well, the final paragraph where Skinner observes that "I acknowledge, of course, that if we are interested in mapping the rise and fall of particular normative vocabularies we shall also have to devote ourselves to examining the *longue durée*" (186–87). Given that Jan-Werner Müller has devoted an essay in this volume to the discussion of *Begriffsgeschichte*, I have elected not to treat it here, though the question of its relationship to a new history of ideas would undoubtedly be interesting to explore.

49. Lovejoy, "Reflections," 4.

50. Lovejoy, *Great Chain*, 15.

51. Ibid.

52. Kelley, *Descent of Ideas*, 300, 313–14.

53. Noel Annan, "Introduction," to Isaiah Berlin, *Personal Impressions*, ed. Henry Hardy (Princeton, NJ: Princeton University Press, 2001), xxi.

54. Jennifer A. Homans, "Tony Judt: A Final Victory," *New York Review of Books*, March 22, 2012, 4–7 (citation on p. 4).

55. Pocock, "Afterword," *Machiavellian Moment*, 554.

2

Contextualism and Criticism in the History of Ideas

Peter E. Gordon

Open thinking points beyond itself.
                    —T. W. Adorno, "Resignation" (1969)

What is meant by the intellectual historian's claim that an idea can only be studied in context? Generally speaking, it suggests that for any given idea we can only understand the meaning of that idea if we reconstruct the unique sphere of meanings to which it once belonged. Although the claim does not lack its detractors, widespread acceptance of its truth has stood for more than forty years as a kind of ideological consensus among those who would characterize themselves as intellectual historians. In what follows I propose to examine some of the underlying principles that support the idea of contextualism as the highest norm for intellectual-historical practice. Specifically, I will argue that intellectual historians should grant contextualism only a qualified allegiance insofar as it runs into serious difficulties once we accept a broader conception of intellectual history as an exercise in critique.

In a spirit of collegial dissent, I will develop this argument in part as a response to the highly influential 1969 essay by the intellectual historian Quentin Skinner, "Meaning and Understanding in the History of Ideas." With the benefit of temporal distance we can now see that its singular prestige was partly due to the way it encapsulated a variety of deeper premises concerning the nature of "meaning" itself, premises that would later gain sufficient adherents as to congeal into a kind of orthodoxy across the interpretive social sciences. I will turn to those broader premises momentarily. For the time being, it will suffice to note that the argumentative strength of the essay lay in its readiness to confront a series of confusions that in Skinner's view bedeviled the practice of intellectual history.[1] The chief complaint was that the history of ideas had ensnared itself in conceptual and methodological difficulties—Skinner called them "mythologies"—that were due most of all to the fact that scholars had paid insufficient notice to the determinative role of context for meaning. Since that time Skinner has not ceased to elaborate and refine a sophisticated defense of contextualism, even if in his later work he has occasionally strayed from his own recommendations. But the original essay can nonetheless stand for the wider consensus. Although many intellectual historians may dispute specific elements of "Cambridge School methodology" (a term that seriously understates the diversity of its representatives), it seems fair to say that the general brief for intellectual history as a contextualist discipline remains a desideratum for the field as a whole. One could also object that Skinner's methodological statement was originally intended only for a specific subfield self-characterized as "the history of political thought." But it is not clear how a discrete realm of thinking about politics can be intelligibly cordoned off from the rest of intellectual inquiry without losing sight of the wider meanings (metaphysical, religious, epistemological, and so forth) that subtend our thinking about politics. The strong version of contextualism must implicate all modes of thought if it implicates any one of them. It is this strong version of contextualism as a general theory of meaning that I hope to question here.

To forgo misunderstanding, I should explain that I am *not* recommending that intellectual historians abandon the use of contextualism in the restricted sense of method that takes notice of context. Contextualism in this restricted sense is a crucial instrument of historical understanding, insofar as it calls our attention to the resonances and ramifications of ideas in different and diverse settings. I will return to this more restrictive and favorable sense of contextualism toward the end of the essay. My aim here is to suggest that intellectual historians should not endorse contextualism as a global and exhaustive theory of meaning, that is, the view that a specific context can *fully* account for all the potentialities of an idea. This exhaustive view depends upon a number of premises whose status is questionable at best. By exposing these premises I hope to unsettle some of our current disciplinary assumptions about the methods and the purposes of intellectual history today.[2]

Two Ideals of Intellectual History

I will begin with the preliminary observation that our modern understanding of history overall is characterized by a peculiar tension between two ideals. On the one hand we tend to think of history as an exercise in reconstruction:

because we are prone to think of the past as a foreign country our chief aim is to rebuild for ourselves its language and its customs while keeping in mind that this world was quite different from our own. But on the other hand we think of history as a discipline that is devoted primarily to the study of change: it is not the past as a location that arouses our interest but the past as passage or transformation. Our very understanding of historical inquiry therefore seems to involve two concepts of time: time as a series of moments (punctual time) and time as the extension between them (differential time).

The distinction between these two understandings of temporality served as a major theme for Walter Benjamin in his celebrated 1940 essay, "On the Concept of History," in which he objected to the normalizing and triumphalist consequences of a historiography grounded in punctual time and recommended instead a species of critical-revolutionary historiography grounded in differential time. But even Benjamin may have drawn too stark a distinction between these two concepts.[3] In fact, neither the punctual nor differential time can be dispensed with entirely. From the logical point of view, they may actually stand in a relation of mutual implication: without the idea of a series, the passage from one to another would be inconceivable, but without temporal separation any series would collapse into a unity. From this observation we can derive the lesson that historical practice involves a productive combination of two distinctive ideals, which we might call the ideal of containment and the ideal of movement. The first is best typified by the classical Hegelian ambition of arriving at a systematic unity that comprehends its moments within an ultimately stabilized whole. The second is typified by the critique of this unity: it seeks to expose the moments of aporia or fracture that volatilize the present and point always to an as-yet unsatisfied beyond. If the first is associated with the more conservative elements of the mature Hegel, the second is associated perhaps most of all with the critique of Hegelian identity-theory developed by left-Hegelians and especially by the later Adorno in *Negative Dialectics*.

Notwithstanding the powerful clash between them, both the ideal of containment and the ideal of movement do and should play an important role in historical practice, perhaps especially in the practice of intellectual history. In this discipline we serve two masters. We obey the ideal of containment when we situate ideas in contexts, insofar as we subscribe to the principle that a context serves as the larger horizon of meaning within whose bounds an idea can be understood. We obey the ideal of movement because it alone awakens us to a sense of the contingency and impermanence of *any* particular horizon of meaning; it reminds us, instead, to attend to the patterns of endless transformation and reformation by which an idea travels through time.

While both of these principles play an important role in the practical business of historical writing, they must be carefully calibrated so as to not come into unworkable conflict. Full and unqualified allegiance to both ideals at once may be impossible. If we obey the ideal of movement without restraint we may lose any sense for the conditioning forces that help to explain why an idea is not merely invariant, and we are disabled from accounting for local changes of meaning. If we obey the ideal of containment without restraint, we may end up imagining a context as a self-stabilizing unity inside of which there is no history whatsoever. Both ideals are therefore one-sided: the ideal of movement on its own runs the risk of breaking up all contexts and creates the illusion that ideas, like privileged passengers on a high-speed train, simply travel through history while taking only the most superficial notice of their surroundings. The ideal of containment, when it governs without restraint, will break up the historical continuum into a set of discrete totalities, each of which exists in a state of sublime isolation, such that even the passage from one station to the next thereby becomes inexplicable.

Contextualism as Containment

With this distinction in place, we are now better positioned to see that, generally speaking, the discipline of intellectual history over the past forty years has taken a marked turn away from the ideal of movement and toward the ideal of containment. The study of conceptual transformation pioneered by Arthur Lovejoy has given way to exercises in contextualist reconstruction.[4] There are, to be sure, countervailing tendencies in the profession, and there are a great many works today by the most accomplished intellectual historians that some describe as "neo-Lovejovian" in their method, insofar as they trace a single "unit idea" through various contexts while presuming that the idea exhibits sufficient identity over time as to survive its own variations.[5] But notwithstanding the occasional gestures of heresy or revolt, the predominant trend for intellectual historians in recent years has been to affirm the dictum that ideas should be studied "in context."

This is especially true of Quentin Skinner, whose muscular polemic against rival conceptions of intellectual history, "Meaning and Understanding in the History of Ideas," was first published over forty years ago but continues to inspire. Since that time Skinner himself has not ceased to elaborate and emend his conception of intellectual-historical method in a variety of statements and debates.[6] It is only right to acknowledge that this corpus of methodological inquiry rivals in its depth and sophistication just about any body of theory ever addressed to intellectual historians. And while in recent years the Cambridge School has come to resemble Saint Sebastian, there can be little doubt that the practice itself has survived the many arrows that critics have shot its way.[7] Indeed, the general ideal of containment still passes for many intellectual historians as a normative guidepost for disciplinary practice, and this is so even for intellectual historians who contest one or another of the particular theoretical statements associated with the Cambridge School itself. At issue, however, is not the precise argumentation articulated by any one historian or historical school; in what follows I do not wish to raise doubts about any particular group, and certainly not about the Cambridge School itself (which may be a misleading name, insofar as its most prominent members have rarely subscribed to one and the same method). Moreover, it seems likely that the normative ideal of contextualism will manage to survive both its various contemporary articulations and the particular challenges that have been directed against it. Indeed one of my claims is that such ideals typically *do* survive bounded historical moments, precisely because contexts do not exhaust meanings.

Before launching into the substance of my argument, it is worth pausing to consider the fact that the contextualist idea allies itself with the principle of containment while it suppresses the principle of movement. The very idea of a context, in other words, implies a cessation or (at the very least) a *slowing down* of historical time, and it affirms a stadial logic that divides time into epochs and eras while resisting the dynamism of a temporality that overflows such limits. Most of all the idea of a context reinforces the thought of an "inside" that is proper to a given time and an "outside" that is improper. One of my purposes in this essay will be to explore the further implications of such ideas. But let us move on to a provisional definition: By contextualism I mean the epistemological and normative (and implicitly metaphysical) premise that ideas are properly understood only if they are studied within the context of their initial articulation. This idea has for some time enjoyed a default status that quite often passes without argument or defense, since it is presumed to be merely the common sense of the profession at large. Borrowing from Louis Althusser, one might call it the "spontaneous philosophy of the historians."[8]

A major characteristic of this spontaneous philosophy is that the historical discipline subscribes to the contextualist premise as defined above as if it were simply the very *meaning* of its own practical activity. Amongst the scholars whose work belongs to the formation of the human sciences, historians are not a group habitually inclined to rarefied debate concerning the philosophical commitments that underwrite their practice. In itself this may not be a fault since the business of philosophy has its own departmental location, and scholarship owes much of its sophistication to a logical (though historically contingent) division of labor. Many historians would therefore feel disinclined to back themselves up out of their actual activity as historians to reflect upon the meta-presuppositions of doing what they do. In raising this observation I wish neither to fault historians nor to imply that they should all quit the archives to become armchair theorists concerning the nature of their own profession. But it is nonetheless crucial to note that no practice is metaphysically innocent: what passes as common sense is merely an unacknowledged metaphysics (and an epistemology and a normativity) that should in principle be susceptible to philosophical defense. It is therefore worth asking whether the spontaneous philosophy of the historians is defensible and whether it captures with any accuracy what it is that historians actually do in their work. One might initiate this inquiry by isolating certain underlying philosophical premises that seem to inhere in the contextualist ideal itself.

The Premise of Origins

Amongst the deepest premises that animates the practice of contextualism in intellectual history is the assumption that, for every intellectual idea, theme, or ideology, the best account of what that idea, theme, or ideology actually means can only be grasped if one restores that idea to the horizon of its *original* articulation. This premise seems almost inseparable from the historian's disciplinary self-conception as someone who aims to recall meanings that may have been forgotten and meanings that are different from those we may deploy today. Now, at first glance this self-conception may strike most historians as unobjectionable. What should at least arouse our curiosity, however, is the normative attitude that typically accompanies this practice, insofar as the historian appeals to the initial context as not merely *different than* but in fact *authoritative over and against* all later manifestations or deployments of an idea. This normative attitude helps to explain why some intellectual historians are moved to describe later deployments of an idea as somehow *improper*, especially if those later articulations do not conform to the original meaning. The original meaning is presumed to be the one that *conformed to its own surroundings*. Animating this premise, in other words, is a very deep conception of "holistic fit" whereby an idea or argument or ideology is seen to be one part within a larger harmonistic whole. The favorable attitude toward origin thus arises from the belief that in later contexts of articulation this original harmony is disturbed or may be altogether lacking.

It is not difficult to see that this premise may occasionally nourish a normative orientation that regards the historical movement of a concept as a movement *away* from proper meaning. This notion of intellectual history (as regression from origins) has found many adherents, perhaps most notoriously Martin Heidegger, who conceived human existence as a condition of thoroughgoing historicity but nonetheless imagined history as a narrative of *Seinsvergessenheit* or ontological oblivion. In Heidegger's philosophy the nostalgia for ideal origins and the declensionist attitude toward later manifestations encouraged a counter-mythology of "authentic" existence according to which the only solution to the predicament of historicity was the resolute claim of proprietary union with the meanings of one's "ownmost" time.[9] To be sure, not all theories of historical authenticity devolve into an unsavory politics of belonging. Still, the theory of a proper "fit" between an idea and its context may carry powerfully normative consequences. The intellectual historian who suggests that the modern appeal to medieval ideas of real universals (an appeal that surely does not harmonize with the principle of uniformity that underwrites modern science's image of nature) is *ahistorical and therefore illegitimate* can only render this verdict on the assumption that the idea of real universals properly belongs only to the medieval context in which it was first articulated. Animating this verdict, then, is an implicit commitment to the distinction between the proper and the improper, the native and the exotic. To be sure, the premise of origins does not always carry the moralistic message that the exotic suffers the stigma of illegitimacy. But of necessity it entails a commitment to a holistic theory of meaning. But with this observation we may be moving closer to the constellation of premises from which contextualism draws its power.

The Premise of Holism

Perhaps the deepest premise in support of contextualism is the belief that, for every idea, principle, or ideology there is *one and only one native context* in which it is properly understood. The exclusion of multiple contexts follows from the notion that a context is like a domestic space, a holistic sphere of self-contained and enclosed meanings that is (like a Leibnizian monad) "without windows." A context is thus conceived as a condition for the intelligibility of a given idea, or a framework of syntactic possibility that is crucial for the proper understanding of its meaning. Now, if this framework were not closed, this would be another way of saying that the conditions for meaning were not wholly internal but might in fact permit the idea to travel outward beyond its initial context of articulation into other contexts in which its intelligibility would remain intact. The premise of domesticity, however, implies that any such travel must be considered illegitimate or at the very least derivative. On this view, the understanding of an idea in its belated articulation seems far less important than the historian's prior understanding of its native meaning at the moment of its initial articulation. The intellectual historian who calls for the *proper* contextualization of an idea thus presupposes that a context is like a discrete and holistic sphere that englobes the idea in question and sharply delimits its capacity for movement. Notice, too, that if there were *more than one* proper context for a given idea the very notion of the *proper* would lose much of its appeal. To believe in the restoration of an idea "to its context" therefore seems to imply (as the propriety "its" indicates) that, at least in principle, there was just one and only one particular holistic and self-contained environment in which the idea enjoyed its native meaning.

The premise of domesticity has won traction in part because it appeals to a concatenation of anthropological, linguistic, and structuralist ideas, all of which gained ascendency over the last half century and contributed to the widespread belief that it makes sense to imagine the world as carved up into self-sustaining cultures or discursive spheres. One important source that has helped to validate the idea of contexts as domestic spaces is the strain of ethnographic holism, inspired in part by the cultural anthropologist Clifford Geertz, that fired the imagination of cultural historians over twenty years ago.[10] The holistic premise was evident, for example, in the notion that a certain event (say, a cockfight in Bali, or a cat massacre in France) might serve as a key by which to unlock an entire system of native meanings. The apparently bizarre or marginal or arcane character of such examples actually helped to reinforce the premise of ethnographic holism, for once one granted the premise of culture as a self-sustaining and quasi-organic unity of logically interconnected parts, it followed (or appeared to follow) that any one component of a culture, even the most unusual, could serve as a synecdoche for the whole. The premise of ethnographic holism may also explain the great attraction of Walter Benjamin's mode of cultural cryptography according to which even the most marginal elements of material culture could be understood as hidden signs for the meaning of the entire age: Benjamin's analysis of the Parisian *passages* is only the most famous example of an interpretative method that became a commonplace in cultural studies over the past half century. This Geertzian-holistic premise was also an important foundation for the so-called new historicism, which carried over from the old historicism the romantic-holist premise that any given culture partakes in a common logic or shared *Zeitgeist*.[11]

The theoretical underpinnings of this idea are legion. If the premise of ethnographic holism has enjoyed tremendous normative authority among intellectual historians in particular, one explanation may be that it could draw freely upon a great variety of theoretical resources from a range of disciplinary movements. For the Cambridge School (which has exhibited a strong preference for methodological insights associated with analytic philosophy) the holist premise derived much of its appeal from post-Wittgensteinian theories of language, according to which the understanding of a term requires an understanding of that term's deployment within a language game and the "form of life" in which that game can be played.[12] This strike against logical-positivism and its atomistic theory of knowledge was to play an important role in validating the holist theory of meaning, especially as it acquired a more accessible and pragmatist character in the speech-act theory of J. L. Austin.[13]

But the holist theory of meaning could draw upon other theoretical resources as well. It gained adherents in linguistics and anthropology thanks especially to the Sapir-Whorf thesis concerning the transcendental function of language in the construction of reality: Differences of languages were supposed to imply differences of worlds.[14] Meaning-holism came in many styles, and it was one of the very few points shared in common across all of the diverse movements of social theory that Skinner summarized in his 1985 collection on "the return of grand theory in the human sciences."[15] It occupied a central place not only in the hermeneutic philosophy of Hans-Georg Gadamer, but also in Thomas Kuhn's theory of paradigm-governed worlds of normal science; it also informed various modes of French structuralism as realized in anthropology by Claude Lévi-Strauss, in Marxism by Louis Althusser, and in the earlier conceptual history of Michel Foucault, especially the archaeological excavations of the historical a priori he undertook in his 1966 masterpiece, *Les mots et les choses*.[16]

The very strength and diversity of these theoretical movements over the last half century may help explain why the holist theory of meaning would have struck so many intellectual historians as an unobjectionable instrument in their methodological arsenal. Partly thanks to this premise intellectual historians were inclined to accept the contextualist notion that the world of human meaning consists in a plurality of holistic spheres, that is, that meaning is conditional upon distinctive and perhaps even incommensurable discursive frames. From all of these various resources intellectual historians could derive the seemingly self-evident truth that a context is a self-contained system or horizon that must be understood *from within* if any of its constituent ideational contents are to be understood at all.

The Premise of Provincialism

One of the more controversial assumptions that has served to underwrite the contextualist model of intellectual history is the notion that a context cannot embrace a very *large* terrain but must instead be sharply delimited in both time and space. The assumption is that such a *localism* is just what it means for something to count as a context: A context, in other words, has to be temporally bounded, because authors can only be said to be in actual conversation with other authors of their own historical moment. This may help to explain why the contextualist imperative tends to fasten the intellectual historian's attention on a context defined by a limited span of years, that is, a sufficiently short framework such that one can plausibly assign a political, generational, or chronological index to an intellectual sphere, defined as, say, "the ancien régime," "the era of the Scientific Revolution," or "the fin-de-siècle." A context has to be geographically bounded for similar reasons (although in the era of transnational history this stricture has considerably relaxed). From the point of view of the practicing historian the emphasis on a local or narrowly defined context may seem to play a truly indispensible role, insofar as it focuses one's research within a specified range and holds in abeyance the welter of facts that might otherwise command one's attention. But as a theory of meaning it is far from uncontroversial.

In "Meaning and Understanding" Skinner sought to defend the narrow conception of context by appealing to the role of intention. Briefly, the thought is that we cannot reconstruct the context of a given idea without understanding what the author of that idea could possibly have meant. Once we have focused our interpretative efforts on an author's *intentions* it may seem we are naturally confined to a quite limited range of semantic possibilities. This emphasis on intention has drawn considerable fire, especially from critics who object on theoretical grounds (especially from psychoanalysis and poststructuralism) that the notion of unitary intention or propriety meaning derives from a mythical notion of a humanist subject who enjoys sovereign control over his own self-expressive utterances and acts. It may be that (as critics such as Jacques Derrida urged us to acknowledge) textual meaning will always exceed the bounds of authorial intention.[17] Challenges to the humanist model have also come from feminist theorists such as Luce Irigaray and Helene Cixous, who have discerned in the privileging of a linear and logo-centric meaning a certain species of "phallogocentrism." Whatever their specific allegiance, all of these complaints partake of the similar insight, that texts are not univocal or grounded in discrete acts of intentionality.[18]

Without minimizing these complaints, however, it is worth considering the proposal that communication itself may depend on a quasi-transcendental commitment to mutual understanding.[19] Even if this were the case, however, there would still be no reason to believe that such a commitment to understanding could be *fully* discharged within the confines of a distinctive chronological or geographical or institutional context. In fact, the ideal of communication may encourage us to exceed any given contextual limits insofar as intentions themselves are not always provincial in scope. After all, when individual philosophers or political theorists articulate their ideas, it is quite often their intention to speak *beyond* their own time and to communicate with a broader audience stretching from the present into the sometimes remote future. Indeed, even intellectual historians who embrace the methodological priority of authorial intent must remain open to the possibility that the textual meanings developed by a particular writer were perhaps *not meant* to be limited to only one place and time. Spinoza, for example, surely did not intend for *The Ethics* to lay out its arguments concerning the one extended substance of the cosmos as arguments only for the inhabitants of seventeenth-century Amsterdam or Western Europe. The appeal to authorial intent might therefore encourage us to imagine a context that reaches across a very wide temporality, and one might even think that the proper horizon as defined by authorial intent would have to be one that considered the meaning of an idea *sub specie aeternitatus*. After all, the finitude of a thinker is a poor measure for the reach of her intentions: if the intellectual historian hopes to sustain her commitment to the empathic reconstruction of past intentions, it is unclear why this responsibility should reach its terminus at the threshold of the dead.

A similar and perhaps rather more intuitive argument might be made regarding the provincial assumption that a context must be sharply limited by space. When Hobbes laid out his theory concerning the State of Nature and the construction of Leviathan, it seems relatively uncontroversial that he intended that theory as a description of the human political condition as such, rather than, say, a description limited in its meaning and validity only to mid-seventeenth-century England. But a certain methodological provincialism seems to inhibit the intellectual historian from endorsing the thought that the context for understanding a given idea may be far more expansive (say, the entire era of early modernity, or the entire era of bourgeois proto-liberalism, or, perhaps, the entire temporal span of European modernity penetrating even our own contemporary age). Intellectual historians often promote a preferred context by announcing the bold truism that no ideas occur "in a vacuum." But if human meaning itself qualifies as a context (albeit one unlimited in scope), there would appear to be no principled or a priori reason why claims to broader validity across greater stretches of time or geography must always invite skepticism, and why they must yield before the ostensibly more "historical" premise that ideas possess their true status only within narrowly bounded fields of meaning.

There is a further reason why the methodological appeal to intention should prompt us to reconsider the premise of provincialism. Two guiding principles for contextualism are that we should, first, "delineate the whole range of communications which could have been conventionally performed on the given occasion by the utterance of the given utterance," and, second, "trace the relations between the given utterance and this wider *linguistic* context as a means of decoding the actual intention of the given writer."[20] Such principles may appear to imply a relaxed and capacious understanding of a context as a field of possibilities that are built up pragmatically if we attend only to what the author *might have meant*: What "could have been" said functions as the sole boundary for interpretation. One difficulty with this principle, however, is that it is still too parsimonious in its conception of possibility. For it is a common strategy of textual interpretation that we try to determine not just *what* an author said but what she *might have said* if pressed to consider a further implication or even a contradiction in her claims. A full reconstruction of *possible* intentions should therefore proceed according to the imaginative scenario where the author would have been responsive to criticism to such a degree that they might even have shifted to views entirely other than the ones they held. Such responsiveness, after all, belongs to the very idea of argument itself. But this interest in conceptual possibility should therefore prompt us to reconsider whether *any determinate field* could ever be fully adequate to the possibilities of a given text. In fact, this more expansive search for possible meaning would seem to reflect with greater accuracy our actual habits of reading and argumentation, insofar as our typical approach to texts is to regard them as *open* rather than *closed* in their range of semantic possibility. This approach is not merely a matter of methodology; it also corresponds to what we should not be embarrassed to call the *wonder* of intellectual inquiry. After all, it is the paradigmatic experience of critical reading that one is confronted by meanings one did not expect to find, and it should be a desideratum for any methodology that it reflect this experience of intellectual astonishment.

Intellectual history is by definition not merely a description of perceptible objects but an inquiry into meaning. From this basic premise intellectual historians have recognized their own hermeneutic implication in the meanings they study, and they have developed sophisticated theories so as to explain the way that any access to past meaning must of necessity involve the historian in an act of interpretation rather than objectivistic description.[21] But this interpretative relation to the past can be easily obscured, and it is especially hard to remind ourselves of our hermeneutic entanglement with the past if we conceive of a context as a singular sphere that pre-exists the act of interpretation. This is because the holistic definition of a context encourages us to believe that a context is an objective thing that can be identified in a purely descriptive and noninterpretive fashion. But is such a belief at all plausible? The ideal of factual reconstruction relies upon the objectivistic ideal of a disengaged observer: the historian, according to this model, is supposed to remain purely external to the world she aims to know. We can call this the *premise of descriptivism*. This premise gains its plausibility only if one accepts the notion that a context is a single objective field that requires empirical reconstruction. But once one abandons the notion of a *single* context, one is confronted with various questions of interpretation and perspective that immediately implicate the historian in the field of meanings she wishes to examine. Doubt regarding the uniqueness of a past context, in other words, should also lead us to doubt the objectivistic methods by which contexts are described.

The Premise of Exhaustion

When gathered together into full-scale doctrine, the various premises sketched here support the view that, for any given idea, there is *one and only one* historical context that both enables and exhausts its meaning. This conclusion—the premise of exhaustion—follows more or less automatically from the quasi-transcendental assumption that a context is a unique and narrowly bounded condition for meaning. But it is a conclusion with some rather startling consequences: Once the historian grants the premise of exhaustion she is forbidden from imagining the possibility of semantic continuities across broad stretches of time, and, more dramatic still, she must be especially skeptical of the possibility that ideas from the past might still be available for *critical appropriation in the present*. An idea that is displaced from the unique context of its initial articulation can no longer be considered the same idea at all: it suffers the stigma of illegitimacy. The premise of exhaustion therefore confronts us with the final and most perplexing consequence of the many premises listed above; namely, it encourages the view that intellectual history should confine itself to the reconstruction of discontinuous contexts, and it discourages the historian from believing in the possibility of long-enduring intellectual traditions.

Most intellectual historians, I suspect, will recognize that the premise of exhaustion continues to hold sway in the spontaneous morality of our discipline. If the cardinal sin of the historical profession is presentism, then the premise of exhaustion is a methodological talisman against it. But there is another, quite different feature of exhaustive contextualism that can make it seem an attractive doctrine for intellectual historians: it can operate as a proxy for direct criticism. Rather than directly grappling with a past idea, the intellectual historian can simply consign it to its context. Historicizing the idea *into the past* thereby serves to *defeat* the idea and marks it as no longer legitimate. This historicizing gesture is a frequent recourse for intellectual historians who wish to condemn past ideas (usually ideas they dislike on political grounds) but who as historians remain uncomfortable with the possibility of engaging in presentist criticism. But the consequences of this genealogical gesture—we might call it "defeatist historicism"—are highly ambivalent.[22] To consign an idea to irrelevancy by revealing its unflattering origins or historicizing it into another time appeals covertly to the logic of historical triumphalism according to which the present enjoys presumptive superiority over the past.[23] The gesture is also suspiciously anti-intellectual, since it refuses to address past arguments *as* arguments and it evades the burden of critical engagement by retreating into the apparently disengaged stance of contextualist reconstruction.

More troubling still, the premise of exhaustion obstructs our access to past ideas whose potentialities may yet remain unredeemed. The premise of exhaustion is especially tempting for historians who aim to expose the unpleasant political consequences of certain high-minded ideals. It is of course a commonplace that political agents often fail the ideals they profess. But ideas from the past may yet retain their potentialities even as we also acknowledge their ideological contamination. Past ideas, in other words, may bear an aspirational significance that remains still unrealized, despite the fact that this significance was betrayed by those who deployed them. This was an insight Habermas wished to proffer in his study of the bourgeois ideology of "public sphere," an idea whose utopian promise retained its validity even as that promise was broken by the fact of its restricted application.[24] To conclude that such ideational aspirations lack all legitimacy is to deny ourselves possible resources of instruction that flow from the past into the present.

This stricture against recognizing the persistence of the past in the present is among the more puzzling consequences of exhaustive contextualism. Skinner's essay gave credence to the notion that intellectual historians should forgo the appeal to anticipations because if we were to permit ourselves such a "mythology of doctrines" we would reify ideas as eternal standards by which to measure their predecessors. Historians who are susceptible to such an error might imagine, for example, that a certain idea "anticipates" a later and more mature articulation, or that another idea does "not yet" or "not quite" embody what it will eventually become. When characterized in this fashion such habits of interpretation can be easily made to look teleological and therefore foolish. But the stricture against them has the unfortunate effect of inhibiting our appreciation for how ideas transform and ramify over the *longue durée*.

In his recent book on human rights Samuel Moyn chastises scholars for their readiness to treat earlier phenomena as anticipations, and he compares them to church historians who saw Judaism as anticipating Christianity.[25] The comparison is noteworthy. Although one might fault Christian supersessionists for their failure to recognize Judaism's integrity and independence, it is not clear why a historian would therefore be wrong for investigating the Jewish roots of Christianity. The ban on anticipations is supposed to relieve us from the error of mistaking earlier views for genuine precedents. But (*pace* Skinner) history in fact is rich with anticipations that are taken up interpretatively in ways that are often difficult to contain. If the intellectual historian insists that an idea make its debut *only* when it bears all the recognizable marks we ascribe to it in a specific temporal moment, he is then saddled with the strangely ahistorical view that a context and its attendant ideas must be born all at once or "in one fell swoop." In this circumstance a great many of the most unlikely and intriguing antecedents that belong to the deeper past will simply drop out of sight. Moyn's skepticism toward more speculative narratives concerning the origins of human rights is from a certain point of view admirable, as it is intended precisely as a *critical* and self-described "genealogical" rejoinder to triumphalist histories of human rights. But it is also symptomatic of the way historians deploy the contextualist imperative to cordon off broad sectors of the historical past. Ironically, historicist contextualism isolates not only the past but also the present; and it thereby fortifies a liberal ideology of thoroughgoing self-authorization. The paradoxical consequence of unqualified contextualism, then, is to assert the deeply ahistorical view of each age as an island unto itself. Ultimately, it may be the present that suffers the greatest impoverishment. Toward the end of his 1969 essay Skinner offered the bracing counsel that "we must learn to do our own thinking for ourselves."[26] To this recommendation we might instead counsel humility and remembrance of the dead: No epoch exists in sublime isolation from its temporal antecedents, and no era should imagine itself as so detached from the past as to flatter itself with the fantasy of intellectual independence.

Intellectual History as a Critical Practice

From the forgoing remarks it should be apparent that I harbor certain reservations about the merits of wholesale contextualism as the highest purpose of intellectual history. Nothing I have said, however, militates against taking contextualism seriously as one among the many gestures to which intellectual historians might have recourse in their labors. Contextualism is not only important, but it is also a vital and even indispensable instrument in the arsenal of historical understanding. When deployed in a modest fashion, it serves to enable understanding and it fortifies the hermeneutic bridge between the present-day historian and her past. Criticism therefore presupposes understanding.

The difficulty arises when the contextualist imperative is deployed in such a way as to disable or to block criticism entirely. Exhaustive contextualism in this sense often serves as a means not of enabling but of *closing down* our critical engagement with the thoughts of the past. If we understand a context as a narrowly delimited sphere of meaning that has long ago exhausted its relevance, we will be discouraged from believing that an idea can enjoy the unbounded freedom of movement across time and space, and we will not permit ourselves to imagine that past ideas have any critical significance for the present world.[27] Once we commit ourselves to the abstemious notion that the context of the past remains separable from the context of the present, we will think of historical inquiry as a disengaged practice, an assumption that will only fortify our sense that the past is a foreign country.

At the beginning of this essay I observed that historical understanding typically involves an allegiance to two distinctive ideals, containment and movement. I noted further one must strive for a certain balance between them. The anatomy of contextualism as presented above was intended to emphasize the risks that attend a one-sided allegiance to the principle of containment alone. For the intellectual historian, these risks may be especially acute. This is because the practice of intellectual history is only possible if one takes up an empathic and communicative rather than merely external and objectivistic relation to the intellectual activity of the past: ideas can only be understood if one believes it is possible to gain hermeneutic access to past meanings. Without such access understanding would be impossible: the past would fall silent, the dead rendered mute. The very practice of historical empathy, in other words, should suffice to show intellectual historians that full-blown contextualism cannot be embraced without serious qualification.[28]

Much of the prestige of contextualism arises from a logical fallacy of collapsing validity into genesis. It is of course an incorrigible fact of human discursivity that due to the very finitude of human existence all meanings necessarily find their articulation *within* sociohistorical contexts. This is not only a truism but also a truth that can only be annulled with an appeal to a Platonism of meaning. But from this truth it does not follow that meanings are thereby exhausted within any given context of articulation. The point was made quite well by Jürgen Habermas when he characterized "today's historicism" as "an empiricism" that "denies seriousness to the validity claim of universalist character that stands behind every affirmation and negation of the subject who takes a position." While any such validity claim is "always held 'here and now,' in a local context," its very character *qua* validity claim necessarily "overflows all merely provincial criteria."[29] If this hermeneutic recovery of past ideas is feasible at all, then our capacity for grasping the potential validity claims of the past *at all* should disallow us from picturing a context as a closed province of meaning. The bridge of empathy does not stop at the threshold of the dead: it demonstrates a movement in human understanding that shatters the boundaries of any possible context and reveals the mobility of ideas against all efforts of containment.

From its beginnings in the early nineteenth century the modern historical profession has always been burdened with a double paternity. On the one hand it ascribes to the identitarian logic of the mature Hegel, which saw in time a principle seeking its own eventual completion. On the other hand it disrupts the ideology of historical closure and sees in time a movement beyond the self-satisfactions of the present.[30] One need only recall the concluding statement of Hegel's *Logic*, where Spirit fulfills its grand tour of its own externalization only to return to itself with the higher knowledge of its mediation as "the self-comprehending pure Notion."[31] To be sure, the logic of narcissism that came to be associated with Hegel's philosophy by the time of his death may not adequately capture what was most dynamic in his thinking: The youthful philosopher discovered in the dialectic an instrument of critique and an occasion for "tarrying with the negative." Indeed, it is this image of Hegel as a restless partisan of ongoing argumentation that has recently enjoyed a revival amongst neo-Hegelians such as Robert Pippin and Terry Pinkard. But the philosopher of negativity ultimately disfigured his own critical impulses to become an affirmative apologist for the merely existent. "The true is the whole" became a gesture of ideological self-satisfaction that gave to the present the metaphysical prestige of completion. The paradox of Hegelian closure is that it misrepresents the eclipse of the mind as its satisfaction, as if an idea reaches a point of stasis beyond which nothing further can be expected.

It is this complacency of the Hegelian dialectic that in the mid-1940s moved Adorno and Horkheimer to condemn identity-theory as a betrayal of the critical intellect:

> The actual is validated, knowledge confines itself to repeating it, thought makes itself mere tautology. The more completely the machinery of thought subjugates existence, the more blindly it is satisfied with reproducing it. Enlightenment thereby regresses to the mythology it has never been able to escape. For mythology had reflected in its forms the essence of the existing order—cyclical motion, fate, domination of the world as truth—and had renounced hope. In the terseness of the mythical image, as in the clarity of the scientific formula, *the eternity of the actual is confirmed and mere existence is pronounced as the meaning it obstructs.*[32]

Taking some interpretative liberties with the above passage, we might say that what Adorno and Horkheimer most feared was the Hegelian ambition to situate thought within a unique and ultimate context. In their view this contextualist ambition would ironically spell the end of thought itself: it would denature the mind's critical energies by bringing it into a quasi-mythic harmony with its surroundings, where all meaning would be identified with "the eternity of the actual."

For this reason the left-Hegelian opponents of identity-theory were eventually moved to adopt a critical posture that disallowed the possibility of contextual reconciliation altogether. For the later Adorno in particular, self-identity was always ideological and as such stood condemned as the enemy of reflection: "The picture of a temporal or extra temporal original state of happy identity between subject and object is romantic," he observed. It was "a wishful projection at times, but today no more than a lie."[33] The critical prospect of an idea that would be more than mere ideology thus presupposed the possibility of an idea's movement beyond any possible context.[34] This prospect prompted Adorno to observe in 1969, "As long as thinking is not interrupted, it has a firm grasp on possibility. Its insatiable quality, the resistance against petty satiety, rejects the foolish wisdom of resignation. The utopian impulse in thinking is all the stronger, the less it objectifies itself as utopia—a further form of regression—whereby it sabotages its own realization. Open thinking points beyond itself."[35]

The passage quoted above from Adorno dates from the same year as Skinner's manifesto for historicist contextualism. If Adorno's critique has any merit, it is that it might serve to chasten the intellectual historian who subscribes to contextualism as the highest principle of understanding. The risk of exhaustive contextualism, in sum, is that it reinforces the ideological notion that it is possible for an idea to come into complete stasis with its surroundings. The quietism of this notion may enjoy a continued allure for intellectual historians who feel untroubled by the thought that their task should be limited merely to the harmonistic containment of ideas. A sociology of knowledge that redescribes thought as mere "strategy" and reduces critical insight to the workings of "habitus" or "persona" commits a similar error of harmonistic reduction of thought to society, even if it believes such redescription serves the interest of a critical unmasking.[36] Genuine criticism, however, must in principle exceed any given limit and cannot permit contextualism to have the last word. This principle is instructive not only for the intellectual historian: Any mode of thinking that does not wish to lapse into thoughtlessness must forbid itself to imagine the past as a closed world that the living would find intolerable.

Criticism without Transcendence

One may be tempted to read the forgoing argument against exhaustive contextualism as a merely reactive plea for the "autonomy" or "transcendence" of ideas. It is entirely correct, as Samuel Moyn suggests, that the argument pursued here endorses the view that there is something about the intellect that resists its wholesale reduction to a given social order. But Moyn is too quick to suppose that the only way for intellectual historians to embrace social theory would be "to anchor" representations in practices. The very notion of an anchor is suggestive insofar as it suggests the desire to bring movement to a stop, the fixing of meaning in something external to itself. If one were to assume that a reduction of this sort is what the reckoning with social theory must entail, then a final reconciliation between intellectual history and social theory would seem unlikely. But such a conclusion rests on a mistake, since, as Adorno's example reminds us, "social theory" can acknowledge the social significance of the intellect itself. It is possible to theorize the relation between intellect and the social whole without collapsing one into the other. Social theorists and intellectual historians alike should be able to agree that the relation between mind and world is one of eternal contestation rather than full reconciliation. Nowhere in this essay have I promoted the view that theoretical activity wholly transcends its discursive (or nondiscursive) context. It is an unfortunate but unsurprising gesture of contextualist holism that it mischaracterizes the critical moment in thinking as a bid for metaphysical transcendence. Nor is this gesture uncommon: Holist theories of meaning have always gained their prestige by characterizing their opponents as partisans of an atavistic metaphysics. This was already true of the contextualist theory that went by the name of Marxism (even if that theory surrendered the critical gesture by which Marxism survived its own context).

To present the possible options of intellectual history as a stark choice between social immanence and intellectual transcendence misses the dialectical entanglement by which immanence and transcendence cannot confront one another merely in a stance of abstract negation: Those who wish to explore the contextual embeddedness of ideas will contribute to this dialectic, but only if they resist the illusory notion of the social as a noncritical and exhaustive totality in which ideas gain an ostensibly final and harmonistic explanation. The methodological stricture against such an illusion arises from the very phenomenology of thinking. If we listen to Socrates (in the *Theaeteus* 155 d) that wonder or "*thaumazein*" is the beginning of wisdom, then our own capacity for astonishment in the face of ideas both past and present may remind us that no single context can ever be adequate to an idea's critical potentialities. To believe in such a final context (that is, an ultimate plenitude for any and all possible meaning) is not a requirement of historical method; it is a species of theology. At the same time, theological motifs may also serve as gestures of critical resistance against the forces of containment, insofar as the act of criticism preserves within itself a memory-trace of the transcendence once ascribed to God. For it is the paradoxical truth inherent in the very meaning of critical reflection that situated thinking exceeds its own situation.

Conclusion

In his celebrated theses "On the Concept of History" Walter Benjamin paid homage to this idea of redemption when he sought to articulate a critical alternative to the style of contextualist historical interpretation he associated with historicism. Ironically, Benjamin felt a properly critical historiography could only resist the logic of historicism if it brought the movement of history to a *standstill*: "Thinking involves not only the movement of thoughts, but their arrest as well." In light of the reflections presented here, Benjamin's conclusion may appear paradoxical, for it would be easy to construe the "arrest" of history as an plea for containment rather than movement. But this would be to misunderstand the real object of his criticism. What is most objectionable in historicism according to Benjamin is its harmonistic ambition to solidify the historical continuum into a closed totality, and its refusal to countenance the critical potentials that point *beyond* any given context. The critical historian, he claims, will resist all such gestures of domestication. Such a historian "blasts a specific life out of the era, a specific work out of the lifework," and ultimately this will "blast open the continuum of history."[37]

These remarks, of course, do not entail an outright rejection of contextualism as such. Contextualism need not imply the *exhaustion* of an idea. On the contrary, when deployed in a more limited way, the recovery of a context that has been neglected or misunderstood may very well facilitate a critical engagement with a given idea and may even help us toward an *enhancement* of that idea's possibilities. My remarks are directed only against the exhaustive or transcendental species of contextualist holism that too often passes for the spontaneous philosophy of historical practice. It is this spontaneous philosophy that we should reject, not contextualism as such. We should, accordingly, take note of the gap between grand statements of method and actual practice. For the irony is that, whenever they venture into a more critical style of analysis, intellectual historians typically violate the principles of exhaustive contextualism to which they claim allegiance.[38]

My reflections may also suggest a reconsideration of the way intellectual historians envision their relationship to neighboring disciplines. Over the past half century, the contextualist imperative has done a great service to intellectual history by deepening its capacities for methodological self-consciousness, but it has also had the unfortunate effect of erecting a barrier against philosophy and political theory (alongside other modes of criticism). The implicit proposal of this essay is that this barrier be dismantled and that we reimagine intellectual history less as a distinctive discipline and more as the eclectic practice that Warren Breckman in this volume calls a "rendezvous discipline," that is, a trading zone *among* the disciplines that could serve as a space for the flourishing of historically informed criticism.[39] This more creative if less definitive understanding of intellectual history might permit us to relax some of the strictures that have gained authority in the field thanks to an overzealous ethic of disciplinary professionalism and technical rationality. And it would embolden us to defend the practice of open thinking in a social order that seems ever more determined to bring it to an end.

Notes

1. Quentin Skinner, "Meaning and Understanding in the History of Ideas," originally published in *History and Theory* 8, no. 1 (1969): 3–53. For a later version of the essay and the most important methodological elaborations, see Skinner, *Visions of Politics*, vol. 1, *Regarding Method* (Cambridge: Cambridge University Press, 2002).

2. For helpful remarks on an earlier draft of this paper, my special thanks to Martin Jay, Warren Breckman, Judith Surkis, Duncan Kelly, and all of the participants in the Radcliffe Workshop. My gratitude also to Samuel Moyn and Darrin McMahon. This paper was completed before the publication of an essay by Martin Jay that develops some similar claims; see Martin Jay, "Historical Explanation and the Event: Reflections on the Limits of Contextualization," in *New Literary History* 42 (2011): 557–71.

3. Thus Benjamin erroneously celebrated the mythological conception of the historical past as a "monad," an idea that I criticize here. See Walter Benjamin, "On the Concept of History," in his *Selected Writings, 1938–1940*, ed. Howard Eiland and Michael Jennings (Cambridge, MA: Harvard University Press, 2003), 389–411.

4. For the original model, see Arthur Lovejoy, *The Great Chain of Being: A Study of the History of an Idea* (Cambridge, MA: Harvard University Press, 1936).

5. See, for example, Jerrold Seigel, *The Idea of the Self: Thought and Experience in Western Europe since the Seventeenth Century* (Cambridge: Cambridge University Press, 2005); Martin Jay, *Songs of Experience: Modern American and European Variations on a Universal Theme* (Berkeley: University of California Press, 2005); Darrin M. McMahon, *Happiness: A History* (New York: Atlantic Monthly Press, 2006).

6. Skinner, *Visions of Politics*, vol. 1, *Regarding Method*.

7. See, for example, James Tully, ed., *Meaning and Context: Quentin Skinner and His Critics* (Princeton, NJ: Princeton University Press, 1989), and Mark Bevir, *The Logic of the History of Ideas* (Cambridge: Cambridge University Press, 2002).

8. I have borrowed and modified this phrase from Louis Althusser, *Philosophy and the Spontaneous Philosophy of the Scientists and Other Essays*, trans. Ben Brewster et al. (London: Verso, 1990), and from John Guillory's brilliant essay on the "Sokal Affair," which he examines against the theoretical background of the metaphysical posture of anti-realism, a posture he calls "the spontaneous philosophy of the critics." John Guillory, "The Sokal Affair and the History of Criticism," *Critical Inquiry* 28 (Winter 2002): 470–508.

9. Martin Heidegger, *Being and Time*, ed. and trans. John Macquarrie and Edward Robinson (New York: Harper and Row, 1962).

10. Clifford Geertz, "Deep Play: Notes on a Balinese Cockfight," in his *Interpretation of Cultures: Selected Essays* (New York: Basic Books, 1973), 412–54; Robert Darnton, *The Great Cat Massacre and Other Episodes in French Cultural History* (New York: Basic Books, 1984).

11. Stephen Greenblatt's brilliant development of this historicist-holist premise introduced, however, a subtle note of dissent from this holism insofar as it demonstrated how a culture (say, Elizabethan England) permits a "swerve" or variation in logic across different domains: Greenblatt's holism, in other words, was a holism of theme *and* variations. See Stephen Greenblatt, *Shakespearean Negotiations: The Circulation of Social Energy in Renaissance England* (Berkeley: University of California Press, 1988).

12. Ludwig Wittgenstein, *Philosophical Investigations (The German Text, with a Revised English Translation, 50th Anniversary Commemorative Edition)*, ed. G. E. Anscombe and Elizabeth Anscombe (Malden, MA: Wiley-Blackwell, 1991). See esp. §241: "It is what human beings *say* that is true and false; and they agree in the *language* they use. That is not agreement in opinions but in form of life" (75).

13. J. L. Austin, *How to Do Things with Words*, 2nd ed. (Cambridge, MA: Harvard University Press, 1975).

14. See Benjamin Lee Whorf, *Language, Thought, and Reality* (Cambridge, MA: MIT Press, 1972), especially the 1939 essay, "The Relation of Habitual Thought and Behavior to Language," 134–59.

15. Quentin Skinner, ed., *The Return of Grand Theory in the Human Sciences* (Cambridge: Cambridge University Press, 1985).

16. Although Gadamer is widely seen as an important resource for proponents of contextualism, it is instructive to note his warning that "a horizon is not a rigid boundary but something that moves with one and invites one to advance further." Quoted from Hans-Georg Gadamer, *Truth and Method* (New York: Continuum/ Seabury, 1975), 238. For a general discussion of the holist theory of meaning in the tradition of analytic philosophy, see John H. Zammito, *A Nice Derangement of Epistemes: Post-positivism in the Study of Science from Quine to Latour* (Chicago: University of Chicago Press, 2004). On Foucault's idea of a historical a priori, see Gary Gutting, *Michel Foucault's Archaeology of Scientific Reason* (Cambridge: Cambridge University Press, 1989).

17. See, for example, Jacques Derrida, "Différance," in *Margins of Philosophy*, trans. Alan Bass (Chicago: University of Chicago Press, 1982), 1–28.

18. See especially the criticism of univocal meaning by Dominick LaCapra, "Rethinking Intellectual History and Reading Texts, " in *History and Theory* 19, no. 3 (October 1980): 245–76.

19. Jürgen Habermas, *The Theory of Communicative Action*, vol. 1, *Reason and the Rationalization of Society*, trans. Thomas McCarthy (Boston: Beacon, 1985).

20. Skinner, "Meaning and Understanding," 49.

21. Gadamer, *Truth and Method*.

22. See Peter E. Gordon, "Continental Divide: Heidegger and Cassirer at Davos, 1929—An Allegory of Intellectual History," *Modern Intellectual History* 1, no. 2 (August 2004): 219–48.

23. The *locus classicus* for this argument is Walter Benjamin's "Theses on the Philosophy of History," which tries to revive the impulses in dialectical materialism that resist historicist containing: criticism, as Benjamin defines it, involves *breaking up* the historical continuum.

24. Jürgen Habermas, *The Structural Transformation of the Public Sphere: An Inquiry into a Category of Bourgeois Society* (Cambridge, MA: MIT Press, 1991).

25. Samuel Moyn, *The Last Utopia: Human Rights in History* (Cambridge, MA: Harvard University Press, 2010), 6.

26. Skinner, "Meaning and Understanding," 52.

27. For further remarks on the ethic of "open reading," see my review of Emmanuel Faye, *Heidegger: The Introduction of Nazism into Philosophy in Light of the Unpublished Seminars of 1933–1935*, trans. Michael B. Smith (New Haven, CT: Yale University Press, 2009), in *Notre Dame Philosophical Reviews: An Electronic Journal*, March 12, 2010, available at http://ndpr.nd.edu/news/24316/?id=19228 (accessed July 13, 2013).

28. On historical empathy, see, for example, Dominick LaCapra, *Writing History, Writing Trauma* (Baltimore: Johns Hopkins University Press, 2001).

29. Jürgen Habermas, "Israel and Athens, or to Whom Does Anamnestic Reason Belong?," *The Frankfurt School on Religion: Key Writings by the Major Thinkers*, ed. and trans. Eduardo Mendieta (New York: Routledge, 2005), 293–301; quote from 297–98.

30. On the critique of Hegel and the origins of modern history, see John Toews, *Becoming Historical: Cultural Reformation and Public Memory in Early Nineteenth-Century Berlin* (Cambridge: Cambridge University Press, 2004), esp. p. 16.

31. *Hegel's Science of Logic*, trans. A. V. Miller (New York: Humanities Press, 1969), 844.

32. Theodor W. Adorno and Max Horkheimer, *Dialectic of Enlightenment: Philosophical Fragments*, trans. Edmund Jephcott (Stanford, CA: Stanford University Press, 2002), 20, my emphasis.

33. Theodor W. Adorno, "Subject and Object," in *The Essential Frankfurt School Reader*, 499.

34. As Walter Benjamin observed, "In every era the attempt must be made to wrest tradition away from a conformism that is about to overpower it." Benjamin, "On the Concept of History."

35. Theodor W. Adorno, "Resignation," rpt. in *Telos* 35 (Spring 1975), as quoted in Martin Jay, *Marxism and Totality: The Adventures of a Concept from Lukács to Habermas* (Berkeley: University of California Press, 1984), my emphasis, quoted at 264.

36. Pierre Bourdieu, *Distinction: A Social Critique of the Judgement of Taste*, trans. Richard Nice (Cambridge, MA: Harvard University Press, 1987).

37. Benjamin, "On the Concept of History," 396.

38. See, for example, Quentin Skinner, *Liberty before Liberalism* (London: Cambridge University Press, 1998).

39. See Warren Breckman, "Intellectual History and the Interdisciplinary Ideal," in this volume.

3

Does Intellectual History Exist in France?: The Chronicle of a Renaissance Foretold

Antoine Lilti

Translated by Will Slauter

Intellectual history has never achieved the same prominence in France that it has in the United States, or that it has enjoyed in England, Germany, and Italy. For French historians, intellectual history barely exists. They tend to know it by other names and in forms that hardly command their respect: first, the history of ideas, which gets bad press for being idealistic, both too abstract and not theoretically grounded enough; then there is the history of philosophy, a territory long held by philosophers and one where few historians dare trespass. When it comes to explaining this situation, the usual culprits are the primacy of social history and the considerable role that the *Annales* has played in French historiography, especially since 1946. Actually, the situation is more complex. The distrust of intellectual history is not as unequivocal as is usually claimed. In recent years more and more French historians have warmed up to intellectual history, or at least to the idea that history cannot simply set aside philosophical and scientific texts. But how should they be integrated into the study of societies? Is it preferable to adopt methods and traditions that have already proven their worth elsewhere, as is periodically suggested, or to develop new approaches? The goal of this article is to reflect on what has been, in some sense, a series of missed opportunities between French historians and intellectual history, but also to provide a critical overview of recent research that reveals the promises of a dynamic form of intellectual history consistent with the main traditions of French historiography, especially the so-called *Annales* school and the deep relations with historical sociology.

The Weight of the Disciplines

The absence of a tradition of intellectual history in France depends first of all on the way that the academic disciplines evolved. It is important to note the lack of a genuine philological tradition among French historians, compared with what prevails in Germany or in Italy. In Germany, philology played a fundamental role in the creation of the Humboldtian university model and in the development of the humanities during the nineteenth century. The legacy of that influence appears in the importance that philological studies accords to historical questions and in the attention that historical studies gives to textual criticism and critical hermeneutics.[1] Such cross-fertilization does not exist in France, where philology has always been a minor and auxiliary field of study, if not a contested one. In France, the theory and practice of history has not been guided by a science of texts so much as by the tension between narrative and knowledge, and between literature and social science. Consequently, the effort to constitute history as an academic discipline distinct from literature has involved a series of rapprochements with the other social sciences, beginning with geography at the end of the nineteenth century, moving on to economics and sociology in the 1920s, and finally anthropology in the 1960s. These disciplinary alliances had legitimate epistemological and methodological consequences for the orientation of research, but they also affected the training of historians, who became seasoned in the methods of statistical analysis and the interpretation of maps rather than the art of textual exegesis. In concrete terms, French secondary schools taught history in conjunction with geography, and all professional historians received training in geography.

Another factor specific to France is that the history of philosophy has always been an essential part of the practice of academic philosophy. A very different situation prevails in England and the United States because of the dominant role of analytic philosophy in those countries. In France the history of philosophy is above all a philosophical activity and is theorized as such by the professors of philosophy who engage in it. Their preferred approach is the monographic study of an oeuvre, considered as a closed system whose coherence and truthfulness need to be evaluated. The strictly philosophical perspective in which this history of philosophy is written—the objective being to develop a conceptual problem—makes this kind of study particularly resistant to social or discursive contextualization.[2] Consequently, the history of philosophy in France has become particularly unreceptive to historical questions and especially to the advances of social and cultural history. Meanwhile, French historians have become uniquely apprehensive of philosophy as a field of study. A wide gulf seems to separate the two disciplines.

The *Annales*' Fault?

Beyond this structural problem, the limited appetite French historians have for intellectual history depends upon the dominant trends of twentieth-century French historiography, especially in the wake of the *Annales* school. The more well-known factors include: the alliances that history has forged with the social sciences rather than with the humanities; the preference for modeling and explanation as opposed to hermeneutics; the importance accorded to quantification and the creation of data series; and, finally, the emphasis on economic and social history, and on material culture more generally. To take an example, the turn toward cultural history that began in the 1970s took a very specific form, *l'histoire des mentalités*, whose practitioners tended to be very suspicious of intellectual history. On one side stood a history of the mental tools of ordinary people based on arranging textual evidence in a series, a quantitative approach to the study of cultural phenomena, whether the subject was religious belief, attitudes toward death, or patterns of literacy. On the other side stood a commitment to the careful study of a few texts produced by the literate elite, analyzed for their uniqueness, their irreducibility, and their internal coherence. The gap between these two approaches seemed too wide to offer any possibility of a common ground.[3]

These developments explain why there have been few great historians of intellectual life in France and why so many of the important works of intellectual history have been written by literary historians. Consider the case of the eighteenth century. From Daniel Mornet to Jean Starobinski and from Paul Hazard to Jean Ehrard, literature professors have contributed some of the most influential studies of the intellectual history of the Enlightenment. Yet this fact should not lead us to presume an incompatibility between the *Annales* tradition—which is much more varied and contradictory than the standard account would have it—and intellectual history. Such a misunderstanding would be based on a caricature of *Annales* historians, as if they have always been interested only in economic and social history and quantifiable collective phenomena. Lucien Febvre, in particular, always showed an interest in intellectual history; in the *Annales* and in the *Revue de synthèse* he reviewed and discussed Ernst Cassirer on the philosophy of the Renaissance, Etienne Gilson on medieval philosophy, Léon Brunschvicg on the "esprit européen," and even the critical edition of Thomas More's *Utopia*. To be sure, he pointed out everything that he saw separating "their history and ours," and he accused historians of philosophy of studying in ahistorical fashion "the generation of concepts issued from disembodied minds, which then acquire their own lives outside of time and space." He did so in order to plea for a rapprochement between the disciplines, between these two "groups of workers who, confined to their respective spaces, remain unaware of each other."[4] Moreover, there are several ways to interpret his *Rabelais and the Problem of Unbelief in the Sixteenth Century*. It can be read as an ancestor of *l'histoire des mentalités*, an effort to present the unique author of the *Pantagruel* as a representative man of the sixteenth century. It can also be read as a kind of intellectual history that sought to explore the evolution of knowledge and science.[5] In 1946, for the second issue of the new *Annales*, Febvre wrote an essay on Etienne Gilson's history of medieval philosophy entitled "Histoire des idées, histoire des sociétés, une question de climat," in which he insisted on the importance of the history of ideas for history more broadly. Taking a stand against reductionism, he extolled a more nuanced historicization of ideas: "The point is not to underestimate the role of ideas in history, much less to subordinate ideas to the role of interests. The point is to show that a gothic cathedral, the halls of Ypres, the victims of eternal barbarism, and one of the great cathedrals of ideas such as those that Etienne Gilson describes in his book—these are all children of the same age. . . . Children who grew up in the same climate."[6] Given such an ambitious program, it might be objected that the climate metaphor would have a hard time standing in for epistemology. Yet his remarks show that at the very moment the term "civilization" appeared in the title of *Annales*, Febvre was not ready to abandon the history of thought to philosophers and literary critics.

The following decades, which saw the triumph of Fernand Braudel's *longue durée* and Ernest Labrousse's economic history as well as the mirage of quantification, were not favorable to the development of such a program. By contrast, the questioning of historical certitudes that began in the 1970s and the redefinition of the *Annales'* paradigm during the 1980s (under the double influence of microhistory and the pragmatic turn in the social sciences)[7] made it much more possible for intellectual history to gain momentum. Evidence of this can be found, for example, in the French reception of the works of Reinhart Koselleck and Quentin Skinner, which was more important than has been claimed.[8] The history of political ideas took off in France thanks to the work of François Furet, Marcel Gauchet, and Pierre Rosanvallon.[9] These authors criticized social history with increasing force and urged historians to turn away from the social sciences and embrace intellectual history and political theory.[10]

On a different note, even though the interest that many historians have shared in Foucault's works was indebted to his rejection of the traditional history of ideas, it paved the way for new forms of history of knowledge, more concerned with discursive moments. Meanwhile, those historians who were committed to the *Annales'* historiographical legacy remained reluctant to publicly support intellectual history. They did so despite the fact that the critical attention then being devoted to the history of historiography had led several members of the editorial board of *Annales* to produce important intellectual histories of their discipline.[11] Admittedly, intellectual history was never explicitly promoted by the *Annales*, probably owing to the long-standing vilification of the history of ideas. However, several fields of research were converging toward it. Michel de Certeau's works on mystic thought and religious writings in the seventeenth century were the product of a highly creative mind, but they were also shaped by his solid philological erudition.[12] Meanwhile, the new history of science offered a fresh historiographical agenda that combined the study of scientific theories with the social, political, and material history of scientific practices.[13] In this context, it was a crucial but difficult task to articulate theoretically how certain questions of intellectual history might be addressed by *Annales* historians in a way that would remain true to their own historiographical legacy.

A Missed Opportunity

The most coherent vision of what intellectual history could look like if liberated from the shortcomings of the history of ideas and the reductionism of *l'histoire des mentalités* came from a specialist in urban history and political economy. Acknowledging the restructuring of historical methodology that was taking place, Jean-Claude Perrot concluded, "Out of this extreme thematic freedom, it is possible to expect a renaissance of intellectual history." Yet he immediately lamented, "In France, it is slow in finding a threshold of growth." He worried in particular about a division of labor that would leave historians with the study of intellectual professions and institutions, false beliefs and collective mentalities, but consign to the specialists of each branch of knowledge the study of the major texts of their respective disciplines. To prevent such fragmentation, Perrot proposed a coherent plan for the intellectual history of political economy. He hoped to reclaim a genuinely historical reading of texts that economists had often interpreted in light of contemporary concerns and the present state of knowledge in their discipline.[14]

J. C. Perrot's approach incorporated several methodological choices. Deploring that "the history of thought at present only explores a small portion of its sources," he called for scholars to expand the corpus of texts well beyond the narrow canon established in political economy. Rather than limit itself to a few major theoretical advances confirmed by subsequent research, intellectual history should consider the numerous texts that have since been forgotten. Meanwhile, the historian should pay careful attention to the social conditions, material apparatus, and publishing techniques at work in intellectual debates in order to avoid the idealism of a disembodied history of ideas. Perrot therefore encourages the practice of intellectual biography, which he conceives as a site of interaction between the sociocultural context and the production of the texts that make up intellectual history. In addition, he borrows a concern from the German hermeneutic tradition, namely a commitment to exploring the range of interpretations applied to a given text, and especially the chain of interpretations that ultimately links us back to the past. Perrot qualifies as hermeneutics this manner of reconciling a commitment to historicism with an interest in the interpretive process itself. In opposition to historians devoted to the classic precepts of social history, Perrot affirms that processes of abstraction are historical objects. In opposition to economists and historians of ideas, he advocates a historical approach to economic thought centered on the complex temporalities of intellectual history: one must situate texts in their own time, guarding against the obvious dangers of genealogy, but also recognize the capacity of these texts to address contemporary issues. It is here that intellectual history can affirm its genuinely historical dimension, in the sense that it presents itself above all as a reflection on the multiple temporalities of those distinct historical objects known as texts.

It is not insignificant that this methodological insight was formulated in the field of political economy. Perrot was evidently encouraging social historians to take a critical look at their own analytic tools. In doing so, he was developing an argument that he had already sketched out in his dissertation on Caen.[15] There he showed that when it comes to early modern cities, urban historians cannot afford to depend exclusively on current methods in demography and economics; they must also study the knowledge about cities that existed at the time, the effects that this knowledge had on the management of cities, and the ways that it has shaped developments up to the present. Acknowledging that the model of urban history based on dividing society into categories and examining how it functions was running out of steam, Perrot cleared the way for a methodological reflection on the historicity of economic knowledge and social thought. His proposal could therefore be seen as an alternative to both the genealogy of knowledge, which is often hampered by a quest for precursors, and the archeology of Foucault, which tends to overemphasize discontinuity.

The lesson could have, and should have, been applied beyond the field of political economy.[16] But has it been? Almost twenty years after Perrot's suggestion, the answer remains ambiguous. One might be tempted to respond negatively, if only because intellectual history still has trouble being recognized as a legitimate field of historical study in France. "That's history of ideas" remains a pet phrase for historians to discount a study that makes texts its primary object, however subtle the historical analysis may be. One would be hard pressed to find institutional forms—journals, conferences, and so on—devoted to intellectual history, and the historians who are committed to it sometimes have the impression of working in isolation. As for the *Annales*, during the 1990s it chose to renew its alliance with the social sciences, especially in the form of pragmatic sociology; meanwhile, by embracing microhistory it confirmed the primacy of social history, albeit in a new form. Nevertheless, this account needs to be nuanced. First, the approach of Jean-Claude Perrot has prospered, most notably in the history of political economy and in the history of social thought more generally, as well as in a journal like the *Revue de synthèse*, of which Perrot is a former editor. Moreover, the recent publication of a number of studies, written from a range of perspectives, testifies to the current vigor of intellectual history. In 2009 the *Annales* even devoted a special issue to "History and Philosophy." Indeed, it seems that the present moment is favorable for French historians to re-appropriate intellectual history.[17] Three areas of inquiry reveal the value of some of the points highlighted by J. C. Perrot: the many forms of mediation between texts and their contexts, the back and forth between the knowledge set of the historian and that of his historical subject, and, finally, the question of biography.

Intellectual Work

One set of recent studies concerns the history of intellectual work. Instead of analyzing thought as a final product, in the form of conceptual systems or fixed texts, these studies seek to understand the conditions in which thought develops. Two approaches become apparent. First is the historical sociology of intellectual labor, which emphasizes the material conditions in which thought is elaborated and transmitted: the role of libraries, the dynamic of controversies, the history of the book, sociability and intellectual networks, places of learning, relationships between teachers and students, institutions of accreditation, censorship, and formalization.[18] The goal is not to reduce intellectual history to a history of intellectuals in the mold of social history, but rather to take seriously the fact that intellectual activity is work that involves a range of social, material, and cognitive tools, as well as regulations, training, and apprenticeship. These aspects of intellectual production have often been obscured by the history of ideas and the history of philosophy. The historian should therefore study the specific forms of learned work, from the mastery of scientific techniques to the organization of intellectual communities.

Specialists in the history of books have played an important role by raising new questions and stressing that the meaning of texts depends on the material and editorial form in which they circulated and were read. These historians also insisted on the active appropriation of texts by different audiences and different reading publics. This double lesson of material bibliography and the history of reading, which has been elaborated by Roger Chartier, makes it possible to historicize how philosophical and scientific works were read in specific contexts. This approach has more frequently been used by historians of literature than by historians of philosophy, who tend to be more reluctant to consider how the meaning of a given philosophical text may have been shaped by its original context of production or reception. Nevertheless, the history of books and reading remains promising common ground for cultural and intellectual history.[19] Cultural historians of science have paved the way by focusing on the material and textual conditions that shape the production and circulation of knowledge, especially in the field of natural history.

Meanwhile, research on the formation of the disciplines and on the phases of intellectual controversies has demonstrated that the very nature of the knowledge being produced depends heavily upon the organization of scientific networks.[20] Even those branches of knowledge that proclaim their universality, such as mathematics and philosophy, must construct this universality through patient effort, often by erasing references to the local conditions in which knowledge is produced.[21] A dual task of intellectual history is therefore to uncover these traces of the knowledge process and to study how such traces were obscured by scientific practitioners or, more subtly, by the ways in which scientific disciplines construct their canon.

Intellectual work can also be analyzed on the level of strictly mental processes that are central to knowledge-making without being the exclusive preserve of any intellectual or philosophical tradition, such as description, comparison, prediction, or generalization. Studying these practices requires contextualization of a different kind. The goal is no longer to document the social conditions of intellectual activity, but to show how modes of thinking migrate from one area of inquiry to another. Rather than reconstructing the *episteme* or mentalities that constrain thinking or direct its focus, the point is to historicize intellectual processes that are too often assumed to be universal. For example, Jacques Revel has shown that the modes of comparison found in certain ethnographic texts from the beginning of the eighteenth century are better understood by analyzing them in relation to the techniques of comparison at work in early modern literature more generally, rather than situating them exclusively within a genealogy of comparative anthropology.[22] Likewise, one of the main characteristics of the intellectual history of the Enlightenment is the reliance on description to make sense of the world.[23] The advantage of this approach is that it brings together texts and mental tools that are usually studied by specialists working in different fields. Doing so reveals the importance of technical innovations that first developed in commerce, finance, or government before being adopted in political economy and in the social sciences more generally, such as double-entry bookkeeping and the calculation of averages. Calling for "a concrete history of abstraction," Perrot encouraged scholars to consider the range of these innovations and the extent of their circulation. The modes of classification so important to the modern sciences, for example, can be shown to depend in large part upon the written forms of merchant accounting.[24]

Such attention to the circulation of intellectual processes through different discursive fields offers an attractive way of distinguishing intellectual history from the history of philosophy or the history of science. By tracking the circulation of modes of thinking, forms of writing, even entire intellectual traditions outside the disciplinary canons, this approach considerably expands the range of texts that matter to intellectual history. It also encourages more daring forms of comparison that could propel intellectual history beyond the realm of European or Western thought. Can the classic tools of intellectual history be adapted to other corpuses? Can we imagine a connected history of thought?[25]

Intellectual History and the History of Social Sciences

Research in the history of the humanities and social sciences has often been separated from methodological advances in the history of science. Paradoxically, when historians look back on the past of their own discipline, they often fall into the very traps that they would otherwise avoid: the heroic cult of ancestors, the futile search for precursors, the genealogy of trends and schools of thought, the history of ideas. Fortunately, a number of recent works are reinvigorating the history of the social sciences, a field that in the last few years has launched a journal and been the subject of much methodological reflection.

The history of intellectual work has opened new perspectives on the history of the humanities and social sciences. Several studies focus on the personal archives of historians and social scientists in order to document precisely how they worked, from note taking to writing, from research methods to course preparation.[26] Previous studies tended to be based on the major works of the great historians of the past, especially their methodological statements (introductions, manifestos, and so on). The availability of a wider range of material enables scholars to move past this idealized version and analyze how history is actually made. This change has been inspired in part by the lively epistemological debate among historians about the nature of their discipline. It is now widely acknowledged that history should be understood both as the production of knowledge and as a literary activity; attention should be paid to how historians work with sources as well as the stylistic or narrative choices that shape their texts.[27] Moreover, the approach is now being extended to the rest of the humanities. Consider, for example, Vincent Debaene's study of French anthropologists' ambivalence toward literary writing or Jean-Louis Fabiani's reflections on French philosophers' stance on authorship.[28]

A second way of historicizing the stakes of the historical debates is to situate historiographic trends within wider epistemological debates. A number of studies have set out to contextualize debates within the historical profession by showing how they depend upon and contribute to broader theoretical and intellectual trends. Such is the case with Enrico Castelli Gattinara's study of epistemological debates during the interwar period.[29] The scope of inquiry can be enlarged further by practicing a sort of historical anthropology of the historian's gaze, as François Hartog has done, moving from reflections on the theoretical stakes of history in Greece to an analysis of regimes of historicity. In this example, as in the later work of Reinhart Koselleck, debates among historians about the function of history are placed in a much broader cultural context—the relationship that societies have with time, the link between their field of experience and their horizon of expectations. Once again the inquiry calls for a wider range of sources, including literary texts.[30]

Finally, the very concepts commonly used by historians need to be treated as material for intellectual history. Whether borrowed explicitly from other social sciences or taken from ordinary language, these notions generally have a history that lexicographic analysis alone cannot reveal. Unfortunately, the reflexivity of historians usually remains limited to discussing the historical uses of a given term within their own discipline, or at best among other social sciences. Yet very often a genuine conceptual history of the notion, in the tradition of *Begriffsgeschichte*, would allow for a more careful and self-conscious use of it. Consider the notion of civilization, for example. After having been one of the banners of French historiography, most famously for Braudel but for many others as well, this term was almost silently abandoned, disappearing from the title of the *Annales* and from general use by historians. Today it is blamed for essentializing cultural differences and dismissed as Eurocentric. However, a genuine intellectual history of the concept, from its invention in the eighteenth century to its transformation into a key word in the philosophy of history during the nineteenth century, would show that the ambiguities of the term "civilization" are inherent to a form of history writing that has always aspired to be both Eurocentric and universalist. Such an approach reveals that Braudel's "grammar of civilizations" should not be read through the prism of contemporary theories of the "clash of civilizations," but rather as an indirect consequence (largely unrecognized at the time) of the inherent contradictions of the Enlightenment historical project, a project that the *Annales* had in many respects inherited. Once again, an intellectual history of concepts in the humanities must move beyond their uses in philosophical texts to take account of all the fields of knowledge, literature, and social activity where those concepts are constructed. For example, a collaborative project on the origins of the notion of society in the eighteenth century analyzed "society" as a social concept, a political principle, and a field of study. Bringing together historians of literature, political culture, and philosophy, the project explored the intellectual conditions for the emergence of social science.[31] This research called into question the way that postwar historiography, under the influence of the linguistic turn, had reified social vocabulary.[32]

Intellectual Lives

Historians have an ambivalent relationship with biography.[33] In the field of intellectual history, biography is simultaneously a convenient temptation, an obligatory step in the research, and a foil, for it can seem dangerously close to the monographic studies characteristic of the history of philosophy or, worse yet, the kind of biographical explanation long central to literary history. One may assume that the cumulative effects of cultural history, the new criticism, and the Foucauldian archeology of knowledge have definitively ended the reign of biography. Yet biography has also sometimes been thought of as a particularly useful subject because it enables historians to test out (in relation to an individual intellectual trajectory) the range of contexts that help make sense of a work.

Intellectual history's relationship to biography has recently been modified in two ways. First, instead of isolating the author's life as a unit of study, the goal is to analyze the significance of the proper nouns that haunt intellectual history. For example, what place does biography occupy in the literary history of philosophy since the early modern period?[34] How does someone become a "grand philosophe"?[35] How does a canon or tradition of intellectual history get established? The biographical referent is no longer taken for granted as something that must be scrutinized for clues that explain an author's work, nor is it rejected in favor of the text alone. Instead, biography is viewed as the result of a number of social, literary, and theoretical operations that enable a given oeuvre to become central in its field.

Second, the influence of Pierre Hadot's work on the philosophy of antiquity and the tradition of spiritual exercises suggests another way that biography can contribute to intellectual history. Hadot took seriously the idea that in certain contexts philosophy is not merely a set of doctrines or coherent theoretical systems, but also a way of life, an ethical ideal toward which the philosopher himself strives. This argument, which calls for historicizing the very notion of philosophy and revitalizing the way its history is written, has been applied in other periods by Hadot himself, such as in the case of Goethe, but also by Juliusz Domanski for the Renaissance or Matthew Jones on major figures of the Scientific Revolution.[36]

In France, several scholars have adopted this approach, which has the virtue of breaking down barriers between fields, reintroducing moral and religious questions into the history of knowledge, and opening a space for dialogue between the social history of intellectuals and intellectual history proper. The history of intellectuals, inspired largely by the history of the professions and the historical sociology of cultural fields, has produced classic works of French historiography by Jacques Le Goff, Daniel Roche, Christophe Charle, Christophe Prochasson, and others. Yet such work has sometimes been criticized for not analyzing the philosophical stakes of the texts themselves. It is this gap—between the intellectual and his work—that current research seeks to fill.[37]

This approach could also benefit from the notion of parrhesia discussed by Michel Foucault in his final lectures at the Collège de France. Parrhesia is a form of truthful speech that requires courage on the part of the person who utters it, and such risk-taking constitutes both a moral and a political act.[38] The example of Jean-Jacques Rousseau suggests the advantages to be gained from such a perspective. Rousseau was of course caught up in the dynamics and internal contradictions of the Enlightenment and is the subject of a massive bibliography. Unfortunately, his works have been divided among specialists who do not speak to one another. While philosophers work on his more theoretical texts (the *Discourse on the Origins of Inequality* and the *Social Contract*), literary historians favor his autobiographical texts and the *Nouvelle Héloïse;* historians, meanwhile, tend to be more interested in his reception and his "influence" on modern sensibility or the French Revolution. Moreover, given the difficulty of pinning down Rousseau's central doctrines, an almost total misunderstanding separates those who view him as a precursor to the Jacobin Republic and those who see him as an enemy of the Enlightenment.

One of the most consistent features of Rousseau's work is its insistence on the equivalence of his life and his thought, with the goal that each could serve simultaneously as a model for the ethical self and as an instrument of social criticism. For Rousseau, a thinker must bring his life into line with his philosophy before his words can be convincing to others. Likewise, his work can be read in part as a reflection on the conditions of an authentic life in the interdependent world of modernity. Such a conception of Rousseau's oeuvre as an ethical and political project encourages us to study his unique position in the literary world of the time (such as his conflicts with other *philosophes* and with his social protectors) in conjunction with his attitudes toward writing and publishing (in particular his rejection of the common practice of anonymity) and his anthropology of recognition. The goal of such an inquiry is obviously not to explain Rousseau's thought as the product of his contradictory position, nor to read his life through the categories of his philosophical work, but rather to make sense of his unique place in the intellectual history of the Enlightenment. Indeed, Rousseau owes much to the ancient philosophical concern for care of the self, both to the Socratic tradition and the parrhesia of the Cynics. But he clearly distinguishes himself by affirming a sense of individuality and uniqueness that belongs entirely to modern subjectivity.[39] In doing so, Rousseau constructs an extremely powerful critical stance that has considerable influence on later conceptions of artistic genius and social activism. This stance turns out to be terribly unstable because it makes the authenticity of critique dependent upon the public's judgment of an author's personality, including his private life. Rousseau discovered a form of social critique based on the performance of an exemplary life in a public sphere open to new forms of celebrity. Recognizing the contradictions inherent in such a project was the tragedy of Rousseau's life, and hence the subject of the dark meditations that characterize his final works.[40]

At a moment when historiography has become transnational, if not global, it may seem strange to have presented the evolution of intellectual history within a national framework. This choice has resulted in an incomplete account, since most of the recent works discussed were part of international trends. Nevertheless, history remains an academic discipline that functions largely within national contexts, not only because of institutional regulations governing the recruitment of scholars and the evaluation of their research, but also because of the distinct ways that students are trained, publications are reviewed, and research priorities are set. There is a widespread notion, in France and abroad, that intellectual history is not genuinely recognized in France. As I have attempted to show, the situation is changing, not through manifestos, journals, and organizations to legitimate intellectual history and bring together those who practice it—as was the case with cultural history during the 1980s—but rather in the form of a constellation of research and publications that share certain strategies and concerns. Focusing on the production and circulation of knowledge and ideas, these works stress the forms, including the material forms, of intellectual work. They strive for a fruitful dialogue with the other social sciences. And they emphasize the kind of critical hermeneutics called for by Perrot: a careful interpretive practice buttressed by solid historical documentation that pays attention to the relationship between our own forms of knowledge and those of the period that we are studying.

Such attentiveness to the temporality of knowledge is especially important for intellectual history. Like literary historians and art historians, intellectual historians study cultural objects that were produced in specific historical contexts, but whose meaning and significance have changed over time, from their earliest reception by readers or viewers up to their most recent interpretation by scholars. Therein lies a major difference between historians of philosophy, who engage in a dialogue with authors of the past and thereby situate their own writing on the same philosophical plane as the texts they cite, and historians, who treat texts of the past as objects of study in themselves. In his contribution to this volume, Peter Gordon defends the idea of approaching philosophical texts of the past with present-day preoccupations in mind, and he cautions against the danger of excessive contextualization. By contrast, the whole tradition of cultural history in France was built upon the premise (sometimes more forcefully stated than others) that an insurmountable distance separates the present of the historian from the past found in his sources. Lucien Febvre's *Rabelais* embodies this insistence on the heterogeneity of the past and the present, and affirms the historian's obligation to avoid anachronism by uncovering the meanings a given text had in the past. This commitment to contextualization is what distinguishes the historian's approach, and it cannot be abandoned without sacrificing the specific contributions that historians make to our understanding of cultural objects. On the other hand, historians also need to recognize that these cultural objects are not stuck in the past. Indeed, the study of Rabelais occupied Febvre for so many years in part because an unbroken chain of commentaries, critical editions, and popular versions had kept Rabelais's work alive in French culture well into the twentieth century. Thus, intellectual history must take into consideration the various mediating forces that enable texts to remain alive and open to interpretation, and then reconstruct the critical tools used by the different interpretive communities that have engaged with these texts over time. Such a perspective implies a different kind of contextualization, one that retains a commitment to the documentation and criticism

of sources while recognizing the historian's own dependence on certain hermeneutic and cultural traditions.

This essay has not attempted to provide a complete or impartial overview of
intellectual history as practiced in France under various names. Rather, I have
tried to better understand the precarious status that intellectual history has long
had within French historiography and to suggest some lines of research that
promise to reinvigorate intellectual history by drawing inspiration and tools
from cultural history and the history of the social sciences. In the works cited,
intellectual history does not appear as an autonomous subdiscipline (in the
model of what exists in the United States), nor does it enter into conflict with
social and cultural history. Instead, intellectual history becomes a special site of
exchange and debate among the fields of history, literary studies, philosophy,
and sciences studies. The strength of such an intellectual history is to encourage
reflexivity, so that the historian experiences the historicity of his or her own
knowledge, as well as to forge links with other disciplines. Because it is not
highly regulated, it may become a place for free experimentation.

Notes

1. Michael Werner, "Le moment philologique des sciences historiques
allemandes," in *Qu'est-ce qu'une discipline?*, ed. Jean Boutier, Jean-Claude Passeron, and
Jacques Revel (Paris: Editions de l'EHESS, 2006), 171–91.

2. A classical definition in Martial Guéroult, *Philosophie de l'histoire de la
philosophie* (Paris: Aubier, 1979). More recently, Charles-Yves Zarka, ed., *Comment
écrire l'histoire de la philosophie?* (Paris: PUF, 2001), 19–32. However, some recent
attempts offer a different history of philosophy, more attentive to historical *moments*,
defined by common questions and networks of texts: Frédéric Worms, *La philosophie
en France au XXe siècle* (Paris: Gallimard, 2009).

3. This point has been stressed by Roger Chartier in "Intellectual or Sociocultural
History? The French Trajectories," in *Modern European Intellectual History:
Reappraisals and New Perspectives*, ed. Dominick LaCapra and Steven Kaplan (Ithaca,
NY: Cornell University Press, 1982), 13–46. Chartier insisted strongly on the
divergences between the two traditions with the implicit aim of advocating a third way,
which he would later call "history of representations" (see "Le monde comme
représentation," *Annales ESC* 44, no. 6 [1989]: 1505–20) and which proved to be very
successful in shaping a new cultural history. In this chapter I will not analyze this
important strand of studies, which remained remote from intellectual history per se.

4. Lucien Febvre, "L'histoire de la philosophie et l'histoire des historiens,"
Revue de synthèse 52, no. 1 (1932): 97–103, and in *Combats pour l'histoire*, in *Vivre
l'Histoire*, éd. B. Mazon (Paris: Robert Laffont/Armand Colin, 2007): 238–44,
quotation on p. 240.

5. History of science is certainly, in France, a field in which a form of intellectual history has existed, in the tradition of historical epistemology, thanks to Bachelard, Koyré, or Canguilhem. I have no place to discuss these authors in this article, but it has to be stressed that they were mostly philosophers and perceived as such by historians.

6. Lucien Febvre, "Histoire des idées, histoire des sociétés, une question de climat," *Annales ESC* 1, no. 2 (1946): 158–61.

7. "Histoire et sciences sociales: un tournant critique?," *Annales ESC* 43, no. 2 (1988): 291–93; "Tentons l'expérience," *Annales ESC* 44, no. 6 (1989): 1317–23; Jacques Revel (dir.), *Jeux d'échelle: La micro-histoire à l'expérience* (Paris: Gallimard/Seuil, 1996); Bernard Lepetit (dir.), *Les formes de l'expérience* (Paris: Albin Michel, 1995).

8. Jacques Guilhaumou, "L'histoire des concepts, le contexte historique en débat," *Annales HSS* 56, no. 3 (2001): 685–98; Julien Vincent, "Concepts et contextes de l'histoire intellectuelle britannique: l''École de Cambridge' à l'épreuve," *Revue d'histoire moderne et contemporaine* 50, no. 2 (2003): 187–207.

9. Above all, Marcel Gauchet, *La Révolution des droits de l'homme* (Paris: Gallimard, 1989) and *La Révolution des pouvoirs, la souveraineté, le peuple et la représentation* (Paris: Gallimard, 1995); Pierre Rosanvallon, *Le moment Guizot* (Paris: Gallimard, 1985) and *Le Sacre du citoyen. Histoire du suffrage universel en France* (Paris: Gallimard, Bibliothèque des histoires, 1992). See also Samuel Moyn's chapter in this volume.

10. Marcel Gauchet, "L'élargissement de l'objet de l'histoire," *Le Débat*, no. 103 (January–February 1999): 131–46, and Roger Chartier's answer in the same issue.

11. Jacques Revel, "Histoire et sciences sociales: les paradigmes des Annales," *Annales ESC* 34, no. 6 (1979): 1360–76; Jean-Yves Grenier and Bernard Lepetit, "L'expérience historique. A propos de C.-E. Labrousse," *Annales ESC* 44, no. 6 (1989): 1337–60.

12. Michel de Certeau, *La fable mystique, XVI–XVIIe siècles* (Paris: Gallimard, 1982).

13. Dominique Pestre, "Pour une histoire sociale et culturelle des sciences. Nouvelles définitions, nouveaux objets, nouvelles pratiques," *Annales HSS* 50, no. 3 (1995): 487–522.

14. Jean-Claude Perrot, *Une histoire intellectuelle de l'économie politique* (Paris: Ed. de l'EHESS, 1992). After an important book on Caen, published in 1975, J. C. Perrot published several articles on the history of political economy, often in *Annales*. See, for intstance, Jean-Claude Perrot, "La comptabilité des entreprises agricoles dans l'économie physiocratique," *Annales ESC* 33, no. 3 (1978): 559–79 and "Premiers aspects de l'équilibre dans la pensée économique française," *Annales ESC* 38, no. 5 (1983): 1058–74. The edition of *Une histoire intellectuelle* was made possible by Bernard Lepetit, then editor of *Annales* and a former student of Perrot, and Jacques Revel, then-director of the EHESS Press and still member of the *Annales* editorial board. Thus, Perrot's work was conspicuously, at the time, in the intellectual proximity of the *Annales*.

15. Jean-Claude Perrot, *Genèse d'une ville moderne, Caen au XVIIIe siècle* (Paris-La Haye, Mouton, 1975).

16. In this field, Perrot's legacy has been important: Eric Brian, *La mesure de l'Etat. Administrateurs et géomètres au XVIIIe siècle* (Paris: Albin Michel, 1994); Jean-Yves Grenier, *L'économie d'Ancien Régime: un monde de l'échange et de l'incertitude* (Paris: Albin Michel, 1996).

17. "Histoire et philosophie," *Annales HSS* 64, no. 1 (2009). See also the special issue: "Regards sur l'histoire intellectuelle," *Revue d'histoire moderne et contemporaine* 59, no. 4bis (2012).

18. Daniel Roche, "l'intellectuel au travail," *Annales ESC* 37, no. 3 (1982): 465–80, reprint in *Les Républicains de letters* (Paris: Fayard, 1986); Etienne Anheim and Sylvain Piron, in the special issue, "Le travail intellectuel au Moyen-Age," *Revue de synthèse* 129, no. 4 (2008); Alain Boureau, *Théologie, science et censure au XIIIe siècle. Le cas de Jean Peckham* (Paris: Les Belles Lettres, 1999); Christian Jacob, ed., "Mondes lettrés, communautés savantes," *Annales HSS* 60, no. 3 (2005) and *les lieux de savoir*, 2 vols. (Paris: Albin Michel, 2007–2011); Dinah Ribard, "Le travail intellectuel: travail et philosophie, XVIIe–XIXe siècle," *Annales HSS* 65, no. 3 (2010): 715–42; Christophe Prochasson and Anne Rasmussen, eds., "Comment on se dispute: les formes de la controverse," *Mil neuf cent. Revue d'hisoire intellectuelle* 25 (2007).

19. See, for example, Jean-Pierre Cavaillé's work on the strategies of writing and publishing by the *libertins* of the seventeenth century: *Dis/simulations. Religion, morale et politique au XVIIe siècle. Jules-César Vanini, François La Mothe Le Vayer, Gabriel Naudé, Louis Machon et Torquato Accetto* (Paris: Champion, 2002); and "Libérer le libertinage. Une catégorie à l'épreuve des sources," *Annales HSS* 64 (2009): 45–80. See also, at the crossroads of the history of books and intellectual history, Jacob Soll, *Publishing the Prince: History, Reading and the Birth of Political Criticism* (Ann Arbor: University of Michigan Press, 2005).

20. Boutier et al., *Qu'est-ce qu'une discipline?*

21. Stéphane Van Damme, *Paris capitale philosophique, de la Fronde à la Révolution* (Paris: Odile Jacob, 2005).

22. Jacques Revel, "The Uses of Comparison: Religions in the Early Eighteenth Century," in *Bernard Picard and the First Global Vision of Religion*, ed. Lynn Hunt, Margaret Jacob, and Wijnand Mijnhardt (Los Angeles, CA: Getty Publications, 2010).

23. B. Lepetit, "En présence du lieu même . . . Pratiques savantes et identification des espaces à la fin du XVIIIe siècle," in *Carnet de croquis* (Paris: Albin Michel, 1999), 186–223.

24. Perrot, *Une Histoire intellectuelle*, 30.

25. Romain Bertrand, "Les 'splendides paroles' du Taj-us Salatin (1603). Pour une histoire à parts égales des idées politiques," in *Les idées en science politique*, ed. Jean-Gabriel Contamin and Jean-Philippe Heurtin (Paris: Presses Universitaires de Rennes, 2013).

26. Jean-François Bert, *L'atelier de Marcel Mauss* (Paris: CNRS Editions, 2013). See also, among works in progress, Patrick Boucheron on Georges Duby, Christophe Prochasson on François Furet, Philippe Artières and Judith Revel on Michel Foucault.

27. Since the seminal works by Hayden White, Paul Ricoeur, Michel de Certeau, Roland Barthes, and Jacques Rancière, many studies have emphasized the importance of such choices. For a striking example, see Paul-André Rosenthal, "Métaphore et stratégie épistémologique: *la Méditerranée* de Fernand Braudel," in *Alter-Histoire*, ed. D. Milo and A. Boureau (Paris: Les Belles Lettres, 1991), 109–26.

28. Vincent Debaene, *L'adieu au voyage, L'ethnologie française entre science et literature* (Paris: Gallimard, 2010); Jean-Louis Fabiani, *Qu'est-ce qu'un philosophe français?* (Paris: Editions de l'EHESS, 2010).

29. Enrico Castelli Gattinara, *Les inquiétudes de la raison. Épistémologie et histoire en France dans l'entre-deux-guerres* (Paris: Vrin/Éd. de l'EHESS, 1998).

30. François Hartog, *Le miroir d'Hérodote. Essai sur la représentation de l'autre* (Paris: Gallimard, 1980), *Evidence de l'histoire. Ce que voient les historiens* (Paris: Editions de l'EHESS, 2005), and *Régimes d'historicité, Présentisme et Expériences du temps* (Paris: Le Seuil, 2003).

31. Laurence Kaufmann and Jacques Guilhamou, *L'invention de la société. Nominalisme politique et science sociale au XVIIIe siècle* (Paris: Editions de l'EHESS, 2003).

32. Keith Baker, "Enlightenment and the Institution of Society: Notes for a Conceptual History," in *Main Trends in Cultural History*, ed. W. Melching and W. Velema (Amsterdam: Rodopi, 1992), 95–120.

33. Sabina Loriga, *Le petit X, De la biographie à l'histoire* (Paris: Seuil, 2010).

34. Dinah Ribard, *Raconter, vivre, penser. Histoire(s) de philosophes, 1650–1766* (Paris: Vrin, 2003).

35. Stéphane Van Damme, *Descartes, essai d'histoire d'une grandeur philosophique* (Paris: Presses de Sciences Po, 2002). See also François Azouvi, *La gloire de Bergson* (Paris: Gallimard, 2007).

36. Juliusz Domanski, *La philosophie, théorie ou manière de vivre? Les controverses de l'Antiquité à la Renaissance*, preface by P. Hadot (Paris: Cerf, 1996); Matthew L. Jones, *The Good Life in the Scientific Revolutions: Descartes, Pascal, Liebnniz, and the Cultivation of Virtue* (Chicago: University of Chicago Press, 2006); Stéphane Van Damme, "Méditations mathématiques. Retour sur une pratique morale des sciences à l'âge classique," *Annales HSS* 67, no. 1 (January–March 2012): 135–52.

37. Etienne Anheim, "Pétrarque, l'écriture comme philosophie," *Revue de synthèse* 129, no. 4 (2008): 587–609.

38. Michel Foucault, *Le gouvernement de soi et des autres I* (Paris: Gallimard/Seuil, 2008) and *Le Courage de la vérité, le gouvernement de soi et des autres II* (Paris: Gallimard/Seuil, 2009).

39. Barbara Carnevali, "Le moi ineffaçable: exercices spirituels et philosophie moderne," in *Pierre Hadot, L'enseignement des antiques, l'enseignement des modernes*, ed. A. Davison and F. Worms (Paris: Editions Rue d'Ulm, 2010).

40. Antoine Lilti, "The Writing of Paranoia: Jean-Jacques Rousseau and the Paradoxes of Celebrity," *Representations* 103 (2008): 53–80.

4

On Conceptual History

Jan-Werner Müller

A consciousness of the history of concepts becomes a duty
of critical thinking.

—Hans-Georg Gadamer

Concepts are like joints linking language and the
extralinguistic world. To deny this distinction is to hypnotize
oneself and, like Hitler, to succumb to a self-produced
ideology.

—Reinhart Koselleck

Words, too, can destroy.

—Reinhart Koselleck

Reinhart Koselleck was the greatest theorist of history in postwar
Germany. Yet, somewhat paradoxically, there exists no real theory of
the approach in intellectual history for which Koselleck became
most famous both in Germany and internationally: conceptual
history, or *Begriffsgeschichte*.[1] While Koselleck throughout his life was
working out his proper *Historik*—that is, a theory explicating the
very conditions of possible histories—conceptual history remained a
related, but in many ways quite undertheorized, project. In the end,
much of what he wrote either about or for the famous lexicon of
Basic Historical Concepts (*Geschichtliche Grundbegriffe*) takes a
pragmatic approach.[2]

   That pragmatism, however, also helped *Begriffsgeschichte* travel.
Apart from the original projects in Germany, there are now great
collective research undertakings in other parts of Europe (especially

northern Europe), but also further afield—with Latin America a particularly important area of development. Yet, the global expansion of conceptual history has also been overshadowed by a number of doubts about the very approach. Some of this skepticism is purely methodological, especially when it takes the form of intellectual sniping from members of the "Cambridge School." In particular, there have been questions about whether concepts can actually change, or whether all that can be investigated is the "changing usage of words." There have also been concerns as to whether conceptual history can really give a coherent account of, broadly speaking, the relationship between language and social history, which in many ways was its most exciting initial promise.

On a more political front, *Begriffsgeschichte* has been suspected of being bound up with—or, less politely put, contaminated by—a profound antimodernism and deeply problematic assumptions about the nature of political and social life that ultimately derive from Carl Schmitt and Otto Brunner, a legal theorist and a historian, respectively, deeply implicated in National Socialism. Many observers think that conceptual history can be disentangled from Koselleck's and Schmitt's diagnoses of modernity as an age of dangerous "ideologizations." At the same time the claim that conceptual history needs to take into account the particular dynamics of modernity (in particular, the rise of "collective singular terms" such as "History" in and of itself, which in its abstract quality is prone to some form of "ideologization") is precisely what made conceptual history as practiced by Koselleck and his followers so stimulating in the first place—as opposed to a pedestrian comparison of the usage of words in lexicons in, let's say, fifty-year intervals (an approach that, alas, can also be found in a number of the chapters in the *Geschichtliche Grundbegriffe*). In what sense, then, might very different modernities need very different conceptual histories? In other words: is conceptual history so far completely bound up with a particular European, or at least Western, experience—and can there be multiple conceptual histories for multiple modernities? Or are there limits to travel, after all?

In this essay I shall start out by reconstructing the origins of conceptual history, before discussing the great success of *Geschichtliche Grundbegriffe*, as well as attempts to export conceptual history beyond its original German contexts. Subsequently, I shall address some of the doubts and concerns about conceptual history at which I already hinted: I shall argue that conceptual history can indeed be dissociated from some of the particular assumptions about modernity that perhaps tell us more about 1950s and 1960s Western Europe than modernity as such. On the other hand, I shall confirm the suspicion that in many ways the actual "method" or, for that matter, the underlying theoretical assumptions of conceptual history are not nearly as clear as might be desirable.

In fact, conceptual history has always remained somewhat indeterminate: it promised to mediate between "social history and the history of consciousness" or, put differently, "between language and reality," without it ever becoming fully clear how that mediation can be carried out coherently, or for that matter whether assuming a split between language and "reality" was actually plausible.[3] This indeterminacy is not the only explanation for conceptual history's success—but, as Hans Ulrich Gumbrecht has pointed out, it probably contributed significantly to it.[4] Put differently: doing conceptual history itself opens certain horizons of expectations about how one can really comprehend very large-scale processes of historical change (not just in intellectual history)—but there are legitimate doubts as to the extent to which these expectations can actually be fulfilled.

Having said that, it is also somewhat naive or at least unimaginative to expect that a method, even with its ambitions of historical understanding some-what scaled down, can somehow mechanically be applied to ever more topics, times, and geographical areas, until all regions and historical experiences have been covered with "their" conceptual histories. What then should one expect, or work toward? This question opens up the final section of the essay, where I offer an explicit assessment of what is dead and what is alive in conceptual history. Conceptual history, in the way initially envisaged by Koselleck (before he moved away from overly normative considerations), can provide a "semantic check" and have a clarifying function for present-day political theorizing, especially if coupled with a convincing account of present-day understandings of the experience of historical time (this may sound rather cryptic—bear with me). I am less convinced, however, that somehow conceptual histories can serve as vehicles to realize lofty ideals such as "mutual European understanding" or even "intercivilizational dialogue," as is sometimes claimed.

Second, I want to encourage more work on how concepts travel and are reworked under very different circumstances of "real history." Finally, I want to suggest that conceptual history could fruitfully be broadened both in its objects and in its ambitions to comprehend lived experience, as opposed to elite discourses. For instance, it could include a focus on political iconology, as has sometimes been suggested. Most important, however, might be a stronger attention to semantic fields, as opposed to single words, especially in everyday use and lived experience, not just among social and political theorists.[5] The last point is not a cheap populist shot. Conceptual history itself, as I shall show, demands an account of historical times and experience, and the broader that account the better. In that sense, "populism" was always a postulate of conceptual history itself.

This essay will offer three recommendations in the end: to undertake a critical conceptual history of the present; to write more histories of translations and appropriations, as well as mistranslations and misappropriations; and, finally, to make more sophisticated use of the idea of conceptual history as a means to theorize processes of historical change—in particular the changing nature of experience itself, and on a broader basis than "basic concepts" or *Grundbegriffe*. In all three areas Koselleck's own theory of history might be productively employed. The exact relationship between conceptual history and *Historik* in Koselleck's own work has not always been entirely clear, but they undoubtedly informed each other profoundly and partly made for such a rich intellectual legacy, the full measure of which has yet to be taken.

Historicizing *Begriffsgeschichte*: Positions and Concepts in Wrestling with European Modernity and Twentieth-Century History

The *Begriffsgeschichte* of *Begriffsgeschichte* tells us that Hegel first used the word.[6] However, as a research program (and much less obviously as a distinct "method") *Begriffsgeschichte* emerged in the late 1950s and early 1960s in West Germany. In a very broad way it can be interpreted as part of the linguistic turn—but with crucial caveats. This point is important to stress because "historical semantics," "discourse analysis," "contextualism," and so on are nowadays often run together with conceptual history, despite their profoundly different objects of study, differing philosophies of language, and, at least in some cases, different normative background assumptions and goals.

German *Begriffsgeschichte* can be understood as a common movement of historians and philosophers—although the movement was internally complex, with many, sometimes deep-seated philosophical and political differences. For instance, Joachim Ritter's project of a philosophical dictionary was not the same as Koselleck's program for specifically investigating historical change and the making of modernity in a national (German) context. Ritter's approach remained much more in the tradition of trying to fix the essential meanings of philosophical terms. To be sure, Hans-Georg Gadamer influenced them all—but different parts of the movement took very different insights from *Truth and Method*.[7]

There are two plausible, but perhaps rather reductionist, readings of why the great wave of *Begriffsgeschichte* happened when it did. On the one hand, it could actually be understood as a form of coming to terms with the past: a tracing and testing of concepts after the Third Reich, with much more obvious examples of examining political languages as part of *Vergangenheitsbewältigung* being Victor Klemperer's *LTI* (*Lingua Tertii Imperii*) and Dolf Sternberger's

Wörterbuch des Unmenschen.[8] Simultaneously, as Gumbrecht has claimed, *Begriffsgeschichte* allowed a broader reappropriation of national traditions.[9] In addition to a more particular process of "semantic chastening" for inherited German languages of politics, conceptual history was both a coming-to-terms with the past and a coming-to-terms with the present—but of modernity more broadly, with its supposedly fateful processes of "ideologization," rather than just the immediate Nazi past.[10]

Begriffsgeschichte had many quasi-official aims originally. In the most ambitious purely philosophical form—which is to say, Gadamer's and, to some extent, Ritter's—it was to provide a firm philosophical foundation for the *Geisteswissenschaften*, or, put more provocatively, hermeneutics and conceptual history were ultimately supposed to become one. The main vehicle for this project was the *Archiv für Begriffsgeschichte* journal (which began in 1955) and later the *Wörterbuch*, initially edited by Ritter, whose first volume appeared in 1971.

In its most ambitious historiographical (or, critics might say, barely veiled political) form, conceptual history was to illuminate the dialectic of the Enlightenment (the original title of Koselleck's dissertation, which was renamed *Critique and Crisis*, when Koselleck realized that the title existed already). The project of *Geschichtliche Grundbegriffe* as a whole was deeply informed by the somewhat skeptical perspective on modernity as an age of "ideologizations" (which is not to say that each individual chapter actually took up this theme). What Koselleck and his contributors called the modern *Sattelzeit*—the period when the basic concepts took on their modern meaning or at least when the range in which their meaning could be contested became limited—was also one of enormous social upheaval, a general sense of acceleration, the "ideologization" and "democratization" of increasingly abstract concepts—and thus a new kind of mass politics, and, not least, the reign of dangerous philosophies of history.[11] The modern age was diagnosed as one of actual or latent ideological civil wars (Koselleck once spoke memorably of a "Feuerkranz von Bürgerkriegen"—a "ring of fire consisting of civil wars"—hinting that they all might culminate in nuclear annihilation during his own time). Why? Because, among other things, modern concepts demanded change, political movement, and, ultimately, conflict.

Who in particular were the formative influences for the *Geschichtliche Grundbegriffe*? Officially the lexicon had three editors: Koselleck, Brunner, and the social historian Werner Conze. But de facto it became Koselleck's project. He oversaw it from beginning to end, edited most of the chapters, and ended up writing a few of them (more than he had ever wanted) himself. Koselleck in retrospect identified "many fathers"—but four major points of reference stood out. First, Otto Brunner and Werner Conze as the main members of the

Arbeitskreis für Sozialgeschichte (working group on social history) were already relating social and conceptual history; second, a tradition stretching back to Hegel, which understood conceptual history as the history of philosophical terms and which found its most important contemporary proponent in Gadamer (and, indirectly, Heidegger, whom Koselleck encountered in various colloquia in Heidelberg);[12] third, Koselleck's dissertation adviser Johannes Kühn, whose historical work on different types of toleration effectively amounted to an analysis of different historical concepts; and, last, but certainly not least, Carl Schmitt, whose book on dictatorship had been a kind of proto-conceptual history and who, in his writings and direct exchanges with Koselleck, insisted on the need to contextualize legal and political concepts—in particular the need to relate the meaning of concepts to the character of a historical epoch as a whole.[13]

Yet the initial official justifications of conceptual history hardly ever evoked any of these names or traditions. No doubt they can only be fully understood in the context of the major trends in the German historical profession during the 1960s and 1970s. This might sound reductionist, but there is little to doubt the sincerity of some of Koselleck's retrospective attempts to relativize some of the original claims for the importance and particular role of *Begriffsgeschichte*. At the time, conceptual history was rather modestly presented as an auxiliary enterprise, a handmaiden even, to social history—all in order to legitimize itself and mark a proper distance to traditional *Ideengeschichte* and *Geistesgeschichte*, which were widely suspected not only of being methodologically flawed, but of having had pernicious political consequences (whether nationalism, conservatism, or simply political passivity).

The marriage to social history was one of convenience, then—and quarrels quickly ensued. Koselleck ever more openly suspected social history in the Bielefeld mode of being more or less teleological (in particular with its theory of a special German path of development, or *Sonderweg*). He also thought social historians were uncritically and, in a sense, ahistorically adopting nineteenth-century concepts such as class, nation, and bourgeoisie.[14] In the end, Koselleck would abandon the term "social history" altogether and speak only of the history of facts or events (*Sachgeschichte* or *Ereignisgeschichte*).

Social historians returned the compliments. In their eyes, conceptual history was at best a "dead end," as Hans Ulrich Wehler, the doyen of social history, once put it. At worst, it was "historicism," or part of a conservative revival of a certain kind of idealism, with dangerous political consequences for the progressive projects of social history in particular.

To be sure, conceptual history had from the beginning also been justified with some present-day concerns. In Koselleck's conception, it could serve as a form of "semantological control" of language use in the present and even lead to "political clarification." Koselleck and his colleagues also insisted that in the present concepts in one sense needed no historical account, as their meaning could be grasped by anyone (his elegant formulation is untranslatable: in one's own time *Begrifflichkeit* collapsed into *Begreifbarkeit*). In other words, according to the official self-presentation, nothing directly normative at all followed from the diagnosis of the modern age.

However, de facto at least a mildly conservative or liberal conservative position[15] resulted (and was advocated by Koselleck in some more occasional writings): a sense that our realm of expectations should be "controlled" by past experience, after all, and that prudence demanded a *Postulat der Prognosenkontrolle*—a postulate carefully to control prognoses about the future.[16] Moreover, Koselleck, who eventually did admit to a "reflexive historicism" (*reflektierter Historismus*), cast suspicion on the "collective singular" terms—especially "History," which suggested a singular, goal-directed global process in the name of which all kinds of atrocities might be justified. There was never History—there were only histories, according to Koselleck, who was memorably described by Jacob Taubes as a "partisan of histories" against single History. This insight into the irreducible plurality of human experience was then translated into a kind of *normative* liberal pluralism.[17]

The research program of the *Geschichtliche Grundbegriffe* arguably had varying success: rather than actually uncovering changing understandings of concepts, at least some of the contributors just traced the changing official or semi-official definitions (and semantic environments) of words, especially from one lexicon entry to another over time. Still, regardless of the more or less lexicometric merits of individual chapters, there was a sense that the roughly 7,000 pages of what often simply came to be called "the *GG*" represented a monumental achievement in scholarship. So much so that a contributor like Gumbrecht later concluded that the lexicon was really a "pyramid of the spirit"—highly impressive, similar to the pyramids, as far as the necessary time for completion was concerned (about twenty years), but never to be built again, even in different versions, and more of a museum really than anything anyone would consider for present-day use.

Yet that conclusion seems hasty. Other projects in Europe and elsewhere have gotten under way. Of course, different concepts were chosen in different contexts (sometimes surprising ones: "simplicity" for the Dutch project, for instance[18]), and different accounts of historical development framed the inquiries. For example, the British or Dutch *Sattelzeit*, that is, the era when concepts took on meanings recognizable for those living today, is clearly a different one than the period 1750–1850, which Koselleck had identified for Germany.[19]

Specialized journals and summer schools were founded. Conceptual history spread north, in particular to Scandinavia, and then the notion of a Europe-wide conceptual history was born.[20] The method then went global, with investigations as to how, for instance, Spanish and Portuguese concepts were received, reworked, and even entirely re-created in a Latin American context.[21] While there might be some suspicion that this is conceptual history in its era of mechanical reproducibility, there is ultimately no doubt that these investigations have not only usefully mapped histories, but also opened wider historiographical questions and facilitated comparative work in the history of social and political thought.[22] Whether they will really help "understanding" or even facilitate the creation of new concepts, as is sometimes promised, are questions to which I shall return.

Decontaminating *Begriffsgeschichte*, Clarifying *Begriffsgeschichte*

Is conceptual history somehow contaminated with deeply problematic political assumptions, or principled kinds of antiliberalism and antimodernism, as some critics have suspected? This suspicion has usually been articulated in the form of some kind of genealogy, rather than as a real methodological or, for that matter, broader historiographical or philosophical argument.[23] Brunner, so the story tends to go, was the first, with his pathbreaking *Land and Lordship*, emphatically and systematically to insist on the historicity of concepts. Schmitt emphasized the need for a "sociology of concepts" in his *Political Theology* and explicitly demanded a kind of conceptual history in one of his lectures from the late 1920s:

> All relevant conceptions of the spiritual sphere are existential and not normative. If the centre of spiritual life constantly shifts in the last four hundred years, then consequently all concepts and words change, too, and it is necessary to remember the multiple meanings [*Mehrdeutigkeit*] of every word and concept. The most and the crudest misunderstandings (of which, however, many con men live) can be explained from the false transposition of a concept at home in one sphere . . . onto the other spheres of spiritual life.[24]

Of course, Schmitt was not just interested in conceptual history as a value-neutral research program. He explicitly practiced a form of political writing that aimed at "capturing" or "occupying" concepts. Schmitt thought of concepts as "real carriers of political energy" that could effectively separate friends and enemies.[25] Successful political action meant, not least, imposing the meaning of concepts on politically weaker or vanquished parties; as he put it, it "is a sign of real political power, when a great people determines the way of talking and even the way of thinking of other peoples, the vocabulary, the terminology and the concepts."[26] In short, "Caesar dominus et supra grammaticam" (Caesar is also the master of grammar), as Schmitt, in this sense not all that different from Hobbes, liked to point out.[27]

Brunner also pursued political goals with his kind of conceptual history: the point of *Land und Herrschaft* was not merely to admonish historians that a nineteenth-century distinction between state and society was profoundly misleading when projected onto feudal orders; he actively sought to undermine and, ultimately, abolish that distinction as such. At the meeting of the German historical profession in 1937 he demanded nothing less than a "revision of basic concepts."[28] To be sure, after the war, Brunner replaced *Volk* with "structure" throughout *Land and Lordship*. Schmitt, barred from teaching, retreated into a semiprivate world that hardly allowed him (at least officially) to further the kinds of histories and sociologies of concepts he had called for earlier. Of course he did influence individual historians, above all sensitizing them to the importance of changing and contested *Begriffe*: Koselleck and the ancient historian Christian Meier are only the best known.

However, none of the above conclusively demonstrates that the *Geschichtliche Grundbegriffe*, let alone conceptual history more broadly, is somehow contaminated by antimodern ideologies, whether Nazism directly or some other *völkisch* set of ideas. Observers have argued that the importance of the "concrete" context and the conception of the essence of politics as conflict are problematic legacies of Schmitt's thought in Koselleck's work—even going so far as to claim that the latter essentially put forward conceptual history as "a form of intellectual military history" (with the historian as a kind of "war correspondent").[29] Others, equally experienced as intellectual war correspondents, have indirectly confirmed this impression: "Koselleck and I both assume that we need to treat our normative concepts less as statements about the world than as tools and weapons of ideological debate. Both of us have perhaps been influenced by Foucault's Nietzschean contention that 'the history which bears and determines us has the form of a war.'"[30] Or so Quentin Skinner observed, probably inventing a Foucauldian influence on Koselleck, but correctly reminding everyone that he and Koselleck share a certain view of politics—even though Skinner appears to have undergone no Schmittian or, for that matter, Brunnerian education in the way that Koselleck obviously did. Put simply, it is not enough to show that Koselleck had a conception of politics as conflict, or that Brunner, like Koselleck, posited a historical break, or "saddle time," to be able to claim that conceptual history is somehow secretly Schmittian. Furthermore,

Koselleck's own account of the modern ideologization of concepts can in a sense explain what happened with intellectuals like Brunner and Schmitt—or, put differently, *Begriffsgeschichte* itself can historicize some of the fathers of *Begriffsgeschichte*, as they self-consciously "ideologized" their concepts and theories.[31]

Such a claim makes it all the more urgent, however, to clarify what *Begriffsgeschichte* really is—because that is in fact far from obvious. How does one know whether one has identified a "basic concept"? What role exactly do concepts play in history? What kind of evidence ought conceptual historians to gather in order to substantiate claims about conceptual history? Ultimately, to what extent can conceptual history really be understood as a "method" or "approach" that is in some meaningful way "transferable" in understanding the relationship between social and political language, on the one hand, and *Sachgeschichte*, on the other?

Arguably *Begriffsgeschichte* never fully worked out its relationship to "real history"—despite the initial self-presentation as being closely linked to social history. The famous formula of a "convergence of history and concept" confused more than it clarified, but it also allowed its representatives to insist that their approach was fundamentally different from that of, for instance, Michel Foucault or Hayden White (as much as Koselleck exhibited warm sympathy for White's thought in particular). Koselleck was adamant that *Begriffsgeschichte* was precisely not one of the "contemporary modern theories that reduce reality to language and nothing else."[32]

To mark the difference from such theories, Koselleck time and again sought to clarify what he called "the key to the history of concepts"—the key to the question, that is, how "the temporal relationship between concepts and factual circumstances [is] configured." He insisted that "every semantics points beyond itself, even if no subject area can be apprehended and experienced without the semantic performances of language." Moreover, "reality" and concepts do not map onto each other, or move in synch: "the meaning and usage of a word never have a one-to-one relationship with so-called reality"; and "concepts and reality change at variable speeds, so that on occasion it is the conceptuality that outpaces the reality, and sometimes the other way around."[33]

This nonsynchronicity implies that there are concepts that above all register experience (*Erfahrungsregistraturbegriffe*) and concepts that actually create experiences (*Erfahrungsstiftungsbegriffe*). Furthermore, there are concepts in modernity that are essentially utopian—that is to say, not based in any existing "reality" at all—and thus purely about creating expectations (*Erwartungsbegriffe*). All concepts contain an "internal temporal structure," but modern basic concepts—especially those ending in "ism"—demand and inspire "movement and change" (and conversely have little or no "experiential content"). As Koselleck famously summed up this thought, concepts are not just *indicators*— they are also *factors* in history. To be sure, concepts and fact (*Sachverhalt*) always diverge—and that divergence keeps driving historical change. But in modernity, or so it seems from Koselleck's account, concepts seek to close the gap ever more urgently, even aggressively.

This raises a further question: conceptual history ought primarily to be after "basic concepts"—but how does one identify them? Basic concepts, according to Koselleck, are in a sense those concepts that are inevitable at a given time: they are "non-interchangeable"; and in their absence it is "no longer possible to recognize and interpret social and political reality." For concepts to acquire this status, they first have to become "exclusive" and lose a range of meanings—only to then turn particularly contentious, as all parties to a semantic (and, ultimately, political) struggle seek to fix their core meaning in their favor, so to speak. In short, concepts—to be basic concepts—have actually to be ambiguous or have multiples meanings (*vieldeutig*).

Concepts can rise—and concepts can fall. They can even become what Ortega y Gasset once called "cadaverous concepts." How does one know whether a basic concept has ceased to be one, or been replaced by another? Koselleck claimed that "only when a word has lost its capacity to bundle together enough of the experiences arising from the concept and to express all its pent-up expectations in that single common term has it been drained of its power to represent a fundamental concept. Then the word will slowly be taken out of circulation."[34]

Such a "life and death of concepts" perspective might easily suggest that conceptual history amounts in the end to nothing more than what Koselleck at one point dismissed as "positivistic registration"—a kind of record of concepts coming and concepts going. However, what makes conceptual history history— in fact what really makes it possible in the first place—is what Koselleck called a "theory of historical times." The particular project of the *Geschichtliche Grundbegriffe* depended on the theory of the *Sattelzeit*, the "saddle-time" of about 1750 to 1850, during which concepts took on their contemporary modern meaning. It was also during this period that the experience of time is said to have changed fundamentally or, more precisely, to have become "denaturalized." Aristotelian meanings waned; topological concepts became replaced by temporalized, dynamic ones; and "collective singulars" emerged, such as History, Progress, and Freedom. In other words, the specific account of conceptual change during the "saddle-time" only became possible against the background of the theory of modernity as an era of acceleration, politicization, temporalization, and democratization.

To be sure, Koselleck always freely admitted that *Sattelzeit* was just a heu-ristic device, not so much a *Begriff* as a *Vorgriff*, literally a theoretical anticipa-tion, an attempt to get ahead of oneself to structure an investigation that otherwise would have amounted to mere "positivistic registration" (though arguably not even that since one would not have known where to look for units of analysis in the first place). Koselleck even nonchalantly revealed that the specific term *Sattelzeit* had occurred to him at the spur of a moment in order to make a funding application during the heyday of social history more plausible.[35]

But the basic point remains: Koselleck and company insisted that no con-ceptual history is possible without some kind of prior theory of historical times, and some account of the experience of time during a particular period. There is no experience without concepts, and no concepts without experience.[36] This does not automatically set limits to where and how conceptual history can be applied, but it does make it clear that conceptual history can never be simply a matter of picking out what might look like important words in a set of national or regional languages of politics and then examining how these words have been used over time. For proper conceptual history, as Kari Palonen has stressed, semasiological and onomasiological approaches proceed together, along with an account not only of changes in "reality" in general, but also a theory of how history and time are experienced.[37]

The seemingly naive talk about "reality" so far might have raised eye-brows. According to Koselleck, conceptual history remains permanently sus-pended in an intermediate position between "pure history of consciousness" and "pure history of reality." Therefore conceptual history is also never enough to comprehend what ought to be comprehended, as Koselleck put it at one point.[38] So, in one sense, the advantage of conceptual history over other ap-proaches is that it at least tries to break out of the kind of explicit or implicit idealism that, as Samuel Moyn points out in his chapter in this volume, char-acterizes so much of twentieth-century intellectual history. Quentin Skinner in a sense conceded the point, claiming that "I have no general theory about the mechanisms of social transformation, and I am somewhat suspicious of those who have."[39] For sure Koselleck et al. also had no "general theory," but they at least tried to relate representations and the "ineradicable remainders of facticity"[40] that cannot be grasped with language, as opposed to retreating to a tracing of what Koselleck had called a "pure history of consciousness." Now Koselleck explicitly stated what to some might seem obvious, namely that "all language is historically conditioned, and all history is linguistically condi-tioned," and that, furthermore, "there is no acting human community that does not determine itself linguistically."[41] But he still sought to hold on to some ontological distinction between the history of languages and *Sachgeschichte*: not all representations are actions, and not all action is somehow linguistic.[42] Here Koselleck insisted on the wisdom of Herodotus: "There are some things which cannot be explained in words, but only in actions. Other things can be explained in words, but no exemplary deed emerges from them." Koselleck made his claim about the "pre- and extralinguistic conditions of human history" more precise by pointing to what he did not hesitate to call "natural givens" (given for all life, that is, including animals): the metahistorical oppositions of "earlier/later," "inner/outer," and "above/below."[43]

Of course, one can fault conceptual history for precisely this *Sonderweg*: that it somehow failed fully to take the linguistic turn; that it wrongly insists on a mysterious "surplus of history" that can never be captured by language; and that Koselleck's "metahistorical" prelinguistic conditions of history were chosen arbitrarily. But especially for discontents of the linguistic turn, or those who think that we have become somewhat lazy in our assumptions about how thought and practices are indissolubly bound up with each other, this peculiarity of conceptual history might prove a fruitful provocation—and hold out a promise of how thought, time, and the invariants of historical existence could be related in novel ways.

Some have conceded that they have no such account at all—but also implied that we do not need one. Skinner, for instance, owned up to having no interest in theorizing Time itself—or even just the possibility of including a temporal dimension in an account of the meaning of certain concepts.[44] But Koselleck's point had been that it is impossible to have any kind of conceptual history—or for that matter to understand modern social and political concepts—without a theory of historical times, and, more particularly, of how experience and expectations are built into the very meaning of concepts. Put differently: we cannot see things *their* way, if we cannot grasp how *they* experienced time. To be sure, this is not a point that can be generalized. I can ask someone on the street for the way to the train station and expect to be able to make sense of their answer without an account of how they conceive time (though there might be curious exceptions). But if I ask about the conceptual history of "progress" or "democracy," the way "hope and action come together" (Koselleck) in these key concepts, or *Leitbegriffe*, and the way they anticipate the future—then I need to understand how, in modern times, these concepts have become "loaded" not just with diverse experiences, but also with expectations of the future and, consequently, particular images of time and history.[45]

One might be tempted to conclude from this that Bielefeld and Cambridge just kept talking past each other, the best efforts of mediators like Melvin Richter notwithstanding, or that the approaches remain fundamentally at odds.[46]

Yet that would be too hasty. In particular, the point that one looks at the *longue durée*, while the other is interested in "epiphanies" or one-off acts is only somewhat plausible. Both in a sense agree that concepts actually do not change at all; what changes is the usage of words, as Koselleck once put it, with Skinner making an essentially similar argument that there is no "conceptual change" at all, but only "transformations in the applications of the terms by which our concepts are expressed."[47] In a sense, Koselleck's "reflective historicism" and what Koselleck himself refers to as Skinner's "rigorous historicism" (according to which all concepts occur as unique speech acts) can converge. As Koselleck puts it, "The historical uniqueness of speech acts, which might appear to make any history of concepts impossible, in fact creates the necessity to recycle past conceptualizations."[48] What we have then are essentially unchanging concepts, but changing conceptualizations in the form of at least some "linguistic recycling"— not quite Cambridge, but also not quite what Skinner had long argued was the central flaw of *Begriffsgeschichte*.

To be sure, there are still important differences: *Begriffsgeschichte* explicitly cares about nonlinguistic contexts, Cambridge does not; *Begriffsgeschichte* needs to engage with "discourses" and "languages," but how concepts interrelate in a language or discourse (almost like a "living thing," according to Pocock) is not the primary focus—and a fateful temptation is indeed to treat single words as units that can be analyzed more or less in isolation (even if de facto, like a Pocockian language, they always have to be seen in relation to what Pocock calls a "semi-specific community of language users").[49] Concepts and discourses are not separate; they are part of a hermeneutical circle—but, as some of the chapters of the *GG* make clear, it is in practice easy to lose sight of this basic point.[50]

What Is Dead and What Is Alive in Conceptual History?

Not so much by way of conclusion but rather by way of tentative recommendations, I would like to suggest three areas in which conceptual history could productively be employed and extended. First is what one might call a critical conceptual history of the present. It was a given for Koselleck and other conceptual historians that, at least in the German context in which they were initially interested, there was no point in tracing conceptual history further than the moment when concepts become immediately comprehensible for the living. This does of course not mean that such concepts turn out to be uncontested. Quite the opposite, for concepts to remain basic they have to be simultaneously unavoidable, ambiguous, and continuously contested.

A critical conceptual history of social and political terms would take on board the point that only that which has no history can be defined and trace the history of contestations up to the very present.[51] At the same time, it might broaden the field of investigation from elite discourses (in particular, academic political and social theory on which the *GG* drew heavily) to lived, everyday experience—an example being Rolf Reichardt's work on French conceptual history, which examines a wide variety of genres, from satires to songs to games, to understand popular *mentalités*.[52] An emphasis on the latter might then generate research into whether some of our basic political and social concepts have not in fact been changing because of different degrees of experience and expectations with which they are invested—in other words, their internal temporality might have been transformed. We might well have similar intuitions to people during the *Sattelzeit* when we talk about democracy, as far as a basic image of political institutions are concerned—but the politics of time associated with democracy might have changed fundamentally, as might have the understanding of the "collective singular concepts" that were representative of a certain ideologization of social and political concepts. Few of us, one would think, believe in unqualified "Progress" or a single, goal-directed process called "History."

Second, the ways concepts travel have yet to be fully explored and understood. If conceptual history depends on a theory of historical times, then what happens when concepts move between different kinds of modernities and their associated temporalities? Concepts do get transmitted and translated, but how—and, not least, why—are questions that, one would think, could only be properly answered if *Sachgeschichte* and the history of experience are meaningfully related through an account of linguistic change. Think, for instance, what "liberalism," or for that matter, "neoliberalism," "globalization," and "democracy" mean once they have traveled outside an Anglo-American context (to take some fairly clichéd examples of our time); and also how such terms are used to come to terms with experiences of "compressed modernity" in ways that seek neither just to copy modernization theory nor to react with some homegrown nationalism.[53] We lack a good theoretical grasp of the contemporary coexistence of the noncontemporaneous, of what one might call "diachronic synchronicity."

Third, I see no reason why conceptual history could not be broadened in two senses. Especially if it ought to focus more on everyday lived experience (as opposed to what is put forward in more or less abstract social and political theory), it might include metaphors and images.[54] It might also shift from a concentration on single terms to a concern with what Willibald Steinmetz has called "elementary sentences"—claims that are frequently repeated and that might expand both the sayable and the doable, to paraphrase the title of Stein-metz's seminal book on British parliamentary debates in the nineteenth century.[55] Of course one can object that this is no longer conceptual history at all—images might indeed make arguments, but they are not unavoidable or contested in the way basic concepts are.[56] Yet both images and metaphors on the one hand, and elementary sentences on the other, might be as important in structuring a social imaginary—if that is indeed a plausible conceptualization of the intermediary between the "pure history of consciousness" and "real history." Of course it is also possible to want to collapse that distinction completely—but then one will have moved decisively beyond the thought of Reinhart Koselleck, and of Herodotus, for that matter.

Notes

I am very grateful to Niklas Olsen, Melvin Richter, Bo Stråth, and Martin van Gelderen for stimulating exchanges on *Begriffsgeschichte*, as well as the two anonymous reviewers for Oxford University Press.

1. To be sure, theory is not the same as method. Kari Palonen has usefully distinguished six ways of conceptualizing the meaning of conceptual history: as "a subfield of historiography," as "a method of historiography," as "a strategy of textual analysis," as "a micro-theory of conceptual change," as "a macro-theory of conceptual change," and, finally, as "a revolution in the understanding of concepts" (with the latter essentially being a judgment about the value of conceptual history). I agree with that judgment—but I also find that the two theories, the method, and the strategy are plagued by problems and lack of clarity. See Kari Palonen, "An Application of Conceptual History to Itself: From Method to Theory in Reinhart Koselleck's Begriffsgeschichte," *Finnish Yearbook of Political Thought* 1 (1997): 39–69; here, 41.

2. While deeply influenced by Martin Heidegger, Karl Löwith, and, in particular, Hans-Georg Gadamer, Koselleck was not himself a philosopher, and certainly had no patience for analytical perspectives and the development of sharp distinctions as such.

3. These phrases are Koselleck's. See "Begriffsgeschichte, Sozialgeschichte, begriffene Geschichte: Reinhart Koselleck im Gespräch mit Christof Dipper," *Neue politische Literatur* 43 (1998): 187–205; here, 188.

4. Hans Ulrich Gumbrecht, "Pyramiden des Geistes: Über den schnellen Aufstieg, die unsichtbaren Dimensionen und das plötzliche Abebben der begriffsgeschichtlichen Bewegung," in *Dimensionen und Grenzen der Begriffsgeschichte* (Munich: Fink, 2006), 7–36.

5. See also Mark Bevir, "*Begriffsgeschichte*," *History and Theory* 39 (2000): 273–84.

6. H. G. Meier, "Begriffsgeschichte," in *Historisches Wörterbuch der Philosophie*, ed. Joachim Ritter, vol. 1 (Basel: Schwabe, 1971), 788–807.

7. See also Hans-Georg Gadamer, *Die Begriffsgeschichte und die Sprache der Philosophie* (Opladen: Westdeutscher, 1971).

8. There have also been much more ambitious explanations on why conceptual history arose in Germany: some have stressed the unique role of Hegel, others the rise of *Dogmengeschichte* in the nineteenth century, and Koselleck himself argued that it was the need to translate from Latin in the modern period that led to a heightened sensitivity to concepts in a German-language context.

9. Gumbrecht, "Pyramiden," and Stephan Schlak, "Am Erwartungshorizont der Begriffsgeschichte: Reinhart Koselleck und die ungeschriebenen *Grundbegriffe* der Bundesrepublik," in *Theorie in der Geschichtswissenschaft: Einblicke in die Praxis des historischen Forschens*, ed. Jens Hacke and Matthias Pohlig (Frankfurt/Main: Campus, 2008), 171–79.

10. Schlak, "Am Erwartungshorizont," 173.

11. Reinhart Koselleck, "Einleitung," in *Geschichtliche Grundbegriffe*, vol. 1 (1972; Stuttgart: Klett-Cotta, 1992), xiii–xxviii. In addition to democratization and ideologization, Koselleck insisted on the "politicization" and "temporalization" (*Verzeitlichung*) of concepts during the *Sattelzeit*.

12. The relationship with Gadamer is not as straightforward as one might think: The *Begriffsgeschichte* of social and political concepts no doubt benefited enormously from Gadamer's philosophical *Begriffsgeschichte*. But later Koselleck insisted that his *Historik*—the theory of the conditions of possible histories—could not be subsumed under hermeneutics. The oppositions that Koselleck identified—dying and the capacity to kill, friend and enemy, public versus secret, as well as "earlier-later," "inside-outside," and "above-below" (or "dominant-dominated") could only be comprehended in language—but they were not themselves necessarily linguistic phenomena. See Reinhart Koselleck and Hans-Georg Gadamer, *Hermeneutik und Historik* (Heidelberg: Carl Winter, 1987). In general, the relationship between *Begriffsgeschichte* and Koselleck's *Historik* has not yet been sufficiently explored.

13. "Begriffsgeschichte, Sozialgeschichte, begriffene Geschichte," 187.

14. Schlak, "Am Erwartungshorizont," 175.

15. Or what might be called methodological conservatism. See Jan-Werner Müller, "Comprehending Conservatism: A New Framework for Analysis," *Journal of Political Ideologies* 11 (2006): 359–65.

16. Then there was also Koselleck's Tocquevillian thesis about the advantages of the defeated: "Im Besiegtsein liegt . . . ein unausschöpfbares Potential des Erkenntnisgewinns." The difference between victor and vanquished in fact forms part of Koselleck's historical anthropology. See also Michael Jeismann, "Wer bleibt, der schreibt: Reinhart Koselleck, das Überleben und die Ethik des Historikers," *Zeitschrift für Ideengeschichte* 4, no. 3 (2009): 69–80, and Stefan-Ludwig Hoffmann, "Was die Zukunft birgt: Über Reinhart Kosellecks Historik," *Merkur* 63 (2009): 546–50.

17. See also Niklas Olsen, *History in the Plural: An Introduction to the Work of Reinhart Koselleck* (Oxford: Berghahn, 2012).

18. For an account of the search for the "typically Dutch," see Karin Tilmans and Wyger Welema, "Applying Begriffsgeschichte to Dutch History: Some Remarks

on the Practice and Future of a Project," *Contributions to the History of Concepts* 2 (2006): 43–58.

19. Though the Iberoamerican Project also takes exactly 1750–1850 as the period of the "advent of modernity."

20. See "The European Conceptual History Project (ECHP): Mission Statement," *Contributions to the History of Concepts* 6 (2011): 111–16. Eight volumes are envisaged, with an introductory one to be followed by collections focusing on *"civilization, federalism, state and market, historical regions, liberalism, parliamentarism,* and *planning."* The project also promises to be "useful in the design of new concepts." One might suspect that the choice of concepts will yield a social–democratic/left–liberal legitimation narrative for European integration—but it is clearly too early to tell.

21. Or rather reborn: Koselleck himself had conceived such a project comparing French, British, and German concepts, with three columns running next to each other to enable direct national comparisons. But he concluded that the nonsynchronicity of national experiences and the lack of a metalanguage for comparison rendered such a project virtually impossible.

22. For instance, the *Diccionario político y social del mundo iberoamericano: La era de las revoluciones, 1750–1850*, ed. Javier Fernández Sebastián, vol. 1 (Madrid: Centro de Estudios Políticos y Constitucionales, 2009), and the Ibero-American Conceptual History Project more generally at http://www.iberconceptos.net/ (see also the interview with Javier Fernández Sebastián by *la vie des idées*, "The Iberian-American Alphabet of Political Modernity," at http://www.booksandideas.net/IMG/pdf/20110610_JFS.pdf [accessed 13 July 2013]), as well as the "Project of Intercommunication of East Asian Basic Concepts" and the "Conceptual Histories of the World and Global Translations: The Euro-Asian and African Semantics of the Social and the Economic," based at the University of Helsinki.

23. For reasons of space I leave out an account of Conze, who also played a highly problematic role during the Third Reich.

24. Carl Schmitt, "Das Zeitalter der Neutralisierungen und Entpolitisierungen (1929)," in *Positionen und Begriffe im Kampf mit Weimar—Genf—Versailles* (Hamburg: Hanseatische Verlagsanstalt, 1940), 120–32; here, 124–25.

25. As Schmitt described this sociology (which was to be neither a form of idealism nor a form of materialism): it ought to "discover the basic, radically systematic structure and to compare this conceptual structure with the conceptually represented social structure of a certain epoch." Carl Schmitt, *Political Theology: Four Chapters on the Concept of Sovereignty*, trans. George Schwab (1922; Cambridge, MA: MIT Press, 1985), 59. See also Schmitt, "Reich-Staat-Bund: Antrittsvorlesung an der Kölner Universität am 20. Juni 1933," in Schmitt, *Positionen und Begriffe*, 190–98; here, 198. In general see my "Carl Schmitt's Method: Between Ideology, Demonology and Myth," *Journal of Political Ideologies* 4 (1999): 61–85.

26. Schmitt, "Völkerrechtliche Formen des modernen Imperialismus," in Schmitt, *Positionen und Begriffe*, 62–80; here, 178.

27. Ibid.

28. Gadi Algazi, "Otto Brunner—'Konkrete Ordnung' und Sprache der Zeit," in *Geschichtsschreibung als Legitimationswissenschaft*, ed. Peter Schöttler (Frankfurt/Main: Suhrkamp, 1997), 166–203.

29. Timo Pankakoski, "Conflict, Context, Concreteness: Koselleck and Schmitt on Concepts," *Political Theory* 38 (2010): 749–79; here, 749–50.

30. Quentin Skinner, "Retrospect: Studying Rhetoric and Conceptual Change," in his *Visions of Politics*, vol. 1, *Regarding Method* (Cambridge: Cambridge University Press, 2002), 175–87; here, 177.

31. Things are different with Koselleck's historical anthropology. Here claims about the anthropological status of the friend–enemy opposition (as well as the inside–outside pair) can look like an unwarranted privileging of a perspective informed by Schmitt.

32. Reinhart Koselleck, "On the History of Concepts and the Concept of History," in *Disseminating German Tradition: The Thyssen Lectures*, ed. Dan Diner and Moshe Zimmermann (Leipzig: Leipziger Universitätsverlag, 2009), 29–49; here, 34.

33. Koselleck, "On the History of Concepts," 40.

34. Ibid., 43.

35. ". . . der Ausdruck 'Sattelzeit' ist natürlich ein Kunstbegriff, den ich benutzt habe, um Geld zu bekommen!," in "Begriffsgeschichte, Sozialgeschichte, begriffene Geschichte," 195. At another point he claimed that "I invented the term and used it for the first time in commercial advertisements created to promote the *GG*—to sell more issues." He also argued in retrospect that the term *Schwellenzeit* (a threshold period) might have been preferable.

36. Which is why Koselleck's claim that the *Sattelzeit* had nothing to do with the method of the *GG* is rather puzzling. See Reinhart Koselleck, "A Response to Comments on the Geschichtliche Grundbegriffe," in *The Meaning of Historical Terms and Concepts: New Studies on Begriffsgeschichte*, ed. Hartmut Lehmann and Melvin Richter (Washington, DC: German Historical Institute, http://www.ghi-dc.org/publications/ghipubs/op/op15.pdf), 60–70; here, 69.

37. Palonen, "An Application."

38. This is a perhaps rather poor translation/allusion to Koselleck's startling claim: "Es ist eine begriffsgeschichtliche Delikatesse, daß die Begriffsgeschichte selber nie hinreicht, um das zu beschreiben, was begriffen werden soll."

39. Skinner, "Retrospect," 180.

40. Elías José Palti, "From Ideas to Concepts to Metaphors: The German Tradition of Intellectual History and the Complex Fabric of Language," *History and Theory* 49 (2010): 194–211; here, 198.

41. Reinhart Koselleck, "Linguistic Change and the History of Events," *Journal of Modern History* 61 (1989): 649–66; here, 649 and 652.

42. See also Martin van Gelderen, "Between Cambridge and Heidelberg: Concepts, Languages and Images in Intellectual History," in *History of Concepts: Comparative Perspectives*, ed. Iain Hampsher-Monk, Karin Tilmans, and Frank van Vree (Amsterdam: Amsterdam University Press, 1998), 227–38. In an interview shortly before his death Koselleck characterized Skinner as a "conventional historian concerned with a load of normative concepts." See "Conceptual History, Memory, and Identity: An Interview with Reinhart Koselleck," *Contributions to the History of Concepts* 2 (2006): 99–127; here, 109.

43. Koselleck, "Linguistic Change."

44. As noted in ibid., 181–82.

45. Reinhart Koselleck, "The Temporalisation of Concepts," *Finnish Yearbook of Political Thought* 1 (1997): 16–24; here, 21.

46. Melvin Richter, *The History of Political and Social Concepts: A Critical Introduction* (New York: Oxford University Press, 1995).

47. Skinner, "Retrospect," 179. Koselleck went so far as to admit that the very concept of *Begriffsgeschichte* was a "logische Lässigkeit."

48. Koselleck, "A Response," 62.

49. J. G. A. Pocock, "Concepts and Discourses: A Difference in Culture? Comment on a Paper by Melvin Richter," in Lehmann and Richter, *The Meaning*, 47–58; here, 47. Another important difference on which I cannot elaborate in this context is the fact that Koselleck in his later *Historik* insisted on the importance of "recurring structures" in history—and, against the background of the oppositional pairs underlying his historical anthropology, came close to endorsing the view that there are indeed what he called "permanent challenges," a.k.a. perennial questions.

50. Van Gelderen, "Between Cambridge and Heidelberg," 234.

51. See also Michael Freeden, *Ideologies and Political Theory* (Oxford: Oxford University Press, 1996).

52. See the multivolume *Handbuch politisch-sozialer Grundbegriffe in Frankreich 1680–1820*, in particular Rof Reichardt, "Einleitung," in *Handbuch politisch-sozialer Grundbegriffe in Frankreich 1680–1820*, ed. Rolf Reichart and Eberhard Schmitt, with Gerd van Heuvel and Anette Höfer, vols. 1 and 2 (Munich: R. Oldenbourg, 1985), 39–148.

53. A good example of such attempts to use conceptual history to negotiate a particular experience of modernity is the survey of conceptual history in South Korea, Myoung-Kyu Park, "Conceptual History in Korea," *Contributions to the History of Concepts* 7 (2012): 36–50.

54. Koselleck himself worked extensively on political iconology later in life. See Hubert Locher, "Denken in Bildern: Reinhart Kosellecks Programm *Zur Politischen Ikonologie*," *Zeitschrift für Ideengeschichte*, no. 3 (2009): 81–96. See also Rolf Reichardt, "Wortfelder—Bilder—Semantische Netze: Beispiele interdisziplinärer Quellen und Methoden in der Historischen Semantik," in *Die Interdisziplinarität der Begriffsgeschichte*, ed. Gunter Scholtz (Hamburg: Felix Meiner, 2000), 111–34.

55. Willibald Steinmetz, *Das Sagbare und das Machbare: Zum Wandel politischer Handlungsspielräume England 1780–1867* (Stuttgart: Klett-Cotta, 1993).

56. The matter with metaphors is both less and more straightforward: metaphors can become concepts, but it is hard to argue that social and political metaphors are somehow inevitable.

5

Of Scandals and Supplements: Relating Intellectual and Cultural History

Judith Surkis

In 1923, Léon Abensour described feminist history as a project to move female activity "away from the level of anecdote and scandal" in order to "place it in the mainstream of history [*grande histoire*]."[1] Writing more than a half century later, Natalie Zemon Davis paid homage to Abensour in a 1976 state of the field essay.[2] She admired many aspects of his work—his critical use of archives and treatment of women of all classes rather than an aristocratic few. But her essay also marked the passage of historiographical time in revising the aims of feminist history: "Our goal is to understand the significance of the *sexes*, of gender groups in the historical past."[3] Davis's strategy in achieving these ends in some ways reversed Abensour's. Rather than moving women away from scandal, Davis placed scandal in the mainstream of history. From her writings on charivari rituals to her imaginative rendering of *The Return of Martin Guerre*, Davis convinced historians that both scandals and women were proper subjects of history.

Writing some years later, Joan Scott described the project of women's history not only as a movement from margin to center, but also as an ongoing project of critical supplementation. Drawing on a deconstructive understanding of supplementarity, Scott argued that new thinking about women as historical subjects filled gaps, but also critically exceeded the ways in which history as a discipline had been conventionally conceived. The project of women's history, as she saw it, was not the completion of "History," but a persistent

RELATING INTELLECTUAL AND CULTURAL HISTORY   95

questioning of the discipline's conventions and boundaries. Such critical disruption could provoke defensive reactions, including to Davis's own provocative work.[4] Informed by anthropologists such as Victor Turner and literary
critics such as Mikhael Bahktin, Davis's interdisciplinary analyses of the social
meanings of scandal were indeed pathbreaking for gender history and for cultural history. Without collapsing feminist history and cultural history, I want
to suggest that the twin themes of scandal and supplement offer productive
ways to conceive relationships between closely related historical fields.

In her dedication to *The New Cultural History*, Lynn Hunt described Davis
as "an inspiration to us all." From the Queen Caroline Affair to the causes célèbres of the ancien régime; from Jack the Ripper to *The Trial of Madame Caillaux*;
from Oscar Wilde to the Eulenberg Affair, scandal emerged as an important
site of historical analysis. Building on insights from Sigmund Freud to Michel
Foucault, scholars used stories of crime, corruption, and intrigue to plumb the
historical connections between politics, culture, and psyche. As Hunt's own
work on pornography illustrated, scandalous representation and the representation of scandal offered new insights into the psycho-symbolic dimensions of
politics and power.[5]

Scandals were an optimal terrain for work in the new veins of cultural
history. At the level of the archive, sensational stories generate troves of both
published and unpublished sources, traversing at once "high" culture and
low. Scandals provide rich resources to mine as historians work to integrate
the analysis of "representation" into their accounts of social and political life.
They also recast ideas of the historical "event" and question grand historical
narratives.

Aesthetically as well as anthropologically revealing, scandals offer insight
into how communities punish or permit perceived transgressions of social
norms. In the process, they demonstrate social fault lines and the disturbing
dynamics of scapegoating in the creation of community.[6] By foregrounding the
relationship between structure and event, the general and particular, work on
scandal invited historians to reflect on the questions of symbolism and narrative that had been sidelined by more economistic and quantitative modes of
historical analysis.

The reconsideration of scandal exemplified by Davis's work arrived at a
crucial moment of methodological transition, especially but by no means exclusively in the field of French history. By the early 1980s, the limits of both materialist models of social explanation and the "*annaliste* paradigm" of the *longue
durée* were increasingly visible. The pursuit of passion-filled scandals provided
historians with seductive ways to work around these methodologically constraining models.

At around the same moment, a parallel but distinct concern with literary and philosophical scandals also drew the attention of intellectual historians. The kinds of questions these scandals raised—about authorship and writers' ethical and political commitments—were distinct from cultural historians' probing of scandal as a political and cultural symptom.[7] While more squarely focused on authors and their works, the issues raised by intellectuals' involvement with scandal nonetheless resonated with those posed by cultural historians: the relationship between texts and contexts, high culture and low, politics and ideas. In the process, intellectual historians probed the broader social and political meanings of "high cultural" texts. From the perspective of the "social history of ideas," Robert Darnton juxtaposed salacious and seditious tracts of "Grub Street" hacks with established Enlightenment auteurs and read the strange story of "the great cat massacre" as dense with social meaning.[8] Dominick LaCapra used the (mis)reading of *Madame Bovary* on trial as an occasion to interrogate the limits of reception histories and social contextualization.[9]

At the end of the 1980s, more historically proximate and more overtly political scandals became a source of controversy and ferment. The publication of literary critic Paul de Man's wartime writings and a series of books focusing on Martin Heidegger's political commitment to Nazism further energized debates about how to relate texts to their contexts. Critiques of communist intellectuals' failure to condemn Soviet crimes likewise focused attention on the political as well as methodological stakes of intellectual history. In the wake of these debates, it was difficult to sustain a vision of intellectual history as a self-contained domain.[10]

Working in parallel and occasionally overlapping veins, European cultural and intellectual history began to pursue affectively and politically charged topics. This is not to say that "scandal studies" is an analytically coherent domain. But at a basic level, explorations of scandal interrupted ideas of both the social and intellectual *longue durée*. They introduced new actors, new texts, and new methodological problems into intellectual history and the nascent field of "new cultural history." The historiography of scandal illuminates what binds and differentiates positions in a now often combined area: "intellectual and cultural history." My focus on scandal here aims to highlight an uneasy, supplementary relationship between them. The fields have become linked *both* because of what they share *and* because of what distinguishes them. They are proximate but not identical. In this sense, they can be seen to have a supplementary relationship to one another, at once exceeding and correcting their respective orientation and aims. In analyzing this supplementarity, we can see points of overlap and identify tensions that render their combination at once frequent and problematic.

Historical Conjunction

The proximity between "intellectual and cultural history" indicated by their conjunction has a history. Digital technology allows us to pinpoint a moment in which this disciplinary pairing began its clear ascendance: it was around 1980.

This quick quantitative experiment finds qualitative confirmation in two signal methodological reflections on this relationship, both published in 1980: Robert Darnton's essay on "Intellectual and Cultural History" in Michael Kammen's state-of-the-field anthology *The Past before Us* and Dominick LaCapra's article "Rethinking Intellectual History and Reading Texts" in *History and Theory* (subsequently republished in the *Modern European Intellectual History* anthology).[11] The two essays inaugurated discussions of the combined field, but they also exemplify the new debates that emerged as a result of this recombination. If intellectual production can be understood to fall under the broad rubric of "culture" (as an expression, for example, of "elite culture"), what, if anything, differentiated these two fields? Was it a distinction between the kinds of texts or practices they treated? The methods they applied? Their respective understandings of "culture"? These problems animated their intradisciplinary discussion from the outset.

Notably, Darnton's essay began with another coupling, that of "social and intellectual history." In his view, these two subfields had worked together since the beginning of the twentieth century in order to contest understandings of "history as past politics."[12] But their union foundered when, by the 1960s, intellectual history appeared to lose interest in broad social contexts, while social history became increasingly radicalized. Darnton's statistical survey of journal articles, dissertations, and course catalogs mapped this parting of the ways. Intellectual history languished as social history pursued a meteoric rise. Rather than despair at this decline, Darnton heralded 1980 as a moment of renewal, as an older, elitist history of ideas ceded place to new trends: Cambridge School contextualism, new approaches to the history of science, the "social history of

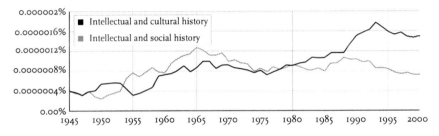

FIGURE 5.1. The ascendancy of "intellectual and cultural history" around 1980. Courtesy Google Books Ngram Viewer.

ideas," and, finally, "cultural history." Darnton's survey of these approaches notably identified "no governing *problématique*," no shared object or method. What they shared was respective positioning in a stacked model of cultural order that descended from the culturally "high" to "low."[13]

In Darnton's spatial mapping, intellectual history focused on literate classes and written texts, while cultural history brought lower social orders into focus, privileging "popular" as opposed to elite culture. Although paired with intellectual history in the title, "cultural history" made a late and separate entrance in his essay. Its difference was not only of degree, but also of kind. As Darnton explained, "In passing to cultural history, one moves below the level of literacy and onto territory where history and anthropology meet."[14] Emerging out of the social history field, "cultural history" did not, in fact, have a genealogical link to "intellectual history."

Darnton's essay thus traveled from the heights of the "great chain of being" to the depths of the new social history before coming to rest on "cultural history" as a field that combined the two and ostensibly brought about their proper reconciliation. In order to arrive at this solution, Darnton appealed to anthropology as a master key. More specifically, he suggested that Geertzian anthropology offered a "coherent conception of culture," which the *Annales* framework of *mentalité* had "failed to provide." For Darnton, Clifford Geertz's idea of culture—as "an historically transmitted pattern of meanings embodied in symbols"—could be applied to "all the varieties of intellectual history, from 'high' to 'low.'"[15] This understanding of "culture" and attendant mode of analysis made an otherwise striated field whole.

While covering some of the same terrain as Darnton's essay, LaCapra's "Rethinking Intellectual History" differed stylistically and argumentatively. It was overtly programmatic, rather than descriptive. Instead of seeking synthesis, it carved out a distinct disciplinary role for intellectual history—"a relative specificity," if not a "specious autonomy."[16] Generated in a shared historiographical context, the two essays showed similar concern for how intellectual history should be articulated with some of its intra- and interdisciplinary "others." But their respective positions on the question contrasted strongly.

LaCapra understood historical writing to have two distinct, if related aims: to document the past and to conduct a dialogue with it. For LaCapra, the combination of the documentary and the dialogical was "a problem relevant to all historiography" and hence "not restricted to intellectual history."[17] The essay nonetheless focused on how to read canonical texts by distinguishing between their documentary or referential aspects and their critical, transformative potential. The later, "worklike" element exceeded the documentary, "supplement[ing] empirical reality by adding to, and subtracting from, it."[18]

LaCapra's approach thus entailed multiple methodologies, at once documentary and dialogic modes to reading. Appealing to a deconstructive sense of "supplementation," he argued that the respective approaches signaled each other's limitations while also adding to one another.[19] Their combination would enhance understanding but also produce "tension," mutual questioning, and contestation.[20] LaCapra's modeling of inquiry drew out these tensions, rather than resolving them. In his view, "culture" was not "harmonistic" and therefore could not serve as a master key.[21]

LaCapra's essay pointedly resisted Darnton's anthropological fix, with its implicit casting of intellectual history as "retrospective symbolic or cultural anthropology."[22] For LaCapra, the anthropological approach reduced texts to cultural symptoms, thus ignoring their "worklike" dimensions. Their holistic understanding of culture remained subject to an *Annales*-style temptation toward "total history." More than cultural symptom, a critical text for LaCapra "supplements existing reality, often by pointing out the weaknesses of prevailing definitions of it."[23] This vision of texts as supplements rather than as symptoms entailed a different understanding of intellectual history's relationship to the broader field of "cultural history." If Darnton took up the "culture concept" to methodologically unify a conjoined field of "intellectual and cultural history," LaCapra expressed skepticism about this resolution. He instead highlighted the supplementary relationship between texts and multiple contexts, including that of "culture." At the same time, LaCapra's method thus resisted generalization, to the extent that it principally addressed select "critical" texts.

Supplementary Scandals

Following up on these methodological essays, Darnton and LaCapra put their programs into practice most notably in two treatments of scandal. Darnton analyzed an eighteenth-century typographical worker's memoir of a "great cat massacre"; LaCapra engaged the obscenity trial of Gustave Flaubert's *Madame Bovary*. Their two studies had themes and problems in common, but they also led "intellectual and cultural history" in distinct directions.[24]

Both studies investigated how close reading could make sense of opaque past events: a symbolically laden cat slaughter in the 1730s and the morals trial of Gustave Flaubert's now classic novel. Both analyses drew out the broader historical and historiographical significance of these "events." The incidents posed problems of historical understanding: why cats? why this novel? Both stories involved sacrificial and scapegoating dimensions as well as carnivalesque ones.

Despite certain thematic overlaps, however, Darnton and LaCapra had fundamentally different conceptions of what historical "reading" should aim to do.

The Great Cat Massacre modeled doing "cultural history" with a lower-rather than upper-case *c*.[25] Following Darnton's vertical sociocultural imaginary, the book's essays ascended a ladder beginning with peasants and ending with Rousseau. Intentionally eclectic, the collection was unified by an "ethnographic" and "exegetical" reading style that reanimated foreign—because past—mental worlds by deciphering their symbols. By dislodging a "false sense of familiarity with the past," Darnton administered "doses of culture shock."[26] In the case of the cat massacre, this treatment was something of an inoculation. While the apparently gruesome cat slaughter scandalizes present-day sensibilities, the essay ultimately ends with an explanation of why contemporaries found the killing funny. By following Darnton's analysis readers are all supposed to get the act's strangely cruel (if familiarly misogynist) joke involving the mistress's "pussy."

In Darnton's essay everyone eventually gets the joke. What is shocking in LaCapra's study is that almost no one does. For LaCapra, Flaubert's trial for moral offenses became an occasion for misunderstanding. It revealed the *mentalité* of Flaubert's contemporaries by showing just how poorly they read *Madame Bovary*. In this account, the trial does not actually help to better explain the novel. Reversing the presumptive relationship between text and context, LaCapra read the trial through the lens of the novel. More specifically, in bringing out the novel's critical dimensions, LaCapra suggested that Flaubert's work questioned the trial's moral framework *avant la lettre*. Calling into question basic distinctions between marriage and adultery, sacred and profane, high art and popular culture, the novel undermined the moral premises on which the court's judgment was eventually based.[27] The irony for LaCapra was that the novel's true scandal was not fully comprehensible to contemporary actors, including Flaubert's own lawyer. In this sense, it had a *supplementary* relationship to its context. The trial's (failed) attempt to capture and contain the novel exemplified this supplementary excess.

On one level, both Darnton and LaCapra foregrounded the importance of "reading." Hence they can be seen to exemplify a broader interest in language—the so-called linguistic turn— in the 1980s. On the other, as this brief review suggests, their understandings of "reading" remained quite distinct. Recent historiographical narratives have tended to collapse or elide such differences when they invoke the "linguistic turn" as a methodologically shared moment.[28] Recalling these differences can help to clarify how we should understand the relationship between "intellectual" and "cultural" history both then—and today.

Darnton's concept of culture and hence "cultural history" was inclusive in both its eclecticism and its populism. Derived from a Geertzian-inspired culture concept, this expansiveness drew considerable scrutiny from critics. Roger Chartier, in a well-known essay, argued that Darnton's metaphorical use of "text"—and of symbolic "reading"—cast writing as a transparent relay of "culture," as a window onto past mental and social worlds.[29] He claimed that, in presuming the stability of "symbolic meaning," Darnton's reading failed to grasp the "unstable, mobile, and equivocal" nature of signs.[30] By assuming the univocality of signs, Darnton effaced distinctions between texts and social worlds. LaCapra similarly questioned Darnton's social and textual holism by reminding readers of the fate of the cats. In his view, this troubling animal sacrifice indicates how Darnton's totalizing account of "culture" obscured questions of difference.[31] The essay's treatment of gender raises similar concerns.

From this perspective, intellectual history might address a "desire" for unified frameworks of meaning, but it also discerns the social and textual forces that disrupt totalizing desires.[32] From LaCapra's perspective, intellectual history ideally effects a critique of unified conceptions of "culture" rather than being contained by such a unifying conception.

Culturalism and Totality

A crucial colleague and collaborator of Darnton's, Geertz was also an important touchstone for Lynn Hunt's pathbreaking 1989 volume *The New Cultural History*. The "culture concept" did not, however, provide the ascendant field's sole methodological orientation. Indeed, Hunt's introduction directly addressed concerns about cultural history as a project of collective meaning recovery. In a formulation that echoed LaCapra's caution about meaningful totalities and their limits, Hunt urged: "Unity is not possible without a sense of difference; difference is certainly not graspable without an opposing sense of unity. Thus, historians of culture really do not have to choose (or really cannot choose) between the two—between unity and difference, between meaning and working, between interpretation and deconstruction."[33] While pointing to a shared use of "language as metaphor," Hunt argued that approaches to "the new cultural history" would not "all fit neatly together as though preplanned."[34] Despite certain overlaps— and indeed precisely because of them—the field was variegated: "it" could not be totalized as an internally coherent domain. The "new cultural history" was open-ended, rather than unified or complete.

As many commentators have noted, that sense of opening seemed to have closed a decade later, when Hunt and co-editor Victoria Bonnell published their anthology *Beyond the Cultural Turn.*[35] In their revisionist introduction, Hunt and Bonnell described a generalized dissatisfaction with what they now referred to as "the cultural turn." What had been diverse methodological departures were now corralled into a common movement. That purported "turn" appeared more and more like a dead end. No longer the key to historians' understanding, Geertz's "culture concept" (or, at least, historians' appropriation of it) became the root of the problem. In the Bonnell and Hunt volume, a Geertzian focus on symbolic interpretation, alongside other "linguistic" epistemologies, appeared to be overly "systematic" (and implicitly totalizing). The volume's introduction and essays questioned the impulse to view "culture as a symbolic, linguistic, and representational system."[36] Contributors, while still critical of reductive materialism, were "just as unhappy with a definition of culture as entirely systematic, symbolic, or linguistic."[37] This hyperbolic definition (that is, of culture as "*entirely* systematic") targeted a totalizing concept of culture—and its inevitable limits—as a new methodological problem.

A tautological ambivalence runs through the *Beyond the Cultural Turn* volume. Contributors both presumed and criticized what they saw as "cultural history's" pretentions to totality and claims to specious autonomy. Of course, the critique was not, in fact, new, if critical reactions to Darnton's work can be seen as one prominent example.[38] Hunt herself raised concerns about a homogenized and unified conception of culture in her introduction to *The New Cultural History.*

Contributions to *Beyond* nonetheless contrasted totalizing accounts of culture with a renewed interest in social context and the diversity of social "practices." Sociologist Richard Biernacki argued that new cultural historians paradoxically treat "culture as an ultimate nonfigural ground."[39] He claimed that this epistemological imperialism relied on the disciplinary scapegoating of social history. William Sewell similarly questioned "the systematic nature of cultural meaning and the autonomy of symbol systems" exemplified by French structuralism and Geertzian anthropology.[40]

Seeking a way out of this impasse, Sewell has argued for a view of culture not as total, but as possessing "thin coherence." In setting forth this less systemic understanding of culture, he has drawn on a different anthropological supplement: Marshall Sahlins. In Sahlins's work, symbols are sites of struggle, rather than essentially shared. The dimension of "practice" thus introduces dynamism and difference into the understanding of culture. Notably for Sewell, the dialectic between system and practice in his vision of "thin coherence" coincides with a "deconstructionist" perspective on meaning. "Deconstruction," he writes, "does not deny the possibility of coherence. Rather, it assumes that the coherence inherent in a system of symbols is thin in the sense that I have described: it demonstrates over and over that what are taken as the certainties or truths of texts or discourses are in fact disputable and unstable. This seems entirely compatible with a practice perspective on culture."[41] In Sewell's "deconstructive" understanding, the play and struggle over symbols within culture necessarily has "thin coherence." By implication, "cultures" should not be viewed as total, homogenous, or bounded.

This view of the contested meanings within "culture" clearly has implications for how one conceives "cultural history" as a field. Perhaps most crucially, it signals that the concept of culture itself is historically contested and not a stable idea to which a fixed method should be applied. "Cultural history" from this perspective invites and even demands supplementation. In recasting the field's animating concept, Sewell has sought to revive dialogues with the social sciences.[42] But these insights into what might be understood as cultural history's own "thin coherence" can extend to its relation with intellectual history as well. By providing genealogies of key concepts such as "the symbolic" and "culture," intellectual histories critically supplement the field.[43]

LaCapra has recently described this relationship as an "articulation," in order to signal both linkage and distinction. He has also pointed to what "cultural history" brings to intellectual history—by at once adding to it and demonstrating its limits. "A source of the appeal of cultural history (as well as of cultural studies in general)," writes LaCapra, "is that its texts (in the broad sense) are not limited to any traditional canon and have an obvious relation to larger social and political processes as well as experiential concerns." Included in this domain are questions of race, religion, colonialism, gender and sexuality, and the human/animal relation. As he explains, "cultural history" directly tackles the "sociopolitical concerns" that "have sometimes been marginalized in intellectual history."[44] Cultural history thus questions intellectual history's potential narrowness as well as its pretensions to transcendence. To extend some of LaCapra's own argumentation, we might think of the relationship as, once again, supplementary.

While crediting cultural history with the opening of intellectual history's social and political horizons, LaCapra continues to caution against its overly "domesticating"—or reductive—forms of contextualization. As in the past, he remains wary of its tendencies to homogenize and objectify "culture" and context. He continues to uphold "intellectual history" as crucially and critically distinct, rather than as subsumable under a general history of culture.

LaCapra's formulation seems to locate questions of sociopolitical difference on the side of context and culture and, in doing so, may risk remarginalizing them. This is of course by no means true of LaCapra's own writing, which consistently attends to questions of social as well as textual difference.

But a broader question remains as to why politicized particularity remains difficult to situate in the conventional framework of intellectual history.[45] When conceived as simultaneously documentary and critical, intellectual history makes significant contributions to the histories of gender, race, religion, and conceptions of "culture," while testing its own boundaries as a field.[46] The consignment of these issues to a distinct field of cultural history may risk limiting or obscuring that doubly critical work. At the same time, cultural history and cultural studies need not be reduced to the role of reduction. In this volume, Peter Gordon has warned against an ideology of native meaning to which cultural history can fall prey. But a "thinly coherent" conception of cultural history can work as a critical supplement rather than as dangerous domestication.

The contributions to this volume demonstrate how supplementarity is integral to recent developments in intellectual history. Drawing on a wide variety of fields (science studies, religious studies, social and political theory, geography, feminist and postcolonial studies, law and international relations), they together suggest that intellectual history has not developed according to a singular or autonomous (disciplinary) logic of ideas. This ramification illustrates intellectual history's ongoing methodological salience, even as it tests its autonomy and internal coherence. Such a claim might appear "scandalous" in a volume devoted to "Modern European Intellectual History." But the embrace of internal diversity or what Warren Breckman has described as *serious* eclecticism should rather be seen as a virtue, a sign of vibrancy rather than vice.

Returning to Scandal

In order to bring this essay full circle (without resolving its tensions), I want to end with a final reflection on scandal. Through the rise and supposed fall of the "cultural turn," work on scandal or what Darnton calls "incident analysis" has remained a staple of historical writing, academic and popular alike.[47] Indicative of broader transformations, new work in this vein reflects preoccupations with colonial and postcolonial violence and exploitation, alongside more familiar themes of war and crime, sex and sensation, anti-Semitism and spectacular trials.[48] A decade's worth of neo-imperial warfare, terrorism, state-sanctioned torture, and corporate malfeasance will no doubt keep the subject of scandal vital for years to come. But, in order to concretize the broader methodological questions broached by this essay, I want to focus on a specific set of scandals whose relationship to "intellectual history" may not be immediately apparent: recent controversies over the *hijab* and "veiling" in Europe.

The question of Muslim headscarves has a significant intellectual history. Since the 1989 crisis surrounding three schoolgirls in the French town of Creil lent public attention to the issue, the headscarf has generated substantial commentary from sociologists, political theorists, philosophers, anthropologists, and historians, alongside journalists and cartoonists. The question of the veil is "intellectual" and more broadly "cultural," provoking heated debates about meaning in multiple and overlapping registers.[49] It is also evidently political.

The vestimentary choices of schoolgirls have tested thinking about core concepts in European intellectual history and Geertzian models of symbolic interpretation. The history of political thinking about republicanism, democracy, secularism, rights, universalism, freedom, equality, consent, conscience, privacy, and the public sphere has all been tested and transformed by these girls' actions and the ongoing debates that they provoke.[50] While the headscarf has operated in public discourse as a synecdoche for the problem of "Islam" in the French body politic, its significance for women who wear it cannot be reduced to this trope.[51] Anthropologists have highlighted what is problematic about viewing the veil as the symbolic exteriorization of hidden subjective meanings or intentions. Their accounts of the headscarf challenge "depth" and hermeneutic models of symbolic interpretation and reveal the limitations of such "readings" of culture.[52]

In her recent study of the headscarf debates in France, anthropologist Mayanthi Fernando outlines these tensions with particular clarity.[53] She signals the contradictions produced by twinned, if mutually exclusive, readings of the headscarf as a sign of *either* girls' personal choices *or* their submission to religious obligation. In the first instance, the headscarf is an expression of a girl's free will (a formulation that is acceptable within a framework that understands freedom as individual autonomy). In the second, it symbolizes a religious obligation to which a girl submits (often interpreted in French public discourse as feminine submission to foreign patriarchal norms). While apparently more liberal, the first interpretation produces a paradox: once cast as a matter of personal choice rather than obligation, the headscarf is no longer protected as a religious freedom. Rather than choosing between the two interpretations, Fernando's ethnography understands the practice as both choice and religious obligation. This doubling continues to scandalize a French public discourse that frames the headscarf's meaning as only ever one or the other. In revealing the discursive and legal bind into which pious Muslim women are placed, Fernando's study indicates the conceptual and practical limits of "secular" republican freedom. It also highlights the limits of "symbolic" reading.

Importantly, Fernando's account resists reading the *foulard* as a sign of a "conflict" between distinct and incompatible cultures. This is not a story of

"Muslim" girls' difference from "French" secular republican culture and a concomitant "crisis of multiculturalism." For Fernando, the practice of veiling and the controversy it has provoked make manifest historical contradictions *within* French republicanism, between rights and obligations as well as freedom and equality. Her account does not provide insight into a cultural totality (either "Muslim" or "French"). By attending to persistent conceptual and historical problems in French republicanism, she unsettles rather than confirms Muslimness and Frenchness as bounded identities.

Such tensions are by no means new to intellectual historians or political theorists. Fernando's study nonetheless supplements conventional intellectual historical work in important ways. By placing the dilemmas articulated by pious Muslim women at the center of her story, Fernando offers more than a specific example of familiar French and contemporary European problems. She locates the politicized relation between secularism and religion by illustrating how those concepts are subtended by ideas of racial and gender difference. In specifying what disembodied concepts overlook, she engages intellectual histories—of secularism, universalism, and selfhood—while critically differing from them.

My point in closing with this ethnography is not to offer yet another "anthropological fix" or better synthesis between "cultural and intellectual history." It is rather to highlight how the twin themes of scandals and supplements underscore the value of difference and distinction, even when relating these fields. Intellectual history's critical and self-critical attention to concepts and their historicity can offer a corrective to totalizing ideas of context and culture. This same engagement should be understood to test rather than reaffirm the field's own limits. Taken together "intellectual and cultural history" are best understood as supplementary or at most "thinly coherent." In participating in a shared discussion, they also provoke vigorous debate. Supplements question boundary designations while resisting autonomy and fusion. Such mutual interrogation should be encouraged rather than ideally resolved.

Notes

My thanks to Warren Breckman, Mayanthi Fernando, Peter Gordon, Dominick LaCapra, Darrin McMahon, Sam Moyn, Joan Scott, and two anonymous readers for their critical feedback on this essay.

1. Léon Abensour, *La femme et le féminisme avant la Révolution* (Paris: E. Leroux, 1923).

2. Natalie Zemon Davis, "'Women's History' in Transition: The European Case," *Feminist Studies* 3, nos. 3/4 (1976): 85.

3. Ibid., 90.

4. Joan Wallach Scott, "Women's History," in *New Perspectives on Historical Writing*, ed. Peter Burke (Oxford: Polity Press, 1992). For one prominent example of a critique and Davis's response, see Natalie Zemon Davis, "'On the Lame,'" *American Historical Review* 93, no. 3 (June 1988): 572–603; Robert Finlay, "The Refashioning of Martin Guerre," *American Historical Review* 93, no. 3 (June 1988): 553–73.

5. Edward Berenson, *The Trial of Madame Caillaux* (Berkeley: University of California Press, 1992); Ed Cohen, *Talk on the Wilde Side: Towards a Genealogy of a Discourse on Male Sexualities* (New York: Routledge, 1992); Alain Corbin, *The Village of Cannibals: Rage and Murder in France, 1870* (Cambridge, MA: Harvard University Press, 1992); Ruth Harris, *Murders and Madness: Medicine, Law, and Society in the* fin de siècle (Oxford: Clarendon Press, 1989); Lynn Avery Hunt, ed., *The Invention of Pornography: Obscenity and the Origins of Modernity, 1500–1800* (New York: Zone Books 1993); Lynn Avery Hunt, *The New Cultural History* (Berkeley: University of California Press, 1989); Thomas W. Laqueur, "The Queen Caroline Affair: Politics as Art in the Reign of George IV," *Journal of Modern History* 54, no. 3 (September 1982): 417–66; Sarah C. Maza, *Private Lives and Public Affairs: The Causes Célèbres of Prerevolutionary France* (Berkeley: University of California Press, 1993); J. D. Steakley, "Iconography of a Scandal: Political Cartoons and the Eulenberg Affair in Whilhelmine Germany," in *Hidden from History: Reclaiming the Gay and Lesbian Past*, ed. Martin B. Duberman, Martha Vicinus, and George Chauncey (New York: NAL Books, 1989); Judith R. Walkowitz, *City of Dreadful Delight: Narratives of Sexual Danger in Late-Victorian London* (Chicago: University of Chicago Press, 1992); Larry Wolff, *Postcards from the End of the World: Child Abuse in Freud's Vienna* (New York: Atheneum, 1988).

6. For a recent effort to map some of these dynamics: Ari Adut, *On Scandal: Moral Disturbances in Society, Politics, and Art* (Cambridge: Cambridge University Press, 2008).

7. Gisèle Sapiro has recently traced how ideas of "authorship" and the modern writer's ethic of responsibility emerged out of literary trials. In this sense, scandals could be seen to play a crucial role in the history of "the intellectual's" social role and political responsibility. Gisèle Sapiro, *La responsabilité de l'écrivain: Littérature, droit et morale en France, XIXe-XXIe Siècle* (Paris: Seuil, 2011).

8. Robert Darnton, "The High Enlightenment and the Low-Life of Literature in Pre-Revolutionary France," *Past and Present*, no. 51 (1971): 81–115.

9. Dominick LaCapra, *Madame Bovary on Trial* (Ithaca, NY: Cornell University Press, 1982).

10. On de Man: Werner Hamacher, Neil Hertz, and Thomas Keenan, *Responses: On Paul De Man's Wartime Journalism* (Lincoln: University of Nebraska Press, 1989). On Heidegger: Pierre Bourdieu, *The Political Ontology of Martin Heidegger* (Stanford, CA: Stanford University Press, 1991); Víctor Farías, Joseph Margolis, and Tom Rockmore, *Heidegger and Nazism* (Philadelphia: Temple University Press, 1989); Dominick LaCapra, *Representing the Holocaust: History, Theory, Trauma* (Ithaca, NY: Cornell University Press, 1994); Hans D. Sluga, *Heidegger's Crisis: Philosophy and Politics in Nazi Germany* (Cambridge, MA: Harvard University Press, 1993); Richard

Wolin, *The Politics of Being: The Political Thought of Martin Heidegger* (New York: Columbia University Press, 1990); Richard Wolin and Martin Heidegger, *The Heidegger Controversy: A Critical Reader* (New York: Columbia University Press, 1991). On intellectuals and communism: Tony Judt, *Past Imperfect: French Intellectuals, 1944–1956* (Berkeley: University of California Press, 1992).

11. Robert Darnton, "Intellectual and Cultural History," in *The Past before Us: Contemporary Historical Writing in the United States*, ed. Michael Kammen (Ithaca, NY: Cornell University Press, 1980), reprinted in Robert Darnton, *Kiss of Lamourette: Reflections in Cultural History* (New York: Norton, 1990). And Dominick LaCapra, "Rethinking Intellectual History and Reading Texts," *History and Theory* 19, no. 3 (1980): 245–76, reprinted in Dominick LaCapra, "Rethinking Intellectual History and Reading Texts," in *Modern European Intellectual History: Reappraisals and New Perspectives*, ed. Dominick LaCapra and Steven L. Kaplan (Ithaca, NY: Cornell University Press, 1982).

12. Darnton, "Intellectual and Cultural History," 329.

13. Ibid., 337.

14. Ibid., 344.

15. Ibid., 347–48.

16. LaCapra, "Rethinking Intellectual History and Reading Texts," 48.

17. Ibid., 50.

18. Ibid.

19. See Jacques Derrida's account of the supplement as that which both adds to and takes the place of "significations whose cohabitation is as strange as it is necessary." Jacques Derrida, *Of Grammatology*, 1st American ed. (Baltimore: Johns Hopkins University Press, 1976), 144.

20. LaCapra, "Rethinking Intellectual History and Reading Texts," 54.

21. For a parallel critique of "harmonistic" conceptions of culture, see Peter Gordon's essay in this volume.

22. LaCapra, "Rethinking Intellectual History and Reading Texts," 83.

23. Ibid., 68.

24. John Toews highlighted this strong contrast at the time and questioned the extent to which a "synthesis" was possible, in "The Historian in the Labyrinth of Signs: Reconstructing Cultures and Reading Texts in the Practice of Intellectual History," *Semiotica* 83, nos. 3/4 (1991): 361–84.

25. Robert Darnton, *The Great Cat Massacre and Other Episodes in French Cultural History* (New York: Basic Books, 1984), 3.

26. Ibid., 4.

27. LaCapra, *Madame Bovary on Trial*, 31.

28. Judith Surkis, "When Was the Linguistic Turn? A Genealogy," *American Historical Review* 117, no. 3 (June 2012): 700–22.

29. Roger Chartier, "Text, Symbols, and Frenchness," *Journal of Modern History* 57, no. 4 (1985): 685. Harold Mah extends this argument and performs a counter-reading of Nicolas Contat's text in "Suppressing the Text: The Metaphysics of Ethnographic History in Darnton's Great Cat Massacre," *History Workshop Journal* 31, no. 1 (1991): 1–20.

30. Chartier, "Text, Symbols, and Frenchness."

31. Dominick LaCapra, "Chartier, Darnton, and the Great Symbol Massacre," *Journal of Modern History* 60, no. 1 (March 1988): 95–112, reprinted in Dominick LaCapra, *Soundings in Critical Theory* (Ithaca, NY: Cornell University Press, 1989). See also "Culture and Ideology: From Geertz to Marx" in the same volume.

32. LaCapra, "Chartier, Darnton, and the Great Symbol Massacre," 98. LaCapra has recently restated this position and foregrounded questions about both animality and violence in "Intellectual and Cultural History, and Critical Theory," in his *History and Its Limits: Human, Animal, Violence* (Ithaca, NY: Cornell University Press, 2009). LaCapra was not alone in raising questions about intellectual and political desires for totality. Indeed, Martin Jay's contemporaneous study of *Marxism and Totality* can be read, albeit in a different vein, as an extended reflection on this same set of questions. Martin Jay, *Marxism and Totality: The Adventures of a Concept from Lukács to Habermas* (Berkeley: University of California Press, 1984).

33. Hunt, *New Cultural History*, 16.

34. Ibid., 21.

35. See, for example, the Forum, especially Ronald Suny, "Back and Beyond: Reversing the Cultural Turn?," *American Historical Review* 107, no. 5 (December 2002): 1476–99. And, more recently, Jay Cook's call to distinguish between "the cultural turn" and "cultural history": James W. Cook, "The Kids Are All Right: On the 'Turning' of Cultural History," 117, no. 3 (June 2012): 746–71.

36. Victoria E. Bonnell and Lynn Avery Hunt, *Beyond the Cultural Turn: New Directions in the Study of Society and Culture* (Berkeley: University of California Press, 1999), 6.

37. Ibid., 26.

38. For a related genealogy, see Darrin McMahon, "The Return of the History of Ideas," in this volume.

39. Richard Biernacki, "Method and Metaphor after the New Cultural History," in Bonnell and Hunt, *Beyond the Cultural Turn*, 73.

40. William Hamilton Sewell, "The Concept(S) of Culture," in Bonnell and Hunt, *Beyond the Cultural Turn*, 44.

41. Bonnell and Hunt, *Beyond the Cultural Turn*, 50. For a further development of this "practice theory," see Gabrielle M. Spiegel, *Practicing History: New Directions in Historical Writing after the Linguistic Turn* (New York: Routledge, 2005). For a critical probing of "practice theory," see "Vicissitudes of Practice and Theory," in LaCapra, *History and Its Limits*.

42. Sewell extends many of these arguments in his subsequent volume, *Logics of History: Social Theory and Social Transformation* (Chicago: University of Chicago Press, 2005). See, in particular, "History, Synchrony, and Culture: Reflections on the Work of Clifford Geertz," where Sewell argues that Geertz can be read in order to attend to differences within "culture," as well as change over time. See, as well, Samuel Moyn's discussion of Sewell and the critique of the presumptive autonomy of "representation" in "Imaginary Intellectual History," in this volume.

43. Camille Robcis, *The Law of Kinship: Anthropology, Psychoanalysis, and the Family in France* (Ithaca, NY: Cornell University Press, 2013); Andrew Sartori, *Bengal in*

Global Concept History: Culturalism in the Age of Capital (Chicago: University of Chicago Press, 2008).

44. LaCapra, *History and Its Limits*, 22.

45. For some further exploration of these themes with respect to sexuality and postcolonialism, see the essays by Tracie Matysik, "Decentering Sex: Reflections on Freud, Foucault, and Subjectivity in Intellectual History," and Shruti Kapila, "Global Intellectual History and the Indian Political," in this volume.

46. Some recent examples include Rita Chin, *The Guest Worker Question in Postwar Germany* (Cambridge: Cambridge University Press, 2007); Carolyn J. Dean, *The Frail Social Body: Pornography, Homosexuality, and Other Fantasies in Interwar France* (Berkeley: University of California Press, 2000); Karuna Mantena, *Alibis of Empire: Henry Maine and the Ends of Liberal Imperialism* (Princeton, NJ: Princeton University Press, 2010); Tomoko Masuzawa, *The Invention of World Religions; or, How European Universalism Was Preserved in the Language of Pluralism* (Chicago: University of Chicago Press, 2005); Tracie Matysik, *Reforming the Moral Subject: Ethics and Sexuality in Central Europe, 1890–1930* (Ithaca, NY: Cornell University Press, 2008); Sandrine Sanos, *The Aesthetics of Hate: Far-Right Intellectuals, Antisemitism, and Gender in 1930s France* (Stanford, CA: Stanford University Press, 2012); Judith Surkis, *Sexing the Citizen: Masculinity and Morality in France, 1870–1920* (Ithaca, NY: Cornell University Press, 2006); Gary Wilder, *The French Imperial Nation-State: Negritude and Colonial Humanism between the Two World Wars* (Chicago: University of Chicago Press, 2005); and a recent review essay that in part discusses my own and Tracie Matysik's work, Sandrine Sanos, "The Subject and the Work of Difference: Gender, Sexuality, and Intellectual History," *Modern Intellectual History* 8, no. 1 (April 2011): 213–25.

47. Robert Darnton, "It Happened One Night," *New York Review of Books*, June 24, 2004.

48. Louis Begley, *Why the Dreyfus Affair Matters* (New Haven, CT: Yale University Press, 2009); Anna Clark, *Scandal: The Sexual Politics of the British Constitution* (Princeton, NJ: Princeton University Press, 2004); Ruth Harris, *Dreyfus: Politics, Emotion, and the Scandal of the Century* (New York: Metropolitan Books, 2010); Sarah C. Maza, *Violette Nozière: A Story of Murder in 1930s Paris* (Berkeley: University of California Press, 2011); Frank Mort, *Capital Affairs: London and the Making of the Permissive Society* (New Haven, CT: Yale University Press, 2010); Samuel Moyn, *A Holocaust Controversy: The Treblinka Affair in Postwar France* (Waltham, MA: Brandeis University Press, 2005); Helmut Walser Smith, *The Butcher's Tale: Murder and Anti-Semitism in a German Town*, 1st ed. (New York: Norton, 2002). For recent work on colonial scandal, see Nicholas B. Dirks, *The Scandal of Empire: India and the Creation of Imperial Britain* (Cambridge, MA: Belknap Press of Harvard University Press, 2006); James Epstein, *Scandal of Colonial Rule: Power and Subversion in the British Atlantic during the Age of Revolution* (Cambridge: Cambridge University Press, 2012); Bertrand Taithe, *The Killer Trail: A Colonial Scandal in the Heart of Africa* (Oxford: Oxford University Press, 2009).

49. Some of the best-known works include Françoise Gaspard, *Le foulard et la République* (Paris: Découverte, 1995); Charlotte Nordmann and Etienne Balibar, *Le*

foulard islamique en questions (Paris: Amsterdam, 2004); Talal Asad, "Trying to
Understand French Secularism," in *Political Theologies: Public Religions in a Post-Secular
World*, ed. Hent de Vries and Lawrence Eugene Sullivan (New York: Fordham University
Press, 2006); Etienne Balibar, "Dissonances within Laïcité," *Constellations* 11, no. 3
(2004): 353–67; John R. Bowen, *Why the French Don't Like Headscarves: Islam, the State,
and Public Space* (Princeton, NJ: Princeton University Press, 2007); Jürgen Habermas,
Between Naturalism and Religion: Philosophical Essays (Cambridge: Polity, 2008);
Christian Joppke, *Veil: Mirror of Identity* (Cambridge: Polity, 2009); Cécile Laborde,
Critical Republicanism: The Hijab Controversy and Political Philosophy (Oxford: Oxford
University Press, 2008); Neil MacMaster, *Burning the Veil: The Algerian War and the
"Emancipation" of Muslim Women, 1954–62* (Manchester: Manchester University Press,
2009); Anne Norton, *On the Muslim Question* (Princeton, NJ: Princeton University
Press, 2013); Joan Wallach Scott, *The Politics of the Veil* (Princeton, NJ: Princeton
University Press, 2007); Todd Shepard, *The Invention of Decolonization: The Algerian
War and the Remaking of France* (Ithaca, NY: Cornell University Press, 2006); Charles
Taylor, "Why We Need a Radical Redefinition of Secularism," in *The Power of Religion in
the Public Sphere*, ed. Eduardo Mendieta and Jonathan VanAntwerpen (New York:
Columbia University Press, 2011); Patrick Weil, "Why the French Laïcité Is Liberal,"
Cardozo Law Review 31 (2008): 2699–2714.

50. Since the passage of the 2004 law on the regulation of religion in French
public space (laïcité), attention to the veils has not ceased, despite the fact that the law
was, in principle, designed to settle the question once and for all. New questions have
arisen about the veiled mothers of schoolgirls as well as the so-called integral veil—the
niqab or burka. See Sylvie Tissot, "Excluding Muslim Women: From Hijab to Niqab,
from School to Public Space," *Public Culture* 23, no. 1 (2011): 39–46.

51. On the veil as synecdoche and the problem of its interpretation, see Scott,
Politics of the Veil.

52. Saba Mahmood, *Politics of Piety: The Islamic Revival and the Feminist Subject*
(Princeton, NJ: Princeton University Press, 2005); Saba Mahmood, "Secularism,
Hermeneutics, and Empire: The Politics of Islamic Reformation," *Public Culture* 18,
no. 2 (2006): 343–44. This account draws on Talal Asad's critique of Geertz in Talal
Asad, *Genealogies of Religion: Discipline and Reasons of Power in Christianity and Islam*
(Baltimore: Johns Hopkins University Press, 1993).

53. Mayanthi L. Fernando, "Reconfiguring Freedom: Muslim Piety and the Limits
of Secular Law and Public Discourse in France," *American Ethnologist* 37, no. 1 (2010):
19–35, and *The Republic Unsettled: Islam, Secularism, and the Future of France* (Durham,
NC: Duke University Press, forthcoming).

6

Imaginary Intellectual History

Samuel Moyn

Intellectual history has never really reckoned with the implications of
social theory, the exceptionally powerful tradition originating in the
Enlightenment discovery of society, reaching an acme in Émile
Durkheim and Max Weber, and continuing in many versions since.
One troubling way of interpreting the itinerary of intellectual history
in the past few decades, in fact, is to register how consistently and
almost definitionally it has skirted engagement with the most serious
consequence of social theory for its practice. I refer to the assault on
the autonomy of representations, as if they were separate from the
making and unmaking of society. In what follows, I argue that several
recent developments in the human sciences—especially the rise of
the concept of the social imaginary—have changed this assault in its
form and left intellectual history well-positioned to incorporate it
rather than merely to continue its strategy of resistance in the name
of the transcendence of concepts.

The rise and fall of approaches and schools in twentieth-century
intellectual history look from the perspective of the autonomy of the
intellectual realm pretty much like a series of variations on a consistent single premise. Arthur Lovejoy and Quentin Skinner certainly
have a bone of contention between them in whether to defend the
border against practices from the citadel of the conceptual "unit" or
that of the linguistic-discursive embodiment of thought—but from
the perspective of those laying siege to the citadel it is the same fight.
In the predominant attention to the theoretical niceties of the

so-called Cambridge School approach, its founding gesture of incorporating discursive context on pain of rejecting all other kinds is not often emphasized, but it shows just how faithful to Lovejoy (and even Leo Strauss) Skinner actually was in the incontestably pathbreaking work that founded his school. What separated Skinner from his adversaries in the beginning was, of course, context—but not a lot of context, for he concurred with his enemies that there was nothing determinative outside texts except other texts. This commitment unites the Cambridge School in its foundations and, in spite of Skinner's own creative later impulses, with most other approaches to writing intellectual history to this day.

In his own version of the famous linguistic turn, to take one example, Dominick LaCapra made much more of a theoretical place for a dialogic and possibly critical relationship between text and (sometimes non-textual) context. But his proposal is still formulated around "reading texts," rather than on the basis of a desire to abrogate the very distinction between representations and practices.[1] Peter E. Gordon, to take a more recent case, vigorously defends the autonomy of ideas against Cambridge-style contextualism. But it is illuminating that Gordon assumes that the Cambridge exclusion of most forms of context goes without saying before moving on to voice his version of the perennial worry about the contextual "reduction" of texts. It suggests how thoroughly he sides with the Cambridge School in viewing the discursive surroundings of texts as the sole potential source of historical explanation in the first place. Turning to Gordon's own writings, they seem to make him nearly a spiritual affiliate of the Cambridge School, given his own emphasis on reconstructing the solely discursive frameworks of past debates, albeit with greater allowance for how concepts can escape the intellectual discussions that only temporarily and partially constitute them.[2] What seems like a major dispute turns out to mask total agreement that theoretical activity in which philosophers engage does not "ramify" into an apparently nontheoretical social world of other practices. (The truth is that practices ramify with equal promiscuity as concepts.)

It is sobering to realize that, from the constitution of the field into the present day, disputes that often seemed most ferocious within the walls of intellectual history mask a deeper pact to guard them. The field has always been defined and unified by its defensive posture more than anything else. But at this late date, the idealism of intellectual history seems a more or less uninteresting stance to take in relation to the lessons of social theory. It may seem noble to shield ideas against waves of external hordes until such time as the civilized sophisticates arrive and the gates can be thrown open not to conquerors but to allies willing to treat thought—and high culture more generally—with the respect it is due. But it does not acknowledge that the basic impulse of social theory to anchor representations in practices is an ongoing project in which intellectual historians should want to participate, not simply promise to join when it is done.

Just as important, commitment to the autonomy of thought does not acknowledge that the savages are unlikely to learn on their own. Given the theoretical illiteracy of the historical profession, the defensive strategy relinquishes one of the intellectual historian's main possible missions, which is to make other historians aware that their own practices are bound up with rather implausible theories about the nature of social identity and agency that need to be replaced by more persuasive ones. I do not purport to offer a more believable approach in what follows, merely to suggest some reasons that the rise of the "social imaginary" is a promising venture precisely because it has the right aspiration: to test and possibly even to overcome the distinction between representations and practices.

Another way to put my claim is that intellectual historians need a theory of ideology in order to avoid self-imprisonment in concepts or language alone. Intellectual historians have generally either avoided having any serious engagement with the problem of ideology, on the premise that beliefs and systems were interesting enough on their own to deserve separate analytical treatment. Or they have worked with a vague definition of ideology emphasizing the contestability of intellectual schemes or—in a kind of Marxism lite—a general legitimating function representations might play.[3] To be sure, such features of ideology matter, but as a specification of the relationship between representations and practices they do not really amount to a serious theory. They merely allude to basic premises all versions of such a theory would have to share; but they systematically avoid the problem of *explanation*, that is to say, what specific roles representations play in the history of the social order.

As with the intellectual historian's typical attitude toward outsiders, such defensive avoidance of the sorts of problems addressed in the Marxist theory of ideology occurred for good reason: the history of the theory of ideology shows that people interested in it tend to make representations secondary reflections of nonintellectualized practices that come first. There were many versions of this position even before Karl Marx. "This kind of froth called the fine arts is the necessary product of a certain fermentation," Stendhal wrote. "If you are to explain the froth, you must explain the fermentation." Of course, "vulgarity" typically triumphed in other forms than Marxism in intellectual history. The most prominent proposal about how to achieve a "social history of ideas"—in Robert Darnton's bracing retread of Peter Gay, who had introduced the notion—left a number of intellectual historians properly worrying whether doing the history of books as a material foundation for intellectual history meant not reading them anymore.[4]

If an idealistic prophylaxis against reduction had its uses, it also has its limits. Bad attempts to connect representations with practices call for good ones. It follows that Marxism—which for all its faults went furthest in exploring this terrain in the twentieth century—remains so relevant to intellectual historians that it seems crucial to keep the dialogue with its theoretical history open, if only out of interest in displacing it with a better approach. In this sense it is ironic that the most high-flown contributors to modern European intellectual history in the last generation did not take up this task, even as they often took Marxism as their subject, in the varieties of its theoretical elaboration. Indeed, in the era of the linguistic turn, their own commitment to an idealist intellectual history became more pronounced.

Deeply impressed by Talcott Parsons's synthesis of social theory, H. Stuart Hughes, probably as crucial for the study of modern European intellectual history as Arthur Lovejoy was for the study of the premodern history of ideas, had already allowed his admiration for the greats he chronicled in his masterpiece no impact on his assumptions and methods. At most he was open to an individualized psychohistory of intellectuals. His students from the "generation of 1968," including Martin Jay and Dominick LaCapra most prominently, often set on rediscovering the theoretical riches of the hidden dimensions of the Marxist past. Yet they treated those very theories as basically autonomous, for the purposes of synoptic narrative or in the name of showing their constitutive tensions. The world outside them rarely intruded. These classic historians expressed at most slight discomfort with the fact that the very bodies of theory they were studying seriously undermined, if they did not rule out, the premises of their own historiography.[5]

Of course, many of the most interesting schools of thought in modern times besides Marxism also reject free-floating ideas. And in the final analysis there is no plausible way—certainly not as a matter of permanent disciplinary practice—to entirely separate and insulate the study of past social theory from some of its own most essential lessons. The short-run decision among intellectual historians to sustain a blatant contradiction between their own theories and methods and those of their protagonists seems understandable. But in the long run, it is unsustainable.

All along in the history of social theory, there were various attempts to devise an alternative to the Marxist theory of ideology. Max Weber, for example, replied in his *Protestant Ethic* that sometimes representations drive practices and not vice versa. But trying to show as much, while he did not revert to idealism, he also did not rethink materialism, nor—much more important—strive to transcend the opposition between idealism and materialism.[6] There the matter stood until the rise of the concept of the "social imaginary," as theorized by Cornelius Castoriadis and others as Marxism entered crisis. This event matters to intellectual historians because it proposed to challenge or even do away with the boundary between representations and practices without simply allowing the territory of the text to be annexed and subdued by the armies of "the context." It may in time allow a new approach to these quandaries without the same result as every other generation has found: a new theoretical defense for the relative autonomy of thought against the barbarians.

The lineage of the notion of the social imaginary is complex, and by now its uses in the humanities are on the verge of boundless and almost random— one reason to recall its original purpose with respect to the antinomy of representations and practices. Castoriadis, the Greek-French theorist, initiated the concept of the "social imaginary" in 1964.[7] It is quite important that Castoriadis, along with his sometime colleague Claude Lefort, began attempting to save Marxism before concluding that it needed to be replaced. They saw two profound difficulties in the Marxism they inherited: determinism and materialism. Even Castoriadis—who could write floridly of human capacities in the creation of novel social worlds—did not introduce these criticisms in order to supplant social theory.[8] What is intellectually significant about the development of the notion of the social imaginary against the backdrop of the powerful tendency to idealism in intellectual history, even among those most open to the project of social theory, is that it was propounded in order to take seriously Marxism's concern with the role of representations in the social order without reducing the former to the latter, understood as something in which representations play no role except as legitimating afterthought.

Concepts and language matter, according to the social imaginary, but not cordoned off from the realm of practices. Thus, the eventual assertion of the imaginary against Marxism was never intended to offer an idealism that one might easily associate with the imaginative or "imaginary" coinage. Rather, it was meant to revise the Marxist aspiration to explain social practices, by insisting on the imaginative or imaginary element or dimension of them. As Lefort put it at one point, "To criticize Marx does not at all imply that we must assert the primacy of representation and fall back into the illusion, which he denounced, of an independent logic of ideas." Indeed, more boldly, the point of the social imaginary was to target the entire distinction of representations from practices, with the former the realm of the conceptual and the latter the domain of non-sapient activity from which intellectual life somehow originated. From the perspective of the social imaginary, Lefort noted, "it turns out to be . . . impossible to fix a frontier between what must be classed in the order of action and what must be classed in the order of representation."[9]

Instead of pursuing the specifics of how Castoriadis and Lefort elaborated this approach, I will abstract from their locale and their details in order to isolate what seems both most theoretically significant about the venture as well as most applicable to the contemporary quandaries of intellectual history. Bluntly, the social imaginary offers an intellectualized view of practices. The essential purpose of the category is that representations help constitute the social order, to the point that there is no choosing between the study of one and the other. Obviously, it is analytically possible and important to separate "concepts" and "ideas" (themselves concepts and ideas with specific histories) for doctrinal or genealogical study. But to do so is to falsify the conditions in which ideas emerge, on the part of agents who are not fully determined but are never exempted from their implication in the creation and sustenance of some social order or other. Castoriadis meant something along these lines in entitling his most famous work "the imaginary institution of society." If society cannot be made or remade without the imaginary, neither does the imaginary appear in the absence of some society it helps bring about (while ruling other societies out). From the perspective of the social imaginary, then, there is really no such thing as a threat of reduction in social explanation, as opposed to an economistic Marxism or a materialist social history that ignores how intellectual categories animate practical identities and activities. There is no idea that is not social, and no society not ideationally founded. In this sense, a proper social history of ideas is the only plausible kind of history of ideas there is.

A few Anglo-American philosophers have arrived at a similar conclusion as Castoriadis and Lefort about the intellectualization of all social practices out of the internal development of Anglo-American debates.[10] Inspired by Maurice Merleau-Ponty, Castoriadis's own source in seeking an alternative to a reductive Marxism, the Canadian philosopher Charles Taylor long ago leveled a similar attack on "the artificiality of the distinction between social reality and the language of description of that social reality"—and indeed developed his own account of the social imaginary to struggle beyond its terms.[11] Robert Brandom has gone even further in his explicit goal of connecting an inferential space of reason-giving with the social reality of changing practices. A neo-Hegelian deeply influenced by phenomenology, much like Taylor for most of his career, Brandom seems an especially valuable guide at present precisely because he has tried to offer an inferentialist account of language that should embed it in the whole practical life of a local place and specific time.[12]

One way to characterize developments in such Anglo-American figures, as well as in their French counterparts, is in part as a return before Marx: to the German philosophy that Marx famously and polemically presented as lost in the clouds, in order to bring it down to earth.[13] Recent students of Marx's "idealist" forebears have shown they were centrally concerned about the imbrication of intellectual schemes and social practices before Marx famously claimed otherwise—certainly G. W. F. Hegel was. The perception that the history of philosophy and the history of society were not separate projects concerning distinctive objects was crucial to German idealism, and in some respects intellectual history should remain defined by the Hegelian imperative to seek their connections. It is simply a matter of making its task more explicit, not least to avoid the air of idealism that brought Hegelianism low for so long, and which led recent intellectual history, in reaction to vulgarizing reduction, into a theoretical cul-de-sac itself.

What, in other words, if the defense of the citadel of intellectual history in view of the primitivism—and occasional savagery—of the invaders no longer makes sense? In terms of my opening metaphor, the conquerors now care about ideas enough to dictate some new attitude toward them, even if their challenge to the autonomy of thought remains as serious as ever. If the new insight into the intellectual foundations of practices is right, then a division of historians between those who attend to intellectual activity and those who attend to non-intellectual matters is wrong at the start. A social history that would depreciate concepts as "elitist," besides reflecting an implausible populism in politics, is misguided as a matter of the philosophy of society itself.

A turn toward the interface between concepts and practices is very different from more ingrained and recently influential views of the history of intellectual life as itself a set of practices or an activity in the public sphere that have been prominent in the field in the past two decades—but which are likewise a surrogate from a turn in the direction of social theory insofar as they most often left completely untheorized the relationship between intellectual concepts and social activity.[14] After all, intellectuals are simply one sort of actor in social life—and one that many societies do not have. If it should turn out that intellectual concepts and principles inform social agency at all levels and in all types of societies, then the crucial preliminary even to studying intellectuals as actors is to work out the relationship between what is "intellectual," on the one hand, and what is "social" or "practical," on the other.

But what, one might ask, is specific about the social imaginary compared to the widespread emphasis in the humanities on the concept of "cultural meaning" and thus of specific relevance to intellectual historians—as opposed to those who might draw their theory of representations from anthropology or literary criticism? The answer, I suggest, is that the social imaginary is much more "high concept" both about the nature of human community and the approaches needed to study it than the notion of culture has traditionally allowed. To gain clarity about both the social imaginary's similarities to and differences from "culture," consider William H. Sewell's *Logics of History*, surely the most cutting-edge and influential Anglo-American argument about the need for historians to take the claims of social theorists seriously (and vice versa).

Sewell organizes his lucid and pathbreaking essays to address the fortunes of social explanation after the "cultural turn"—a turn that Sewell took in moving from his training as a quantitative social historian to his analysis of the linguistic-cum-cultural constitution of the categories of social history.[15] Only now, Sewell concludes in retrospect, the cultural turn has shown its own limits, in part because it has lost all moorings in the study of the making of the social order it was originally supposed to supplement. Sewell indeed gives a structural interpretation of the move from structural toward cultural explanation—a reading that should promote their marriage in the future. In this respect, Sewell's desire to move beyond the idealism of the cultural turn seems completely plausible.[16]

For Sewell, it goes without saying that structures are culturally shaped and that it would be foolish to elaborate a theory of structure without acknowledgment of (indeed insistence on) how meaning infuses them. Labor, for example, is not a natural fact about human social interaction; instead the relations it fosters are ones that follow from meaningful symbolic constitution as much as from other sorts of forces and imperatives. In part because Sewell thinks the cultural shaping of all structures goes without saying, their exact relation rarely becomes a target of explicit theoretical attention. It is obvious why: he is battling reductionist social theories that accorded culture no role whatsoever in the making of social order. In his exploration of culture, not surprisingly, Sewell proves much more committed to securing the "relative autonomy" of culture than to exploring and explaining its precise relationship to the structural determination of society.

What Sewell achieves in showing is the reason one might have to isolate culture analytically given its own internal logic and the irreducibility of cultural meaning to any specific use in context that may nonetheless shape it. But he does not have any particular approach to the corresponding heteronomy of culture to match his discussion of its autonomy. In a related examination of Clifford Geertz's materialism, Sewell offers a fascinating discussion of the adaptive (because open-ended) role of culture in the natural order of which humans are a part. But this does not do much to explain how culture relates to the social orders that humans construct in an ongoing way. Even if there are the biological foundations to human practices of making meaning, for example, there is no cause to consider structural features of the social order nonsymbolic in the same way that the natural order is. The real emphasis—which in some respects Sewell takes so much for granted conceptually that he then goes on to slight it compositionally—has to fall on exactly how structures are symbolically founded, maintained, and undone.[17]

The structure/culture interface, if it is not to be dropped altogether as an irresolvable antimony worth replacement, is one of the most difficult conundrums social theory currently faces, and I do not want to suggest that the social imaginary provides a decisive alternative to the culture concept in any respect. But I suspect that it really does matter whether one starts from the premise that meaning is—as Martin Heidegger argued—first of all practical and low, rather than in part theoretical and high, no matter how tacit or unspoken the theory is. Though strongly influenced by the phenomenological and existentialist traditions, Lefort, by comparison, insisted on "the notion that relations between human beings and the world are generated by a principle or body of principles"— a position poles apart from the culture concept in its usual models.[18] Castoriadis and Lefort spoke constantly of the symbolic constitution of society, but in a way that emphasized specific concepts rather than generalized "meaning." Put boldly, the difference credits all humans with commitment to theoretical propositions, which are as influential as unreflective imperatives in shaping one social order rather than another.

There is no need to force the contrast between social imaginary and cultural meaning. It is not the purpose of the social imaginary to suggest that intellectuals found the social order, only that concepts that elites may well theorize most explicitly pervade the social order and structure its conflicts. One could thus read the concept of the social imaginary as a controversial version of the concept of culture. Geertz himself, like Sewell in his brilliant conceptual genealogy of the meaning of labor in French history (with much attention accorded to theological discourses and leading figures), clearly assumed that elite conceptual discourse was an instance of culture. It was Darnton, with his folksy anti-intellectualism, who distracted readers from this possibility in ways that were to be fateful for the entire understanding of what cultural analysis might look like—especially among intellectual historians who responded with a phobia to a culture concept that perhaps might otherwise have given their evidence and analysis considerable importance.[19] Ironically, the social imaginary was received by Anglo-American historians in a perverse episode of garbling that forestalled for a generation its potential uses in overcoming any strong distinction between ideas and society or culture and structure. Lynn Hunt, reading François Furet's Lefortian text

Interpreting the French Revolution, theoretically liquidated the social imaginary's emphasis on concepts and principles in the name of a history of "political culture" focusing vaguely on "the values, expectations, and implicit rules that expressed and shaped collective intentions and actions." Some, like Keith Baker, responded to this move by simply dropping all inquiry into how culture related to structure on the idealist grounds that "social and political changes are themselves linguistic," while others assimilated Hunt's political culture to ethnographic thick description as the key to the deciphering of symbolic worlds.[20]

In the shuffle, both the problem of how to connect culture to structure and the role of concepts were lost. None of this intrinsically follows from the idea of culture itself, though no one—not even Geertz and Sewell—took up the challenge of theorizing the role of concepts in making the social order even when they described that role. If one wanted, in other words, one could rephrase the notion of the social imaginary as the premise that there is no way to study representations as culture without taking into account the concepts that make up culture, which is not simply a system of thick meaning but also one in which principled rationales for and justifications of the social order always matter and indeed inhabit social practice to the core. If there is ultimately no ground for a liquidation of the culture concept in the name of the social imaginary, the latter does nevertheless provide a prophylaxis against some of the least plausible implications of the former. Evidently, one wouldn't want to choose an account of ideology even in part because it made intellectual history indispensable (unlike the anthropological history of the last generation). But the fact is that recent historiography suggests just this move from "representations" as culture to an intellectualized insistence on the relevance of concepts in the making of social order.

What would an intellectual history look like that took account of the abolition of the frontier between what is intellectualized and what is not? Lefort's approach is best examined in practice in Pierre Rosanvallon's wide-ranging historical works—its best available intended exemplification. The social imaginary led Rosanvallon to what Americans like Darnton were calling the social history of ideas, yet in a completely different form—one much friendlier to the substance of intellectual history.

Lefort famously defined the social as unthinkable apart from "the political," a phrase he helped popularize. It was the inevitably political constitution of the social order, in particular, that lent credence to the study of concepts, for concepts of justice have always been intellectual by definition but pervasive in their ramifications for every bit of society. The history of society as Rosanvallon and others practiced it initially resembled a return to great texts and idealist history, in part because intellectual history had "for so long been forsaken by

French academics that it was often necessary to start from the most traditional historical reconstruction before attempting a more conceptual account of it."[21] It immediately drew fire from the heirs of the *Annales* school in France who considered it (as Rosanvallon put it) "a trite, idealistic attempt to restore the old philosophy of the free subject, whose luster had been somewhat tarnished by the social sciences." To this charge, Rosanvallon responded by emphasizing that the point of an approach that incorporates intellectual history into its explanation of society is to grasp the social imaginary that allows for society to take shape at all. "It is precisely of the essence of the philosophical history of the political," Rosanvallon wrote, "to consider that social representations cannot simply be assimilated to the order of ideology; they cannot be reduced, either, to prejudices reflecting a given state of social relationships. The philosophical history of the political maintains that beyond ideologies and prejudices there are positive representations that . . . need to be taken seriously: they constitute real and powerful infrastructures in the life of societies. In contrast to an idealist vision, which disregards the economic and social determinants structuring the field of human action, this approach sets out to enrich and make more complex the notion of determination."[22]

Such slogans represent perfectly the call for a history that finds the intellectual only in its joinder with all other aspects of social life—amounting to a call for a renewed interest in the problem of ideology to skirt an idealist account of representations. (Rosanvallon seems to have avoided this implication as he faced down vulgar accounts of "ideology" that made representations into mere reflections of the social order as thoroughly as idealism had made them independent of that order.) Remarkably, in recent years the *Annales* school has rediscovered, after the waning of its more social scientific and functionalist heyday, the concept of *mentalités* that animated the school's founders—and that now seems to justify the widespread use of the notion of the imaginary rather than its dismissal. In his recent history of the school, André Burguière cites Castoriadis in order to conclude that "the imaginary preserves the dynamic of the Annales historians' concept, which allows us to consider mentalities not simply as the distinctive color of an age or the consequence of the relations of domination structuring the social field but also as the profound driving force of changes."[23] As with culture, a "social history" that may once have seemed the implacable enemy of a high-concept intellectual history turns out to overlap in its agenda with it.

Following Lefort, Rosanvallon identified democracy as a crucial part of the modern social imaginary—the heart of the political in modern circumstances— and the key concept in a first trilogy on the history of French democracy.[24] The democratic principle according to which the people rule—for it is a principle rather than simply a matter of diffuse cultural meaning—is the first step for

understanding the nature of modern society and especially the constitutive dilemmas of modern life. One might note, in passing, the correspondence or
homology between the methodological assumption of the social imaginary that
humans make their social world in part through principles and the modern
notion of popular sovereignty, in which what is true of all human communities
becomes self-conscious as a principle.

Obviously, it would be possible to approach the doctrine that the people do
or should rule themselves idealistically, asking which philosopher invented it
and how it admits of different philosophical readings from place to place and
moment to moment. But the "history of the political" is not the Anglo-American history of political thought. Rosanvallon's intention was to write a history
that connected intellectual history "to the most intimate and decisive matters
of social experience": "Contrary to the classical history of ideas, the material for
this philosophical history of the political cannot be limited to an analysis of and
the commentary upon the great texts, even though such texts, in certain cases,
can justifiably be considered as poles around which the questions raised in a
period of history as well as the answers that it sought to offer crystallized. . . .
No subject matter is really excluded from this type of history of the political."[25]
If histories about the political constitution of the social always include concepts, those histories must seek their concepts wherever they are to be found.

Whatever the specifics of one's approach to the social imaginary, it is hard to
avoid the impression that the most interesting work in the field of European
intellectual history today is attempting a history of ideas as (constitutive) ideology. The ecumenical variety of possible ways to move intellectual history
beyond its inherited and tenacious idealism in order to explore the role of representations in the constitution of practices may actually matter more than the
particular version of this campaign. Several promising interventions express
that variety in fashions that neither revert to the vulgar priority of practice, nor
resort to vague or belletristic calls for contextualism, whether biographical, cultural, political, or anything else. They all share the goal of focusing on constitutive representations in the making of the social order.

Consider Quentin Skinner's own struggle against his inaugural idealism. It
is perhaps surprising to do so given his main legacy in founding an idealist
school of practitioners in the history of political thought. It is true that his later
theoretical moves—which one could not interpret otherwise than in minute contexts on pain of violating his own strictures against the mythology of coherence—
have so far proved far less influential among his followers. It is also true that
Skinner's acquaintance with a fuller range of social theory, mainly though not
exclusively in the so-called Continental tradition, opened him up rather early to

the fact that a linguistic turn could have many forms, but not in ways particularly friendly to seeking a path beyond the impasse of representations and practices.[26]

Yet since that pantextualist era in the humanities and his own career, which occasionally risked a deepening of his early anti-Marxist idealism, Skinner has seen the promise of, and need for, an account of sapient practices. This is not so much because Skinner, pleasingly willing to see correspondences between his intricate evolution and a large variety of other theoretical ventures with which he became acquainted over the years, actually invoked the "social imaginary" at one point as his goal: "We need, in short, to be ready to take as our province nothing less than the whole of what Cornelius Castoriadis has described as the social imaginary, the complete range of the inherited symbols and representations that constitute the subjectivity of an age," Skinner wrote in 2002. For note that his own interpretation of what the "social imaginary" is has already converted it into subjective culture rather than seeking its interface with structure or practices.[27]

But more generously, one might well claim that much of Skinner's impulse harmonizes with that very goal, though he failed ever to frontally theorize it. It seems clear that Skinner—perhaps for most of his career—worked based on a profound insight into the relevance of historically situated normative vocabularies for shaping and constraining human action, with intellectual life itself pioneeringly theorized as a sort of action in context. If this is right, the challenge for the school, therefore, is much more one of clarifying its aims in moving beyond the exploration of linguistic context *stricto sensu* in its many studies and exploring more directly the interface between language games and social life than it has so far either in its theoretical work or its historical practice.

Take now the example of Judith Surkis's recent intellectual history, inspired by Michel Foucault above all.[28] In Mark Poster's contribution to a classic theories and methods volume or Ian Hacking's writings in the history of science, it was typically Foucault's archeological moment, in *The Order of Things*, that was taken as a model.[29] Meanwhile, Foucault's turn to the relationship (or identity) of knowledge and power after the high tide of his structuralism appeared in historical circles in large part as "cultural history," not least due to its prominent appropriation by new historicists like Stephen Greenblatt and some historians in the Berkeley *Representations* group.[30] As a result, a Foucauldian intellectual history has by and large awaited our own time. To read Judith Surkis's study of the regulatory function of crises of masculinity in the late nineteenth century is to be introduced to an innovative sort of such an approach.

In it, the antinomy of representations and practices is not easily interpreted as involving a knowledge simply or ultimately reducible (or identical) to power, as many Americans read Foucault as suggesting. To be sure, Surkis's main concern is social regulation. Yet her theme is far more than conceptualization as a proxy for control, especially given her emphasis on the constitutive instability of gender concepts. Surkis declares that her topic is "the powerful hold of married love on the social imagination" of her place and time, how "this 'sex' was continually imagined and re-imagined." Arguably, Surkis's study actually depends on an implicit theory in which the subject matter is not mere "concepts" but the interface between representations and practices in which no fundamental distinction between them is really discernible. Across her book, Surkis's attention falls primarily on public debate, rather than the density of social practices it must have informed—potentially begging the question of the exact relationship between regulatory discourse and regulated practice, as in her statement that idealized conceptions of masculinity "both relied on and instituted" practical enterprises. *Sexing the Citizen* does incontestably succeed, however, in showing the profound relationship between the texts of an elite theorist like Durkheim and the overall regulatory enterprise of his time—a relationship not of one-way dependence but of common constitution. As a result, and far more than in common instances of Foucauldian approaches, Surkis's version lays explicit emphasis on avoiding the choice between respect for the conceptual and attention to the practical.[31]

Finally, consider a pathbreaking study by Andrew Sartori that attempts to renovate (or more faithfully conceptualize) Marxism as a framework for "global concept history." It is telling, and provocative, that Sartori relies on a version of (Western) Marxism that incorporates subjective representations and rejects a hierarchical material/ideational divide. Sartori's study is dedicated to explaining how the notion of "culture" could be taken up around the world, in analogous fashion in far-flung locales, including in Bengal. To do so, he claims, requires discovering "structures of practice which are socially generally rather than linked either to specific language communities or to concrete institutional apparatus or practical conventions that necessarily vary from place to place." Such "structures," however, are for Sartori not simply the material underpinnings of intellectual life but an interpretation of Marx's abstract mediation under modern conditions that cuts across more simpleminded oppositions from his tradition like that of "consciousness" versus "existence." Sartori has no truck with superstructural analysis, because, he says, "the structure of subjectivity . . . is a real moment of social reproduction that, insofar as it is brought into conflict with external constraints, can have consequential, and potentially transformative, effects. . . . Practical activity [is] the constitutive groundwork of both *objectivity* and *subjectivity*."[32] One could also say that, just as subjectivity is "objectively" constituted, the objective is always, in a sense, subjective: practical activity is never without subjective constitution and participation. Concepts are in part constitutive of the social, not least when it takes the critical analyst to reveal their implication in and reflection of it.

There is a welcome variety in approaches to European intellectual history today. But it combines with programmatic quiescence, to the point that the discipline complacently accepts styles of reconstructing past thought that should rule one another out rather than peaceably coexist. The paradox is that where programs contended violently with one another in the age when everyone appeared to agree on "the linguistic turn," today the opposite temptation rules, and every intellectual historian feels justified in his or her own unique approach in the absence of programmatic calls for new directions. Against this backdrop, it seem appropriate to group together those recent ventures in the field that, however much they may differ, together suggest the relevance of the new category of the social imaginary to future styles of work. Across apparently rival schools, the creation of an intellectual history that targets the distinction between representations and practices without reducing representations to practices seems to be under way—even in Marxist thinking. (Of course, this does not mean that these various approaches don't diverge from there.)

To these promising developments, it is worth adding in conclusion another event within the larger discipline of history itself—an event that requires some rethinking of the traditional place of the subdiscipline of intellectual history within its broader home. With the crisis of social history and the waning of cultural history, intellectual history has become familiar today, so much so that it is not clear where it ends and other forms of inquiry into the past begin. A huge number of historians, in fact, have gladly incorporated intellectual history as a dimension of their approach to the past, which spreads the fire that a few intellectual historians guarded when it flickered in a former age, while also risking a loss of expert control. If it goes much further, one might legitimately worry that this otherwise exciting development will leave a distinctive intellectual history faced with disappearance—because it is everywhere. Yet even as this scenario progresses, it seems to me that there is a continuing task for the field in brokering the relationship between history and social theory.

As noted above, historians are often wary of (or bad at) theorizing their own practices and thus considering how they propose to integrate representations and practices—even in an age in which many historians take not simply the high culture but also the high theory of the past seriously. Much is at stake in whether history incorporates intellectual material unthinkingly or on the basis of some richer approach to the role of representations in the creation, sustenance, and transformation of the social order. In this situation, an intellectual history that focuses on the social imaginary seems even more relevant.

Notes

1. Arthur O. Lovejoy, *The Great Chain of Being: A Study of the History of an Idea* (Cambridge, MA: Harvard University Press, 1936); Lovejoy, "The Historiography of Ideas," in his *Essays in the History of Ideas* (Baltimore: Johns Hopkins Press, 1948); Q. R. D. Skinner, "Meaning and Understanding in the History of Ideas," *History and Theory* 8, no. 1 (1969): 3–53; Skinner, *Visions of Politics*, vol. 1, *Regarding Method* (Cambridge: Cambridge University Press, 2002); Dominick LaCapra, "Rethinking Intellectual History and Reading Texts," *History and Theory* 19 (1980): 235–76, rpt. both in LaCapra and Steven L. Kaplan, eds., *Modern European Intellectual History: Reappraisals and New Perspectives* (Ithaca, NY: Cornell University Press, 1982), and LaCapra, *Rethinking Intellectual History: Texts, Contexts, Language* (Ithaca, NY: Cornell University Press, 1983).

2. Peter E. Gordon's *Continental Divide: Heidegger, Cassirer, Davos* (Cambridge, MA: Harvard University Press, 2010) and his essay in this volume for his critique of "exhaustive" Cambridge contextualism, without recognizing his goal of achieving more consistently the Cambridge school's commitment to the autonomy of thought from other sorts of social practices.

3. Keith Baker, writing in the famous intellectual history approaches volume, used "ideology" that way; citing him, David Armitage defined ideology "in two senses: first, in the programmatic sense of a systematic model of how society functions and second, as a world-view which is perceived as contestable by those who do not share it." Keith Michael Baker, "On the Problem of the Ideological Origins of the French Revolution," in LaCapra and Kaplan, *Modern European Intellectual History*; David Armitage, *The Ideological Origins of the British Empire* (Cambridge: Cambridge University Press, 2000), 4. More recently, Quentin Skinner refers to "the role of our evaluative language in helping to legitimate social action." Skinner, "On the Idea of a Cultural Lexicon," in *Visions of Politics*, 174.

4. See Peter Gay, "The Social History of Ideas: Ernst Cassirer and After," in *The Critical Spirit: Essays in Honor of Herbert Marcuse*, ed. Kurt H. Wolff and Barrington Moore (Boston: Beacon, 1967), and especially Robert Darnton, "In Search of the Enlightenment: Recent Attempts to Create a Social History of Ideas," *Journal of Modern History* 43 (1971): 113–32, rpt. in Darnton, *The Kiss of Lamourette: Reflections in Cultural History* (New York: Norton, 1989).

5. H. Stuart Hughes, *Consciousness and Society: The Reorientation of European Social Thought, 1890–1930* (New York: Knopf, 1958); Martin Jay, *Marxism and Totality: The Adventures of a Concept from Lukács to Habermas* (Berkeley: University of California Press, 1984), 19 for the "Generation of 1968" and its members. There were dissenters to the defensive pact to guard the walls, to be sure, including other of Hughes's students, but they did not win a comparable audience. John Toews famously appealed—albeit vaguely—to "experience" as a necessary complement to "the autonomy of meaning" in "Intellectual History after the Linguistic Turn: The Autonomy of Meaning and the Irreducibility of Experience," *American Historical Review* 92, no. 4 (October 1987): 879–907. Compare Gerald Izenberg, "Text, Context,

and Psychology in Intellectual History," in *Developments in Modern Historiography*, ed. Henry Kozicki (New York: St. Martin's, 1993), for the most persuasive argument on behalf of Hughes's tentative ventures into psychological biography.

6. "The following studies could, then, perhaps play a modest part in illustrating the manner in which 'ideas' become effective in history. . . . However, it cannot, of course, be our purpose to replace a one-sided 'materialist' causal interpretation of culture and history with an equally one-sided spiritual one." Max Weber, *The Protestant Ethic and the "Spirit" of Capitalism and Other Writings*, ed. Peter Baehr and Gordon C. Wells (New York: Penguin, 2002), 35, 122.

7. One of the first expositions of the contours of this development remains one of the most accessible and relevant: John B. Thompson, "Ideology and the Social Imaginary: An Appraisal of Castoriadis and Lefort," *Theory and Society* 11 (1982): 659–81, rpt. in *Studies in the Theory of Ideology* (Berkeley: University of California Press, 1984). I am likewise grateful to Warren Breckman, whose major study *Adventures of the Symbolic: Post-marxism and Radical Democracy* (New York: Columbia University Press, 2013), gives the best view of Castoriadis's concept, for sharing some thoughts and writings on this topic.

8. The voluntarist flavor of the social imaginary, due to its assertion against Marxism, has led to both its celebration and vilification among those who have not recognized its continuities with Marxism and the tradition of social theory. See, for example, Richard Rorty, "Unger, Castoriadis, and the Romance of a National Future," in his *Essays on Heidegger and Others (Collected Philosophical Papers 2)* (Cambridge: Cambridge University Press, 1991).

9. Claude Lefort, cited in my "On the Intellectual Origins of François Furet's Masterpiece," *Tocqueville Review* 29, no. 2 (2008): 72–73.

10. Robert Brandom, *Making It Explicit: Reasoning, Representing, and Discursive Commitment* (Cambridge, MA: Harvard University Press, 1994. See also Gillian Rose, *Hegel contra Sociology* (Atlantic Highlands, NJ: Humanities Press, 1981).

11. Charles Taylor, "Interpretation and the Sciences of Man" (1971), in Paul Rabinow and William M. Sullivan, eds., *Interpretive Social Science: A Reader* (Berkeley: University of California Press, 1979), 8; Charles Taylor, *Modern Social Imaginaries* (Durham, NC: Duke University Press, 2004).

12. But compare Stephen Turner, *Explaining the Normative* (Cambridge: Polity, 2010), for some extremely compelling worries that Brandom severs reason-giving from social practices.

13. Consider Paul Redding, *Analytic Philosophy and the Return of Hegelian Thought* (Cambridge: Cambridge University Press, 2007).

14. Tony Judt, *Past Imperfect: French Intellectuals, 1944–1956* (Berkeley: University of California Press, 1992), is the most prominent work. Of course, it is possible to study the history of intellectuals in ways that combat idealistic explanation, as in the sociology of knowledge; see, for example, Jean-Louis Fabiani, *Qu'est-ce qu'un philosophe français?* (Paris: Editions de l'EHESS, 2010).

15. William H. Sewell, Jr., *Work and Revolution: The Language of Labor from the Old Regime to 1848* (Cambridge: Cambridge University Press, 1980).

16. William H. Sewell, Jr., *Logics of History: Social Theory and Social Transformation* (Chicago: University of Chicago Press, 2005), 147–48 and chap. 5, passim. See also Sewell, "Language and Practice in Cultural History: Backing Away from the Edge of the Cliff," *French Historical Studies* 21, no. 2 (1998): 241–54. I am grateful to Sewell for help in reframing the discussion that follows, even though he will definitely not concur with it.

17. Sewell, *Logics*, 164–65, 185–89.

18. Claude Lefort, *Essais sur le politique, XIXᵉ-XXᵉ siècles* (Paris: Seuil, 1986), 8; in English, *Democracy and Political Theory*, trans. David Macey (Minneapolis: University of Minnesota Press, 1988), 2.

19. See esp. Dominick LaCapra, "Chartier, Darnton, and the Great Symbol Massacre," *Journal of Modern History* 60, no. 1 (March 1988): 95–112.

20. Lynn Hunt, *Politics, Culture, and Class in the French Revolution* (Berkeley: University of California Press, 1984), 10; Keith Michael Baker, *Inventing the French Revolution* (Cambridge: Cambridge University Press, 1990), 8; Moyn, "On the Intellectual Origins," for the original intent and garbled reception of Furet's "revisionism." The later process of vulgarization of the "social imaginary" among Anglo-Americans only made the detour of the social imaginary more pronounced—converting it into a linguistic idealism it was in fact introduced to avoid. See in particular Sarah Maza, *The Myth of the French Bourgeoisie: An Essay on the Social Imaginary 1750–1850* (Cambridge, MA: Harvard University Press, 2003), and Jan Goldstein's excellent critique, "Of Marksmanship and Marx: Reflections on the Linguistic Construction of Class in Recent Historical Scholarship," *Modern Intellectual History* 2, no. 1 (2005): 87–107.

21. Pierre Rosanvallon, "Towards a Philosophical History of the Political," in Rosanvallon, *Democracy Past and Future*, ed. Samuel Moyn (New York: Columbia University Press, 2006), 66; see also his Collège de France inaugural lecture, in English in the same book, as well as Antoine Lilti's essay in the present volume for a narrative of France and intellectual history.

22. Rosanvallon, "Towards a Philosophical History," 72, discussing Roger Chartier, "L'histoire aujourd'hui: des certitudes aux défis," *Raison présente* 108 (1993): 45–56. See also the Lefortian approach in Marcel Gauchet, "L'élargissement de l'objet historique," *Le Débat* 103 (January–February 1999): 131–47, with responses from Chartier and others.

23. André Burguière, *The Annales School: An Intellectual History*, trans. Jane Marie Todd (Ithaca, NY: Cornell University Press, 2009), 242.

24. Rosanvallon has recently concluded a second trilogy on democracy today. Rosanvallon's first trilogy has been summarized in English in my article, cowritten with Andrew Jainchill, "French Democracy between Totalitarianism and Solidarity: Pierre Rosanvallon and Revisionist Historiography," *Journal of Modern History* 76, no. 1 (March 2004): 107–54.

25. Rosanvallon, "Towards a Philosophical History," 73, 63.

26. I am very grateful to Joel Isaac for insisting that I pay heed to Skinner's later permutations, though for the reasons stated I do not think Isaac is right in boldly claiming "the roots of Skinnerian contextualism in an early conception of the social

imaginary"—given the anti-Marxist idealism of Skinner's early and most influential (indeed school-founding) theoretical pronouncements (personal communication).

27. Q. R. D. Skinner, "Motives, Intentions, and Interpretation," in *Visions of Politics*, 102. Note that this line was belatedly added after the millennium to a text with roots in two others published in 1972 and 1996 and whose own contexts were much more Anglo-American ordinary language philosophy and Continental pantextualism, respectively.

28. Judith Surkis, *Sexing the Citizen: Morality and Masculinity in France, 1870–1920* (Ithaca, NY: Cornell University Press, 2006).

29. Mark Poster, "The Future According to Foucault: *The Archaeology of Knowledge* and Intellectual History," in LaCapra and Kaplan, *Modern European Intellectual History*; Ian Hacking, *The Emergence of Probability: A Philosophical Study of Early Ideas about Probability, Induction and Statistical Inference* (Cambridge: Cambridge University Press, 1984).

30. See esp. Patricia O'Brien's significantly entitled "Michel Foucault's History of Culture," in *The New Cultural History*, ed. Lynn Avery Hunt (Berkeley: University of California Press, 1984).

31. Surkis, *Sexing the Citizen*, 1, 7, 13 (the concept of imagination is one of those most frequently invoked throughout the book). In early modern studies, Foucault (together with Pierre Hadot) has influenced the creation of a school, including Ian Hunter and Matthew Jones, treating philosophy as ascetic spiritual exercises; but so far as I know no modernists have followed their lead.

32. Andrew Sartori, *Bengal in Global Concept History: Culture in the Age of Capital* (Chicago: University of Chicago Press, 2008), 48, 61, footnote omitted, emphasis in original. I am very grateful to Andrew Sartori for helpful thoughts on this essay.

7

Has the History of the Disciplines Had its Day?

Suzanne Marchand

The study of history is not as ancient as the night sky, but it has boasted almost as many points of light. Some of these unfixed stars organize themselves into galaxies—such as "economic history" or "cultural history," which themselves are never stagnant, but have some enduring permanence. Other, more specific, types of historical inquiry might be said to form constellations within these galaxies— for example, "microhistory" might count as a constellation within the "social history" galaxy. Stellar constellations, of course, appear or disappear for us as the seasons change and the earth revolves; historical constellations may shine brightly for a time, and then fade forever. In this essay, I want to chart the waxing and waning of a set of inquiries known as "the history of the disciplines" from the 1970s to the present. Though never more than a constellation within the much more enduring galaxy we might call the history of scholarship, "the history of the disciplines" was, for a time, a widely practiced and much discussed field of intellectual history. Although it seems to me that this constellation is now in eclipse, perhaps the time has come to evaluate what we learned from it, and to discuss what new shapes related inquiries might take in the future.

Astrological metaphors aside, "the history of the disciplines" was very much a product of earthly time and space. It was practiced chiefly by North American scholars, and especially by intellectual historians and historians of science, working under the influence of two pioneering thinkers, the physicist and historian of science

Thomas Kuhn and the French philosopher Michel Foucault—although as we shall see, there were other founding fathers and mothers, formative contexts, and strains of inquiry. As I practically grew up in this sub-universe, as an avid participant in the workshop entitled "History of the Human Sciences" at the University of Chicago between 1985 and 1991, I probably have an exaggerated view of this constellation's importance, and may not be the proper person to map it. More than twenty years on, I feel indebted to this set of inquiries and proud of what it achieved, but disinclined to recommend it to the students of the next generation for reasons that will become clear at the end of this essay. I do not particularly lament what I see as the eclipse of my subfield; it is in the nature of scholarship to move on. But it also might be useful to see where we have been, in part because it seems to me that the history of the disciplines, at least in the form we once knew it, had a formative impact on intellectual history, building, for one thing, bridges between the history of science and intellectual history proper that neither subfield, today, can do without.

Of course, scholars have been interested in some way in the history of scholarship from at least the Renaissance forward; one needed periodically to review past achievements and absurdities, to praise or blame forefathers, or to argue for the superiority or inferiority of supposedly new views. Self-conscious pursuit of "craft" histories dates at least to Giorgio Vasari's *Lives of the Painters* (1550), which heroized the Italian painters of his day over those of medieval times, and offered a model for championing individuals on the basis of their new ideas. The "quarrel of the ancients and moderns" provoked the adoption of a Vasarian model, substituting the achievements of Galileo or Newton for those of Raphael and Michelangelo. The eighteenth century churned out numerous histories of astronomy as well as histories of civilization that championed progress in the sciences and the arts—and also saw J. J. Rousseau's publication of a major inversion of this model, his "Discourse on the Arts and Sciences" (1749), which claimed that scientific and cultural enrichment had come at the cost of human moral declension: as institutions and manners evolved, humans lost their freedom and naturalness, becoming slaves to conventions, to institutions, and to one another. This moral critique of scientific progress endured, *sotto voce*, even as nineteenth-century scholars threw themselves into celebrating the achievements of a multitude of disciplinary founders and heroes, often championing, as did Hegel, the emancipation of the secular sciences from the overlordship of the great mother discipline, theology. In the mid- to late nineteenth century, as scholarly change (and disciplinary divergences) accelerated, one can find massive numbers of these celebratory histories as well as hagiographic biographies of founding fathers such as the German philologist Franz Bopp or the French chemist Antoine Lavoisier. Accompanying this ballyhoo but largely out of academic earshot, one can find strong echoes of Rousseau's reservations, for example, in Marx, who added an essential bit about the ways in which "ruling ideas" are used simply to rule while at the same time trying to fashion a scientific critique of capitalism that would change the world. Famously, too, Nietzsche took on sciences that sought to rip off nature's veils, only to dissect and destroy a living and often resistant body beneath; the will to knowledge, in his view, is also very clearly a will to power. Here, of course, are the sources of later discussions of relationships between knowledge and power, but we should keep in mind that these were discussions going on outside of academia (when academics did discuss Nietzsche, Rousseau, or Marx, it was not to critique their own scholarly efforts, but to understand other social forces). The later nineteenth and early twentieth centuries abound with disciplinary histories—some of them critical of other disciplines (as orientalists were critical of classicists, or sociologists critical of theologians), but most of them written by disciplinary insiders, and devoted to celebrating the progress of the field.[1]

In the wake of the First World War, one finds a resurgence of moral and political critiques of scientific institutions and scholarly specialization; some of this was neo-romantic (as in attacks on the "killing of the Greek spirit" by specialized philologists, or the failure of anatomical dissections as a means to understand the holistic functions of living beings), some of it Marxist, some of it what we might call proto–counter cultural. The 1920s and 1930s teem with philosophical and psychoanalytical challenges to positivist models of science and Freudian theories of subjectivity; this is the world of Heidegger and Horkheimer, of Gramsci and the young Gaston Bachelard, of C. G. Jung and Alexandre Koyré. It was also a world in which a very old tradition of seeking the origins of Western science and philosophy in Eastern climes revived in the works of Otto Neugebauer and Joseph Needham and discussions of cultural relativism flourished along a spectrum running from Ruth Benedict to Oswald Spengler. Deepening and radicalizing some of these lines of thought were the experiences of fascism and the Second World War, which, for the second time in a still young century, demonstrated the disastrous destructiveness of European "civilization." In the United States, a more strictly historical and sociological set of inquiries into the history of the sciences was set in motion after 1918 by George Sarton, who brought the journal *Isis* to the United States and established the History of Science Society in 1924. Sarton served on the Harvard dissertation committee of the great sociologist of science, Robert K. Merton, whose first real foray into the field, an essay on science and society in seventeenth-century England, was published in 1938. It was also at Harvard that

Thomas Kuhn began teaching the history of science after 1946, and here that he wrote *The Copernican Revolution* (1957).

All of this work was crucial preparation for an important, but not directly linked, series of developments in the 1950s and early 1960s, as American and also British anthropologists, sociologists, and psychologists (the three disciplines featuring centrally in early studies of the history of the behavioral sciences) began to reflect on the checkered histories of their fields, and to worry about the overly positivist, presentist, and self-congratulatory character of their work. For some, like George W. Stocking, Jr., the point of entry was through personal contact; as a student of American history at the University of Pennsylvania in 1957–1960, he took courses in historiography with a strong social scientific orientation, including several from Murray Murphey, who favored an anthropological approach, and Irving ("Pete") Hallowell, who was an anthropologist, and taught what must have been one of the first courses on the history of anthropology. Hallowell, Stocking notes, treated the history of anthropology as a success story, tracking an evolution from "proto-anthropology" to "scientific" anthropology in his own day; by no means would this be Stocking's historicist position, but Hallowell was, at least, taking the history of his discipline seriously.[2] Other social and natural scientists, too, were becoming interested in and rather more critical of the history of their disciplines, in part, like Stocking, as a reaction to the Cold War expansion of the military-industrial state,[3] or to the development of more coercive medical, social, and psychoanalytical forms of "normalization."

In 1960, a newsletter devoted to the history of the behavioral sciences was founded, and just two years later, Thomas Kuhn—who had recently moved to the University of California at Berkeley, and to the philosophy department—published his epoch-making *The Structure of Scientific Revolutions* (1962). The *Journal of the History of the Behavioral Sciences* appeared in 1965; as an editorial by Stocking, one of the founding members, made clear, there were now a considerable number of social scientists who had read Kuhn, and found his discussion of "paradigms" and "revolutions" useful, if still too internalist, mostly because it was helpful in expiating the "sins of history written 'for the sake of the present.'"[4] After 1965, there would be a boomlet in histories of the behavioral sciences, like Stocking's own *Race, Culture and Evolution: Essays in the History of Anthropology* (1968), J. W. Burrow's *Evolution and Society: A Study in Victorian Social Theory* (1966), Philip Rieff's *The Triumph of the Therapeutic: The Uses of Faith after Freud* (1966), Dorothy Ross's *G. Stanley Hall: The Psychologist as Prophet* (1972), and Steven Lukes's *Émile Durkheim, His Life and Work: A Historical and Critical Study* (1973). Many of these authors would go on to write Kuhnian histories; in a move I think typical for others, Stocking started off interested in one disciplinary founder, Franz Boas, and then expanded his studies to encompass the "normal science" of the field more generally, producing *Victorian Anthropology* in 1987 and *After Tylor* in 1995. Ross, similarly, began with Hall, and moved on to the magisterial *The Origins of American Social Sciences* (1991); Lukes began a series of more theoretical inquiries into power and individuality, producing (among other works) *Moral Conflict and Politics* (1991). Although this generation did read Foucault, and perhaps thought of him as a sympathetic fellow traveler in some respects, they were not in the first instance inspired by him nor did they adopt his methods.[5]

If I can characterize further what motivated this generation, I would point to concerns about the transformation of social thought into invasive, ahistorical, hubristic, and sometimes persecutory forms of social *science*; major anxieties included the medicalization of psychology, the application of racial sciences to minority populations, and the use of demographic data to generate social norms, or to undermine democracy. All three disciplines were undergoing enormous intradisciplinary battles over method, which took the form (in part) of battles over founders such as Boas and Malinowski, Freud and Jung, Durkheim and Max Weber. Among evolutionary biologists, too, the works of the founders had come under fire. Peter Bowler and Stephen Jay Gould, among others, were posing questions about Darwin's legacy, and about the "scientificness" of evolutionary theory (beginning with Gould's *Ever since Darwin*, 1977), questions that other historians of science also found deeply provocative.[6] Freud in particular was scrutinized and denounced, but other "fathers" too were found wanting. Even a few "mothers" felt the wrath of a younger generation unwilling to take foundational scholarship on faith. The widely celebrated— and still living—Margaret Mead was denounced in Derek Freeman's *Margaret Mead and Samoa: The Making and Unmaking of an Anthropological Myth* (1983), a highly controversial book that raised deep questions not only about Mead's personality, but about methods of fieldwork more generally. In the midst of a general discussion about "whither anthropology?" (involving among others Clifford Geertz, James Clifford, and Claude Lévi-Strauss), questions were raised about where the field had been, and why it existed at all. Connections to colonialism were mentioned, but only in passing, it seems to me, in this era; the real question was one of "scientific" method: could the other be known? This question, and its equivalent for the natural sciences, could nature be known? had of course been asked by philosophers, at least since Nietzsche; but the more radical historians of the sciences (still, mind you, mostly renegade insiders) were now transporting it back into those sciences themselves.[7]

Contextually speaking, we can probably say that this first version of the history of the disciplines was a reaction to Cold War positivism, and occurred in the context of a massive expansion of both state and private university systems after 1960, which permitted so much more "normal science" to go on. Quite suddenly, after *Sputnik*, there were a lot more labs, a lot more textbooks, and a lot more publications that replicated similar results. Perhaps, too, it was a humanistic reaction to the movement of the social sciences toward quantification: telling their histories as constructed ones allowed some means of reminding hard-core economists, for example, that much of what they were championing as "scientific" was in fact the product of struggles with other disciplines, of the need to define the world in a particular way, of attempts to claim power over others. But at least at the outset, the idea was certainly that historicizing the disciplines would remind fellow insiders that the concepts they were deploying had a history, and sometimes a tainted and outdated one; the object was not to delegitimize disciplines, but to push back against presentism, especially a presentism that seemed all too likely to serve the interests of the powerful.[8]

In the 1970s, Americans began to read the works of Michael Foucault, the French philosopher who combined structural linguistics with a deep countercultural critique of the "liberal" institutions and sciences whose origins lie in the Enlightenment. Foucault's French texts appeared chiefly in the 1960s, and began to be translated into English in the 1970s, beginning with *The Order of Things* (1970), and then followed by *The Archaeology of Knowledge* (1972), *The Birth of the Clinic* (1973), *Discipline and Punish* (1977), and *The History of Sexuality*, volume 1 (1978). Foucault's works were recognized for their originality and welcomed for their critical treatment of the history of the sciences; as early as 1971, Foucault participated in a famous debate with Noam Chomsky, and by 1975, he was cited favorably (but only twice) in British philosopher Ian Hacking's *The Emergence of Probability* (1975). But by no means did most Anglophobe writers greet Foucault's work with unstinting praise. On the contrary, most of the early reviews, especially by historians, were negative.[9] Foucault's facts were faulty; his periodization was wrong; his neo-romantic prose was impenetrable; he generalized about "man" on the basis of a few quotations from random Frenchmen. A 1976 review essay on Foucault's work in the *Journal of the History of the Behavioral Sciences*, written by psychologist David Leary, acknowledged that Foucault's work might "contribute to the development of a more full-bodied approach to the history of science," but thought Foucault's "archaeological" method had simply been invented to justify the scholar's findings (in *The Order of Things*), and was impracticable, even by Foucault himself; Leary compared Kuhn's paradigms favorably to Foucault's epistemes.[10] And in 1978, Clifford Geertz disapproved of the stifling pessimism of Foucault's analysis of "the Panoptic society" in *Discipline and Punish*.[11]

By the late 1970s and the early 1980s, this view had changed, at least in part. Historians continued to object to Foucault's shoddy research methods, overly sharp and inexplicable epistemological breaks, and obscure prose; few were ready to go the whole discursive nine yards. But Foucault now seemed to offer a promising way to deconstruct not only the ideas of disciplinary founders, but whole disciplinary discourses as well. His work was, as Daniel T. Rodgers has argued, a means to address a more general problem, that of finding a concept of power adequate to an age of "the financialization of management decisions, the precipitous rise and fall of corporate entities, the offshoring of production, and the decline of labor union membership"; the apocalypticism of the 1970s was gone, but big government, big business, and an elaborate structure of "disciplining" and "normalizing" institutions remained.[12] In the social sciences, most scholars gave up seeking an overarching social theory, but that left many fields in existential, if not professional, crisis. In a 1986 book seeking new ways forward, two leading anthropologists wrote: "At the broadest level, the contemporary debate is about how an emergent postmodern world is to be represented as an object for social thought in its various contemporary disciplinary manifestations."[13]

Foucault's wave came in as beachcombing intellectuals were already seeking the imbrication of power in cultural forms, and attuned to the ways in which experts and elites, rather than elected officials, seemed to run the world; even communist countries such as China and Cambodia continued to harbor fierce nationalisms. In this situation, old-fashioned Marxism failed to explain the world—one reason for the great appeal of the newly published prison notebooks of Antonio Gramsci, and for Benedict Anderson's decision to investigate the cultural origins of what he claimed remained not age-old nations but "imagined communities."[14] Nor could liberal models offer much assistance. "Liberalism, the political theory of the ascendant bourgeoisie, long ago lost the capacity to explain events in the world of the welfare state and the multinational corporation," wrote Christopher Lasch in 1978; "nothing has taken its place."[15] Lasch—speaking as something of a left-wing populist—actually voiced rather more hope than Gramsci, Anderson, or Foucault that individuals might extricate themselves from all-encompassing and stultifying cultures that had been "invented" but then imposed on docile populations; and Jürgen Habermas's *Structural Transformation of the Public Sphere* (published in German in 1962, translated into English in 1989), addressing the problem from a left-liberal position, was even more optimistic about reestablishing the conditions for rational, inclusive, transformative discourse. But Habermas's analyses of modern power relations, too, were of a piece with these other attempts to comprehend what Rodgers calls "the soft faces of power."[16]

By the mid-1980s, then, scholars in search of ways to investigate these "soft faces" were finding their way to Foucault, and finding in Foucault a means to locate the very deep roots of this "soft power" in what the Frankfurt School Marxists had described as "the Enlightenment project." Foucault's *Discipline and Punish*, when added to *The Order of Things*, allowed thoroughgoing indictments of the "disciplinary" power of medical, penal, and military institutions— and the scholarly disciplines linked to those institutions (medicine, sociology, criminology, psychology, and so on).[17] The method of discourse analysis allowed scholars to focus on language—perhaps the ultimate form of "soft power"— and to see how words were being deployed to do things, such as sort "normal" and "abnormal" people, or divide "amateurs" (such as midwives) from "professionals" (such as male physicians). The origins of the institutional apparatus were not located in the turn from social thought to social *science* in the later nineteenth or early twentieth centuries, but in a far earlier moment of modernization, the later eighteenth century. All of what historians knew as "modern knowledge," then, had been complicit in creating the microphysics of modern power and the "iron cages" of modern institutional life.

Foucault's disarming habit of demonstrating the ways in which the seemingly most innocent ideas, and those cherished by liberals—including healing, law, and the self—served as linguistic illusions, simply obscuring the ways in which we had lost our freedoms, appealed to those already inclined to embrace Rousseavian counternarratives or wish the 1960s and 1970s had produced more thoroughgoing social changes. This was more than a critique of presentism; it was, in its way, a Rousseauvian thought experiment: what if scholarship had not developed in the ways it had done? Would we be better people, and have a more humane society? Would we know the world and ourselves in fundamentally different ways? Perhaps no passage of Foucault's work was quoted as often as the opening of *The Order of Things*, though scholars should perhaps have worried that what is being quoted there is a twentieth-century short story and not an ancient Chinese encyclopedia. But Foucault's three-volume *History of Sexuality* also provoked even those historians already sensitized to what the great scholar of late antiquity Peter Brown called "the disturbing strangeness of the past" to consider carefully, in Foucault's words, "the question of knowing if one can think differently than one thinks, and perceive differently than one sees."[18] And, of course, Foucault's works, especially perhaps *Discipline and Punish*, showed readers who couldn't quite buy Gramsci's hegemony theory how to understand modern forms of power, and their pervasiveness in Western societies, in new and eye-opening ways.[19]

But Foucault offered something more than a means to get at the origins and extent of "soft power," and that was an excavation of the process of identity formation. Edward Said's (still) enormously influential *Orientalism* in 1978 explored a critical dimension of this process in demonstrating the ways in which "Western" and "Eastern" identities and power relations were made in the imperial age. But just as influential were Foucauldian discussions about individual identity and sexuality. Important explorations of these questions were made by Ian Hacking, in his widely circulated essay "Making up People" (1986), and by Thomas Laqueur, in *Making Sex* (1990). One could list many more, including Elizabeth Lunbeck's *The Psychiatric Persuasion: Knowledge, Gender and Power in Modern America* (1994), and a very large literature on the body and on the "construction" of homosexuality, whose debts to the French philosopher are perhaps only slightly exaggerated by the title of David M. Halperin's 1997 study, *Saint = Foucault*. Foucault's works, as David Hollinger has described, "accelerated the movement Kuhn had stimulated from 'objectivist' to 'constructivist' theories of knowledge" and played a key role in launching American debates about "identity."[20] Here, too, Foucault left a very deep imprint on North American scholarship, not just in history, but in the humanities and social sciences broadly defined.

I would say that the 1980s and 1990s were the era *par excellance* of the history of the disciplines. Many of these were written not by insiders, but by professional historians, writing from outside the discipline, and never intending to practice it themselves (viz. one I know well, titled *Down from Olympus: Archaeology and Philhellenism in Germany, 1750–1970*). The Chicago School is strongly represented in my list, and it may be that Foucauldian influence was stronger here than elsewhere (though even here, most practitioners were not uncritical Foucauldians). There were histories of mathematics and of musicology, of physics and of sociology, many of them titled "Inventing the X" or "Professionalizing the X." Those who know the history of the natural sciences will be able to list numerous works on the histories of medicine, psychiatry, physics, biology, chemistry, botany, and zoology published in the 1980s and 1990s, and some in the 2000s—although many of these were shaped equally, or even more powerfully, by the older tradition of Thomas Kuhn's *Structure of Scientific Revolutions*, or by more recent work in the sociology of science (see below).

Having just laid out this general trajectory, I must immediately note that throughout the period I have sketched, there were always those who did not jump on the history of the disciplines bandwagon, and pursued the history of knowledge production in different ways. Numerous disciplinary histories of the 1980s and 1990s did without explicitly Foucauldian frameworks; examples include Michael Ann Holly's *Panofsky and the Foundations of Art History* (1984), Woodruff Smith's *Politics and the Sciences of Culture in Germany, 1840–1920*

(1991), and Michael Podro's *The Critical Historians of Art* (1982). I have just mentioned the ongoing importance of the tradition of Kuhn and the sociology of science; similarly, in the history of the social sciences and of the humanities, the sociology of knowledge, dating back to the work of Max Weber and Karl Mannheim, continued to exert influence. Many early modernists, like Anthony Grafton, Donald Kelley, Mark Phillips, and Joseph Levine, though keenly interested in the development of knowledge, never found the Foucauldian model useful, and tended instead to point to the careful historiographical essays of Arnaldo Momigliano; but then again, Foucauldian ideas have always been more compelling for those who focus their attention on the nineteenth or twentieth centuries. Still, the work of John Toews, Carl Schorske, and Peter Gay on Freud did not depend on Foucauldian categories.[21] When Daniel T. Rodgers sought a model for discourse analysis, he found Raymond Williams rather than Foucault more compatible; Dorothy Ross turned to J. G. A. Pocock.[22] Even Stocking, though he read and thought about Foucault's work, remained committed to a historicist approach, one that could not give up pursuing the questions of "influence" and details of authorial biographies that Foucault had ruled out of court.

Nor was the Foucauldian model nearly so widely adopted in Europe itself. Many German and French scholars hesitated to follow either Kuhn's or Foucault's models; perhaps they didn't need them. On the European continent, updated forms of the sociology of knowledge, as found in the work of Pierre Bourdieu and Niklas Luhmann, or of the Frankfurt School and Habermas, or the methodology known as *Begriffsgeschichte*, have been more influential in shaping how books about knowledge production were written. Bruno Latour, whose work seems to me to owe less and less to Foucault as time goes on, has been on the cutting edge of the sociology of science, producing probing and insightful studies of how scientists do their work; there are some individuals, such as Claudine Cohen, Dominique Pestre, and Maurice Olender, who regularly write about the history of the sciences or humanities, and important centers such as the Centre Alexandre Koyré in Paris and the Max Planck Institut für Wissenschaftsgschichte in Berlin. There is a new spate of work in both countries about the histories of the natural sciences, archaeology, and philology.[23] But there is still a powerful tradition of hagiographic biography, which flourishes outside of these centers and is especially on view in the ongoing world of the Festschrift, or museum exhibition; most of the work is very detailed but not very critical, and focuses on people who are still thought to be great achievers, rather than "normal scientists" or mavericks—except, of course, for those studies that deal with scholars who collaborated with the Nazis (which are, tellingly, usually NOT written by disciplinary insiders).

In Britain, Roy Porter read *Madness and Civilization* in 1970, and claimed that his "admiration, for both its erudition and its vision," grew with every rereading[24]—although his own histories of madness favored careful historical reconstruction over the analysis of medical discourses. At the Wellcome Institute for the History of Medicine in London (beginning in 1977), Porter surely helped to diffuse Foucauldian ideas through the community of Brits interested in the history of the sciences and in his more general field, the history of the Enlightenment in Britain. But the Edinburgh school of sociologists of science did not particularly need or want Foucault; and when Steven Shapin and Simon Schaffer acknowledged their methodological debts in the pathbreaking *Leviathan and the Air-Pump*, the laurels went not to Foucault, but to Wittgenstein, "because of his stress on the primacy of practical activity."[25] They also thanked Cambridge's enormously influential historian of ideas Quentin Skinner, who has long worked on political rhetoric but never seems to have been attracted by Foucauldian discourse theory. Intellectual historians who study eastern Europe, Russia, or the non-Western world have not tended to be attracted to the subject; or, as Laura Engelstein noted long ago, there are good reasons for hesitating to apply a critique of Western institutions to Russian conditions.[26] All of this is to say that the "history of the disciplines" may really have been a North American phenomenon, and one practiced chiefly by and for social scientists and modern intellectual historians of a particular generation, and particularly by those who felt themselves in the grip of "soft" rather than "hard" power. This helps us to map our constellation (and to remind us that it was never alone in intellectual history's firmament, or even in the history of scholarship's much smaller galaxy)—and perhaps to understand why it may be facing eclipse.

Before we describe this eclipse, it is worth remembering what disciplinary histories in the Foucauldian mode achieved. Discourse theory allowed us to look beyond genre differences and individual biographies, and even to dispense with an analysis of what impact ideas actually made; the main game was simply to understand the logic, or what Foucault called the "rules" of the discourse itself. Bracketing the proverbial problems of documenting the origins of an idea (one of the key reasons Foucault opted for the study of "rules"[27]) made it possible to avoid the elaborate and erudite but endless backward regressions found in works such as Arthur Lovejoy's *Great Chain of Being*; we could, then, sideline the problems of ur-origins and of "influence" and seek to understand the circulation of ideas in new ways. Inquiries into the history of disciplinary knowledge gave us important new insight into nineteenth-century struggles between forms of expertise and between professionals and amateurs; they helped us understand why it was that things were ordered as they were (even if those classifications did not follow Foucault's rules, or win over to all classifiers). The history of the disciplines gave us critical purchase on the supposedly progressive institutions around us and encouraged us to look at minor writers, trivial publications, and throwaway lines in the text.[28] This form of inquiry has not always been welcomed by practitioners of those disciplines, many of whom continued to write Festschrifts and obituary tributes in the same way they had always done, as celebrations of individual achievements and of intellectual progress. But that is one of its strengths, as it sometimes made possible the exposure of truths insiders would not or could not divulge, either because of the "family ties" that often link one generation of researchers to particularly revered ancestors, or because insiders were warned not to foul their own nests. When done well, disciplinary histories demonstrated linkages between institutions, social and cultural norms, and methods of knowledge production that tell us a very great deal about the history of ideas, but are obscured or obliterated by the study of ideas or individuals in isolation. Unfortunately, disciplinary histories (and discourse theory as a whole) can also be done badly, by sloppy scholars who selectively assemble lines and phrases from disparate texts, and link the political to the intellectual in ways that would have made Hegel blush.[29] I have also grown concerned about the tendency of this literature to condemn knowledge-making in general as simply a power grab, and to refuse to consider motivations for knowledge-production other than disciplinary expansionism or social control. But there is nothing like reading a few context-adverse disciplinary hagiographies to make one see just how much we have learned from the history of the disciplines.[30]

Yet even for North American intellectual historians some aspects of this project now seem dated, unsatisfying, or simply so widely accepted that the subject no longer seems an interesting one to pursue. I think there is a general sense that many of the stories of disciplinary development have been told, and the genre is becoming repetitive, and it is time to move on. There are a number of reasons for this, one of which is simply scholarship's need to change horses after the old ones have carried us as far as they can go. But there are other reasons, too, which I would like to suggest in the following paragraphs. First of all, modern intellectual historians have grown more and more dependent (and this is by no means a bad thing) on the history of science for our epistemological underpinnings, and historians of science have moved far beyond Foucault. In a sense they had to; the "science wars" of the 1990s forced them to describe in very careful detail how scientists work on and shape nature with their hands and instruments as well as with their minds.[31] To get a closer look at these processes, some have returned to intellectual biography.[32] Others, like Bruno Latour and Steven Shapin, have expanded sociological models to help explain knowledge production;[33] their colleagues have introduced us to the study of material culture, laboratory practices, and instruments (something paralleled by early modern studies of the history of the book, of collecting, of memory technologies).[34]

Historians of science have also been at the forefront of those seeking sensitive and precise ways to link knowledge production with information technologies, with market forces, with political pressures, and with military imperatives.[35] They have shown us—in works like James Secord's magnificent *Victorian Sensation: The Extraordinary Publication, Reception and Secret Authorship of the Vestiges of the Natural History of Creation* (2003)—how to study influence directly, rather than simply to infer it from the texts themselves. Volumes like Lorraine Daston and Peter Galison's *Objectivity* (2006) start from something that seems like Foucauldian observations (that definitions of objectivity and subjectivity are inextricably intertwined, and historically situated). But their Foucault is rather the philosopher interested in "the care of the self," not the quasi-intellectual historian of *The Order of Things*, and their intention is to understand the creation of specific types of scientific personae, not to tell the history of objectivity as a discourse. An important recent volume that reaches out to garden-variety social historians, *Science and Civil Society* (edited by Lynn Nyhart and Thomas H. Broman, 2002), takes its starting point from Habermas rather than from Foucault. Historians of science surely owe debts—some more than others—to Foucault; but they know that power is not enough to explain why some ideas work and last and others do not, and they take contingencies and personalities seriously in a way the Foucauldian model never could; they know that human beings, as well as nature itself, do not always follow the "rules of discourse."[36] The one worry I have about the future of the history of science is that as it delves more deeply into internal dynamics and practices, it invokes vocabularies that most garden-variety historians can't understand. Thus these disciplinary historians' audiences are very small, and publishers are rather wary of printing their books.[37] That, in the long term, is not a recipe for institutional success, even if it produces high-quality scholarship.

Another rich field of inquiry, the study of colonial knowledge production, has also arisen of late, and taken up a great deal of the space once inhabited by the history of the disciplines. This field owes a great deal, of course, to Edward Said's Foucauldian *Orientalism*, but also the work of Bernard Cohn and the scholars who pushed forward the creation of subaltern studies in the later 1980s and 1990s.[38] To generalize broadly, one might say that the first series of these works was heavily devoted to critiquing knowledge production from the European side, and there is still a great deal of interest in this topic.[39] There are now many books on the history of racial science, for example, on the history of imperial (and imperious) linguistics, archaeology, geography, ethnography, botany, and art.[40] Studies of "the image of the other" have branched out into careful work on the history of museums, of photography, and of advertising.[41] Although some of these stick to analyzing European and American discourses, some historians also began to ask questions about the impact and reception of Western ideas in the non-Western world, about the brokering of ideas by particular individuals, and about knowledge transfers between peoples.[42] Thanks to this body of work, we have learned, to a certain extent, anyway, to "provincialize" Europe, as Dipesh Chakrabarty pressed us to do—to see Europe not only as a "center of calculation," to use a term coined by Bruno Latour, but also as the recipient of ideas made elsewhere, or the maker of ideas that others—at least in some circumstances—could use to their own ends.[43] While there are some key Foucauldian or Saidian concepts embedded in some of this work— governmentality, orientalism—over time the disciplines and their imperatives no longer matter much here, and individuals seem to be mattering more.[44] All of this work owes debts to the history of the disciplines; but as it evolves, it makes Thomas Kuhn—and even Foucault—look indeed provincial, and Foucault's inexact linking of context and ideas seems less helpful, perhaps, than some of the older sociology of knowledge or richly detailed historicist cum biographical work of the generation of Stocking, Ross, Momigliano, and Donald Lach.[45]

A third reason I believe the history of the disciplines has had its day is rather less cheering than the new departures in the history of science and the study of colonial knowledge and that is the waning of intellectual historians' interest in the nineteenth century. I have written about this elsewhere,[46] so shall not belabor the point, but it does seem to me that it is harder and harder to interest students in studying the nineteenth century, especially if one wants them to undertake topics other than imperialism or Nietzsche. The flight from the nineteenth century is partly the result of the expansion of the twentieth century: it is now safe to work on the post-1945 period and not be thought a mere "journalist." There has also been a very exciting and rich development of early modern studies, something that has attracted talented cultural historians who might once have devoted their efforts to studying Balzac, Ruskin, or Theodor Mommsen. I do think the Foucauldian trajectory—which suggests that epistemic ruptures occurred sometime in the 1780s and in the 1960s—has contributed to this problem, for all too many of us have been convinced that the discourses of the late Enlightenment radically broke from previous modes of thought, and then remained essentially unchanged until almost the present day. We have perhaps convinced our readers that the nineteenth century was a period in which virtually everyone trotted along happily in the wake of the "stars" of *The Order of Things* (Cuvier, Darwin, Adam Smith, Marx), or spent their lives devising nasty things to say about "abnormal" people and ethnic "others." Who would want to study that? Of course, I am overstating the case to make this point: there are excellent historians, and historians of science, still beavering away in this world. But journal contents and conference programs do seem to demonstrate that the nineteenth century is rapidly diminishing in proportion to other subjects, and part of that may both be blamed on the history of the disciplines, and may result in the further waning of the subfield itself.

I would like to suggest two further, unsettling, reasons the history of the disciplines might be a fad that is fading. First of all, positivism in the natural and probably behavioral sciences seems to have won; or where it is questioned, those questions come not from historians, but from environmentalists, or from proponents of alternative medicine, or from critics of the penal system—and even they are desperate to have "scientific" experts side with them. I fear the hope that disciplinary histories would undercut the hubris of the scientists has not been realized, and we may be too cynical now to dream this dream again soon. Secondly, we all surely recognize that we are entering a new era of utilitarianism in higher education, and perhaps in intellectual life more broadly, our choices are to be useful, or to entertain. Disciplinary histories were never particularly entertaining, and their usefulness was a usefulness proper to the 1960s–1980s: of questioning authority, of deconstructing our present-day hubris, of making us understand just how much our knowledge relied on interest, serendipity, patronage, and power relations. Perhaps these critical disciplinary histories did help to increase at least scholarly acceptance of homosexuality, alternative medicine, and mental illness in our society; though perhaps they also helped to spread the cynical view that all identities, sentiments, cures, and words of consolation are constructed, and that all institutions seek only their own perpetuation or further empowerment. The work this line of thought accomplished was largely destructive, or more positively, deconstructive; but in the end, did not answer the question, where to from here? Few of those who wrote disciplinary histories, including myself, had much to offer those seeking a less repressive and more honest future for, say, classical archaeology, or physical anthropology.

We are in a different moment now, and it seems that the time has come to develop models for the history of scholarship and intellectual history more generally that do not throw the proverbial baby out with the bathwater. We are quite well aware, now, that our foremothers and -fathers invented particular kinds of "objectivity" to suit their own purposes—but didn't they also learn things in the process? Can we remain critical of some developments, like, say, "shock therapy," without delegitimizing the study of psychology as a whole? We also do not need to undermine our own credentials any further (and here is where things get very uncomfortable); in the present situation, it is actually incumbent upon us to explain to students, deans, and taxpaying citizens that we actually do know things, in more or less stable and defensible ways, and that this knowledge is worth transmitting and cultivating further.[47] To do this, we may find we need to take two steps backward in order to take a step ahead, to go back to good, pre-Foucauldian studies like those of Stocking or of Steven Lukes, of Momigliano and Dorothy Ross. The "sociology of knowledge" sounds old-fashioned—but as the recent work in the history of science shows, it continues to show us new things. Early modern historians, too, have developed many rich and powerful models for understanding how scholars do their work; those who work in modern history could surely learn much by reading more of their work, and by observing longer-term intellectual developments.[48] By tapping, or returning to, these sources we might recover a sense of the nineteenth century's richness and its own "disturbing strangeness"—and learn to treat it not just as an era of repression, competition, and conquest (which it surely was), but also as a period of liberation, creativity, and lasting achievements.

Perhaps, in retrospect, writing the history of the disciplines was a luxurious indulgence for North American scholars, men and women lucky enough to be employed during a period in which scholarship was valued in and for itself sufficiently that we could turn around on our own tails, and critique ourselves. The time for critique is not over, and should never be over; self-examination, we have learned, is a critical means of discovering (and hopefully diminishing, if not doing away with) our own prejudices. The flourishing of the history of science and the history of colonial knowledge these days should give us heart—the history of scholarship has by no means disappeared from intellectual historians' horizons. There is much interesting work going on today, too, in the history of the humanities, an area that was little touched by Foucauldian disciplinary history.[49] Nor is the influence of Foucault entirely gone; his work on the "care of the self" continues to be of use, and his late lectures on governmentality have inspired new lines of inquiry.[50] As the constellation fades, we ought to use its remaining light to uncover earlier formations as well as chart future ones; we should not despair that the history of the disciplines has had its day; the "constellation" provided considerable illumination, and some of us, at least, will continue to soldier on in its crepuscular afterglow, and perhaps forge new constellations. Indeed, it should be a consolation to historians that there is so much in our starry skies that does endure, in some form, and continues to provide us with inspiration and the courage to know more.

Notes

I thank the editors of this volume and its two anonymous reviewers; together, their critical comments prompted me to rethink and revise this essay. It remains a rather impressionistic piece, and I hope readers will take it as provocation to further discussion rather than as the "final word" on the subject or, worse, as proof that it is no longer important to read Foucault, or to write disciplinary histories.

1. See, for example, Sir John Edwyn Sandys, *A History of Classical Scholarship*, 3 vols. (Cambridge: Cambridge University Press, 1903); Ernst Windisch, *Geschichte von Sanskrit-Philologie und Indischen Altertumskunde*, 2 vols, (Stuttgart: K. J. Trübner, 1917–1920); Karl Hugo Bauer, *Geschichte der Chemie*, 2 vols. (Leipzig: G.-J. Göschen, 1905).

2. George W. Stocking, Jr., *Glimpses into My Own Black Box: An Exercise in Self-Deconstruction* (Madison: University of Wisconsin Press, 2010), 70–71.

3. Ibid., 155.

4. George W. Stocking, "Editorial: On the Limits of 'Presentism' and 'Historicism' in the Historiography of the Behavioral Sciences," *Journal of the History of the Behavioral Sciences* 1, no. 3 (1965): 214–15, quotation on 215.

5. In *The Origins of American Social Science*, Ross described J. G. A. Pocock's *The Machiavellian Moment: Florentine Political Thought and the Atlantic Republican Tradition* (Princeton: Princeton University Press, 1975), as "the largest single intellectual stimulus for this book" (xxi); Foucault does not even rate a mention in the index.

6. To cite one by another member of the Chicago History of Human Sciences Workshop: Robert Richards, *Darwin and the Emergence of Evolutionary Theories of Mind and Behavior* (Chicago: University of Chicago Press, 1987).

7. Perhaps Hayden White's *Metahistory: The Historical Imagination in Nineteenth-Century Europe* (Baltimore: Johns Hopkins University Press, 1973) belongs here, as a version of that radical questioning for historians, by an historian.

8. Thomas Kuhn—who envisioned the readership of his book as philosophers of science, rather than, as it turned out they mostly were, social scientists—opened his book with this statement: "History, if viewed as a repository for more than anecdote or chronology, could produce a decisive transformation in the image of science by which we are now possessed" (Kuhn, *The Structure of Scientific Revolutions* [Chicago: University of Chicago Press, 1962], 1).

9. See, for example, G. S. Rousseau, "Whose Enlightenment? Not Man's: The Case of Michel Foucault," *Eighteenth-Century Studies* 6, no. 2 (Winter 1972–1973): 238–56. Rousseau's final footnote concluded: "If Foucault wishes to be taken seriously ever again, he ought to abandon the past altogether and concentrate exclusively on the present. Then his audience will agree or disagree but never label him a scholarly naïf." Ibid., 256, n. 51.

10. David E. Leary, "Essay Review: Michel Foucault: An Historian of the *Sciences Humaines*," *Journal of the History of the Behavioral Sciences* 12, no. 3 (1976): 286–93; quotation on 293.

11. Daniel T. Rodgers, *Age of Fracture* (Cambridge, MA: Belknap Press of Harvard University Press, 2011), 104.

12. Ibid., 80–81; quotation on 81.

13. George E. Marcus and Michael M. J. Fischer, *Anthropology as Cultural Critique: An Experimental Moment in the Human Sciences* (Chicago: University of Chicago Press, 1986), vii.

14. Benedict Anderson, *Imagined Communities: Reflections on the Origins and Spread of Nationalism*, 2nd ed. (London: Verso, 2006), xi.

15. Christopher Lasch, *The Culture of Narcissism: American Life in an Age of Diminishing Expectations* (New York: Norton, 1978), xiii.

16. Rodgers, *Age of Fracture*, 106.

17. Examples here would include Robert Nye, *Crime, Madness and Politics in Modern France: The Medical Concept of National Decline* (Princeton, NJ: Princeton University Press, 1984); Jan Goldstein, *Console and Classify: The French Psychiatric Profession in the Nineteenth Century* (Cambridge: Cambridge University Press, 1987); Richard Wetzell, *Inventing the Criminal* (Chapel Hill: University of North Carolina Press, 2000); and most of the essays collected in *Knowledges: Historical and Critical Studies in Disciplinarity*, ed. Ellen Messer-Davidow et al. (Charlottesville: University Press of Virginia, 1993). Interestingly, all of these examples do not really buy into Foucault's chronologies, but define their own, often identifying turning points much later than the Enlightenment.

18. Foucault, quoted in Peter Brown, *The Body and Society: Women and Sexual Renunciation in Early Christianity* (New York: Columbia University Press, 1988; 2nd ed., 2008), xviii.

19. For some examples of the application of Foucault to the history of historical and statistical thinking, see Philippa Levine, *The Amateur and the Professional: Antiquarians, Historians, and Archaeologists in Nineteenth-Century England, 1838–1886* (Cambridge: Cambridge University Press, 1986); Peter Novick, *That Noble Dream: The "Objectivity Question" and the American Historical Profession* (Cambridge: Cambridge University Press, 1988); Ian Hacking, *The Taming of Chance* (Cambridge: Cambridge University Press, 1990); David Lindenfeld, *The Practical Imagination: The German Sciences of State in the Nineteenth Century* (Chicago: University of Chicago Press, 1997); Bonnie Smith, *The Gender of History: Men, Women and Historical Practice* (Cambridge, MA: Harvard University Press, 1998).

20. David Hollinger, "The Disciplines and the Identity Debates, 1970–1995," *Daedalus* 126, no. 1 (1997): 333–51; quotation on 344.

21. See, for example, John E. Toews, "Historicizing Psychoanalysis: Freud in His Time and for Our Time," *Journal of Modern History* 63 (1991): 504–45; Carl Schorske, *Fin-de-siècle Vienna: Politics and Culture* (New York: Knopf, 1980) and *Thinking with History: Explorations in the Passage to Modernism* (Princeton, NJ: Princeton University Press, 1998); Peter Gay, *Freud, Jews, and Other Germans* (New York: Oxford University Press, 1984); among other titles. Nor is Toews's history of the historicizing disciplines, *Becoming Historical: Cultural Reformation and Public Memory in Early Nineteenth-Century Berlin* (Cambridge: Cambridge University Press, 2004), a Foucauldian disciplinary history.

22. Daniel T. Rodgers, *Contested Truths: Keywords in American Politics since Independence* (Cambridge, MA: Harvard University Press, 1987).

23. Claudine Cohen, *La Méthode de Zadig: La trace, le fossil, La preuve* (Paris: Seuil, 2011); Maurice Olender, *Les Langues du paradis: Aryens et sémites, un couple providentiel* (Paris: Seuil, 1989); Sabine Mangold, *Eine "weltbürgerliche Wissenschaft": Die deutsche*

Orientalistik im 19. Jahrhundert (Stuttgart: F. Steiner, 2004); Céline Trautman-Waller et al., *Ignác Goldziher: Un autre orientalisme?* (Paris: Geuthner, 2011); Alain Schnapp, *La conquête du passé: Aux origines de l'archéologie* (Paris: Editions Carré, 1993); Michel Espagne, *L'histoire de l'art comme transfert culturel: L'itinéraire d'Anton Springer* (Paris: Belin, 2009); Amy Dahan-Dalmédico, Dominique Pestre, et al., *Les sciences pour la guerre, 1940–1960* (Paris: Editions de l'EHESS, 2004); Veronika Lipphardt, *Biologie der Juden: Jüdische Wissenschaftler über "Rasse" und Vererbung, 1900–1935* (Tübingen: Vandenhoeck und Ruprecht, 2008).

24. Roy Porter, "Foucault's Great Confinement," *History of Human Sciences* 3 (1990): 47. Porter's works on the subject include *A Social History of Madness: Stories of the Insane* (London: Weidenfeld and Nicholson, 1987) and *Mind-Forg'd Manacles: A Social History of Madness in England from the Restoration to the Regency* (Cambridge, MA: Harvard University Press, 1987).

25. Steven Shapin and Simon Schaffer, *Leviathan and the Air-Pump: Hobbes, Boyle, and the Experimental Life* (Chicago: University of Chicago Press, 1985), 15, n. 32.

26. Laura Engelstein, one of this generation of Russian historians most interested in Foucauldian methods, contributed an important essay to the *Foucault and the Historians* volume in which she explains why it is that Foucault is hard to apply to the Russian world—where oppression is so much more a matter of the imposition of overt force than of more subtle microphysics of power. See Engelstein, "Foucault, Russia and the Question of Legality," in *Foucault and the Writing of History*, ed. Jan Goldstein (Oxford: Basil Blackwell, 1994).

27. See Michel Foucault, *The Archaeology of Knowledge and the Discourse on Language*, trans. A. M. Sheridan Smith (New York: Pantheon, 1972), 135–45.

28. There is an interesting relationship here to the kind of science of reading "clues" Carlo Ginzburg described in the lead essay in his *Clues, Myths and the Historical Method*, trans. John and Anne C. Tedeschi (Baltimore: Johns Hopkins University Press, 1992).

29. I fear I have to some extent earned that criticism myself in this essay, though I will excuse myself by saying that I am not trying to offer a full history of the disciplines here, but merely a provocative overview.

30. Two of these have recently come across my desk: Annette M. Baertschi and Colin G. King, eds., *Die modernen Väter der Antike: Die Entwicklung der Altertumswissenschaften an Akademie und Universität in Berlin des 19. Jahrhundert* (Berlin: Walter de Gruyter, 2007) and Wolfgang Hardtwig and Philipp Müller, *Die Vergangenheit der Weltgeschichte: Universalhistorisches Denken in Berlin, 1800–1933* (Göttingen: Vandenhoeck und Ruprecht, 2010).

31. See, for example, Andrew Pickering, *The Mangle of Practice: Time, Agency, and Science* (Chicago: University of Chicago Press, 1995).

32. Cathryn Carson, *Heisenberg in the Atomic Age* (Cambridge: Cambridge University Press, 2010); Mary Terrall, *The Man Who Flattened the Earth: Maupertuis and the Sciences in the Enlightenment* (Chicago: University of Chicago Press, 2006); Janet Browne, *Darwin: A Biography*, 2 vols. (New York: Knopf, 1996, 2003); Gerald Geison, *The Private Science of Louis Pasteur* (Princeton, NJ: Princeton University Press, 1996).

33. Bruno Latour, *Science in Action: How to Follow Scientists and Engineers through Society* (Cambridge, MA: Harvard University Press, 1988); Steven Shapin, *A Social History of Truth: Civility and Science in Seventeenth-Century England* (Chicago: University of Chicago Press, 1995); Jessica Riskin, *Science in the Age of Sociability: The Sentimental Empiricists of the French Enlightenment* (Chicago: University of Chicago Press, 2002); Deborah Harkness, *The Jewel House: Elizabethan London and the Scientific Revolution* (New Haven, CT: Yale University Press, 2007).

34. A new collection of papers offers a good selection of recent approaches from some of the leading figures in the field. See Mario Biagoli and Jessica Riskin, eds., *Nature Engaged: Science in Practice from the Renaissance to the Present* (New York: Palgrave Macmillan, 2012).

35. Anke te Heesen, *The World in a Box: The Story of an Eighteenth-Century Picture Encyclopedia* (Chicago: University of Chicago Press, 2002); Ann Blair, *Too Much to Know: Managing Scholarly Information before the Modern Age* (New Haven, CT: Yale University Press, 2011); Lynn K. Nyhart, *Modern Nature: The Rise of the Biological Perspective in Germany* (Chicago: University of Chicago Press, 2009); Robert N. Proctor, *Cancer Wars: How Politics Shapes What We Know and What We Don't Know about Cancer* (New York: Basic Books, 1996); Daniel J. Kevles, *The Physicists: The History of a Scientific Community in Modern America* (New Haven, CT: Yale University Press, 1995).

36. Bernard Cohn, *Colonialism and Its Forms of Knowledge: The British in India* (Princeton, NJ: Princeton University Press, 1996).

37. See Paula Findlen's interesting essay attempting to deal with this problem: "The Two Cultures of Scholarship?," *Isis* 96 (2005): 230–37.

38. See, for example, Cohn, *Colonialism and Its Forms*; Partha Chatterjee, ed., *Texts of Power: Emerging Disciplines in Colonial Bengal* (Minneapolis: University of Minnesota Press, 1995); Dipesh Chakrabarty, *Provincializing Europe* (Princeton, NJ: Princeton University Press, 2000); Gyan Prakash, *Another Reason: Science and the Imagination fo Modern India* (Princeton, NJ: Princeton University Press, 1999).

39. See, for example, Ronald Inden, *Imagining India* (Oxford: Basil Blackwell, 1990); Timothy Mitchell, *Colonising Egypt* (Cambridge: Cambridge University Press, 1988); Mary Louise Pratt, *Imperial Eyes: Travel Writing and Transculturation* (New York: Routledge, 1992).

40. Ronald Meek, *Social Science and the Ignoble Savage* (Cambridge: Cambridge University Press, 1976); C. A. Bayly, *Empire and Information: Intelligence Gathering and Social Communication in India, 1780–1870* (Cambridge: Cambridge University Press, 1996); Harry Liebersohn, *The Travelers' World: Europe to the Pacific* (Cambridge, MA: Harvard University Press, 2006); Felix Driver, *Geography Militant: Cultures of Exploration and Empire* (Oxford: Blackwell Publishers, 2001); Jim Endersby, *Imperial Nature: Joseph Hooker and the Practices of Victorian Science* (Chicago: University of Chicago Press, 2008).

41. For example, H. Glenn Penny, *Objects of Culture: Ethnography and Ethnographic Museums in Imperial Germany* (Chapel Hill: University of North Carolina Press, 2002); James R. Ryan, *Picturing Empire: Photography and the Visualization of the British Empire* (Chicago: University of Chicago Press, 1997); David Ciarlo, *Advertising Empire:*

Race and Visual Culture in Imperial Germany (Cambridge, MA: Harvard University Press, 2011).

42. See for example Simon Schaffer, ed., *The Brokered World: Go-Betweens and Global Intelligence, 1770–1820* (Sagamore Beach, MA: Science History Publications, 2009); Tapati Guha-Thakurta, *Monuments, Objects, Histories: Institutions of Art in Colonial and Post-Colonial India* (New York: Columbia University Press, 2004); Daniel T. Rodgers, *Atlantic Crossings: Social Politics in a Progressive Age* (Cambridge, MA: Harvard University Press, 1998); Donald M. Reid, *Whose Pharaohs? Archaeology, Museums, and Egyptian National Identity from Napoleon to World War I* (Berkeley: University of California Press, 2002).

43. See Kris Manjapra, "From Imperial to International Horizons: A Hermeneutic Study of Bengali Modernism," *Modern Intellectual History* 8, no. 2 (2011): 327–39; Edwin F. Bryant, *The Quest for the Origins of Vedic Culture: The Indo-Aryan Migration Debate* (New York: Oxford University Press, 2004).

44. See, for example, Lucette Valensi, *Mardochée Naggiar: Enquête sur un inconnu* (Paris: Stock, 2008); Jack Harrington, *Sir John Malcolm and the Creation of British India* (New York: Palgrave Macmillian, 2010); Lynn Zastoupil, *Rammohun Roy and the Making of Victorian Britain* (New York: Palgrave Macmillan, 2010).

45. I will cite only two of Momigliano's essay collections and Lach's magnum opus here: Arnaldo Momigliano, *New Paths of Classicism in the Nineteenth Century* (Middletown, CT: Wesleyan University Press, 1982), Momigliano, *The Classical Foundations of Modern Historiography* (Berkeley: University of California Press, 1992), and Donald Lach, *Asia in the Making of Europe*, 9 vols. (Chicago: University of Chicago Press, 1965–1993).

46. Suzanne L. Marchand, "Embarrassed by the Nineteenth Century," in *Consortium on Revolutionary Europe, 1750–1850: Selected Papers, 2002*, ed. Bernard Cook et al. (Consortium on Revolutionary Europe, 2004), 1–16.

47. I tried to do a bit of this in my *German Orientalism in the Age of Empire: Religion, Race and Scholarship* (Cambridge: Cambridge University Press, 2009).

48. In addition to works cited above by Lorraine Daston, Steven Shapin, and the other historians of science, I will mention here just a few recent and a few older works: Frank E. Manuel, *The Eighteenth Century Confronts the Gods* (Cambridge, MA: Harvard University Press, 1959), and other titles; Jonathan Sheehan, *The Enlightenment Bible: Translation, Scholarship, Culture* (Princeton, NJ: Princeton University Press, 1985); Paolo Rossi, *The Dark Abyss of Time: The History of the Earth and the History of Nations from Hooke to Vico*, trans. Lydia G. Cochrane (Chicago: University of Chicago Press, 1984); Anne Goldgar, *Impolite Learning: Conduct and Community in the Republic of Letters, 1680–1715* (New Haven, CT: Yale University Press, 1995); Blair, *Too Much to Know.*

49. To cite just a few: Anthony Grafton, *What Was History? The Art of History in Early Modern Europe* (Cambridge: Cambridge University Press, 2007); Jonathan Sheehan, *The Enlightenment Bible: Translation, Scholarship, Culture* (Princeton, NJ: Princeton University Press, 2005); Margarita Diaz Andreu, *A World History of Nineteenth-Century Archaeology: Nationalism, Colonialism, and the Past* (New York: Oxford University Press, 2007); Philip L. Kohl, Mara Kozelsky, and Nachman

Ben-Yahuda, eds., *Selective Remembrances: Archaeology in the Construction, Commemoration and Consecration of National Pasts* (Chicago: University of Chicago Press, 2007); Tuska Benes, *In Babel's Shadow: Language, Philology and the Nation in Nineteenth-Century Germany* (Detroit, MI: Wayne State University Press, 2008). See also the works cited in note 14, on European developments.

50. For example, James C. Scott's influential *Seeing Like a State: How Certain Schemes to Improve the Human Condition Failed* (New Haven, CT: Yale University Press, 1998).

8

Cosmologies Materialized: History of Science and History of Ideas

John Tresch

For most historians of science trained in the past thirty years, doing history of science has meant avoiding the history of ideas. Our teachers warned us against traditional intellectual history's neglect of practice, material culture, and complex, pluralistic contexts in favor of artificially tidied, abstract systems of thought. The distrust may have been mutual. Despite the innovations in Dominick LaCapra's *Rethinking Intellectual History* (1983), none of its chapters addressed natural science. Unfortunately, the standoff between these fields has hidden the close relationship they previously enjoyed. Many of the works that defined early twentieth-century history of ideas took natural science as a central topic, and for the scholars who set the history of science on its feet in the 1940s and 1950s the two fields were nearly inseparable. The gap that has opened between them has made it hard to see in what ways the new history of science resembles the old—and why that might be a good thing.[1]

The split occurred in the 1970s and 1980s with the appearance of sociologically informed studies of laboratories and scientific controversies in their detailed historical settings. Among academic historians of science, biographies celebrating isolated geniuses who transcended their time and place have gone out of vogue. Equally absent from our accounts—or at least in abeyance—are the normative preoccupations that had guided many earlier histories. Our case studies no longer aim to demonstrate the emergence of a universal rationality overcoming obstacles, or the progress of scientific thought

toward certainty. As Steven Shapin, a scout of "the social turn," argues, historians' new focal points—the institutional basis and political economy of struggles between schools of thought, the precariousness of proof and replication,
the historical variability of methods and standards of certainty, and the physical
idiosyncrasies and frailty of researchers and their equipment—may be argument enough. These new interests have all contributed, however modestly, to
"lowering the tone" in discussions of science, a goal he sees as a laudable realization of the historian's vocation: "to try to tell it as it really was in the past."[2]

Shapin offers an inclusive credo for today's historians of science: "[We] are
telling stories—rich, detailed, and, we hope, accurate—about a tone-lowered,
heterogeneous, historically situated, embodied, and thoroughly human set of
practices."[3] Yet as suggested by a recent exchange over whether the affections
of history of science ought to lie with sociologists or with philosophers, the split
between history of science and history of ideas still rankles.[4] Some worry that
the field has lost its critical edge by abandoning its role as epistemological tri-
bunal; others fear a collapse into a morass of isolated case studies disconnected
from broader narratives or explanatory aims.

This chapter insists, on the contrary, on the vitality of today's history of
science. More counterintuitively, it suggests that some of its promise lies in its
past: in its long-standing, underappreciated allegiance to the history of ideas.
This alliance should be acknowledged and deepened. To this end, I undertake
a review of the history of science's early, happy union with intellectual history—
while making a distinction between Lovejoy's embracing, ecumenical approach
and what I call the "neo-revolutionary" mode. I then present the developments
that led to the apparent split between the fields, though the divorce was neither
so thorough nor so final as we have been warned. Although the narrative of
modern science has been decentered, tilting away from an assumed unity of
method and doctrine whose roots go back to Newton, one key aspect of traditional history of ideas has remained central: its interest in cosmological ideas.[5]

In the new approaches, scientific ideas have been materialized, while "science" has been disaggregated into a multiplicity of methods, styles, disciplinary
arrangements, and practices. What is now required, I suggest, is a principled
reassembly of these fragmentary shards, especially in the light of major reori-
entations in understandings of the origins and consequences of modern science. With the growing recognition that "Western science" emerged along with
European nation-states and movements of exploration, trade, and conquest,
scholars increasingly consider science's contents as well as its sense of itself as
a distinct tradition to be inseparable from both internal politics and myriad
engagements with other cultures. Further, the outsized impact of the sciences
in the age of industrial technology and global capitalism has vertiginously

intensified historians' understanding of science's role in "the construction of nature": scientifically informed industry has altered and destabilized processes of planetary equilibrium.

Reframing the history of science as the comparative study of materialized cosmologies—ideas of the order of nature that are enacted, embodied, elaborated, and contested in concrete settings, institutions, representations, instruments, and practices—helps us grapple with science's culturally hybrid and stratified past, as well as with its profound and growing impact on the earth. These pressures make the history of science an exceptionally fruitful and necessary perspective from which to trace the roots of today's global condition.

Eclectic Lovejoy and the Neo-revolutionaries

From its first issues in the early 1940s, the *Journal of the History of Ideas* under Lovejoy's editorship displayed a persistent interest in scientific ideas and their connections to wider intellectual patterns. Readers encountered articles on Ficino's astrology, Darwin's effect on American theology, Boyle's alchemy, and Pascal's liberalism. It featured authors who demonstrated the variety and richness of Western knowledge traditions in studies of magic, the poetics of mountains and moon voyages, and the fate of evolutionary thought.[6]

The field's wide compass was nowhere more apparent than in Lovejoy's own highly readable—suspenseful, even!—*Great Chain of Being* (1936), which followed a single "unit-idea" through metaphysics, theology, astronomy, and natural history over twenty-three centuries.[7] Understandings of the Great Chain—a hierarchical continuum joining the lowliest of worldly entities up to God—shifted depending on whether it was allied with the notion of an otherworldly, self-sufficient deity, or with an overflowing creator expressing his perfection through incessant creation. Touching upon poetry, politics, and landscape gardening, Lovejoy followed the shifting combinations of three notions—gradation, continuity, and plenitude—with a range of "dialectical motives" and forms of "metaphysical pathos." According to Lovejoy, the fate of the Great Chain was tied up with the assumption of a rational and knowable plan of nature. Its ultimate failure—signaled by romanticism's embrace of irrationality and nationalism's championing of individual identity—prepared the impasse faced by Western thought at the start of World War II.[8]

The Great Chain revealed that Lovejoy's true obsession, despite his declared interest in "unit-ideas," was large-scale, synchronic ensembles of ideas—cosmologies or worldviews—and their modifications over time. This preoccupation ran through early twentieth-century history of ideas. Ernst Cassirer's philosophy of symbolic forms—forged in contemplation of Aby Warburg's collection of the products of the human mind—connected mythical, expressive systems of thought to empirical knowledge and mathematical methods from the Renaissance to relativity.[9] Under the influence of Hegel, Oxford philosopher R. G. Collingwood presented actors' ideas as historical driving forces: his *Idea of Nature*, posthumously published in 1945, concisely expounded a series of conceptions of the cosmos from the pre-Socratics to Henri Bergson, ending at the "modern" view of nature as an organic and historical process. Romanticism was also an inflection point for Alfred North Whitehead—one of Lovejoy's mentors—whose *Science and the Modern World* (1925) depicted "the romantic reaction" as a sane, holistic response to the seventeenth century's reduction of nature to primary qualities and mechanisms—a view he expanded in *Process and Reality* and *Adventures in Ideas* into his own organic cosmology.[10] These authors' engagement with organicism testifies to their debt to Bergson and romanticism.

Those influences were largely undetectable among the scholars responsible for establishing the discipline of history of science in the United States and England at the end of World War II in the form of professorships, departments, journals, degrees, and a canon. These scholars invented the synthetic narrative of "the Scientific Revolution": the breakdown of geocentric cosmology and the virtues and appetites of Aristotle's natural philosophy, the rise of mathematical idealization and mechanical explanations, the move from thought experiment to actual experiment, and the coronation of Newton as the synthesizer and founder of the new "scientific worldview." These "neo-revolutionaries" held that all fields of physical science underwent the same transformation at roughly the same time (even if chemistry's "revolution" was deferred until the late eighteenth century), replacing one worldview—traditional, scholastic, and dependent on theology—with another that was forward-looking, empirical, mechanical, and free-thinking.[11]

British neo-revolutionaries included Cambridge historian Herbert Butterfield, author of the *Origins of Modern Science* (1949), who coined the expression "the Whig interpretation of history," or the tendency to see events in the past leading inevitably toward the most valued aspects of the present. Butterfield argued that a specialist profession of history of science—one conducted not by scientists but by historians, leaving aside the political valences or uses of science—could avoid this pitfall.[12] His Cambridge colleagues Rupert Hall and Mary Boas Hall joined him in isolating the intellectual changes of the seventeenth century as the field's center of gravity.[13] In the United States the discipline's emergence was embroiled with postwar pedagogy. As president of Harvard, former physicist and federal administrator James Bryant Conant created a humanities-based general education program in which science and liberal democracy were presented as crowning achievements of Western civilization.[14] Conant was patron to both George Sarton, the Belgian-born historian who launched the journal *Isis*, and I. Bernard Cohen, the first American Ph.D. in history of science. In Paris and Princeton, Russian émigré Alexandre Koyré honed the study of science's unfolding conceptual structures to a fine edge; his works cast a potent influence on subsequent neo-revolutionaries, including Richard Westfall and Charles Gillispie, whose 1960 epic, *The Edge of Objectivity*, was subtitled *An Essay in the History of Scientific Ideas*.[15]

The works of this first generation of professional historians of science carried a normative insistence on the unity of scientific method, science's internal consistency, and its epistemological, political, and ethical value. They often presented the scientific revolution as shorthand for all that was best in the modern worldview as a whole.[16] In contrast to Lovejoy's model of history of ideas—eclectic, cosmological, attuned to aesthetics, ethics, and politics—for the neo-revolutionaries, the seventeenth century's empiricism and mechanism were the hallmarks of rationality and progress. Ironically, their view that science transcended politics and economics often went hand in hand with an interpretation of science as an outgrowth and reinforcement of democracy and capitalism; the central role they gave Newton and Galileo reinforced the preeminence of physics in the military-industrial order of the early Cold War.[17]

From this perspective, Koyré, who had studied with Bergson and Husserl, and presented Galilean physics as a peculiar, alienating form of idealization, might have less in common with his neo-revolutionary successors than with Whitehead, Collingwood, Cassirer, and Lovejoy (whose *Great Chain* shared many topics with Koyré's *Closed World*). Though the philosopher-historians working in Lovejoy's mode did not refuse normative judgments, their evaluations of cosmological conceptions placed greater weight on ideas' ethical, aesthetic, and existential implications than on their epistemological validity.[18]

Ideas in situ, in vivo, in Action

Despite their distinctive slant, the neo-revolutionaries often wrote for the *JHI*, nesting comfortably within the broader terrain prepared by Lovejoy. The field was united by a concern with worldviews (even if the neo-revolutionaries focused on a single, "scientific" worldview) and with intellectual change over time; it also tended to relegate ideas' social origins and political provocations to asides and footnotes.[19] By the late 1960s—as Quentin Skinner took aim at Lovejoy's neglect of ideas' settings and prompts—new approaches appeared, defining themselves against decontextualized and "internalist" histories of science.[20]

A turning point was Kuhn's *Structure of Scientific Revolutions* (note the plural), which spelled out the sociological dimensions of scientific communities, including journals, meetings, and institutional hierarchies, as well as training programs, textbooks, and, crucially, *exemplars*—problems that teach students to see certain situations as like others.[21] Those who adhered to different paradigms, he claimed, inhabited "different worlds," and successive paradigms did not imply increasing truth or improved fit to nature. If anything set science apart, Kuhn argued, it was not its certainty, but rather the quotidian activity of "normal science," defined, deflatingly, by routine work "solving puzzles." Regardless of his own much-debated intentions, Kuhn was enshrined as the pioneer of a politically and sociologically informed study of science, one that left behind internalist history and resonated with Vietnam-era critiques of science and rationalism as weapons of militarism, capitalism, and patriarchy.[22]

Kuhn was seen as an ally by historians of the 1970s who sought to reinvigorate earlier traditions of sociology of knowledge.[23] Those who launched the sociology of scientific knowledge (SSK) in Edinburgh and England in the mid-1970s claimed Kuhn as a founder. SSK used case studies to argue that scientific knowledge relied on trust, testimony, and the acceptance of assumptions that could never be irrefutably confirmed; revisiting Wittgenstein and Durkheim, they insisted on the practical and social grounding of epistemic conventions and on the link between scientific and political authority.[24] Kuhn's emphasis on the unspoken rules behind scientific concepts also harmonized with Michel Foucault's work. Though *epistemes* were vaster than paradigms, and Foucault's later "genealogies" gave power relations a primacy absent from Kuhn, Foucault's analyses of bodily discipline, the normative force of classifications, and the "breaks" between internally coherent discursive formations helped align *Structure*'s tacit knowledge, conceptual schemes, and incommensurability with critical reflection on enlightenment and modernity. Further, Foucault's excoriation of "magical" concepts such as influence, the author, and the "mentality" or "spirit" of the age also strengthened the notion that the traditional history of ideas was an obstacle to a politically attuned history of science.[25]

Foucault, Kuhn, and SSK were staples of the smorgasbord that came to be known in the 1980s as science studies or science and technology studies (STS). They joined philosophers who argued against the notion of a single scientific method and ethnographers who showed how the frontiers between society and nature, humans and nonhumans, truth and falsity dissolved and recrystallized in practice both inside and beyond the lab.[26] Historians also contributed to and made use of STS. Influentially, Shapin and Schaffer's *Leviathan and the*

Air-Pump demonstrated that the controversy between the founders of the Royal Society and Thomas Hobbes was waged not just with words but with presses and pictures, air pumps and barometers, rules of sociability and rituals—what the authors called literary, material, and social technologies.[27] Under the sign of "technologies" and "forms of life," *Leviathan* set contrasting ideas about the vacuum, the nature of matter, God's action in the world, and the proper methods of proof within their practical, theological, and political contexts.

Subsequent works have likewise aimed to disaggregate the neo-revolutionaries' "unity of science" into particular cases and components.[28] Science historians no longer see it as their job to separate the wheat of "real science" from the chaff of error and superstition; instead, they detail how "universal" concepts such as truth, proof, and objectivity, as well as science's double aims of doing and knowing, have been applied and transformed in various specific settings.[29] If a "revolution" is said to occur, they examine through what arguments and routes of persuasion is it recognized—when, where, and by whom.[30] Of course, scientific concepts and "themata" continue to capture historians' attention—life, matter, energy, probability, relativity, descent, proof, norms, mechanism, universality, the economy, or time, to name just a few.[31] But such ideas are relentlessly shown to be woven into skillful practice with things: scientific instruments, collections and displays of objects and facts, and methods and media of inscription, analysis, accounting, and transmission. The focus on objects has a tripled valence. First, historians of science insist (against both scientific idealism and a thoroughgoing "constructivism" that exists primarily as a straw man) on the reality of material entities, their capacities, and the constraints they impose. Further, inspired by the history of technology, science itself is examined as a "technological system": facts and theories extend only as far as the concrete networks or infrastructures that carry them. Finally, specimens, instruments, or artificially and naturally encountered phenomena are also considered as semiotic supports and embodiments of epistemological and cosmological commitments.[32]

Alongside scientific concepts and objects, historians have also isolated "ideas" of different sorts. Instead of a single "scientific method" they recognize a range of "styles of reasoning" and "ways of knowing." They also follow shifting disciplinary boundaries, discursive formations, and "forms of positivity" that have organized research, tracing the limits of, for instance, natural philosophy, mixed mathematics, and natural history. Another element they have identified is ideas of practice—implicit or explicit theories about the right way to get to grips with the material world, as well as the ethical codes that organize knowledge practices. Scholars have, for instance, examined the "artisanal epistemology" of early modern alchemists and natural philosophers, the division of labor between public virtuosi and "invisible technicians" behind the scenes in the early Royal Society, and the "moral economy" allotting credit and encouraging exchange of *drosophila* samples in T. H. Morgan's laboratory.[33] Along these lines, Daston and Galison's *Objectivity* matched successive articulations of its titular concept to historically favored modes of representation and epistemic ideals, such as the delicate paintings of idealized plants in the era of "truth to nature" and the gritty, particular photographs of "mechanical objectivity."[34]

In the self-understandings and "epistemic virtues" of scientists, *Objectivity* also isolated a further dimension of science. Eighteenth-century empiricists experienced the self as a sensitive tablet on which fragmentary external impressions were written, arriving at general ideas only after long observation, while post-Kantian experimentalists fretted that the desires of an excessive will had to be kept in check by machines. Such analyses resonate with arguments of feminist epistemologists who have shown how gender norms shape and reflect scientific values. These norms also bear upon ethics and the emotions, or affect, as Tracie Matysik explores in this collection.[35] Even if the pursuit of truth has been presented as a struggle against the passions, suppressed emotion remains an emotional state—one as significant for the history of science as it is for histories of Western subjectivity.[36]

The new historians have revealed that "science" contains a multitude of elements, each with its own types and variations. Further, replacing the single line that the neo-revolutionaries drew between the seventeenth century and the technocratic arrangements of the Cold War, alternative historical trajectories are now drawn: laterally to other domains of culture (politics, arts, technology), and transversally to other historical predecessors and cultures.

Concrete and Fragmentary Wholes

These new cartographies of knowledge have not gone unchallenged. Notions of linear progress and unity still dominate mainstream understandings of science; internalist, idealist histories are still written and taught. A reaction flared up in the 1990s with the "Science Wars" and the "Sokal Hoax," when a disgruntled physicist wrote an article peppered with exaggerations and jargon that interpreted his own field in the light of critical theory; at its publication, he declared his article a joke that should have been recognized as such.[37] The ensuing fracas—along with the discovery that STS arguments were being used to promote Intelligent Design and to undermine scientific consensus on global warming—contributed to a dampening of theoretical agitation. This quietism fit well with the sense that in the 2000s the humanities were entering a "post-theory" era.[38]

As a result, some within the field have critiqued what they perceive as narrowed horizons and a dulled critical edge.[39] Even if the polemical volume has dropped, however, philosophical questions remain, though on new ground. Many authors now serve a constructivist cake that can be realistically eaten. Donna Haraway's "semiotechnologies" and Andrew Pickering's "mangle of practice" present entities of biology, chemistry, physics, or engineering— quarks, human bodies, bespoke mice, and electronic brains—as both intellectual and material, as constructs with concrete effects; likewise, Bruno Latour insists that he has always been a realist, though now in the characteristically gonzo form of "multinaturalism."[40] Further, one of the preferred genres of STS and history of science—the detailed case study—can itself be read as an epistemological argument: by showing scientific ideas and objects bound up with historically specific and variable systems of practice, reasoning, and technique, case studies offer support for pluralist epistemologies and ontologies.[41]

Yet this virtue matches a vice. Disconnected from the unities of the neo-revolutionaries, case studies risk closing in on themselves, in a celebration of the singular recalling early modern cabinets of curiosity.[42] To arrive at more general perspectives, one solution might be to heed the invitation to return to the *longue durée* emphases of earlier history of ideas.[43] Various components of "science" may be linked, compared, and contrasted across time and location, replacing the neo-revolutionaries' grand narrative with new "serial contextualizations." *Objectivity* points in this direction; following suit, others may isolate general topics to guide transhistorical investigations.

Yet the methodological innovations of the past thirty years of history of science have raised the stakes for contextualization. If transhistorical genealogies are to be more than annotated N-grams, it is worth reflecting on the ways in which scholars reassemble the material fragments into which "science" has been broken. How should we consider the diachronically separate conjunctures— the "cases"—that "serial contextualizations" would connect? Here, once more, we might draw upon the salutary resources of traditional history of ideas. Despite the variety of their topics, Lovejoy and his fellow travelers were driven by a fascination for ideas about the composition, extent, and structure of the universe, and the place of humans within it. Like cultural anthropologists (and inspired by similar post-Kantian impulses), they undertook comparative studies of cosmology. Even the neo-revolutionaries, though privileging a single "scientific" cosmology, shared this vocation.

The cosmological impulse surreptitiously remains at work in the newer histories of science. Yet this continuity is rarely acknowledged, much less celebrated.

In jettisoning the normative unities of the neo-revolutionaries, historians of science encouraged a renunciation of the history of ideas as a whole. Further, their chosen allies—Wittgenstein, poststructuralism, cultural anthropology—all contributed arguments that could be applied not just against "grand narratives" and "scientific absolutism," but against generalizing concepts of all kinds. Any notion that claimed to convey a shared system of thought—worldview, cosmology, mentality, *episteme*, culture, *Zeitgeist*, conceptual scheme, even Kuhn's "paradigm"—provoked suspicion.[44]

There were and are excellent reasons for such skepticism. Worldviews float everywhere and nowhere, operating through spooky action at a distance when not enclosed in skulls. Cosmologies have often been presented as uniform, coherent, and widely shared, rather than in the motley, variable, idiosyncratic forms through which they are lived and practiced. Philosophers have asked whether there is even such a thing as a conceptual scheme; others claim that formalized systems of thought are invented by researchers out of partial, discordant observations; others pronounce the notion of a "subject" experiencing "objects" through "representations" as just one possible mode for the disclosure of being.

Despite endorsing many of these very critiques, the new historians of science have maintained the study of cosmology as a central organizing principle. This is precisely what was at stake in many of the exemplary works of the past thirty years: those that examined conceptualizations of wondrous particulars and natural laws, reconstructed the natural philosophical detours of Newton's successors, stalked computationally masterable chance from astronomy to sociology and statistical mechanics, detailed the contributions of geologists, Jacobin journalists, and Goethe to the different shadings of "evolution," or perused the railway schedules that grounded Einstein's relativity. Like the earlier historians of ideas, the new historians of science study the ways in which facts, concepts, and arguments form a world, a nature, a cosmos. Yet the cosmologies they study are materialized—not "reduced to" or "determined by" a material base, but instantiated in concrete actions, texts, and institutions, even when (as is often the case) the very definition of matter and "materiality" is what is at stake. Cosmological ideas take on realist force when they are anchored, housed, and transmitted in objects, technical networks, routine practices, and social institutions. Acknowledging this connection with the older history of ideas allows us to reclaim a rich heritage that adds depth and perspective to local situations and particular cases.

Yet this affirmation has to incorporate not just the materializing turn but the skepticism toward totalizing concepts and seamless holism mentioned above. Materialized cosmologies involve potentially incompatible elements;

they are riddled with gaps and counterpoints. The challenge, then, is to follow the elements that make a cosmos as they arise from and feed back into concrete activities, settings, and objects. While studying the habitual, entraining, mutually constraining relationships among humans and other beings, we must also attend to the openness, changeability, and contradictions of the conceptual, practical, and cosmological orders that may arise, hold, or dissolve through their interactions.

To this end historians can continue to learn from anthropology's attention to the meshing (and the splitting) of the quotidian and the cosmological and to the embodiment of natural and social hierarchies in practice and ritual, as well as from its insistence on the dialogical, perspectively shifting, contested nature of public life. Systems of knowledge are riven with divisions, such as those among disciplines, research programs, and roles. Furthermore, actors may spend time in labs, offices, or lecture halls, while involved in religious, governmental, or artistic activities, all of which are underwritten by distinct concepts and principles of value. To reckon with the tensions between the phenomenological and pragmatic worlds of complex societies—what Weber called "the struggle that the gods of the various orders and values are engaged in"— sociologists have developed many helpful frameworks.[45] STS has contributed the notion of "boundary work," efforts to mark divisions between disciplines, groups, and metaphysical domains. Thomas Gieryn, for instance, showed the Victorian physicist John Tyndall using lectures and popular writings to raise the status of science by distinguishing it both from religion (emphasizing its empiricism and utility) and from mechanics (emphasizing its abstraction and freedom from utility). Similarly, we can study the ways, whether internally consistent or not, in which actors try to make plain the overall arrangement of the entities they recognize by making and using concrete representations of the universe, or cosmograms; such objects—maps, diagrams, buildings, calendars, poems, encyclopedias—are not transparent, uncontested encapsulations of a bounded world, but performative assertions, entries into debates, points of reference for further elaboration. Paying attention to the locally situated acts and objects through which historical actors divide and connect parts of the universe keeps us at the level of observable, material practices, while showing how they assemble and situate themselves within greater wholes—however incomplete or fragmented these may be.[46]

In short, doing history of science means contributing to the comparative study of materialized cosmologies. It means undertaking the description, narration, and analysis of embodied, concrete, totalizing but unavoidably incomplete and equivocal systems of natural and social order. This modest reframing of our field picks out a level from which to think comparatively and genetically about the diverse case studies assembled in the past thirty years. It reconnects us to the wider field of intellectual history, both ancestors and contemporaries—a renewed alliance encouraged by Antoine Lilti and Suzanne Marchand in this book. It also encourages a robust engagement with history of religions, archaeology, area studies, and anthropology, whose interest in comparative cosmology has recently been reaffirmed.[47]

When Material Cosmologies Collide

Defining our field as the study of materialized cosmologies may also help address some of the most pressing questions historians of science currently face. I conclude with a glance at three closely connected sites of inquiry: modern scientific cosmologies and their complexities, the global origins and settings of Western knowledge, and science's environmental impacts. Arising out of concerns of the present, these topics exert a reorienting pressure on understandings of the past and future.

One challenge is to make sense of the cosmological complexities of the industrial past and postindustrial present. For historians of the medieval and early modern periods, consideration of large-scale cosmological frameworks connecting science, religion, commerce, politics, and the arts has been a matter of course.[48] In studies of the period after 1800, however, the question of a general natural order is often swiftly glossed with notions such as secularization, standardization, disenchantment, mechanization, normalization, or discipline. Yet the material turn pushes us to ask: in what diverse practices, settings, and objects do these general tendencies reside? What sort of world do they gather together? How do they incorporate or exclude other possibilities? Indeed, such questions can lead to the realization that the uniformity of the modern world has been greatly exaggerated. Throughout the nineteenth century, even as many administrators, scientists, and entrepreneurs worked on various fronts to standardize entities and sites including schools, industries, and markets, wildly variable theological, metaphysical, and epistemological conceptions proliferated. Alternative modernities, often grounded in heterodox sciences and challenges to existing social hierarchies, flourished within Europe as well as in those regions forced into new global routes of labor, production, and trade; these cosmologies need to be shown materially, dialectically, and critically engaging with more familiar "modern" patterns of action and thought.[49]

Further, the more we learn about the knowledge practices that administered the nineteenth-century global order, the more we realize the necessity of following their transformations forward into the scientific orders consolidated in the North Atlantic and worldwide after World War II. Mining the archives of the "Strangelovian sciences" has begun to reveal Cold War rationality not as a self-evident unity, but a varied set of calculating practices, organizational logics, and attitudes toward nature, the state, the public, "the enemy," and "the Third World" that demands further excavation.[50] The perspective of material cosmologies also leads to questions not just about the theoretical complexity of twentieth-century sciences but about their experiential complexity and the ways they have been implemented. How were fields as disparate as post-Copenhagen physics, molecular biology, or neuropsychology linked by personnel, research, and funding institutions, computational techniques and metaphors, and conceptions of knowledge, self, and nature? How did scientific explanations align or clash with the views of "humanity's place in the universe" inculcated by advertising, entertainment, economics, government propaganda, mainstream religions, or new-age philosophies? Such questions guide recent works that show how cosmological ideas from physics, information science, business, and the 1960s counterculture were assembled, more or less comfortably, into new forms of life.[51] Comparable questions can be raised about the cosmologies juxtaposed and synthesized in Western science's postwar transfers and frequent hybridizations with "local" knowledge traditions; they resonate with interest in the theory and practice of "development" as a novel, quasi-imperial mode of coordinating states, populations, and natural resources.[52]

Positioning natural knowledge within stratified global political economies is a challenge being taken up by scholars not just of the recent past but of all periods. As a result, the contours of "Western science" have begun to shift. In 1931 Boris Hessen demonstrated the connections between the "pure science" of Newton's age and the rise of commercial and professional classes, European states' military and administrative apparatus, and the extension of empires.[53] Much of today's most interesting scholarship arguably continues Hessen's work, showing the entanglement of natural knowledge with trade networks, state formation, class conflicts, and imperial ambitions. Renaissance collections housed curiosities of art and nature while cementing exchange relations among courts, merchants, and explorers. Newton's *Principia*, created in a furious correspondence with traders, plantation owners, natural philosophers, and sailors from the Americas to Japan and the Gulf of Tonkin, was a node in the British Empire's emerging information order. In the eighteenth and nineteenth centuries, natural history flourished on board survey, trade, and military expeditions, while new social sciences steered interventions in declining populations, dangerous urban classes, and defiant colonial subjects. Physicists instituted a cosmos of energy and ethers and prophesied the heat-death of the sun, while building networks to streamline productive forces at home and abroad.[54]

In all of these cases, material cosmologies set the stage for cultural contacts. Western science was not a neutral "tool of empire," using value-free facts
to accomplish utilitarian ends; it carried culturally specific values (not least
accuracy, efficiency, commensuration) and sought to redraw the map of the
world, both metaphysically and geographically. Further, many of its orientations emerged in confrontation with other traditions. Increasing attention has
been paid to the elusive and mercurial "go-betweens" who served as ambassa-
dors, translators, negotiators, procurers, and enablers in the distributed admin-
istration of empires.[55] The knowledge of indigenous experts was incorporated
into "universal" science in various ways, as in maps of New Spain that inscribed
native views of landscape, flora and fauna; Serge Gruzinski's arguments about
the "mestizo" knowledge in the Americas can extend to "hybrid" knowledge
formations in Asia and Africa.[56] As Marwa Elshakry has argued, the very notion
of a distinct "Western science" was only consolidated around 1900, through
the historiographical construction of past "Golden Ages" (in Greece, India, and
Islam) and the modernizing efforts of pedagogues outside the West.[57]

Rewriting another chapter of the origin story of Western science, Bernal's
Black Athena set the knowledge traditions of Egypt, Mesopotamia, and India—
recrafted as Greek—within the imperial intersections of the ancient world,
while George Saliba has helped reconstruct the role of Islam in the European
Renaissance. To re-imagine other points of transmission and reconstitution of
diverse knowledge traditions requires deep familiarity with diverse learned
practices, local and imperial formations, and the variable diagrams that connect commerce, statecraft, and religion—in short, it demands a grasp of multiple materialized cosmologies.[58] From this perspective, the comparative history
of civilizations urged by George Sarton and Joseph Needham in the early twentieth century might appear strikingly avant-garde, suggesting multiple starting
points from which to trace our own moment's "globalization."[59]

A final challenge for the history of science set by the present is to help make
sense of the impact of ideas of nature on the natural world itself. The idea that
nature is not a different kind of being "out there," but rather a given that accompanies, constitutes, and yet can be transformed by human activity has a long,
varied history. Some of its turns were tracked by Georges Canguilhem in his genealogy of the concept of "milieu," or the nutritive envelope surrounding organ-
isms, an idea central for Alexander von Humboldt's biogeography, and through
him, for Darwin and those who study "the environment." A further elaboration
came with the ethologist Jacob von Uexkull's concept of *Umwelt*: the world inhabited by different species depends on the configuration of their senses.[60]

In the earth sciences, the notion that humans construct their worlds has
recently moved from pragmatic metaphor and phenomenological speculation

to quantified fact. With discussions of the "Anthropocene," the proposed geological era defined by industry's impact on the planet, we are forced to acknowledge "ideas of nature" as instruments for permanent modifications of "external" and "objective" nature itself.[61] Accordingly, history of science joins forces with environmental history. There is considerable interest in the history of the earth sciences, climatology, and space sciences: their extreme settings and aesthetic motivations as well as the role various fields (geology, agronomy, chemistry) have played in shaping landscapes, from uranium mines and oil fields to hill stations and urban research centers. A further tendency, one with outstanding precursors in the history of ideas, addresses the aesthetic and moral valences of ideas about nature—as garden, wasteland, wilderness, standing reserve—and how these have directed practical engagements with the landscape. Following the convolutions of such ideas as they shape the material conditions of our existence in the hands not only of "thinkers" but of engineers, politicians, corporate managers, farmers, citizens, consumers, and activists, the history of science can help ground our understanding of the most pressing challenges of today.[62]

To come to grips with the disorientingly plural, technologically modified, politically and environmentally precarious worlds we now inhabit, the new history of science examines ideas of nature in their complex and concrete ecologies, tracing their roots, movements, and mergers as they have coordinated actions and interventions, defining the contours of the real. The study of materialized cosmologies goes beyond the neo-revolutionaries' insistence on a single method and idealized scientific worldview. Yet in an important sense it lands us back where we began: in productive dialogue about concepts of natural order with our neglected ally, the history of ideas.

Notes

1. This paper began in conversation and collaboration with Graham Burnett, whose suggestions and encouragement were indispensable. Thanks also to Darrin McMahon, Samuel Moyn, the conference participants, Robert Kohler, and especially James Delbourgo for helpful comments.

2. Steven Shapin, "Lowering the Tone in the History of Science: A Noble Calling," in *Never Pure: Historical Studies of Science as If It Was Produced by People with Bodies, Situated in Time, Space, Culture, and Society, and Struggling for Credibility and Authority* (Chicago: University of Chicago Press, 2010), 13.

3. Shapin, "Lowering the Tone," 14.

4. In "Science Studies and the History of Science" (*Critical Inquiry* 35 [2009]: 798–813), Lorraine Daston argues that the partnership in the 1980s between the

history of science and science studies has run its course, concluding with a sporting invitation: "Philosophy, anyone?" In reply, Peter Dear and Sheila Jasanoff ("Dismantling Boundaries in Science and Technology Studies," *Isis* 101 [2010]: 759–74) point to a tradition of sociologically informed histories, rejecting Daston's interpretation of a splintering.

5. According to Andrew Cunningham and Perry Williams, "Historians are ceasing to believe in a single scientific method which makes all knowledge like the physical sciences, or that science is synonymous with free intellectual enquiry and material prosperity, or that science is what all humans throughout time and space have been doing as competently as they were able." "De-Centring the 'Big Picture': 'The Origins of Modern Science' and the Modern Origins of Science," *British Journal for the History of Science* 26 (1993): 407–32.

6. Lynn Thorndike, *The Place of Magic in the Intellectual History of Europe* (New York: AMS Press, 1967); Marjorie Hope Nicolson, *Mountain Gloom and Mountain Glory: The Development of the Aesthetics of the Infinite* (New York: Norton, 1959); John C. Greene, *The Death of Adam: Evolution and Its Impact on Western Thought* (Ames: Iowa State University Press, 1959). Greene's work intersects with classics such as Carl Becker's *Heavenly City of the Eighteenth Century Philosophers* (New Haven, CT: Yale University Press, 1932) and Karl Löwith's *Meaning in History* (Chicago: University of Chicago Press, 1949).

7. Arthur Lovejoy, *The Great Chain of Being: A Study of the History of an Idea* (1936; Cambridge, MA: Harvard University Press, 1976).

8. Daniel J. Wilson, "Lovejoy's The Great Chain of Being after Fifty Years," *Journal of the History of Ideas* 48 (1987): 187–206; Isaiah Berlin, *The Roots of Romanticism* (Princeton, NJ: Princeton University Press, 1999).

9. Ernst Cassirer, *The Individual and the Cosmos in Renaissance Philosophy* (Chicago: University of Chicago Press, 1963); see Peter Gordon, *Continental Divide: Heidegger, Cassirer, Davos* (Cambridge, MA: Harvard University Press, 2010).

10. Arthur Lovejoy, "The Meaning of Romanticism for the Historian of Ideas," *Journal of the History of Ideas* 2 (1941): 257–78; R. G. Collingwood, *The Idea of Nature* (Oxford: Clarendon Press, 1945); Alfred North Whitehead, *Science and the Modern World* (New York: Macmillan, 1925).

11. Michael Dennis, "Historiography of Science: An American Perspective," in *Companion to Science in the Twentieth Century*, ed. John Krige and Dominique Pestre (New York: Routledge, 2003), 1–26; I. B. Cohen, *The Birth of a New Physics* (New York: Doubleday, 1960); Richard Westfall, *The Construction of Modern Science: Mechanism and Mechanics* (Cambridge: Cambridge University Press, 1977).

12. The first informal group of Cambridge historians of science led by Joseph Needham included scientists who favored "leftish" historical and sociological approaches; Butterfield encouraged a far less contextual approach. Anna-K. Mayer, "British History of Science and 'the End of Ideology,' 1931–1948," *Studies in History and Philosophy of Science Part A* 35 (2004): 41–72.

13. Herbert Butterfield, *The Origins of Modern Science, 1300–1800* (London: Bell, 1950); A. Rupert Hall, *The Scientific Revolution, 1500–1800: The Formation of the Modern*

Scientific Attitude (London: Longmans, Green, 1954); Mary Boas Hall, *The Mechanical Philosophy* (New York: Arno, 1981).

14. *General Education in a Free Society: Report of the Harvard Committee* (Cambridge, MA: Harvard University Press, 1945); John Rudolph, "Epistemology for the Masses: The Origins of 'The Scientific Method' in American Schools," *History of Education Quarterly* 45 (2005): 341–76.

15. Alexandre Koyré , *From the Closed World to the Infinite Universe* (Baltimore: Johns Hopkins Press, 1957); Charles Coulston Gillispie, *The Edge of Objectivity: An Essay in the History of Scientific Ideas* (Princeton, NJ: Princeton University Press, 1960).

16. See Butterfield, *Origins of Modern Science*, chap. 10, for jaw-droppingly ethnocentric expressions of this view.

17. See Karl Popper, *The Open Society and Its Enemies* (Princeton, NJ: Princeton University Press, 1966); David Hollinger, "Science as a Weapon in Kulturkampfe in the United States during and after World War II," *Isis* 86 (1995): 440–54.

18. The distance between the neo-revolutionaries and the warier, humanistic approach associated with Lovejoy is made plain by comparing many of the contributions to Gerald Holton, ed., *Science and the Modem Mind: A Symposium* (Boston: Beacon, 1958), with Jacques Barzun, *Science: The Glorious Entertainment* (New York: Harper and Row, 1964).

19. Literally in Koyré's *Closed World*, where the notes provide detailed contextualization of the ideas of the text.

20. Quentin Skinner, "Meaning and Understanding in the History of Ideas," *History and Theory* 8 (1969); for discussion see Donald R. Kelley, *The Descent of Ideas: The History of Intellectual History* (Aldershot: Ashgate, 2002).

21. Thomas S. Kuhn, *The Structure of Scientific Revolutions* (Chicago: University of Chicago Press, 1970).

22. Against the canonization of Kuhn as a radical, Steve Fuller aligns his aims with Conant's, who saw a science independent of external review as critical for postwar national security. *Thomas Kuhn: A Philosophical History for Our Times* (Chicago: University of Chicago Press, 2000), 179–226.

23. Arnold Thackray and Robert K. Merton, "On Discipline Building: The Paradoxes of George Sarton," *Isis* 63, no. 4 (1972): 473–95.

24. Barry Barnes, *T. S. Kuhn and Social Science* (New York: Columbia University Press, 1982); David Bloor, *Knowledge and Social Imagery* (London: Routledge, 1976).

25. Michel Foucault, *The Archaeology of Knowledge* (New York: Pantheon, 1972), 3–20.

26. Andrew Pickering, ed., *Science as Practice and Culture* (Chicago: University of Chicago Press, 1992); Mario Biagioli, ed., *The Science Studies Reader* (New York: Routledge, 1999).

27. Steven Shapin and Simon Schaffer, *Leviathan and the Air-Pump: Hobbes, Boyle and the Experimental Life* (Princeton, NJ: Princeton University Press, 1985).

28. Rudolf Carnap, *The Unity of Science* (London: Kegan Paul, 1934).

29. See Cunningham, "De-Centring the 'Big Picture'"; Peter Dear, *The Intelligibility of Nature: How Science Makes Sense of the World* (Chicago: University of Chicago, 2006).

30. Adrian Johns, *The Nature of the Book: Print and Knowledge in the Making* (Chicago: University of Chicago Press, 2000).

31. Gerald Holton, "On the Role of Themata in Scientific Thought," *Science* 188 (1975): 328–34.

32. Lorraine Daston, ed., *Things That Talk: Object Lessons from Art and Science* (New York: Zone, 2004); Joseph O'Connell, "Metrology: The Creation of Universality by the Circulation of Particulars," *Social Studies of Science* 23 (1993): 129–73; Crosbie Smith and M. Norton Wise, *Energy and Empire: A Biographical Study of Lord Kelvin* (Cambridge: Cambridge University Press, 1989); focus section on "Thick Things," ed. Ken Alder, *Isis* 98 (2007): 80–142.

33. Steven Shapin, "The Invisible Technician," *American Scientist* 77 (1989): 554–63; Pamela Smith, *The Body of the Artisan: Art and Experience in the Scientific Revolution* (Chicago: University of Chicago Press, 2006); Robert Kohler, *Lords of the Fly: Drosophila Genetics and the Experimental Life* (Chicago: University of Chicago Press, 1994).

34. Lorraine Daston and Peter Galison, *Objectivity* (New York: Zone, 2007).

35. Helen Longino, "Taking Gender Seriously in Philosophy of Science," *Proceedings of the Biennial Meetings of the Philosophy of Science Association* 2 (1992): 333–40; Sandra Harding, *Sciences from below: Feminisms, Postcolonialities, and Modernities* (Durham, NC: Duke University Press, 2008).

36. Matthew Jones, *The Good Life in the Scientific Revolution: Descartes, Pascal, Leibniz, and the Cultivation of Virtue* (Chicago: University of Chicago Press, 2006).

37. Keith Ashman and Philip Baringer, eds., *After the Science Wars* (New York: Routledge, 2001).

38. W. J. T. Mitchell, "Medium Theory: Preface to the 2003 *Critical Inquiry* Symposium," *Critical Inquiry* 30 (2004): 324–36; Bruno Latour, "Why Has Critique Run Out of Steam?," *Critical Inquiry* 30 (2004): 238–39.

39. Steve Fuller, "CSI: Kuhn and Latour," *Social Studies of Science* 42 (2012): 429–34.

40. Bruno Latour, *Politics of Nature: How to Bring the Sciences into Democracy* (Cambridge, MA: Harvard University Press, 2004); Andrew Pickering, *The Mangle of Practice: Time, Agency, and Science* (Chicago: University of Chicago Press, 1995); Donna Haraway, *Simians, Cyborgs and Women: The Reinvention of Nature* (New York: Routledge, 1991); Ian Hacking, *The Social Construction of What?* (Cambridge, MA: Harvard University Press, 1999).

41. Daston, "Science Studies," 812–13; Ian Hacking, *Historical Ontology* (Cambridge, MA: Harvard University Press, 2002).

42. Peter Galison asks, "If case studies are the paving stones, where does the path lead?," in "Ten Problems in History and Philosophy of Science," *Isis* 99 (2008): 120. In the blog of Will Thomas (http://etherwave.wordpress.com), the disciplinary reflex of case studies is a recurrent *bête noire*.

43. See David Armitage, "What's the Big Idea? Intellectual History and the *Longue Durée*," *History of European Ideas* 38 (2012): 493–507, and Darrin McMahon's chapter in this volume.

44. Jean-François Lyotard, *The Postmodern Condition: A Report on Knowledge*, vol. 10, *Theory and History of Literature* (Minneapolis: University of Minnesota Press, 1984); Harold Garfinkel, *Studies in Ethnomethodology* (Englewood Cliffs, NJ: Prentice-Hall, 1967); Johannes Fabian, *Time and the Other: How Anthropology Makes Its Object* (New York: Columbia University Press, 1983); Peter Galison, "Computer Simulations and the Trading Zone," in *The Disunity of Science: Boundaries, Contexts, and Power*, ed. Peter Galison and David Strump (Stanford, CA: Stanford University Press, 1996), 118–57. For a discussion and rehabilitation of anthropological uses of cosmology, see Eduardo Viveiros de Castro, "Cosmologies: Perspectivism," *Hau Master Class Series*, vol. 1 (2012).

45. Max Weber, "Science as a Vocation," *Daedalus* 87 (1958): 111–34; Andrew Abbott, *Chaos of Disciplines* (Chicago: University of Chicago Press, 2001); Howard Becker, *Art Worlds* (Berkeley: University of California Press, 1982); Pierre Bourdieu, *Practical Reason: On the Theory of Action* (Stanford, CA: Stanford University Press, 1998); Luc Boltanski and Laurent Thévenot, *On Justification: Economies of Worth* (Princeton, NJ: Princeton University Press, 2006); Latour proposes a new grounding for modernity's pluralist values in *An Inquiry into Modes of Existence* (Cambridge, MA: Harvard University Press, 2013).

46. Thomas Gieryn, *Cultural Boundaries of Science: Credibility on the Line* (Chicago: University of Chicago Press, 1999); John Tresch, "Technological World-Pictures: Cosmic Things, Cosmograms," *Isis* 98 (2007): 84–99.

47. Philippe Descola, *Par-delà nature et culture* (Paris: Gallimard, 2005).

48. William Ashworth, "Natural History and the Emblematic World View," in *Reappraisals of the Scientific Revolution*, ed. David C. Lindberg and Robert S. Westman (New York: Cambridge University Press, 1990), 303–32.

49. See for instance Timothy Mitchell, ed., *Questions of Modernity* (Minneapolis: University of Minnesota Press, 2000); Alex Owen, *The Place of Enchantment: British Occultism and the Culture of the Modern* (Chicago: University of Chicago Press, 2004); John Tresch, *The Romantic Machine: Utopian Science and Technology after Napoleon* (Chicago: University of Chicago Press, 2012).

50. See Focus Section: "New Perspectives on Science and the Cold War," ed. Hunter Heyck and David Kaiser, *Isis* 101 (2010).

51. Fred Turner, *From Counterculture to Cyberculture: Stewart Brand, the Whole Earth Network, and the Rise of Digital Utopianism* (Chicago: University of Chicago Press, 2006); David Kaiser, *How the Hippies Saved Physics: Science, Counterculture, and the Quantum Revival* (New York: Norton, 2011).

52. Fa-ti Fan, "Redrawing the Map: Science in Twentieth-Century China," *Isis* 98 (2007): 524–38; Timothy Mitchell, *Carbon Democracy: Political Power in the Age of Oil* (New York: Verso, 2011).

53. Boris Hessen, "The Social and Economic Roots of Newton's Principia," in *Science at the Crossroads*, ed. Nicolai Bukharin (New York: Howard Ferting, 1974).

54. See for instance Simon Schaffer, *The Information Order of Isaac Newton's Principia Mathematica* (Uppsala: Office for History of Science, Uppsala University, 2008); N. Jardine, J. A. Secord, and E. Spary, *Cultures of Natural History* (Cambridge:

Cambridge University Press, 1996); the Focus Section on "Global Histories of Science," ed. Sujit Sivasundaram, *Isis* 101 (2010); James Delbourgo and Nicholas Dew, eds., *Science and Empire in the Atlantic World* (New York: Routledge, 2008); Londa Schiebinger and Claudia Swan, eds., *Colonial Botany: Science, Commerce and Politics in the Early Modern World* (Philadelphia: University of Pennsylvania Press, 2005); D. Graham Burnett, *Masters of All They Surveyed: Exploration, Geography, and a British El Dorado* (Chicago: University of Chicago Press, 2000); Suman Seth, "Putting Knowledge in Its Place: Science, Colonialism, and the Postcolonial," *Postcolonial Studies* 12 (2009): 373–88.

55. Marie-Noëlle Bourguet, Christian Licoppe, and H. Otto Sibum, eds., *Instruments, Travel and Science: Itineraries of Precision from the Seventeenth to Twentieth Century* (London: Routledge, 2002); Simon Schaffer, Kapil Raj, Lissa Roberts, and James Delbourgo, eds., *The Brokered World: Go-Betweens and Global Intelligence, 1770–1820* (Sagamore Beach, MA: Science History Publications, 2009).

56. Serge Gruzinski, *The Mestizo Mind: The Intellectual Dynamics of Colonization and Globalization* (New York: Routledge, 2002); Christopher Bayly, *The Birth of the Modern World, 1780–1914* (London: Blackwell, 2003).

57. Marwa Elshakry, "When Did Science Become Western?," *Isis* 101 (2010): 146–58.

58. Martin Bernal, *Black Athena: The Afroasiatic Roots of Classical Civilization* (New Brunswick, NJ: Rutgers University Press, 1987); George Saliba, *Islamic Science and the Making of the European Renaissance* (New York: MIT Press, 2007); Sheldon Pollack, ed., *Literary Cultures in History: Reconstructions from South Asia* (Berkeley: University of California Press, 2003).

59. Joseph Needham, *Science and Civilisation in China* (Cambridge: Cambridge University Press, 1954); George Sarton, *An Introduction to the History of Science*, 3 vols. (Baltimore: William and Wilkins, 1927–1948); Nathan Sivin and Geoffrey Lloyd, *The Way and the Word: Science and Medicine in Early China and Greece* (New Haven, CT: Yale University Press, 2005).

60. In Georges Canguilhem, *Knowledge of Life* (New York: Fordham University Press, 2008), 98–120.

61. Dipesh Chakrabarty, "The Climate of History: Four Theses," *Critical Inquiry* 35 (2009): 197–222; for a longer history of the "climatic paradigm," see Fabien Locher and Jean-Baptiste Fressoz, "Modernity's Frail Climate: A Climate History of Environmental Reflexivity," *Critical Inquiry* 38 (2012): 579–98.

62. James Fleming and Vladimir Jankovic, eds., "*Klima*," *Osiris* 26 (2011); Carolyn Merchant, *The Death of Nature: Women, Ecology, and the Scientific Revolution* (San Francisco: Harper and Row, 1980); Karl Appuhn, *A Forest on the Sea: Environmental Expertise in Renaissance Venice* (Baltimore: Johns Hopkins University Press, 2009); William Cronon, "The Trouble with Wilderness; or, Getting Back to the Wrong Nature," *Environmental History* 1 (1996): 7–28.

9

Decentering Sex: Reflections on Freud, Foucault, and Subjectivity in Intellectual History

Tracie Matysik

The relationship between the history of sexuality and European intellectual history is a rich if vexed one. Especially in the twentieth century, sexuality has been framed routinely as intimately connected to the problem of knowledge, albeit in diverse ways. As early as 1913 Sigmund Freud identified the entire project of knowledge production—and with it art, literature, morality, and culture as a whole—as the sublimation of sexual drives.[1] In this framework, sexual desire is primary; it is the origin of subjectivity, of culture, if in indirect and displaced form. Conversely, and in a more historically specific fashion, Michel Foucault maintained in the first volume of his *History of Sexuality* that "sexuality" as a concept was an explicitly modern invention operating between juridical and medical practices that combined to produce a certain subject whose "truth" was his or her sexuality. To know the subject, for the subject to know him- or herself, is to know his/her sexuality.

In light of the strong—if competing—Freudian and Foucauldian claims about the close relationship between sexuality and knowledge, one might expect to see the intellectual history of the European twentieth century as one ubiquitously tied to sexual matters. And indeed, at least since the late nineteenth century, sexuality has been a topic of serious and sustained consideration by intellectuals: sexologists made sexuality the primary object of their study, while psychoanalysts

from Freud to Jacques Lacan and most of their disciples along the way continued to see sexual desire as central to both subjective and social formations. But
sexologists and psychoanalysts have not been alone. Social theorists and philosophers as diverse as Georges Bataille, Simone de Beauvoir, Claude Lévi-Strauss,
Herbert Marcuse, Wilhelm Reich, Niklas Luhmann, Judith Butler, and Slavoj
Žižek, to name just a few, have also understood sexuality as a crucial category
of analysis when considering ideology, politics, and cultural formations.
Indeed, the European twentieth century seems in retrospect to have been one
in which the relationship of sexuality to forms of knowledge was scrutinized
from every possible angle, most urgently in fields of inquiry about the structure
of subjectivity and the structure of social relations, including fields of law,
ethics, political theory, and medicine.

Moreover, if thinkers in the twentieth century turned comfortably to the
topic of sexuality, their work helped illuminate the centrality of sexual matters
in the intellectual production of previous centuries that authors of the time
may or may not have so explicitly thematized. From historians, for instance, we
have learned that matters of sexuality played a far more central role in medieval, early modern, and modern legal regimes than the authors of those
regimes may have recognized.[2] From more theoretical circles, we have had
claims about the close relationship between seemingly nonsexual philosophical developments and their explicitly sexual counterparts. From Horkheimer
and Adorno as well as from Lacan, for instance, we have had arguments that
the philosophy of Immanuel Kant had far more in common with the sexual
fantasies and experiments of the Marquis de Sade than Kant would ever have
acknowledged.[3] Even earlier, we were told by Nietzsche that the history of philosophy and the pursuit of truth as a whole had for centuries been the history
of the denial of the will and, with it, of sexual desires.[4] Again, in a more scholarly fashion, philosophers from Plato and Aristotle through Descartes,
Wittgenstein, Arendt, and beyond have been featured in the "Feminist Interpretations" series from the Pennsylvania State University Press, with sexuality
always emerging as a highlighted theme. In addition, there have been the
sweeping claims by philosophers such as Luce Irigaray and Michèle Le Doeuff
about the centrality of gender and sexuality in the history of Western philosophy as a whole.[5]

Yet despite all of this activity, the subfields of European intellectual history
and the history of sexuality have remained relatively segregated, as a brief
glance at the major journals in the field would suggest. In the last ten years the
Journal of the History of Ideas has published two articles pertaining to sexuality,
while *Modern Intellectual History* has published three in its eight years of existence, though both have included a smattering of articles and reviews on closely

related topics such as gender and selfhood. Conversely, a brief review of the *Journal of the History of Sexuality* reveals countless articles on topics pertaining explicitly to the production, formation, and distribution of knowledge—all topics that could easily be considered under the rubric of intellectual history. The point of this admittedly very superficial observation is not to suggest that some sort of injustice is being done, that somehow the two subfields *should* be better integrated. Rather, the point is simply to highlight the fact that the actual practices of intellectual historians and historians of sexuality would not seem to support the claims by either Freud or Foucault about the centrality of sexuality to modern forms of knowledge. Sexuality has been *a* theme in the intellectual-historical treatment of knowledge but by no means a privileged theme. Moreover, historians of sexuality writing about the production of sexual knowledge are more likely to be talking to historians of other aspects of sexuality (for instance, aspects such as subjective experience, marketing and consumption, state interest in its subjects' sexual practices) than to intellectual historians broadly understood. Thus, we see from one angle—from the subfield of the history of sexuality—that the twentieth century fused the history of sexuality to the field of intellectual history in a comprehensive and undeniable fashion, that intellectual inquiry is always enacted by sexed, desiring subjects. Yet we see from another angle—the subfield of intellectual history—that in both thematic and institutional ways the subfields have never fully converged in the way that Freud or Foucault might have expected.

The question is what this discrepancy tells us about one or the other subfield. In what follows, I want to historicize the problem itself, seeing how the fusion of sexuality to the production of knowledge is a story very much marked by tensions of the twentieth century, intellectually framed by the poles of Freud and Foucault. I then want to conclude by examining some of the points of departure that have been opened up in recent years, as practitioners and theoreticians of both traditions have begun decentering sexuality as a privileged site of knowledge production and as a distinct category of analysis.

The Foucauldian Revolution

Over the last several decades, much of the intellectual history of sexuality has fallen into two camps: one camp informed by Foucauldian theories of disciplinarity, regulation, and the constitution of subjects; the other an examination of sexualized subjectivity itself as something that precedes and/or exceeds discursive constructions. It pays thus to examine these two developments individually and in their interactive evolution.

To be sure, the history of sexuality was being written well before the break-through of Michel Foucault's three-volume study by the name. One could view as early examples of this kind of history tracts such as Marianne Weber's *Wife and Mother in the Development of Law* or Magnus Hirschfeld's *Sexual History of Humanity*.[6] In the domain of academic histories written in more recent years, a subdiscipline began to appear in the 1960s and 1970s. Emerging from the concerns of social historians, these early studies were interested particularly in the nature of the family and demographics.[7] More closely related to the methods and interests of intellectual history were studies about sexual liberation, on the one hand,[8] and psychobiographies and histories, on the other.[9]

Yet especially in terms of overlap with the subdiscipline of intellectual history, Foucault's first volume of *The History of Sexuality* was positively transformative for the field. Most poignantly, and most famously, Foucault contested what he called the "repressive hypothesis," the premise that the Victorian era was dominated by the repression of sexuality and that the post-Victorian era had somehow seen its gradual liberation. In its place, he suggested that the modern era in Europe has been one of incitement to discourse, the proliferation of talk about sexuality, and, with that talk, of mechanisms for the production of particular kinds of sexed subjects and particular ways for those sexed subjects to manifest their desires. While he did not remove the state from the equation, he painted the rise of sexology, psychoanalysis, modern medicine, and modern law in particular as co-productive of the modern sexed subject. Psychoanalysis was a particularly offensive institution in (this moment of) Foucault's analysis, as it so effectively elicited discourse from its subjects, turned them into "confessing animals" who sought their own truth in their supposedly repressed sexual fantasies and expressions.[10]

The result of Foucault's challenge was the opening of vast new ways to explore the place of sexuality in intellectual and social formations, and historians turned subsequently to the production of sexual knowledge with a new energy and critical lens. The areas of sexology and eugenics emerged as specially targeted areas of renewed investigation. What really linked the study of sexology with the study of eugenics was the broad medicalization of society and its treatment under the rubric of biology.[11] On this front, Thomas Laqueur's *Making Sex* was an important contribution that tracked the modern transformation in European thought through which sexual difference came to be understood in biological terms.[12] In addition, a range of more targeted synthetic studies emerged that concentrated on the normative and regulative effects of sexology and eugenics, their joint tendency to simultaneously produce and pathologize particular types of sexual proclivities.[13] Although Foucault's intervention had deemphasized the role of the sovereign state as a center of power, many of the Foucault-inspired studies of twentieth-century eugenics brought the modern state squarely back into the picture, detailing the profound interest that modern states—across the political spectrum—demonstrated in managing the reproductive capacities of their subjects.[14]

Much of the contention amongst researchers in the history of sexology and eugenics has pertained to the homogeneity or heterogeneity of the field of knowledge. In the German domain in particular, a thesis from Detlev Peukert established a paradigm for research into the relationship between social- and sexual-reform campaigns seemingly aligned with liberal political projects of the Kaiserreich, on the one hand, and the later practices of the National Socialist state, on the other. While Peukert found the tools for the murderous eugenics of Nazism to have roots in those liberal reform campaigns,[15] others have maintained that no easy transition can be made across the line of 1933 in large part because of the multifaceted nature of the reform campaigns.[16] The discussion about the homogeneity of the sexology and eugenics discourse, however, by no means pertains solely to the German—or even the European—case. In a series of articles Howard Chiang, for instance, has recently been insisting not only on the vast diversity and often very non-normative components of European sexology but also on the importance of recognizing that diversity when trying to understand the complicated ways in which sexology was imported to China.[17] In a similar vein but perhaps closer to Foucault's own emphasis on the productive and normative quality of scientific debates and dissent has been a spate of recent publications exploring the globalization of sexology in the twentieth century.[18]

In the late 1980s and into the 1990s, extremely sophisticated studies informed by the *spirit* of Foucault's challenge but less devoted to his explicit narrative also began to find the centrality of sexuality in a range of areas of knowledge production not so immediately tied to sexology itself. For example, Carolyn Dean's study of Bataille and Lacan found the origin of the decentered subject—a concept central to so much poststructuralist thought—to have emerged in the interwar crisis of masculinity.[19] In another register, Isabel Hull's study of the role of sexuality in seventeenth- and eighteenth-century Germany demonstrated how vast elements of German Enlightenment thought—from legal theory to theories of statecraft to Idealist philosophy—were infused with questions about sexuality, sometimes more and sometimes less explicitly stated. Additionally, groundbreaking have been studies led by Ann Stoler and others about the place of sexual knowledge in the colonial project, that is, in the knowledge necessary for European colonialism and in the formation of scientific racism.[20]

The Challenge of Psychoanalysis and the
Decentering of Sexuality

If Foucault's work thus revolutionized the history of sexuality as a subdiscipline, the status of psychoanalysis in his narrative has nevertheless remained a
point of contention. Both theoretically and historiographically, the stakes have
been high, and the relationship simultaneously troubled and productive of
important questions. One especially provocative analysis of the standoff
between Foucault and psychoanalysis came from the Lacanian theoretician
Joan Copjec in an introduction to her edited collection, *Supposing the Subject*.
According to Copjec, Foucauldian thought assumes that discourse can account
entirely for the subject: it brings the subject into being and shapes the choices
the subject confronts. Conversely in psychoanalysis, she claims, the subject
exceeds discourse, in that it effaces itself from discourse with its every gesture
and statement. Copjec turns to the category of foreclosure to explain the
working of the psychoanalytic subject as that which cannot be fully represented
in the past and present.[21] Foreclosure, she explains, pertains to something that
is fully eliminated from discourse, something that can never return, in the
sense of the repressed, except "*in* its very effacement."[22] Understood in the
sense of foreclosure, the subject does not simply disappear or somehow slip
out of discourse. Rather, in its effacement—in its distancing itself always from
its own statements and acts—it makes itself *felt* as subject. In its own negotiation of discourse, this subject as foreclosure is not to be understood as predis-
cursive; yet it can nonetheless never be located or made fully present—neither
to the self nor to the historian. "To state it somewhat differently," Copjec argues,
"in psychoanalysis the subject is not hypostatized, but hypothesized—that is, it
is only ever *supposed*: we never actually encounter it face to face."[23]

   For Copjec there is no means to reconcile the Foucauldian and psychoanalytic frameworks because they operate with such different starting points concerning the make-up of the subject: psychoanalysis assumes a distinctive subject
with a distinctive formation of desire, while Foucauldian thought assumes a
subject that is fully constituted by discourse. Yet not all would accept her presentation of the problematic, and indeed much more theoretical energy has gone
into finding sites of overlap between psychoanalysis and Foucauldian approaches to subjectivity than to insisting on their incompatibility. We could take
Suzanne Stewart-Steinberg's *The Pinocchio Effect* as an example of a historically
informed negotiation of the two poles. Tracing the evolution of sexed subjects—
and especially of the masculine subject—in post-unification Italy, Stewart-
Steinberg identifies a paradox she calls the "Pinocchio Effect," in which the
masculine subject embodies an anxiety about its own existence, "self-conscious

of its own fictional status."[24] Yet Stewart-Steinberg finds in the language of ideology—understood as the social mechanisms that produce subjects both as free agents who choose to respond to the call of those mechanisms, and as subjects mastered by their law or their call—the best means to think about this self-consciously fictional subject. Ideology in this sense, she explains, relies on the pleasure that the subject experiences in its relationship to social norms—a pleasure that controls or drives the subject but that "is not reducible to the effects of ideology," or is not merely the subject's joy in meeting social norms. Citing the Lacanian political theorist Slavoj Žižek, she adds that "the modern form of ideology is grounded in a disavowal: we know that the subject is not a preconstituted being, but nevertheless we must *pretend* that he/she is."[25] While Stewart-Steinberg ultimately continues to understand the subject as a discursive product, thus enabling her to recreate historically the process of modern masculine subject-formation, her approach to ideology allows her to thematize how subjects get produced in historically specific ways so as to make them inaccessible to full discursive disclosure. Stewart-Steinberg is thus not making transhistorical claims about the make-up of subjectivity, but rather is attuned to the historically specific ways in which "post-liberal" subjects of Italian modernity functioned. Akin to the psychoanalytic prompt, however, she is sensitive to the kinds of historical methods that researchers might take if they want to understand their subjects as not fully open to discursive demonstration, pursuing their traces rather than their manifestations in discourse.[26]

If Stewart-Steinberg's argument demonstrates in a historically informed way how theories of depth-subject and discursive construction are not necessarily at odds, other theoretical interventions have sought even more directly to demonstrate the compatibility of elements of Foucault's thought with elements of psychoanalysis. A particularly careful and sustained effort is Arnold Davidson's *The Emergence of Sexuality: Historical Epistemology and the Formation of Concepts*. In this book, Davidson—one of the rare analytical philosophers to be deeply indebted to Foucault's methodological innovations—defends psychoanalysis with some of Foucault's own tools. First, he uses Foucault's "archaeological" method of inquiry to indicate what he sees to be the truly revolutionary accomplishment of psychoanalysis within the fields of sexology and psychiatry, namely that it denaturalized the relationship between sexual drive and sexual object. Even if Freud at times replicated many of the practices and assumptions of sexology and psychiatry about the so-called perversions, Davidson maintains, this denaturalizing of the sexual drive and object, this claim that there is no "normal" object for the drive, marked a definitive break in the "regime of truth" governing nineteenth-century science.[27] Recognizing that his reading of Freud counters the letter of Foucault's *History of Sexuality*, Davidson nonetheless maintains that it coincides not only with its spirit but also with a longer and more complex relationship between Foucault and psychoanalysis. He thus concludes his study with an effort to fuse Foucault's thought to certain elements of psychoanalysis. He notes that throughout his career Foucault, following Lacan, was interested fundamentally in the epistemological project that countered existentialism, phenomenology, and all theories involving a free subject. In this reading, Foucault, like Lacan, was interested in the structures of language that cannot be controlled by the intentional, conscious subject. Davidson writes that "however odd it may sound, the existence of the unconscious was a decisive component in Foucault's *antipsychologism*," and he thus reads Foucault's archaeological histories as complements to the psychoanalytic focus on the structures of the unconscious.[28] Davidson then asserts that Foucault's real objection to psychoanalysis pertained not to its focus on the unconscious but rather to its centering of that unconscious on the problem of desire as that which reveals the truth of the subject. He concludes by citing Foucault's own preference for Freud's *The Interpretation of Dreams* over the *Three Essays on the Theory of Sexuality*. "It is not the theory of development, it is not the sexual secret behind the neuroses," Foucault had explained, in his effort to clarify his admiration for elements of psychoanalysis, "it is a *logic of the unconscious*."[29] Davidson sees Foucault's later interest in *ars erotica* as a discourse about "body-pleasure-intensification," in contrast to *scientia sexualis*—itself a discourse about "subject-desire-truth"—as a turn away from sexuality not only as that which provides the truth of the subject, but also as the privileged object of study for both Foucault and psychoanalysis. "Just as Foucault wanted to divorce the psychoanalytic theory of the unconscious from the theory of sexuality," Davidson concludes, "so he wants to detach the experience of pleasure from a psychological theory of sexual desire, of sexual subjectivity."[30]

Interestingly, it is by turning away from sexuality and toward pleasure and intensity that Davidson finds the real coalescence between Foucault and Freud, as well as a promising alternative way to think about subjectivity. According to Davidson, if Foucault took issue with the psychoanalytical focus on desire as the truth of the subject, he had turned to pleasure as something that could never be true or untrue, right or wrong. "Although we have no difficulty talking about and understanding the distinction between true and false desires," he maintained, "the idea of true and false pleasures (and Foucault understood this point even if he never put it in exactly this way) is conceptually misplaced. Pleasure is, as it were, exhausted by its surface; it can be intensified, increased, its qualities modified, but it does not have the psychological depth of desire. It is, so to speak, related to itself and not to something else that it expresses, either truly or falsely."[31]

Although he does not identify the influence, Davidson's analysis harkens back in surprising ways to elements of Deleuze and Guattari's *Anti-Oedipus*, a book that has not played a significant role in the historiography of sexuality but that ran parallel to Foucault's own development and even earned his enthusiastic endorsement in the preface to the English-language translation. Ostensibly a screed against psychoanalysis, the book can also be read to evince a rather nuanced relationship to it.[32] In the course of the argument Deleuze and Guattari aligned themselves closely with Foucault not in the rejection of psychoanalysis as such but rather in an all-out assault on the normative familial politics enforced by psychoanalysis as an institutionalized practice.[33] As the title suggests, they took the Oedipus myth as the primary object of their critique, maintaining that institutionalized psychoanalysis had so overly internalized its logic as to shape its very understanding of the unconscious as deriving from the Oedipus-related notion of castration anxiety; likewise, drives and desires took on a derivative connotation. In short, institutionalized psychoanalysis had tamed the unconscious, drives, and desires to accommodate the Oedipus myth, while talk therapy aimed primarily to help the analysand accommodate him- or herself to the normative nuclear-family model. If Freudian psychoanalysis claimed to be discovering and interpreting a mechanism through which the sexual self had come into being, it was also setting the parameters of that operation. In the language of Deleuze and Guattari, psychoanalysis always "territorializes" desires in advance, giving them (Oedipal) orientation and normative aims. Lacanian psychoanalysis had seemed to open itself to alternative formations of desire and the unconscious through its recourse to the symbolic and chains of signification, chains that exist in multiple and heterogeneous formation. According to the authors of *Anti-Oedipus*, however, Lacan regrettably understood these chains as rather detached from physicality, repeating the "idealism" of the Freudian recourse to an unconscious that expresses itself in fantasy, in territorialized representations. In doing so, he, too, allowed his followers to convert the inherent heterogeneity of desires into an Oedipalized, normative structure.[34]

Yet Deleuze and Guattari did not reject all that psychoanalysis had to offer. Rather, in their call for "schizoanalysis," they sought to return the unconscious and the drives to their antinormative, heterogeneous, productive potential. "The great discovery of psychoanalysis," they explained, "was that of the production of desire, of the productions of the unconscious." In this project, they began with "desiring machines," nonoriented and noncoordinated processes that are not motivated by "lack" or "need," but rather are "desiring productions," activities that constantly produce new realities. "If desire produces, its product is real," they wrote, adding: "If desire is productive, it can be productive only in the real world and can produce only reality. Desire is the set of *passive syntheses* that engineer partial objects, flows, and bodies, and that function as units of production." Desire and its relationship to partial objects is easily territorialized, directed to normative ends. The task of schizoanalysis is thus to deterritorialize desiring machines, to open them up to their schizophrenic and heterogeneous potential, and thus to eliminate the depth-subject that is the product of the Oedipal norm. They insisted that the sum is a diffusion of sexuality from any origin or telos. "The truth is," they explained, "that sexuality is everywhere." It is not the primary drive, produced and oriented through the Oedipal process and then "sublimated" into seemingly desexualized cultural forms. Rather, schizoanalysis implies a pansexualization of the world, a multiplicity of desire and sex and simultaneously a decentering of sexuality—of any single sexual aim, orientation, or desire—as the truth of the subject.[35] Much like Foucault who would soon call for a decentering of sexuality from the privileged position that psychoanalysis had granted it but who was not necessarily rejecting all that psychoanalysis had to offer, Deleuze and Guattari were challenging a particular formation of psychoanalysis and the constraints it placed on sexuality, the unconscious, drives, and desires while recognizing a non-normative potential in certain elements of psychoanalytic inquiry.

Decentering Sexuality

We thus see in the work of both Davidson and Deleuze and Guattari a move beyond sexuality itself as a distinct concept or even as the most important dimension of psychoanalytic theory. In this regard, it is interesting to note that in recent years those practicing historians who have engaged psychoanalytic theory have also ventured quite far from sexuality as its center or base. Indeed, amongst professional historians in recent decades, psychoanalysis itself has had its most regular and sophisticated influence not in the history of sexuality but in questions of historiographical method itself. Dominick LaCapra, for instance, a leading spokesperson for trauma as a theoretical category for historical investigation, has mobilized such psychoanalytic categories as "working through," "acting out," "*nachträglichkeit*" (belatedness), "transference," and especially the "repetition compulsion" to indicate not just how one might think about developments in the past but also about the implicated subjectivity of the historian in the present.[36] Recently Joan Scott has made an argument for the productive "incommensurability of history and psychoanalysis." Drawing heavily on the work of Michel de Certeau and Lyndal Roper,[37] she maintains that the benefit of psychoanalytic theory to the writing of history is its ability to question the "certainty about facts, narrative, and cause." If it opens up to the historian matters of fantasy and unconscious motivation on the part of both subject and object of historical inquiry, its strength lay in its resistance to master narratives. Indeed, it loses its potential when it becomes just another master framework or explanatory matrix in the historian's toolbox—a tendency, she maintains, to which psychohistory as informed by ego psychology was inclined.[38]

These turns by historians to matters of trauma, transference, and more generalized modes of critical inquiry inspired by psychoanalysis do not necessarily divorce psychoanalytic theory from matters of sexuality. Indeed, Bonnie Smith's *The Gender of History* and its investigation into the problem of sustained trauma in the form of domestic violence and its gendered impact on the discipline of history as a whole fused trauma and sexuality together again. Yet for the most part, the tendency to de-emphasize sexuality itself as the privileged component of psychoanalysis echoes tendencies in the history of psychoanalysis itself. The earliest major institutional conflict within the circles of "depth psychology" revolved at least in part around Carl Jung's move away from Freudian libido theory.[39] Less obviously confrontational, Lou Andreas-Salomé's Spinozist approach to psychoanalysis subtly decentered the sexual, while Freud's own daughter, Anna Freud, helped to inaugurate "ego psychology" with Erik Erikson and others, a psychoanalytic offshoot that would free up the development of the ego from the monopoly of the sexualized id.[40] The subdiscipline of psychohistory, too, if at times interested especially to unearth sexual conflicts that might explain behaviors of historical figures, also evolved in diverse directions that could accommodate complex and not wholly sexual explanations for personality development and behaviors.[41] Even Freud's own intellectual evolution and his ultimate embrace of the theory of the death drive evince a gradual opening to nonsexual interpretations of the unconscious. Resistant at first, he ultimately recognized the death drive as a phenomenon that must be understood as distinct from the sexual drives even if it might manifest itself together with those sexual drives.[42]

In reference to the death drive itself, it is worth noting that theoreticians have been divided on its place both in psychoanalysis and in the latter's relationship to Foucauldian thought. Deleuze and Guattari had found the death drive to be, after the Oedipus complex, the most offensive development in Freudian thought, a development that established the death drive as a transcendent principle aimed to make bearable the ascetic ideal imposed by the Oedipus complex.[43] Conversely, Jacques Derrida found in the death drive a development that might make psychoanalysis more compatible with the Foucauldian project, albeit in the latter's earlier attention to madness and its confinement. In "To Do Justice to Freud," Derrida suggested that Freud's death drive might actually be a recognition of a profound and irremediable madness in psychoanalytic theory, a conception that in his eyes moved Freud's thought out of the camp of disciplining technicians and into a domain that perpetually exceeds all discursive control.[44] One thing that is certain is that, whether through the death drive or through notions of the unconscious or pleasure and intensity, theoretical efforts to articulate a meeting-of-the-minds between Foucault and Freud have consistently landed on a general decentering of sexuality as the privileged category of psychoanalytic theory.

In this regard, I want to discuss one final theoretical intervention of more recent vintage that could hold particular value for historians interested in the formation of fields of knowledge and moral valuation, namely developments in affect theory. In relationship to the history of sexuality, Eve Kosofsky Sedgwick's *Touching Feeling: Affect, Pedagogy, Performativity* is especially relevant. In this book Sedgwick expresses a frustration she had begun to feel over the years with the Foucauldian treatment of sexuality. She had always understood Foucault to be suggesting that there might exist some form of alternative to the repression/liberation dynamic he had exposed.[45] Her own hope in thinking through Foucault's work had been placed in the possibility that it might provide some way "to think of human desire quite to the side of prohibition and repression" and its often displaced but always dualistic "chameleonic guises."[46] Yet her frustration lay in her sense that both Foucault in his *History of Sexuality* and subsequent scholars in the field have remained bound to the idea of prohibition in some fashion, that "even beyond the repressive hypothesis, some version of prohibition is still the most important thing to understand."

Sedgwick's response is not to abandon Foucault's challenge and all that it provocatively offered the theorist of sexuality, a gesture that could only repeat the duality she finds troublesome; nor is it to embrace or reject psychoanalysis. Rather, her response is to appeal to affect theory in an effort to move poetically *beside* the two. Sedgwick's main concern is that the literary-theoretical treatment of sexuality has been too narrow, permitting a "diagrammatic sharpness" that fails to account for the rich array of sensual experience that subjectivity includes. As an alternative she proposes the category of affect, a category that, she maintains, makes dualistic thinking impossible. Indebted especially to the work of the psychologist Silvan Tomkins, Sedgwick explains that "the difference between the drive system and the affect system is not that one is more rooted in the body than the other; [Tomkins] understands both to be thoroughly embodied, as well as more or less intensively interwoven with cognitive processes. The difference instead is between more specific and more general, more and less constrained: between biologically based systems that are less and more capable of generating complexity or degrees of freedom."[47] She thus finds in Tomkins a theory of affect that embeds what she calls the "digital," "on-off" character of sexual drive—especially as theorized by psychoanalysis—in a textured "analog" or "multiply differentiated" context. With its modification through a network of affects, sexual drives disappear as a central or organizing element in the formation of subjectivity.

There are clear overlaps between Sedgwick's project and recent work in the history of emotions. For instance William Reddy finds in the study of emotions a means to get beyond the distinct gender, class, racial, and sexual identities that preoccupy historians. Recently he has turned to the history of love as a means to denaturalize sexual desire itself as a universal category.[48] Yet if Reddy's work resonates with Sedgwick's thought, one might be wary of too quickly fusing the history of emotion generally with recent developments in affect theory. Indeed, one implicit aim in Sedgwick's project is to surround sexuality in a framework of affect in order to decenter it from its privileged place in identity formation and as an object of knowledge and normative morality. On this front her work echoes a common trend in humanist approaches to affect theory. Drawing on research in cognitive- and neurosciences, theorists such as Charles Altieri and Brian Massumi both distinguish between "affect" (Massumi) or "feeling" (Altieri) and "emotion."[49] In the former they find a non-normative mode of being-affected and expressing human experience—which Massumi labels as "post-ideological"—and in the latter a dimension of human experience that gets aligned with moral and cognitive judgment and identity formation. Albeit forwarding quite different projects, they share a joint aim to valorize those dimensions of affective human experience that are not reducible to the "self," or are not subject to judgments of right and wrong, true and false. While some work in the history of emotion may also decenter sexuality and may be equally concerned with pre- or post-subjective dimensions of affective experience, the field as a whole has also understandably been interested in reconstructing precisely those kinds of communal and normative frameworks—"emotional regimes," "emotional communities"—in and through which subjects develop emotional identities and learn to embrace and reject emotional norms.[50] In short, the field may overlap with shifts in the history of sexuality and critiques coming out of affect theory, but it also has its own set of questions, of which the status of the depth-subject as a privileged site for normative and cognitive judgment is only one small part.

If historians have thus not yet fully embraced affect theory as an inquisitive aid, one can speculate what its implications could be. Here I want to take Seth Koven's work *Slumming* as an example of the potential affect theory might offer in a post-Foucauldian, post-psychoanalytic project to decenter sexuality. To be sure, Koven's book is not immediately an obvious choice, as its aim is explicitly to reveal the unstated sexual politics he finds lurking behind middle-class Londoners' attraction to the slums of the city. And yet, the work is richly attentive enough to a range of affective expressions on the part of the individuals it treats that it makes alternative readings possible. If it is not exactly a study in affect theory *avant la lettre*, it does make possible some observations on what such a work might do.

Koven refers just once to his own affective ambivalence toward his subjects, but that one reference opens up an interpretive potential for the rest of the book.[51] If Koven aims throughout to tie his subjects' various affective expressions to a complex formation of conflicted sexual desires and regulation, his own ambivalence—his own effort to not overly discipline or orient the statements and actions of his subjects—also creates a dynamic in which those affects are allowed their own nondetermined expression. Thus Koven interprets utterances by his historical actors such as the "attraction of repulsion" as pertaining to sexual attraction and repulsion, while still allowing those utterances simultaneously to express themselves in more immediate, nonoriented fashion. Attraction can be simple sympathy or pity without erotic overtones, while repulsion can manifest itself as simple disgust or fear.[52]

As a result of Koven's willingness to let both of these tendencies work, to attend to the ways in which "politics and erotics, social and sexual categories, overflowed their boundaries," *Slumming* proves particularly suggestive for thinking about the relationship between affect and sexuality. In this regard there are two moments of tension worth noting. On the one hand, as a cultural history of altruism situated within the history of sexuality, the book exhibits a tendency at once to attach or orient affects to the field of the sexual *while simultaneously* allowing those affects to exceed such a constraining orientation. At the same time, it reveals a similar dynamic on the part of the actors it treats. Here, addressing precisely the period Foucault identified with the modern invention and disciplining of sexuality, the book reveals the tendency of nineteenth- and early twentieth-century writers and activists to express a variety of nonoriented affects such as fear, pleasure, disgust, and pity *and* to quickly channel those affects into a sexual direction that they may or may not have wanted to avow. Yet in both moments, in that of Koven as historian and in that of his historical actors, we see the kind of work that a turn to affect theory could potentially enable. That is, we see the expression of affect as nonrepresentational, uncontained, not tied to ideological or discursive explanation; and we see the ideological work that interprets and orients that affect, in this case toward the sexual. The combination in this case allows for an at least partial decentering of sexuality as the dominant explanatory matrix for a range of human affects and their expression.

Ruth Leys has issued a rather convincing critique of the humanist appropriation of affect theory and the neurosciences that undergird it, claiming that
the scientific foundations themselves are uncertain.[53] However, it is not clear
that her incisive critique necessarily undermines the interpretive potential of
affect theory for intellectual history or the history of sexuality. Indeed, much as
Scott says of psychoanalysis, the strength of affect theory is its resistance to
becoming a tool for the production of master narratives. Affect theory attends
to subjective expression and response—on the part of both subjects of history
and historians as subjects—that are not immediately available for moral or
cognitive capture, or for causal explanation in the narrative of history. Its value
for the field of work taking place at the intersection of intellectual history and
the history of sexuality is not in its ability to provide a *better* account of historical
actors or their desires, but solely in shifting a frame of investigation and reading
practices that might enable historians to attend to a wider array of affective experiences than just the sexual desires that came to such prominence in the
twentieth century. Affect theory may thus prove valuable in decentering sexuality as an explanatory category of human behavior and motivation without
necessarily becoming a new master framework for historical interpretation.

Conclusion

So where do these developments leave us? We began with the observation that
the history of sexuality had been somewhat segregated within the field of intellectual history despite the fact that questions of knowledge formation are of
central importance to both fields. Yet going through the literature, we are
reminded that, at least from the Foucauldian perspective, the central role that
sexuality came to play in modern fields of knowledge about the self was always
a matter to be critiqued, not embraced. One could even say that the decentering
of sexuality on the part of Sedgwick, Davidson, and even Deleuze and Guattari
is more of a positive realization of the critical potential in the Foucauldian project than its surpassing. Moreover, as we witness the decentering of sexuality in
psychoanalytic theory, we see far less distance between psychoanalytic and Foucauldian thought than we might once have expected. It may well be that psychoanalysis inherently "supposes" a different kind of subject than the
discursively constituted subject of Foucauldian thought, even a depth-subject
of sorts, but that subject is no longer so clearly defined by its sexual desires or
by a primal repression as it once was.

In fact, at this point and in light of developments in Foucauldian, psychoanalytic, and affect theory, one might wonder if the seeming standoff between

Foucault and Freud might best be seen historically and as framed loosely by the twentieth century. There can be little doubt that sexuality did emerge in that era both as a privileged site of knowledge and as a highly politicized one. Neither the twentieth-century biopolitical state that existed throughout Europe nor such parallel phenomena as the feminist or homosexual-emancipation movements would have been conceivable without developments in sexology and reproduction-management. This is not to suggest that sexual knowledges and sexual politics were not significant long before the twentieth century, as pre- and early modern historians will remind us; nor is it to suggest that they will not remain pressing issues into the future (as current debates in the United States about abortion or insurance-funded contraception and Viagra remind us, not to mention those about immigration, birthplace, and citizenship). But it is to suggest that the particular prominence that sexuality played as the object of contention between two such significant theoretical developments could only have played out in the sex-obsessed twentieth century. Seen in this light, it may be that the seeming segregation of the history of sexuality from intellectual history broadly speaking is both symptomatic of twentieth-century developments and an indicator of developments to come—that is, symptomatic of the twentieth-century elevation of sexuality as such a specific category of knowledge that it was best treated in isolation, and indicative also of a perhaps desirable decentering of sexuality as a privileged analytical category in favor of related but broader categories such as affect, emotion, intimacy, or embodiment.

Notes

1. Sigmund Freud, *Totem und Tabu*, in *Gesammelte Werke, chronologisch geordnet*, vol. 11 of 18, ed. Anna Freud, Edward Bibring, Willi Hoffer, Ernst Kris, and Otto Isakower (London: Imago, 1940–1952), 172.

2. See for instance Isabel Hull, *Sexuality, State, and Civil Society in Germany 1700–1815* (Ithaca, NY: Cornell University Press, 1996); Helmut Puff, *Sodomy in Reformation Germany and Switzerland, 1400–1600* (Chicago: University of Chicago Press, 2003).

3. Theodor Adorno and Max Horkheimer, *Dialectic of Enlightenment*, trans. John Cumming (New York: Continuum, 1993), 81–119; Jacques Lacan, "Kant with Sade," trans. James B. Swenson, Jr., *October* 51 (1989): 55–75.

4. Friedrich Nietzsche, *On the Genealogy of Morality*, trans. Keith Ansell-Pearson and Carol Diethe (Cambridge: Cambridge University Press, 2006), 68–120.

5. Luce Irigaray, *Speculum of the Other Woman*, trans. Gillian C. Gill (Ithaca, NY: Cornell University Press, 1985); Michelle Le Doeuff, *Hipparchia's Choice: An Essay Concerning Women, Philosophy, etc.*, trans. Trista Selous (Cambridge, MA: Blackwell, 1991).

6. Marianne Weber, *Ehefrau und Mutter in der Rechtsentwicklung: eine Einführung* (Tübingen: J. C. B. Mohr, 1907); Magnus Hirschfeld, *Sexualgeschichte der Menschheit* (Berlin: P. Langenscheidt, 1929).

7. See for example Lawrence Stone, *The Family, Sex, and Marriage in England 1500–1800* (New York: Harper and Row, 1977); James Woycke, *Birth Control in Germany: 1871–1933* (New York: Routledge, 1988);

8. Examples include Edward Shorter, *The Making of the Modern Family* (New York: Basic Books, 1975); Paul Robinson, *The Modernization of Sex: Havelock Ellis, Alfred Kinsey, William Masters, and Virginia Johnson* (New York: Harper and Row, 1976): James Steakley, *The Homosexual Emancipation Movement in Germany* (New York: Arno Press, 1975).

9. See for example Erik Erikson, *Young Man Luther: A Study in Psychoanalysis and History* (New York: Norton, 1958); Peter Loewenberg, *Decoding the Past: The Psychohistorical Approach* (New York: Knopf, 1983); Robert Waite, *The Psychopathic God: Adolf Hitler* (New York: Basic Books, 1977).

10. Michel Foucault, *The History of Sexuality, Volume I*, trans. Robert Hurley (New York: Pantheon, 1978).

11. A good discussion is Edward Ross Dickinson and Richard Wetzell, "The Historiography of Sexuality in Modern Germany," *German History* 23, no. 3 (2005): esp. 294.

12. Thomas Laqueur, *Making Sex: Body and Gender from the Greeks to Freud* (Cambridge, MA: Harvard University Press, 1992).

13. On sexology, see for example Robert Nye, ed., *Sexuality* (New York: Oxford University Press, 1999); Vern Bullough, *Science in the Bedroom: A History of Sex Research* (New York: Basic Books, 1994); Jeffrey Weeks, *Sex, Politics, and Society: The Regulation of Sexuality since 1800* (New York: Longman, 1981); Roy Porter, *The Facts of Life: The Creation of Sexual Knowledge in Britain, 1650–1950* (New Haven, CT: Yale University Press, 1995); Roy Porter, ed., *Sexual Knowledge, Sexual Science: The History of Attitudes to Sexuality* (New York: Cambridge University Press, 1994).

14. The literature on eugenics and the modern state is vast. A select sampling includes Robert Proctor, *Racial Hygiene: Medicine under the Nazis* (Cambridge, MA: Harvard University Press, 1988); Paul Weindling, *Health, Race, and German Politics between National Unification and Nazism, 1870–1945* (Cambridge: Cambridge University Press, 1989); Gisela Bock, *Zwangssterilization im Nationalsozialismus: Studien zur Rassenpolitik und Frauenpolitik* (Opladen: Westdt. Verlag, 1986); Lutz Sauerteig, *Krankheit, Sexualität, Gesellschaft: Geschlechtskrankheiten und Gesundheitspolitik in Deutschland im 19. und 20. Jahrhundert* (Stuttgart: Steiner, 1999). Although this listing seems slanted especially toward the German case, Mark Mazower's *Dark Continent* (New York: Vintage, 2000) makes a compelling case that the eugenical project stretched across Europe in a variety of forms in the middle decades of the twentieth century, from Britain and France to Spain, Italy, Russia, and beyond.

15. Detlev Peukert, "The Genesis of the 'Final Solution' from the Spirit of Science," in *Re-Evaluating the Third Reich*, ed. Thomas Childers and Jane Caplan (New York: Holmes and Meier, 1993); Anna Bergmann, *Die verhütete Sexualität: Die medizinische Bemächtigung des Lebens* (Hamburg: Rasch und Röhring, 1992).

16. Atina Grossmann, *Reforming Sex: The German Movement for Birth Control and Abortion Reform, 1920–1950* (New York: Oxford University Press, 1995); Cornelia Usborne, *The Politics of the Body in Weimar Germany* (Ann Arbor: University of Michigan Press, 1992).

17. Howard H. Chiang, "Liberating Sex, Knowing Desire: *Scientia Sexualis* and Epistemic Turning Points in the History of Sexuality," *History of the Human Sciences* 23, no. 5 (2010): 42–69.

18. Examples include Sabine Frühstück, *Colonizing Sex: Sexology and Social Control in Modern Japan* (Berkeley: University of California Press, 2003); Vincanne Adams and Stacy Leigh Pigg, *Sex in Development: Science, Sexuality, and Morality in Global Perspective* (Durham, NC: Duke University Press, 2006).

19. Carolyn Dean, *The Self and Its Pleasures: Bataille, Lacan, and the History of the Decentered Subject* (Ithaca, NY: Cornell University Press, 1992).

20. See especially Ann Stoler, *Race and the Education of Desire* (Durham, NC: Duke University Press, 1995); Anne McClintock, *Imperial Leather: Race, Gender, and Sexuality in the Colonial Contest* (New York: Routledge, 1995).

21. Joan Copjec, "Introduction," to *Supposing the Subject*, ed. Copjec (New York: Verso, 1994), ix.

22. Here Copjec suggests that the subject returns in the Lacanian "real." Ibid., xi.

23. Ibid., xi.

24. Suzanne Stewart-Steinberg, *The Pinocchio Effect: On Making Italians (1860–1920)* (Chicago: University of Chicago Press, 2007), 5.

25. Ibid., 9.

26. Stewart-Steinberg's historical argument resonates well with Judith Butler's argument in *The Psychic Life of Power: Theories in Subjection* (Stanford, CA: Stanford University Press, 1997), in which Butler tries to read psychoanalysis and Foucault together. She maintains first that it is conceivable to understand the unconscious as open to—even attached to and shaped by—forms of social power and discipline; additionally, she finds in the Foucauldian conception of the permanently reiterated subject at the intersection of varieties and at times inconsistent moments of social power a space for misrecognition and incompletion. As a result, the "subject" that emerges is at once produced by those social discourses but, akin to the psychoanalytic subject, exceeds those discourses (83–105).

27. Arnold Davidson, *The Emergence of Sexuality: Historical Epistemology and the Formation of Concepts* (Cambridge, MA: Harvard University Press, 2001), 79, 180.

28. Ibid., 210. Davidson draws his conclusions about Foucault's proximity to Lacan from Michel Foucault, "The Death of Lacan," in *Homosexuality and Psychoanalysis*, ed. Tim Dean and Christopher Lane (Chicago: University of Chicago Press, 2001): 57–58; and Michel Foucault, "Lacan, le 'liberateur' de la psychanalyse," in *Dits et écrits*, vol. 4, ed. Daniel Defert and François Ewald with collaboration of Jacques Lagrange (Paris: Edition Gallimard, 1994), 204–5.

29. Michel Foucault, "Le jeu de Michel Foucault," in *Dit et écrits*, vol. 3, ed. Daniel Defert and François Ewald with collaboration of Jacques Lagrange (Paris: Edition Gallimard, 1994), 315 (cited in Davidson, *Emergence of Sexuality*, 211).

30. Davidson, *Emergence of Sexuality*, 211.

31. For complementary studies that seek to read Foucault and Freud together, see John Forrester, *The Seductions of Psychoanalysis: Freud, Lacan and Derrida* (New York: Cambridge University Press, 1990), 286–316; Judith Butler, *The Psychic Life of Power* (Stanford, CA: Stanford University Press, 1997), 83–105; Joel Whitebook, "Freud, Foucault und der 'Dialog mit der Vernunft,'" *Psyche* 52, no. 6 (1998): 505–44.

32. A good historical discussion of the text and its relationship to Lacanian psychoanalysis is Camille Robcis, *The Politics of Kinship: Anthropology, Psychoanalysis, and Family Law in Twentieth-Century France* (Ph.D. diss., Cornell University, 2007), 222–41; see also Tim Dean, *Beyond Sexuality* (Chicago: University of Chicago Press, 2004); Slavoj Žižek, *Organs without Bodies: On Deleuze and Consequences* (New York: Routledge, 2004).

33. Gilles Deleuze and Félix Guattari, *Anti-Oedipus: Capitalism and Schizophrenia*, trans. Robert Hurley, Mark Seem, and Helen R. Lane (Minneapolis: University of Minnesota Press, 1983), 13, 20.

34. Ibid., 38–39, 53, 73.

35. Ibid., 24, 26–27, 296, 293, 296.

36. These terms are best formulated in Dominick LaCapra's *Representing the Holocaust: History, Theory, Trauma* (Ithaca, NY: Cornell University Press, 1994) and *History and Memory after Auschwitz* (Ithaca, NY: Cornell University Press, 1998). Other examples of historians' interest in trauma include Bonnie Smith, *The Gender of History: Men, Women, and Historical Practice* (Cambridge, MA: Harvard University Press, 2000); Henri Rousso, *The Vichy Syndrome: History and Memory in France since 1944*, trans. Arthur Goldhammer (Cambridge, MA: Harvard University Press, 1991); Alison Frazier, "Machiavelli, Trauma, and the Scandal of *The Prince*: An Essay in Speculative History," in *History in the Comic Mode: Medieval Communities and the Matter of Person*, ed. R. Folton and B. Holsinger (New York: Columbia University Press, 2007), 192–202.

37. Michel de Certeau, *The Writing of History*, trans. Tom Conley (New York: Columbia University Press, 1988); Lyndal Roper, *Oedipus and the Devil: Witchcraft, Sexuality, and Religion in Early Modern Europe* (New York: Routledge, 1994); *Witch Craze* (New Haven, CT: Yale University Press, 2004).

38. Joan Scott, "The Incommensurability of Psychoanalysis and History," *History and Theory* 51 (2012): 63–83. See also Elizabeth Wilson, "Another Neurological Scene," *History of the Present* 1, no. 2 (2011): 149–69.

39. Carl Gustav Jung, *Symbols of Transformation: An Analysis of the Prelude to a Case of Schizophrenia*, trans. R. F. C. Hull (Princeton, NJ: Princeton University Press, 1956).

40. See for examples Lou Andreas-Salomé, *The Freud Journal*, trans. Stanley A. Leavy (New York: Basic Books, 1964); Anna Freud, *The Ego and the Mechanisms of Defense* (New York: International Universities Press, 1966); Erik Erikson, *Childhood and Society* (New York: Norton, 1963).

41. On the de-emphasis of sexuality in psychohistory, see Scott, "Incommensurability of Psychoanalysis and History," 74–76. She suggests that Erik Erikson, a founding father of psychohistory with his *Young Man Luther*, was also a leader in the turn away from sexuality and to stages of individual development as the core of psychoanalysis. Scott identifies this desexualization, also associated

with Karen Horney, Erich Fromm, and others, as helping to fortify psychohistory as a master narrative that seeks to contain and explain historical development, cordon it off in the realm of rational explanation, and thereby to divert the more productively disruptive implications that psychoanalysis may have for historical explanation. Yet, as I think she would agree, her main argument that psychoanalysis troubles conventional historical narrative need not rely on libido theory or the primary emphasis on sexuality; rather, the disruptive capacity relies on the work of the unconscious, belatedness, the uncontainability of the past and the present, the deferred and displaced representation of desires.

42. Sigmund Freud, "Einleitung zu 'Zur Psychoanalyse der Kriegsneurosen'" and *Jenseits des Lustprinzips*, in *Gesammelte Werke, chronologisch geordnet*, vols. 12 and 13 of 18, ed. Anna Freud, Edward Bibring, Willi Hoffer, Ernst Kris, and Otto Isakower (London: Imago, 1940–1952).

43. Deleuze and Guattari, *Anti-Oedipus*, 332–33.

44. Jacques Derrida, "'To Do Justice to Freud': The History of Madness in the Age of Psychoanalysis," *Critical Inquiry* 20, no. 2 (1994): 227–66.

45. Eve Kosofsky Sedgwick, *Touching, Feeling: Affect, Pedagogy, Performativity* (Durham, NC: Duke University Press, 2003), 9.

46. Ibid., 10.

47. Ibid., 18.

48. Jan Plamper, "The History of Emotions: An Interview with William Reddy, Barbara Rosenwein, and Peter Stearns," *History and Theory* 49 (May 2010): 238–39. See also William Reddy, *The Navigation of Feeling: A Framework for the History of Emotions* (Cambridge: Cambridge University Press, 2001) and *The Making of Romantic Love: Longing and Sexuality in Europe, South Asia, and Japan, 900–1200 C.E.* (Chicago: University of Chicago Press, 2012).

49. Charles Altieri, *The Particulars of Rapture: An Aesthetics of the Affects* (Ithaca, NY: Cornell University Press, 2003); Brian Massumi, *Parables for the Virtual: Movement, Affect, Sensation* (Durham, NC: Duke University Press, 2002). For useful empirical studies informed by similar theories of affect, see Patricia Ticineto Clough, ed., *The Affective Turn: Theorizing the Social* (Durham, NC: Duke University Press, 2007).

50. "Emotional regimes" is the term from Reddy, *Navigation of Feeling*; "emotional communities" derives from Barbara Rosenwein, *Emotional Communities in the Early Middle Ages* (Ithaca, NY: Cornell University Press, 2006); see also her "Worrying about Emotions in History," *American Historical Review* 107, no. 3 (2002): 821–45.

51. Seth Koven, *Slumming: Sexual and Social Politics in Victorian London* (Princeton, NJ: Princeton University Press, 2004), 5.

52. Ibid., 38, 39, 4.

53. Ruth Leys, "The Turn to Affect," *Critical Inquiry* 37, no. 3 (2011): 434–72. See also the response from William Connolly, "The Complexity of Intention," *Critical Inquiry* 37, no. 4 (2011): 791–98.

10

Can We *See* Ideas?: On Evocation, Experience, and Empathy

Marci Shore

Pure Seeing

In 1888 Anton Chekhov wrote to his publisher:

> It seems to me it is not for writers of fiction to resolve
> questions such as those of God, pessimism, and the like.
> The writer's business is simply to describe who has been
> speaking or thinking about God or about pessimism, how,
> and in what circumstances. The artist should be not the
> judge of his characters and what they speak about, but only
> an impartial witness. I heard a confused conversation of two
> Russians about pessimism—a conversation resolving
> nothing—and I should convey that conversation in the very
> form in which I heard it; the jury—that is, the readers—will
> decide its value. My business is simply to be talented—that
> is, to know how to differentiate the important from the
> unimportant, to cast light on the characters and to speak
> their language.[1]

Unlike some of his contemporaries, Chekhov did not believe it was
the writer's task to save the world. His task, Chekhov insisted, was
rather to enable the reader to *see* that world in its dilemmas.

Pure seeing—a seeing that reaches the essence, *Wesensschau*—
was a preoccupation of Edmund Husserl. The goal of phenomenology,

Husserl wrote in 1900, was *"erkenntnistheoretische Klarheit und Deutlichkeit"*—epistemological clarity of a kind never before achieved.[2] Husserl's phenomenological method involved the philosopher's "bracketing" his assumption of the world's existence in order to reach a higher state in which he could analyze the contents of his own perceptions. In this state of sharpened self-consciousness, the so-called phenomenological reduction, he was to focus his attention on how objects *appeared* to him, on his unmediated experience of them.

For the Russian literary theorist Viktor Shklovsky, the purpose of literature was analogous: *truly seeing*. Poetic language accomplished this through *ostranenie*—"defamiliarizing" or "making strange." By disrupting usual (non-) perceptions, art jarred objects into the reader's consciousness. *Ostranenie* awakened readers from sleepwalking, shook them from their automated way of being in the world. "And so," Shklovsky wrote in 1917,

> in order to return sensation to our limbs, in order to make us feel
> objects, to make a stone feel stony, man has been given the tool of
> art. The purpose of art, then, is to lead us to a knowledge of a thing
> through the organ of sight instead of recognition. By "enstranging"
> objects and complicating form, the device of art makes perception
> long and "laborious."[3]

This disruption of the process by which all of us unthinkingly "recognized" an object on the basis of our preexisting, habitual assumptions was a good and necessary thing, Shklovsky believed. *Ostranenie* in literature was meant to startle the reader, to wrench something out of its taken-for-granted context in order to truly see it.

Chekhov, Husserl, and Shklovsky—in their different ways—were all concerned with clarifying perception, with sharpening consciousness, with awakening us to the world. Historians engage in a similar pursuit: to help the reader truly see the past. We aim to put aside our present meanings and, as in Husserl's slogan, *"auf die 'Sachen selbst' zurückgehen"* (go back to the "things themselves").[4] For historians *"die Sache selbst"* is the past and our experience of it. We—historians—want to enable our readers to "suspend disbelief," to make an imaginative leap into that past. In a lengthy essay distinguishing between "presence effects" and "meaning effects," Hans Ulrich Gumbrecht called upon humanists to engage in "the production of presence."[5] One way of casting the historian's "calling" is arguably this: to conjure up the past in the present, to make it vivid, palpable, illuminated.

Returning to Chekhov's distinctions: it falls not to us, intellectual historians (as opposed to philosophers), to make pronouncements regarding philosophical truth claims—to decide, for instance, which conceptualization of the human subject was "correct": the Cartesian cogito, Husserl's transcendental ego, or Heidegger's *Dasein*. Rather it falls to us to evoke what was at stake—and for whom—at different moments. The philosophical question of determinism versus responsibility, for example, acquired a particular weight in eastern Europe in the years after Stalin's death; it acquired this weight above all among intellectuals who had been engaged in Stalinism. Our mandate here is a tactile one: our readers should be able to *feel* this weight, to touch the contours of the burden.

A Caveat

I am not an opponent of "idealist" intellectual histories—or of the history of ideas or of philosophy or of the history of philosophy or of the Cambridge School or of a history of political thought. On the contrary, I am deeply indebted to "idealist" intellectual histories—Charles Taylor's epic *Sources of the Self* being one among many.[6] Writing is a personal thing, and what follows are my own principles for my own writing, in no way meant to devalue those of other historians.

The Intrusion of Life

We all write from our own commitments, which perhaps inevitably express a self-awareness of our own peculiar abilities. My own commitment has been to overcoming an idealist-empiricist divide and to capturing the equal reality of both people and ideas, that is, to respecting the "heaviness" of both individuals and their thoughts. There are, after all, no ideas produced outside of time and place and the lives of concrete persons. Ideas do not move around independently of people. There is always involvement; "life" intrudes. While situation in time and space might not be a necessary condition for all knowledge, it is a necessary (we could say "Kantian") condition for *historical* knowledge. Only by grounding ideas temporally and spatially can we understand their stakes historically.[7]

Further, ideas are "always already" dialogical. They are always already shaped, reshaped, and inflected by their encounters with other ideas from the past and present. Dialogue demands actors; there are no pure ideas uncontaminated by human encounter. This is a problem with many attempts to locate "purely indigenous" national intellectual traditions. A "purely indigenous" idea is always to some extent a myth—or, less harshly, a misunderstanding. The intellectual history of nation-building itself is inextricably intertwined with cosmopolitanism. To take one example: in *Jewish Renaissance in the Russian Revolution*, Kenneth Moss describes how his protagonists, nationally-minded intellectuals devoted to the creation of "Jewish culture" (then a neologism), were themselves multilingual monolingualists (people who spoke multiple languages but wished for this new Jewish culture to speak in only one), who took inspiration not only from Jewish folk culture and ancient Judaic tradition, but also from Spinoza and Cassanova, from Byron, Pushkin, and Mickiewicz, from Maupassant and Tolstoy and Przybyszewski and Nietzsche.[8]

If ideas come into being through dialogue, then friendship is historically significant. Friendship is a site of disclosure, a reminder that intellectual production is by nature dialogical, and an illumination of the interplay between emotions and intellect. Friendship offers a window into the infinite complexity of human relations and into the infinite mysteries of the minds producing the ideas that interest intellectual historians. The shift in Derrida's approach to certain ethical questions in his later years takes on a fuller meaning when viewed through the lens of his friendship with his fellow deconstructionist, literary theorist Paul de Man. After de Man's death, Derrida was faced with revelations of his friend's youthful contributions to a collaborationist newspaper in Nazi-occupied Belgium. Confronting these deeply upsetting, in some sense devastating, texts, Derrida initially performed a deconstructionist analysis of the most egregious one, revealing how language subverted itself, how the apparent anti-Semitic meaning was not a stable one. The exercise was both the most lucid example of deconstruction and its bankruptcy. Yet the essay as a whole was remarkably poignant: it laid bare the rawness of Derrida's pain and deconstruction's palpable inability to resolve this pain. As time passed, Derrida implicitly grappled with this friendship from a very different, in some sense antithetical, angle. In *On Cosmopolitanism and Forgiveness*, written over a decade later, Derrida made the argument that forgiveness must mean to forgive the unforgivable if it was to mean anything at all.[9]

Correspondence is accordingly an invaluable historical source. A philosopher can learn Husserl's phenomenology from reading Husserl's philosophy. A historian often needs more; letters provide insights beyond those given by philosophical texts alone. In Husserl's case, his letters reveal different sides to his self-absorption; they reveal the tension between his German patriotism and his attachment to his non-German students during the First World War; they reveal both his generosity and his egoism; they reveal his desire for his students to be true disciples, to work on his project, to refrain from following intuitions leading in other directions; they reveal the depth of his distress at Martin Heidegger's *philosophical* betrayal (which predated and did not necessarily foreshadow his political betrayal). The letters reveal as well how Husserl responded to Nazism, to his exclusion from his own university, to the arrest of his son: with an increased desperation to clarify the phenomenological reduction, the path to clarity and certitude, to a truth that alone could save European civilization from barbarism.[10]

"The burning need for an understanding of the spirit announces itself; and lack of clarity about the methodical and material relation between the natural sciences and the humanistic disciplines has become almost unbearable," Husserl said in May 1935 during a lecture in Vienna.[11] He began to repeat "unbearable," and he began to speak more frequently not only about "das transzendentales Ego" (the transcendental ego), but also about "der Geist" (the spirit) and "die Seele" (the soul). The transcendental ego became heavier and more introspective. History became more palpable. The telos of Europe, Husserl insisted in the 1930s, was reason. Europe was in crisis; the source of the crisis appeared to be the failure of reason—but in fact the problem was superficial reason as opposed to profound reason. There were only two possibilities: the triumph of a deeper reason or the descent into barbarism. The calling of the philosopher was to ensure that we not abandon faith in truth, in philosophy, in the possibility of finding answers.[12]

The philosophical despair at the core of Husserl's 1935 lectures in Vienna and Prague (which became *The Crisis of European Sciences*) testifies to the fact that the emotional versus the intellectual is a divide that exists in theory but not in practice. In real life the personal and the political, the emotional and the intellectual, are always already—sometimes subtly, sometimes ostentatiously— bound up in one another. Historian Mary Gluck, in *Georg Lukács and His Generation 1900–1918*, understands the rejection of positivism, the social critiques, and the modernist aesthetic crises of Georg Lukács and his friends through a common "psychological condition": the obsession with alienation; the hunger for wholeness; the need to transcend the solitude of the self.[13] In "Did Friedrich Schelling Kill Auguste Böhmer and Does It Matter? The Necessity of Biography in the History of Philosophy," Robert J. Richards provides another illustration of how an emotional-philosophical divide reveals itself to be deceptive. At the very beginning of the nineteenth century, Schelling broke with Johann Gottlieb Fichte's subjective idealism in favor of a "new objective idealism." The shift to a conviction of a reality transcendent of the self, Richards argues, can only be understood in the context of the death of Schelling's lover Caroline's teenage daughter Auguste (with whom Schelling was perhaps in love as well), with Schelling's feelings of both responsibility and helplessness when faced with passion and tragedy.

Aleksander Wat was a Polish avant-garde poet born at the fin-de-siècle who, in the 1920s, renounced futurist poetry and embraced communism. At the end of a tragic life, he told the younger Polish poet Czesław Miłosz that it was one thing for people who came from the working classes and truly knew their misery to be drawn to communism, or for people like Miłosz's friends at the University of Vilnius in the 1930s, who through their battles with increasingly violent nationalist extremists were drawn to communism. For these people, after all, there were some "objective" reasons. There was a certain logic. Wat believed that for himself the decision was a purely personal one, bound up with his psychic state, his emotional proclivities, his longings to anchor himself in the world. "But that was a pure choice," he told Miłosz, "subjective, not especially conditioned by anything outside of my own will, my own outlook, my own attempt to orient myself in the world, my own spiritual needs. Do you understand?"[14] Wat, too, of course, like the workers and the students drawn to communism, lived in a certain social world to whose influence he was not immune. His self-awareness of the inseparability of his own psychic state from his intellectual response to that world highlights a more general fact: namely, the belief that an intellectual realm can be purified from an emotional realm is an illusion—and a kind of hubris.

The Question of Why

The problem of emotional-intellectual disentanglement is related to the problem of causality. "I think it is the job of the historian," Robert J. Richards writes, "not merely to show the development of a series of ideas but to explain them causally, to render those ideas, as best one can, as the absolutely determined outcome of their psychological, social, logical, and natural environments."[15] This is an understandable ambition. Yet for historians, causality—unlike situation in time and space—will always prove elusive; our arguments about causality will always be necessarily speculative and thereby presumptuous. There is no way to do a control study on real life. We cannot go back and replay scene X holding variables A and B constant in order to determine if variable C is the causal one. History is always underdetermined, in the sense that other outcomes were always possible had individuals made different choices. History is at the same time always overdetermined, in the Freudian sense that multiple and potentially overlapping causes are always at play. I would argue for modesty in attributing causation; in its place, we have to fall back on a mandate to capture complexity, nuance, and idiosyncrasy.

And yet—to continue the Kantian analogy—our minds need causation as well as space and time in order to structure reality. We are always working with some implicit assumptions as to what the answer to "why" might be. (We are always doing this in a way reminiscent of Heidegger's hermeneutic circle: we must have, Heidegger points out in the early passages of *Being and Time*, some assumption of what "to be" means in order to be able to pose the question "what is being?" at all.)[16] We are always already engaged in feeling out the boundary between the necessary and the contingent, between the realm of historical determination and the realm of human agency. We must assume contingency, without disregarding the force of historical circumstances. In this way, existentialism, an object of study for intellectual historians, can also itself help us to understand history, and in particular, biography. *Geworfenheit* ("thrownness") and "facticity" suggest that each of us is thrown into a particular time and place, not of our choosing. Within these constraints we then must make choices. To fail to acknowledge either the situational constraints or human freedom would be *mauvaise foi* ("bad faith"), as Sartre understood it.[17]

The "Heidegger Affair" illustrates well that the questions of causality most haunting in intellectual history are the ones that cannot be definitively answered. The empirical contours of Heidegger's engagement with Nazism can be ascertained, but that fails to resolve the more compelling question: what drew Heidegger to Nazism? How determined was his engagement—that is, was his decision to opt for Nazism necessary or contingent?[18] Were the origins of Heidegger's engagement in Nazism always already present in his philosophy itself? If yes, then is all of Heidegger's philosophy—and all of the subsequent thought of those influenced by it—"contaminated"?

Czech philosopher Jan Patočka was among Edmund Husserl's last students and one of his close friends; in 1935 Patočka invited Husserl to Prague after Husserl, as a "non-Aryan" in Nazi Germany, was banned from his own university in Freiburg. Forty years later, responding to Heidegger's posthumously published *Der Spiegel* interview, Patočka expressed empathy for Heidegger's decision in 1933 to become the National Socialist rector of University of Freiburg. Patočka pointed to historical context: to Nazism as a child of the First World War; to the feeling that one of the great European societies was on the threshold of a new epoch; to the understandable desire of philosophers to take part in the reorganization of the world. Of course in 1976 it was clear what Nazism had been. "The question is," Patočka said, "whether that was and could have been clear to a German in 1933. And whether a German in 1933, in certain circumstances, might have had no other choice than to try it out." Heidegger's position in 1933, Patočka argued, was not so different from Husserl's position in 1914: "Husserl himself belonged among the very nationalistic scholars . . . to the 'Griff nach der Weltmacht', Husserl did not say no."[19] Husserl, too, believed that European culture was the culture of philosophy, that it had its own telos, and that philosophy had a special role to play, that it should not stand to the side.

Patočka even wondered whether Husserl himself might have engaged similarly in 1933, had he had such a possibility—that is, were it not for the contingent factor that Husserl was (at least by the National Socialists' definition) a Jew.

An Imaginative Leap

If we can never determine for certain why, what then *can* historians do? "The narrative of the novelist or historian, which follows the historical course of events," Wilhelm Dilthey wrote, "makes us re-experience it." This "re-creating or re-living"—*Nacherleben*—was for Dilthey "the highest form of understanding in which the totality of mental life is active."[20] The task of the intellectual historian, no less so than the political or diplomatic or social historian, it seems to me, remains precisely "*Nacherleben*," which demands an imaginative leap into another time and another place. This means an attempt to achieve full immersion, to write in such a way that the reader—as when reading an engrossing novel or watching an absorbing film—"suspends disbelief" (in the fictional nature of the story). Only in this way do we have a chance to make the impact of ideas—their historical heaviness—felt. The risk is that, otherwise, the weight of the ideas is lost. This imaginative leap involves at least two closely related aspects: first, this involves "bracketing" (analogous to the "bracketing" Husserl called for in the phenomenological reduction, when the phenomenologist does not doubt, but simply suspends his belief in the existence of the world) our knowledge of what came afterward—putting that knowledge aside, as if out of our minds. Second, this imaginative leap involves an immersion in *Zeitgeist* that can only be effected through context—and not merely the context of other texts, but also the social and political, in short, the empirical, historical context. To continue the phenomenological analogy, we face the classical epistemological problem of transcendence: how can we move from the immanent realm to the transcendent realm? Can we ever truly reach the transcendent realm? For historians, the transcendent realm is the past. How can we cross over the boundary, step outside our own lives into the past lives of others?

In 1996 I was working at the University of Toronto on my master's thesis about the Czechoslovak Writers' Union during the Stalinist period. I was trying to understand how Czechoslovak writers constructed a Stalinist idiom and, later, how they extricated themselves from it. At a certain moment I stopped reading the current newspapers—and I stopped reading anything at all that might remind me that I was living in Toronto in 1996. Instead I went to the microfilm room at the university library and read the Czechoslovak daily newspapers from the early 1950s. I wanted to wake up in the morning and put in my head what would have been put there had I been waking up in Stalinist Prague.[21]

This imaginative leap from the present to the past parallels the leap from the immanent subject to the transcendent object. I would draw on an (imperfect) analogy here to the Polish philosopher Leszek Kołakowski's evaluation of Husserl's phenomenology. Kołakowski admired Husserl, but argued that Husserl's project ultimately failed, that epistemological certainty was an impossibility, that the gap between immanence and transcendence could not be overcome. "The problem of the bridge is insoluble," Kołakowski concluded, "there is no logical passage."[22] And yet—Kołakowski insisted—the moral imperative remained: we must continue the search for epistemological certainty, for absolute truth—and this necessarily involved putting outside our minds the impossibility of ever reaching such truth.

A perfect historical imagination is a bit like absolute truth. My time in the microfilm room was an imperfect exercise: I always knew that I was, in fact, living in Toronto in 1996 and not in Prague in 1952. Yet it was not an ineffectual exercise—and I believe it was even, for me, a necessary one. In a certain sense, only once I was "inside" the *Zeitgeist*, once that atmosphere and the attitudes bound up with it became palpable to me, was I able to feel the meaning of my protagonists' linguistic and aesthetic decisions, the weight of them. Related to yet more ineffable than *Zeitgeist* is *Stimmung*, the "mood" of a place and a moment. As historians we need not only to discern, but also to recreate *Stimmung*. "*Stimmung*," contains within itself "*Stimme*," Gumbrecht tells us. He explains that voice plays a critical role: to feel *Stimmung* means to feel the voice of the other wrap itself around you.[23] As writers conjuring up the dead, we must then, as Chekhov insisted, "speak their language." For me this has meant much direct quotation and a certain kind of writing. It has meant softening my own voice to allow the voices of the others of times past to wrap themselves around the reader.

Understanding Lived Experience

Because intellectual history deals with ideas, with the intangible, with what, not being solid, can all the more easily "melt into air," the imperative to render those ideas in a way that the reader truly feels them, imaginatively experiences them, is all the more present.[24] For Husserl, *die Sache selbst*—the true, essential thing—was not the Kantian *Ding-an-sich*, not the object itself, but rather our experience of the object. Similarly, for an intellectual historian the essential thing to capture is not only the ideas themselves, but also the experience of those ideas. Reading history should be not only *Erfahrung*, but also *Erlebnis*; just as the reading done by the protagonists of our histories was not only cognitive experience, but also lived experience. The distinction here is the one

Walter Benjamin articulates between *Erfahrung* as digested and reflected experience, and *Erlebnis* as the immediate, sensuous, unreflected-upon experience.[25] Perhaps it is being an east Europeanist that has given me a particular bias toward *Erlebnis* (although, then again, perhaps not—perhaps this is equally true of intellectuals elsewhere even if not always quite so conspicuously). Isaiah Berlin has written movingly about the fanatical dedication of the Russian intelligentsia to ideas: ideas were to be lived integrally and wholly, with one's entire being. (Russia was unique, Berlin argues, not in its philosophical inventiveness, but in its peculiar responsiveness to philosophy.)[26] Eastern Europe, I would argue, is a place where, at least in the past two hundred years, intellectuals truly lived ideas. Self-consciously they rejected a public-private divide as a bourgeois artifice. Mary Gluck captures well how the distance between subject and object was not simply an epistemological problem Lukács struggled with, but also a distance he truly suffered over.[27] In *The House in the Garden: The Bakunin Family and the Romance of Russian Idealism*, John Randolph portrays Russian Idealism as domestic intimacy—and domestic ordeal, as a romance that "as always . . . ends with Hegel."[28] Hegel was not only something to be learned, but also something to be lived. "I even think," Randolph quotes Alexander Herzen's memoirs, "that a man who has not *lived through* Hegel's *Phenomenology* and Proudhon's *Contradictions of a Political Economy*, who has not passed through that furnace and been tempered by it, is not complete, not modern."[29]

If intellectuals lived ideas, then in order to understand those ideas historically we need to understand the lives of those who lived them. Ilinca Zarifopol-Johnston, in her unfinished, posthumously published biography of the Romanian-turned-French philosopher Emil Cioran, insists on the "need to interpret Cioran's texts in a closer relation to his life than has yet been done: not as direct reflections of the life but as his own interpretations of it."[30] She does more than this: she communes with Cioran. She writes of a teenager frequenting Transylvanian brothels with a copy of Kant's *Critique of Pure Reason* in his pocket; of a macabre obsession with birth; and of the deadly emptiness of Sunday afternoons in provincial Sibiu that prompted epileptic fits. Of course, Zarifopol-Johnston writes with no sarcasm, one can empathize: Sunday afternoons *are* unbearable. She channels Cioran's voice, a voice of metaphysical despair, the author's gentle mediation only partially tempering Cioran's violence.

Yet something renders Zarifopol-Johnston's striving for empathy, which is so essential, somehow "uninnocent": Cioran's youthful sympathy for the fascist Iron Guard. This was a Romanian movement prone not only to virile xenophobia, but also to orgiastic violence. And of course this political engagement is the elephant so often in the room when we talk abstractly about the relationship between ideas and lives, the idealist realm and the empirical realm: the political tends often to dominate the empirical realm of "real life." It forces us to ask a further question: where, then, is the boundary between empathy and apologetics?

Ideas are never pristine. In Peter Gordon's *Continental Divide*, his close reading of the 1929 Davos debate between Ernst Cassirer and Martin Heidegger, the yearning for the pure philosophical idea is like the yearning for the *Ding-an-sich*, a theoretical possibility but a practical impossibility. "Can we restore to philosophy its innocence in the face of historical disruption? While I appreciate the longing," Gordon answers, "the *necessity*, even, for such restoration of original meaning, its prospects seem to be dubious at best."[31] Yet nor can abstract ideas be abridged to their empirical political manifestations. In his hysterical diatribe against Heidegger (or more accurately, against Heidegger's French apologists) Emmanuel Faye makes one simple philosophical argument: namely, once one breaks with the rationalist Cartesian cogito, one is on a slippery slope toward the dissolution of the individual subject, be it in the *Volksgemeinschaft* or in the gas chamber.[32] Faye's argument is clear, but reductionist. As Gordon argues in a review of Faye's book *Heidegger: The Introduction of Nazism into Philosophy in Light of the Unpublished Seminars of 1933–1935*, "Any genuinely philosophical texts are open rather than closed in their interpretative possibilities."[33] To interpret *Being and Time* as nothing more than Nazi ideology lightly disguised by philosophical jargon is to have understood very little about this moment in the history of philosophy. Heidegger was a Nazi, but he was not only a Nazi. The historian's challenge is to work between the two oversimplified positions: we cannot dismiss Heidegger's engagement in Nazism as irrelevant for understanding Heidegger's philosophy, nor can we reduce one to the other. We have to work in the ambivalent space in-between and accept the tension that this involves.

This raises a related question: breaching the gap between idealist and empiricist narrative (between a history of ideas and a history of the "real life" surrounding them) creates an often irresistible temptation to judge, to draw normative, if not moralizing, conclusions from that narrative. Intellectual history by its nature involves a grounding of ideas in time and space. Once we additionally ground ideas in individual lives, we open the question of responsibility. Once we locate ideas in individuals, can we judge the ideas and the individuals separately? Can we separate ideas from acts? Are both Heidegger and his philosophy guilty—or is the guilt only Heidegger's? Does an invocation of "historical context"—such as Jan Patočka's in reference to Heidegger—serve as a mitigating factor for the accused? Can we use biography to illuminate intellectual history without reducing biography to politics—and politics to either condemnation or apologetics? Is this a matter simply of restraint? "To judge a thing that has substance and solid worth is quite easy," Hegel wrote in the preface to *Phenomenology of Spirit*, "to comprehend it is much harder."[34] Above all, the task of the historian is to see what happened, to see in Husserl's meaning-laden sense of *erfassen*, to grasp it, to understand. Understanding (to return to Sartre's existentialism) requires negotiating a continual tension between the realm of "facticity" and the realm of "transcendence," of our power of self-creation. Our obligation is to have enough empathy to understand—and to distinguish this understanding from justifying, or excusing, or forgiving.

Moreover, to (re)call into being *Stimmung* means to forgo some interventionist normativity. (But do—can—we forgo all interventionist normality? All moral judgment? Even in extreme cases, which give evidence to Hegel's observation that changes in scale can become so great as to become changes in kind?) In order to hear that "voice of the Other" the historian has to soften his (or her) own voice—this does not mean to endorse that voice of the Other, but rather only to conjure it up, to give it expression, to allow the reader to hear it. Historians, in Chekhov's spirit, cannot resolve the past, we can neither normalize nor overcome it—in the best case we can only allow our readers to imaginatively experience it.

Guilt

In its Husserlian origins phenomenology was a passionate search for epistemological certainty, grounded in an aspiration to pure *Wissenschaft*. Yet the history of phenomenology has become inextricably entangled with questions of guilt. Heidegger was a Nazi, Cioran a supporter of the Iron Guard, Merleau-Ponty a (qualified) defender of Bolshevik terror, Sartre an apologist for Stalinism. The German existentialist Karl Jaspers's postwar writing described "metaphysical guilt" as survivor's guilt, "the lack of absolute solidarity with a fellow human being."[35] Guilt was a postwar preoccupation of Jaspers's friend Hannah Arendt as well: "For many years now we have met Germans who declare that they are ashamed of being Germans. I have often felt tempted to answer that I am ashamed of being human."[36]

Biography is inextricably bound up with guilt: the guilt of the protagonist and the guilt of the historian—a guilt of a different kind. We read other people's diaries, we read letters never meant for us. Truly seeing the past—the lives of others—is voyeurism. In an uncompleted, probingly self-reflective memoir, Zarifopol-Johnston describes her own presence around Cioran's deathbed: her affection for Cioran and her acquisitiveness, her sadness at his passing and her desire for his diary, a desire that made her feel like a vulture.[37]

In the last chapter of Margaret Atwood's *The Handmaid's Tale*, the gruesome events related in the dystopian novel have long passed. The setting is an academic conference, a gathering of historical scholars. "We must be cautious about passing moral judgment," says the historian presenting a paper about the recently discovered manuscript by "The Handmaid." "Surely we have learned by now that such judgments are of necessity culture-specific." The sentiment is entirely reasonable. Yet this last chapter of Margaret Atwood's novel is very disturbing. The reader is not sympathetic to the historians, despite their scholarly integrity. The combination of voyeurism and restraint from moral judgment feels cold, perhaps even immoral.

How can we temper our impulses to judge without retreating into coldness? Does this require muting our "warmer" responses? Affect, as Tracie Matysik describes, is relevant to historians as a category of analysis applied to our protagonists. Yet it is a relevant category of analysis applied to ourselves as well. As an immediate, prereflective response, an intensity with which we react to certain historical moments, affect is both elemental and elusive, precisely because in order to grasp it we have to reflect upon it, at which point it is no longer itself. Yet it is at the center of what we do.

I was once reading a correspondence from the 1920s between a young Polish poet, Władysław Broniewski, and his fiancée, Janina Kunig. Broniewski was at the time a Polish patriot and a proletarian poet, a socialist and a Romantic, an enormously vain man capable of absolute devotion to a selfless cause. He wrote love letters to Janina Kunig in a grandiloquent language of ecstasy and despair. Then suddenly it emerged from his letters that there was a woman living in another city who was pregnant with his child. Broniewski wanted nothing to do with her, she was being very irritating; he would insist she do away with the pregnancy, his fiancée was not to worry. When he wrote about this woman his language shifted abruptly: the elevated neo-Romanticism vanished and his tone became crude. Reading these letters, I felt a kind of visceral disgust. This was not so much a thoughtful moral condemnation of Broniewski's unfaithfulness to his fiancée or his heartlessness toward the woman pregnant with his child (whom he wrote of as if she had raped him), but rather a visceral disgust at the ugliness of it all. What does a historian do with those feelings? Do they matter? Do they influence how we write (inevitably they do)—and should they? An attempt to make ourselves affectless would involve an undesirable muting of our sensitivity. Yet at the very least we have an obligation of self-awareness, an obligation to interrogate our own initial responses.

Affect bears parallels to the stage of consciousness Hegel describes in *The Phenomenology of Spirit* as "sense-certainty" (*die sinnliche Gewißheit*): a naive, primitive certainty, un-self-aware, outside the realm of reason, seemingly—perhaps deceptively so—unmediated.[38] In *The Phenomenology of Spirit*, sense-certainty (as all the other stages of consciousness) is soon *aufgehoben*, superseded by a higher state of consciousness, yet in such a way (as is always the case for Hegel) that this earlier, more primitive state is not only negated, but also in some way preserved. This is arguably true of historians' affective responses to our material as well: while "sublated," they never entirely disappear. In what form, then, do—should— they remain?

Death, Wholeness, Meaning

For a historian, biography has an aesthetic appeal beyond the guilty pleasure of voyeurism: ideas always go on, while an individual life always comes to an end. Death (as Heidegger, Rosenzweig, and Lukács, each in his own way, tell us) is what gives form and wholeness; for historians it is the only "natural" telos. Hence the attraction to individual lives: an individual life provides a narrative arc; an individual's death is the only non–artificially imposed semblance of narrative closure.

But is any life a whole? "To produce a life history or to consider life a history, that is, as a coherent narrative of a significant and directed sequence of events," Pierre Bourdieu warns in "The Biographical Illusion," "is perhaps to conform to a rhetorical illusion."[39] The warning is one reminiscent of postmodernism's central critique: namely, that there is no grand narrative, no coherent subject, no stable meaning. These are all illusions, for in reality narrative is vulnerable to self-subversion, the subject to diachronic and synchronic inconstancy, meaning to flux.[40]

These inherent vulnerabilities haunted, for instance, Artur Domosławski's biography of the Polish author Ryszard Kapuściński. Having spent decades as a foreign correspondent for communist Poland in the third world, Kapuściński was a literary giant famous for his novelistic reportage. After his death, his biographer became obsessed with Kapuściński's multiple subjectivities, which disturbed Domosławski the way those of a father disturb the son. Kapuściński was not who Domosławski had thought he was. Or rather he was that but also more, and these multiple subjectivities were full of tensions and contradictions: bravery and cowardice, egoism and generosity, conviction and opportunism were disconcertingly all mixed together. Domosławski's biography is unsatisfying not because Kapuściński's life was vulnerable to fragmentation, but rather because Domosławski experiences this (by now rather classical postmodern) revelation as such a personal betrayal that the book is, in the end, as much about the biographer's psychoanalytic journey, the working through of his trauma in confronting these multiple subjectivities, as about the intellectual journey of his subject.[41]

Postmodernism's skepticism toward stable narrative, stable subjectivity, and stable meaning has forced historians to think harder and more critically. Yet in the end, historians cannot be historians without narrative. We can—and should—become ever more self-aware of the problems and entrapments, the necessary distortions and reductions involved in historical narrative. Yet ultimately we differ from literary critics in that the balance between deconstructing and constructing narrative must always, for us, be weighted (even if at moments only very slightly) toward the latter. We tell stories. When we stop telling stories, the practice of history is finished.[42]

Hayden White tells us that historians have an irresistible impulse to bestow coherence on the past. For this reason we are always biased in favor of order; we subliminally edit out what does not fit; we desire a narrative arc.[43] I believe he is right. This raises then the further question: do historians have an irresistible impulse to bestow not only coherence, but also meaning? Bourdieu says yes. The author of a life history, Bourdieu insists, is never disinterested: on the contrary, he always has an interest "in accepting the *postulate of the meaning* of narrated existence." The historian-author wants to deny what Shakespeare tells us in *Macbeth*, that life "is a tale told by an idiot, full of sound and fury, signifying nothing."[44] Death is in some sense our partial remedy to the condition White diagnoses. Death provides wholeness—but does it provide meaning? Or does it merely provide a "teleological temptation"—that is, a temptation to understand earlier events through the perspective of the narrative's ending? In "The Second *Mahābhārata*," Sudipta Kaviraj makes the point that "fiction is teleological in a way that history is not" because in fiction the author can choose the moment of ending. Yet while history itself might not be teleological, the writing of history inescapably leaves us with the same "teleological" feeling as fiction does, for it is difficult, if not impossible, not to read the ending point of a given narration as an implicit telos. And this makes the historian's choice of an ending point never an innocent one.[45]

If we reject the "teleological temptation," does, then, death provide meaning? No, it does not. And perhaps nothing does. In October 1888, several months after Chekhov had written that it was not his job to be the judge of his characters, but only to speak their language, Chekhov explained further to his publisher: "but you are confusing two concepts: the resolving of a question and the correct formulation of a question. Only the second is obligatory for an artist. In *Anna Karenina* and *Eugene Onegin* not a single problem is resolved, but they satisfy you completely, simply because all of the questions are correctly presented."[46]

The questions posed in great novels are questions about meaning. In May 2011 I had a long conversation with my editor about the book manuscript I was completing. My editor was happy with it. It was almost ready, she believed; in the text only one small thing still needed to be clarified.

"What was that?" I wanted to know.

"What does it mean?" she answered.

"What does *what* mean?" I asked her.

"You know, *everything*: life, history. What does it *mean?*"

(An excellent question—to which I did not have an answer.)

If historians then cannot provide answers to the question of meaning, then does history have a moral purpose? In arguing for the importance of *Stimmung* in literature, Gumbrecht writes that *Stimmung* potentially allows the reader an "especially intensive and intimate experience of alterity."[47] "Communing" with minds of the past is a communing with the other, and as such is necessarily personal—even intimate—and so different not only for each historian, but also for each reader. For Husserl and Heidegger's student Emmanuel Levinas encountering the other was an "ultimate" situation, in some sense the deepest experience of one's own subjectivity. This experience of alterity was fundamentally about ethics: "It involves a calling into question of oneself, a critical attitude which is itself produced in face of the other and under his authority."[48] Like Levinas's "face-to-face" encounter with the other, and Shklovsky's poetic *ostranenie*, the writing of good history should disrupt a certain intellectual and emotional complacency. Perhaps, then, while history unto itself has no intrinsic meaning, the *writing* of history does. And that meaning is the cultivation of the ability to make an imaginative leap into the minds and lives of others—that is, the cultivation of empathy itself.[49]

Notes

I am very grateful to Ute Frevert, Hans Ulrich Gumbrecht, Sudipta Kaviraj, Norman Naimark, and Timothy Snyder for their comments on earlier versions of this text, and to the ever-congenial Institut für die Wissenschaften vom Menschen in Vienna, where I wrote this essay.

1. Anton Chekhov to A. S. Suvorin, Moscow, May 30, 1888. А. П. Чехов, *Полное собрание сочинений и писем*, Т. 2. Письма, 1887—сентябрь 1888 (АН СССР: Ин-т мировой лит. им. А. М. Горького.—М.: Наука, 1975), 277–82.

2. The phrase was inspired by René Descartes. Edmund Husserl, *Logical Investigations* vol. 1, trans. J. N. Findlay, ed. Dermot Moran (London: Routledge, 2003), 168; Edmund Husserl, *Logische Untersuchungen I: Prolegomena zur reinen Logik* (Tübingen: Max Niemeyer Verlag, 1993), 6.

3. Viktor Shklovsky, "Art as Device," in *Theory of Prose*, trans. Benjamin Sher (Normal, IL: Dalkey Archive Press, 1990): 1–14, quotation on 6.

4. Husserl, *Logische Untersuchungen I*, 6.

5. Hans Ulrich Gumbrecht, *The Production of Presence: What Meaning Cannot Convey* (Stanford, CA: Stanford University Press, 2004).

6. Charles Taylor, *Sources of the Self: The Making of Modern Identity* (Cambridge, MA: Harvard University Press, 1989).

7. The interplay between the discursive and the empirical—in particular between the conceptual and the social—was central to Reinhart Koselleck's model of *Begriffsgeschichte*. For Koselleck one sphere was not derivative of the other. Rather he emphasized the "live tension between actuality and concept" and maintained that "[a] 'society' and its 'concepts' exist in a relation of tension which is also characteristic of its academic historical disciplines." See "*Begriffsgeschichte* and Social History," chap. 5 of Reinhart Koselleck, *Futures Past: On the Semantics of Historical Time*, trans. Keith Tribe (New York: Columbia University Press, 2004), 75–92, quotations on 76 and 92.

8. Kenneth B. Moss, *Jewish Renaissance in the Russian Revolution* (Cambridge, MA: Harvard University Press, 2009).

9. See Jacques Derrida, "Like the Sound of the Sea Deep within a Shell: Paul de Man's War," *Critical Inquiry* 14, no. 3 (Spring 1988): 590–652, and Derrida, *On Cosmopolitanism and Forgiveness* (New York: Routledge, 2001).

10. See, for example, Edmund Husserl, *Briefe an Roman Ingarden* (The Hague: Martinus Nijhoff, 1968).

11. Edmund Husserl, "The Vienna Lecture," in *The Continental Philosophy Reader*, ed. Richard Kearney and Mara Rainwater (London: Routledge, 1996), 7–14, quotation on 12.

12. See Edmund Husserl, *The Crisis of European Sciences and Transcendental Phenomenology*, trans. David Carr (Evanston, IL: Northwestern University Press, 1970).

13. Mary Gluck, *Georg Lukács and His Generation 1900–1918* (Cambridge, MA: Harvard University Press, 1985).

14. Aleksander Wat, *Mój Wiek. Rozmowy z Czesławem Miłoszem* (London: Polonia Book Fund, 1981), 161.

15. Robert J. Richards, "Did Friedrich Schelling Kill Auguste Böhmer and Does It Matter? The Necessity of Biography in the History of Philosophy," *Biography and Historical Analysis*, ed. Lloyd Ambrosius (Lincoln: University of Nebraska Press, 2004), 133–54, quotation on 135.

16. Martin Heidegger, *Being and Time*, trans. John Macquarrie and Edward Robinson (San Francisco: HarperCollins, 1962), 21–28 (paragraphs 1 and 2).

17. See the chapter "Bad Faith" in Jean-Paul Sartre, *Being and Nothingness*, trans. Hazel E. Barnes (New York: Washington Square Press, 1956), 86–116.

18. In this sense the Heidegger debate can be read as a variation on the much larger intentionalist versus functionalist debate about the Holocaust.

19. Jan Patočka, komentuje rozhovor Martina Heideggera "Už jenom nějaký bůh nás může zachránit," Prague 1978 [*sic*, should be 1976], Jan Patočka Archive, Institut für die Wissenschaften vom Menschen, Vienna, 38, 37.

20. Wilhelm Dilthey, "The Understanding of Other Persons and Their Life-Expressions," in *The Hermeneutics Reader: Texts of the German Tradition from the Enlightenment to the Present*, ed. Kurt Mueller-Vollmer (New York: Continuum, 1998), 152–64, quotation on 159–60.

21. That research became the following article: "Engineering in the Age of Innocence: A Genealogy of Discourse inside the Czechoslovak Writers' Union, 1949–1967," *East European Politics and Societies* 12, no. 3 (Fall 1998): 397–441.

22. Leszek Kolakowski, *Husserl and the Search for Certitude* (South Bend, IN: St. Augustine's Press, 2001), 80.

23. See Hans Ulrich Gumbrecht, *Stimmungen lesen: Über eine verdeckte Wirklichkeit der Literatur* (Munich: Hanser Verlag, 2011).

24. "All that is solid melts into air": Karl Marx and Friedrich Engels, "Manifesto of the Communist Party," in *Modern Europe: Sources and Perspectives from History*, ed. John S. Swanson and Michael S. Melancon (New York: Longman, 2002), 72–88, quotation on 74.

25. Walter Benjamin, "On Some Motifs in Baudelaire," trans. Harry Zohn, in *Illuminations: Essays and Reflections*, ed. Hannah Arendt (New York: Schocken, 1968), 155–200, see esp. 163.

26. Isaiah Berlin, "Russian Intellectual History," *The Power of Ideas*, ed. Henry Hardy (Princeton, NJ: Princeton University Press, 2000), 68–78.

27. Gluck, *Georg Lukács and His Generation*.

28. John Randolph, *The House in the Garden: The Bakunin Family and the Romance of Russian Idealism* (Ithaca, NY: Cornell University Press, 2007), 225.

29. Quoted in Randolph, *House in the Garden*, 4. See also Alexander Herzen, *My Past and Thoughts*, trans. Constance Garnett (Berkeley: University of California Press, 1982), 236.

30. Ilinca Zarifopol-Johnston, *Searching for Cioran*, ed. Kenneth R. Johnston (Bloomington: Indiana University Press, 2009), 13.

31. Peter E. Gordon, *Continental Divide: Heidegger, Cassirer, Davos* (Cambridge, MA: Harvard University Press, 2010), 325.

32. Emmanuel Faye, *Heidegger: The Introduction of Nazism into Philosophy in Light of the Unpublished Seminars of 1933–1935* (New Haven, CT: Yale University Press, 2009).

33. Peter E. Gordon, review of Faye, *Heidegger*, *Notre Dame Philosophical Reviews* 2010 (3); available at http://ndpr.nd.edu/review.cfm?id=19228 (accessed June 25, 2011).

34. G. W. F. Hegel, *Hegel's Phenomenology of Spirit*, trans. A. V. Miller (Oxford: Oxford University Press, 1977), 3.

35. Quoted in Suzanne Kirkbright, *Karl Jaspers: A Biography—Navigations in Truth* (New Haven, CT: Yale University Press, 2004), 196.

36. Hannah Arendt, "Organized Guilt and Collective Responsibility," *The Portable Hannah Arendt*, ed. Peter Baehr (New York: Penguin, 2003), 146–56, quotation on 154.

37. Zarifopol-Johnston, *Searching for Cioran*.

38. Hegel, *Phenomenology of Spirit*, 58–66.

39. Pierre Bourdieu, "The Biographical Illusion," *Identity: A Reader*, ed. Paul de Gay, Jessica Evans, and Peter Redman (London: Sage, 2000), 297–303, quotation on 298.

40. Compare here Husserl's idea that it is precisely the diachronic inconstancy of the "I" that provides us with a model for understanding the other: that is, we understand intersubjectivity through analogy with the past and present "I"s. See Husserl, *Crisis of European Sciences*, esp. 184–86.

41. Artur Domosławski, *Kapuściński: Non-Fiction* (Warsaw: Świat Książki, 2010).

42. This raises the question of whether there can be nondiachronic—that is, synchronic—narrative. See, for instance, Hans Ulricht Gumbrecht, *In 1926: Living at the Edge of Time* (Cambridge, MA: Harvard University Press, 1997).

43. Hayden White, *Tropics of Discourse: Essays in Cultural Criticism* (Baltimore: John Hopkins University Press, 1978).

44. Bourdieu, "Biographical Illusion," 298.

45. Sudipta Kaviraj, "The Second *Mahābhārata*," *South Asian Texts in History: Critical Engagements with Sheldon Pollock*, ed. Yigal Bronner, Whitney Cox, and Lawrence McCrea (Ann Arbor, MI: Association for Asian Studies, 2011), 103–24, quotation on 113.

46. Anton Chekhov to A. S. Suvorin, Moscow, October 27, 1888. А. П. Чехов, *Полное собрание сочинений и писем*, Т. 3. Письма, Октябрь 1888—декабрь 1889 (АН СССР: Ин-т мировой лит. им. А. М. Горького.—М.: Наука, 1976), 45–48.

47. Gumbrecht, *Stimmungen lesen*, 23.

48. Emmanuel Levinas, *Totality and Infinity*, trans. Alphonso Lingis (Pittsburgh: Duquesne University Press, 2007), 81.

49. This is a sentiment I share with Emma Winter, to whom I am grateful for an exchange at the Princeton University workshop "Beyond Concepts and Discourses? Framing Inquiry" in April 2011.

II

The Space of Intellect and the Intellect of Space

John Randolph

"Ubique" was the hopeful motto chosen for the American Geographical Society in 1851; and indeed, 150 years later, space does seem to be "everywhere."[1] This is not just because of the already two- or three-stage "spatial turn" that has been properly announced in multiple scholarly discourses, over the past forty years or so. More important, spatial thinking and practices have become a popular and widespread form of intellectual life. To judge by academic laments, students arrive to classrooms today no more prepared than ever to perform most kinds of textual analysis, pre-, post-, or just plain modern. But they are increasingly likely to have a spatial imagination rooted in Internet and smart-phone technologies such as Google Maps and Facebook.[2] As of 2008, Google Earth had been downloaded 350 million times; and of course that was an eternity ago.[3] If the essay remains a largely academic enterprise, a geographical form of spatial thinking has gone viral, not simply as a set of keywords or concepts, but as a practice.[4]

From one point of view, this recent popularity of geography may not seem relevant to the topic of this essay: namely, the utility and importance of spatial analysis for intellectual history. I certainly don't intend to argue that *actualité* demands scholars turn their attention to space. Instead, I hope to ask: How important were spatial concepts to the foundation of intellectual history in the early twentieth century? What role did spatial questions play in cultural-historical challenges to intellectual history in the 1980s and 1990s? What might the more definitive "reassertion of space"[5] of the past decade—and the rise of "geo-humanistic" digital technologies such as HGIS (historical geographic information systems)—mean for intellectual histories to come? Nonetheless, I mention the recent explosion of geographic genres to flag a different sort of question, to which I hope to return at the end. On what terms might intellectual historians enter the new modes of intellectual activity being born with the mass proliferation of spatial technology: a world in which visualizations (most notably, maps) are more native than texts?

We might begin by recalling that when intellectual history was first articulated as a scholarly project in the early twentieth century, the category "space" was surrounded by controversies far more profound than our own.[6] The Theory of Relativity had just prompted physicists to declare traditional distinctions between time and space exploded, alongside universal notions of scale or chronology. "Henceforth space by itself, and time by itself, are doomed to fade away into mere shadows," Hermann Minkowski announced to his fellow physicists in 1908, "and only a kind of union of the two will preserve an independent reality."[7] As others perceived, this called into question not only the Newtonian vision of a single, continuous, "absolute" space, but also the Cartesian distinction between space and thought, *res extensa* and *res cogitans*, that had long governed scientific investigation. In 1929, the philosopher Alfred North Whitehead argued that the analysis of "relatedness" of things must now take precedence over that of their unique "quality"; his contemporary Herbert Wildon Carr claimed "concrete Nature is not matter but movement, and concrete mind is not contemplation, but activity." With universal scales and common geometries collapsing before Theory, it seemed, there could be no pure space and no pure mind, but rather a spatialized intellect akin to the new space-time, for which he chose Leibniz's monads as emblem.[8]

These physical and philosophical debates were accompanied by an emerging conceptual detachment between space and social phenomena in other forms of intellectual life. This "subordination of space in social theory," as Edward W. Soja calls it, has been variously explained by scholars, since it first began to be critiqued in the late 1960s.[9] In his account, Soja accuses late nineteenth-century obsessions with time—alongside capitalism's ambitions to conceal its rearrangement of space—of fostering this division. One might also cite a growing sense that geographical determinism—a beloved scholarly paradigm—had finally played itself out, even as the Newtonian universe on which it stood was being detonated.[10] In any event, the field of "social space," as a distinct, nongeographical field of inquiry, came to the fore. "Social space is something quite different from geometrical space," Pitirim Sorokin emphasized in his paradigmatic classic, *Social Mobility* (1927): "Social space is a kind of universe composed of the human population of the earth."[11] Instead of studying humanity in the "everywhere" of geographical societies, Sorokin proposed to study it in the manmade geometry of its social relations.[12]

An unexpected corollary of this calving away of "social space" from its New-tonian counterpart was a tendency to also detach the study of movement from that of social "mobility." In the end, Sorokin paid as little attention to physical movement as to physical location, failing to attribute to geographical mobility any great significance for the "vertical" social mobility that was his prime concern.[13] This deepened the detachment of social from geographical space by excluding motion as well as location. "Much of the social mobility literature regarded society as a uniform surface and failed to register the geographical intersections of region, city and place, with the social categories of class, gender and ethnicity," comments John Urry, a leading theoretician of "mobility studies" today.[14] Indeed, we may say that many current questions about both space and movement stem from this paradoxical intellectual moment, when the emergence of space-time in philosophy and the physical sciences helped loosen the bonds between the two in the social.[15]

There were, of course, important exceptions. Both spatial analysis and mobility studies draw inspiration from the social philosopher Georg Simmel (1858–1918), for whom movement possessed a defining significance. In *his* sociology of space, rooted in the study of relations, Simmel contended that "humanity in general only gains the existence that we know through mobility." People must move to live, Simmel observes; yet this "miracle of the road," as he calls it, contains within it a continual, dialogical process that reshapes the space so crossed. A bridge establishing a connection between two points must stand on moorings that simultaneously fix and define their division; likewise, a door separates realms that in another sense it connects. As a result, human life and with it human intellect reside within a giant technological edifice of their own invention: a landscape of starts and stops, anchors and thoroughfares, limitations and freedoms, all defined not by abstract location but by the relational geographies created by constant processes of separation and connection.[16]

The decades that surrounded the formation of intellectual history, then, contained a variety of speculations about the future meaning of space for mind: from a detachment into social abstraction, to a renewed interest in Leibnizian monads, to a vision in which mind forms through spatial extension, and the technologies developed to enable it.

Rereading some of the classics from the early days of intellectual history against this backdrop, it is clear they share a creative interest in—and uncertainty about—possible new conceptions of space. On the one hand, spatial metaphors are both plentiful and foundational to the field's conception. Arthur Lovejoy presents the historian of ideas as a mental geographer of sorts, whose fundamental task is to trace an idea "through more than one—and ultimately indeed through all—of the provinces of history in which it figures in any important degree—whether those provinces are called philosophy, science, literature, art, religion or politics." Yet even as he embraces the relativistic idea of a plenitude of possible historical spaces for exploration, Lovejoy leaves the question of how these "provinces" connect hanging without much theoretical comment.[17] His "unit idea" seems to serve as both the maker and the marker of relation across time—that is, it somehow both establishes and represents an interaction between "provinces." Without explaining how this is so, it seems, Lovejoy joins Sorokin in selecting spatial relations out, to focus on more simply on absolute shifts in cultural location. The result is a kind of intellectual geometry—the positioning of ideas in abstract social or cultural fields—rather than intellectual geography: leaving what that latter expression might mean as yet unclear.[18]

One profoundly influential answer to this question was provided, of course, by Lovejoy's contemporary, Daniel Mornet, with his *Les origines intellectuelles de la Révolution française, 1715–1787*.[19] Mornet's ambition in describing the "intellectual origins of the French Revolution"—rather than the history of individual "revolutionary ideas"—was to understand the "diffusion" of radical concepts across different regions of French society.[20] Such a geographical vision was no doubt partly encouraged by the geographical orientation of French historical science, beginning in the late nineteenth century.[21]

That said, Mornet focused on the placing of ideas within institutional and sociological locations: academies, journals, and salons, on the one hand, and "high," "middle," and "popular" milieux, on the other. As a result, his intellectual vision again seems more geometrical than geographical, more fixed on the position of mental processes within an abstract mapping of society than on their communicative production within physical space-time. While his method of plotting the "diffusion" of radical concepts within sociological and institutional spaces succeeded in decentering the role of the eighteenth century's famous "maîtres de l'esprit," it had much less to say about the questions of relationship, process, and communication that are at the heart of spatial analysis today.

Depending on how one defines it, the "spatial turn" has by now occurred so many times and in so many disparate ways in different fields that it seems best to abandon the term altogether, and adopt (more simply) Soja's phrase, "the reassertion of space."[22] One of this phrase's virtues is that it helps remind us that space never went away (though its position within American academia long remained unclear).[23] Perhaps even better, letting go of the idea of a single "spatial turn" also allows us to capture the multifaceted and sometimes self-contradictory nature of this process, which drew inspiration from competing strands of humanist, critical-Marxist, and postmodern geography, as well as from emerging digital technologies, such as Geographic Information Systems, or GIS.[24]

Most generally speaking, as Derek Gregory and John Urry have observed, renewed calls for attention to space achieved prominence in academic thought in the late 1960s and early 1970s, "on the marchlands between human geography and sociology."[25] Historians who embrace the notion of a "spatial turn" tend to credit either poststructuralist philosophical texts or critical Marxist geography with making it (citing, most typically, Henri Lefebvre's 1974 *The Production of Space* on the one hand, and the British geographer David Harvey's numerous studies on the other).[26] But one could make a good case that humanistic or even computational approaches shook up the realm of spatial analysis first, at least within geography.[27] As has already been mentioned, scholars often look to Whitehead's process philosophy or Simmel's connective sociology as precedents. Within the field of geography itself, one should mention John K. Wright's "Terrae Incognitae: The Place of the Imagination in Geography" (1947). Here, Wright tried to turn geographers' attention away from attempts to expand the one "known world," and to get them to chart the innumerable "worlds as known," by individuals and communities, across space and time.[28]

By the early 1960s, meanwhile, considerable strides had been made in the application of the first computers to problems of spatial analysis. Starting in 1960, the Canada Geographic Information System was developed by the Canadian government to store, analyze, and visualize geospatial data, resulting in what has been called the first "industry-scale computer-based GIS." The phrase "geographic information system" emerged thereafter, as a descriptor of this layered approach to relating spatial shapes (points, lines, and polygons, as drawn on a defined map) to other forms of quantitative and qualitative data.[29] While the continued development of this technology—whose concepts and uses will be discussed more fully below—sparked accusations that it marked an unreconstructed return to positivistic, "absolute" space (a controversy that has by no means fully died), GIS's undoubted utility for governance, commerce, and war helped drive its rapid development up until the early 2000s, when the Internet helped make it truly ubiquitous.[30]

Over the long term, these humanistic and computational approaches to space have become popular, if somewhat opposing, strands in recent geographical thought. Scholarship outside geography, however, was more immediately affected by postmodern and critical-Marxist thinkers interested in space, such as Lefebvre and Harvey. Both are credited with turning scholars' attention to the social construction of space. Inspired by the Marxist tradition, both see the production of space as a crucial realm of political activity, with forms of capitalist domination and with them inequality being indelibly written into the landscape in which we live. Yet despite being united by their critical desire to reveal how social power is made and unmade in the creation of space, they define this central concept rather differently, as David Harvey has recently observed.

Lefebvre presents his study of *The Production of Space* as the recovery of an inherently living, social artifact from the clutches of abstract mathematics. "Not so many years ago, the word 'space' had a strictly geometrical meaning," Lefebvre claims: "To speak of 'social space,' therefore, would have sounded strange."[31] He proposes to rectify this situation by identifying three different processes, that together create this "social space": *spatial practice* (the modes of production and reproduction that make "the particular locations and spatial sets characteristic of each social formation"); *representations of space* ("conceptualised space," as by scientists, planners, and so on); and *representational spaces* (space "as directly lived through its associated images and symbols").[32]

Respectful of Lefebvre's description of the various processes by which society produces relationships in space, Harvey nonetheless has recently urged scholars to consider—without confusing—at least three different definitions of space itself. We might, varyingly, think of space as an *absolute* phenomenon (that is, as referring to set locations in a fixed, Newtonian universe); as a *relative* one (whose locations shift within the variable geometries of Einsteinian space-time); or as a more *relational* concept, internal to subjective consciousness itself. (In this last understanding, processes internal to consciousness gradually produce reflective geographies, out of the web of past, present, and anticipated future experiences. From this point of view processes do not take place *in* space at all, Harvey comments, for "the concept of space is embedded in or internal to process," as in the lives of Leibniz's monads.)

Thus, to take Harvey's example, a Lefebvrian "spatial practice" might take the form of a physical door in *absolute* space; the way new transport systems affect position in *relative* space; and the affect of sudden shifts in sensory experience (smells, sounds, sights) on the lived cosmology of *relational* space. Denying that there is an ultimate philosophical solution as to whether space should be conceived solely in any of these terms (absolute, relative, or relational), Harvey posits that the utility of each meaning (both for life and for scholarship) depends upon the "nature of the phenomena under investigation." To take another of his examples, the whole point of property is to create divisions in absolute space, and thus an absolute approach may help explore it. The same approach, applied to the analysis of the cultural power of Sacré-Coeur or Tiananmen Square, might in itself say little about practice, conceptions, or experience (to recur in rough form to Lefebvre's triad).[33] Here the extension of research into other definitions of space would seem necessary.

All of these strands of spatial scholarship were in rapid development in the 1970s and 1980s, but to judge from the widespread perception that "the spatial turn" is just now happening in history, one might imagine the concept found little response among historians.[34] Offering a few hypotheses as to why may help set the stage for considering current and future attempts to "spatialize" intellectual history.

The first thing, perhaps, that needs to be said is that the philosophical and geographical texts commonly perceived as marking the beginnings of a "spatial turn" in scholarship could with some justice be seen, at least initially, as simply catching up with history's traditional concern for the social dimensions of human experience—that is, other disciplines were taking a "social" turn history had already made. Lefebvre's accusation that scholarship had previously been concerned with physical rather than "social space" does not seem to apply to the founding era of intellectual history discussed earlier. To be sure, the emerging sociocultural critique of intellectual history argued that Lovejoy's history was too displaced from social reality to have much descriptive or analytical power.[35] Even as he built from the tradition Mornet established, Robert Darnton argued (in 1971) for the need to situate "the Enlightenment within the actualities of eighteenth-century society."[36] Yet these criticisms were not primarily aimed at spatial or geographical lacunae in intellectual historical works, at least not yet. As Lynn Hunt has noted, by the 1970s, even among the *Annales* school—deeply influenced by geography and the home of Fernand Braudel's call for truly large-scale *géohistoire*—the "geographical dimension, though present, appeared only as a kind of formula at the beginning of each study, not as a guiding spirit."[37]

Rather, the advent of social-, sociocultural, and eventually textual and pragmatic critiques of intellectual history centered on the social part of "social space." In retrospect, this seems to be one of the few things that holds the so-called cultural turn (in reality containing heterogeneous sociological, hermeneutic, discursive, psychoanalytic, material, and technique-driven components) together.[38] Take, for example, the debate about contextualization—and more specifically, how one should contextualize—that is one of the major running threads, linking various strands of cultural criticism together (even in debate) over the last several decades. In almost every case—Geertzian "deep reading"; Foucauldian discursive analysis; Skinnerian analyzes of intention; cultural semiotics (such as that practiced by the Soviet scholar Iurii Lotman); Lacanian analysis—the space being analyzed is sociotextual in nature, the system of communicative statements as they relate to the operations of power and meaning within human community, often implicitly imagined on an epochal or societywide scale.[39]

To point this out, of course, is not to denigrate the lasting importance of cultural contextualization for intellectual history; nor, indeed, is it even necessarily to criticize the "cultural turn" for failing to pay attention to space. Indeed, many aspects of the "spatial turn" (as conceptualized by humanist geographers, the philosophical and geographical traditions represented by Lefebvre and Harvey, or even as tabularized and visualized by GIS technologies) can be seen as existing with the daily practice of historians at the time. Local and microhistories such as Le Roy Ladurie's *Montaillou* and Carlo Ginzburg's *Cheese and the Worms* provide striking portraits of the meaning of place and the creation of cosmologies; William Cronon's *Nature's Metropolis* situates American geographical consciousness within the new relative spaces created by railroad development and commodity exchange; the tradition of book history sponsored by Darnton and Chartier has been more relentlessly geographic than any other in thinking about the realm of culture, in its attention to the geographies ordering the production, distribution, and consumption of books.[40]

Even so, the question for intellectual history going forward would seem to be twofold.[41] First, on what grounds, and to what extent, should space be considered not just a subcategory of social context, but a topic or method worth prioritization in its own right? Second, what benefit can intellectual history get from it?

Perhaps one place to begin this evaluation is with the critiques of traditional historical procedures mounted by Soja, Lefebvre, and Harvey. In Soja's opinion, the failure of modern scholarship to maintain a proper, dialectical sense of the relationship between time and space has allowed history to be instrumentalized in the name of political oppression. He believes that historical explanations that focus too heavily on time and social being as the active variables tend to either ignore or obscure the spatial dimension of human experience, and in so doing help reify inequality and injustice as mere features of the landscape.[42] Harvey has contended that an all-too-easy sense of the "social construction of space" often amounts to the same thing. Even as scholars casually speak of a dialectical relationship between space and society—and of a world in which these two spheres constitute and are constituted by each other—the failure to pay close attention to space often results in "a much more prosaic presentation in which social relations occur *within* some pre-constituted and static framework."[43] Thus for Harvey, as for Soja, paying attention to space is an important counterweight to history's rationalizing tendencies. To place space (absolute, relative, or relational) alongside time serves to highlight a whole new realm of causes, contingencies, and consequences that might otherwise be obscured.

In *The Production of Space*, Lefebvre advances a similar argument about the ideological obscurantism encouraged by a failure to pay attention to space.[44]

(Indeed, his account inspired both Harvey and Soja.) But he also identifies space itself as a kind of sociocultural artifact: "The spatial practice of a society is revealed through the deciphering of its space."[45] Thus, in addition to stressing their value as a context for existing intellectual canons, Lefebvre argues that spatial relations can themselves be read as kind of intellectual corpus, one that has yet to be systematically studied, published, or analyzed, but that should occupy a substantial place in our histories of the mental world.

How guilty is intellectual history before these allegations of bias and omission? Perhaps the most robust case to use to consider this issue is Enlightenment historiography, transnational in geographical conception from its earliest incarnations and long inspired, in turn, by Mornet's project of tracing the "diffusion" of *philosophie* in (social) space.[46] In *Enlightenment Contested: Philosophy, Modernity and the Emancipation of Man, 1670–1752*, Jonathan Israel has argued that despite these commitments, Enlightenment historiography remains bedeviled by a persistent national bias; and that furthermore the "cultural sociology" of Mornet's "diffusionism" has exhausted itself. On the one hand, Israel argues, the "diffusionist" approach encourages the sort of abstract vision of intellectual life for which Lovejoy's history of "unit ideas" has long been criticized, in which ideas float from place to place in a manner seemingly unrelated to the evolution of larger social structures.

On the other hand, in Israel's view, such an approach promotes the notion that the real mental life of the past is represented less by conscious arguments and interventions and more by deep, socially driven changes in attitudes and mentalities.[47] The end effect, in Israel's view, is to assign ideas too *little* importance in the life of humanity, as consciousness becomes utterly structural in nature. To replace both this "cultural sociology" and the traditional history of ideas, Israel proposes a new "controversialist" approach. By this, he means the study of great debates or "controversies" as they are registered across a large bed of sources, from the complete texts and systems that have long been intellectual historians' purview, to critical philosophy as it expresses itself across the whole of human life, from legal and scientific discourses to "popular protests and interventions." By recognizing that such large "controversies took place and provide masses of evidence," Israel argues, his "'controversialist' approach" will allow for a truly transnational intellectual portrait, tracing "public events" that "occurred everywhere in the western Atlantic world throughout the Enlightenment era."[48]

Will an attention to controversies, as opposed to the cultural-sociological "diffusion" of texts or ideas, cure the persistent national-areal biases or structuralist assumptions about the position of ideas in life Israel has identified? From a strictly spatial point of view, there would seem to be questions. Israel's immensely learned reconstruction of critical controversies, even as it moves "up" and "down" the social scale fluidly and from one end of the greater European world to another, seems to have little rigorous concept of how the sites of controversy and the communication between them are formed. To be sure, he can and does draw on "diffusionist" studies—as well as his own formidable investigations of early modern economy—to argue about the *social* breadth of changes in attitude, or to invoke the likely influence of migrations and diasporic communities on the spread of Enlightenment. In the end, however, he seems content to situate his "controversialist" approach within the social geometry generated by "cultural sociology," whose notions of causation he criticizes, but whose analysis of the social dimensions of Enlightenment he finds impressive (as it no doubt is).[49]

Yet can this controversialist approach be made to account for the way, as Philip Ethington observes, in which human action both *"takes* and *makes* place"?[50] By this Ethington means that events create locations in space-time, rather than simply being phenomena diffused or distributed across the surface of absolute geography. How did early modern intellectual activity—whether conceived of as the flow of ideas, or as the expression of broad communicative controversies—participate in the creation of eighteenth-century spaces, whether understood in absolute, relative, relational, or (ultimately) archival terms?[51]

In his work on "placing the Enlightenment," Charles W. J. Withers argues that consideration of "place as social practice and of placing as a process" may help explain the "uneven movement of ideas over space."[52] To recur to the insights of Lefebvre and Wright, one might equally productively turn this statement around: the study of the geography of mental life—in the motion of its shifting rearrangement—may have a lot to say not only about the landscape of meaning, but of the operations of power and society in time. From this point of view, it would seem less important whether the object of study is "ideas" or "controversies." Ultimately our choice of which object to trace as a way of following the production of space-time in its absolute, relative, or relational dimensions would seem to depend on the phenomenon we wish to study, rather than on the absolute nature of mental processes, abstractly conceived. In his essay for this collection, for example, Antoine Lilti argues for attention to the circulation of intellectual tools or epistemes, while John Tresch and D. Graham Burnett, from within the history of science, stress the distribution of physical artifacts and site- or institution-based forms of life.[53]

Regardless of tracing element, in the end, as Richard White has observed in his recent essay, "What Is Spatial History?," the most direct means to observe phenomena and examine their relation to the production of space is through the study of motion. This procedure has an additional advantage in that it encompasses the whole of the natural world:

> We produce and reproduce space through our movements and the goods that we ship and the information we exchange. Other species also produce space through their movements. Spatial relations are established through the movement of people, plants, animals, goods, and information.[54]

Thus, we move from the geographies of points in isolated space to the geography of the flows and scapes that connect them, not least (as in Wright's "geosophy") through the study of how these scapes are known and practiced.

Yet studying motion across historical space-time is considerably more difficult than plotting the position or distribution of events across a snapshot of absolute, Cartesian space. Part of the problem lies in the source base. Just as we can reconstruct the movements of ordinary French people only through the rather gloomy records provided by their births and their deaths (rather than any systematic recordings of the paths they crossed in life, plotted across any kind of coordinates), so too the tracks of intellectual processes can be hard to discover and analyze.[55]

Here is where increasingly large-scale efforts are being made to develop historically useful forms of GIS, in an effort to track movement and "place" history.[56] At its heart, GIS rests on databases that relate qualitative or quantitative "attribute" data to locations on a user-specified map grid (which itself may be absolute [Cartesian] or relative in nature). Typically developed from the metadata produced as textual corpuses are being digitized, such databases can then be used to conduct spatial queries. Where did an artifact circulate in 1767? What were the further relations of people who had contact with it? What was the radius of invocations of a given topic, or the nature of the social network (mapped in relative space) of the people who entertained it? Perhaps just as important, these relations can then be visualized in digital form, and animated diachronically to create a sense of temporal process.

Thus, for example, the "Circulation of Knowledge and Learned Practices in the 17th Century Dutch Republic" project, funded by the Netherlands Organization for Scientific Research (NWO), aims to gain "insight into the transfer of knowledge between 17th century scholars via their correspondence." Building from a database of some 20,000 letters exchanged by Dutch scholars, they have created a web application (called ePistolarium) that allows scholars to layer geographical and social-network analysis, to reveal both the absolute and the relative dimensions of how knowledge circulated in this early "information society."[57] Working from metadata provided by the

Electronic Enlightenment Project—a vast collection of correspondence curated by Oxford University—historians at Stanford University's "Mapping the Republic of Letters" are creating similar visualization tools, in an attempt to identify and analyze the correspondence networks in which intellectual activity was situated, in the eighteenth century. What can we learn about such commonplaces of Enlightenment life as the Grand Tour or the opinions of Voltaire, if we can use digital technology to improve our ability to see and represent their spatial dimensions?[58]

During their advent in geography, GIS technologies caused great controversy, centered on the question of whether the analyses and visualizations they generated marked a heuristic advance, or simply a powerful recursion, in technological dress, of imperious, absolute conceptions of space. These controversies seem sure to repeat in history, as most scholars engaged in this field admit.[59] Most obviously, historical data rarely conform to either the standards or the categories employed by modern digital databases; creating visualizations that distort more than they illuminate is a constant danger for historians.[60] More subtly, as Richard White has observed, "GIS often ends up emphasizing not the constructedness of space but rather its given-ness, which is fine if you are setting out to bomb something or go out to eat, but not so good if you are trying to understand a wider spectrum of human constructions of space over time."[61]

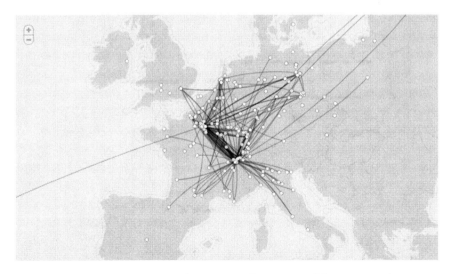

FIGURE II.I. Voltaire's Correspondence Network, courtesy of the Mapping the Republic of Letters Project, based on data from the Electronic Enlightenment Project at the University of Oxford.
Source: http://republicofletters.stanford.edu/tools/, accessed December 4, 2012.

How can we learn to visualize the production of various kinds of historical space—the "placing," say, of the Enlightenment, to use Charles Withers's terms—in a suitably open-ended, transparent, and heuristically flexible way? Confronting this dilemma will no doubt require both interpretive imagination and technological innovation, as historians feel their way into the realm of data visualization in the years to come.

In this essay, I have tried to sketch some points of contact between intellectual history and the analysis of space, across the past century. To put my hypothesis, for the moment, in David Harvey's terms, I would say that intellectual history has always been alive to the idea of relative space—of mapping intellectual productions within the "provinces" of socially constituted fields of expression—but that its very strength in this dimension left it weak on questions of absolute (physical) location, as well as on questions of relational geography (the meaning of mental life within the cosmology arising around a place, and the swirl of imagined pasts, presents, and futures that are reflected in it). The best way, perhaps, to rectify this situation is to bring, more fully, the production of space into intellectual historical scholarship, not least through the study of movement and the processes that sustain it. Whether this can best happen through the sort of massive, database-driven, and digitally realized visualizations produced by GIS—or whether it will depend on more traditional techniques of research and narration—remains to be seen.

Left hanging, however, so far, are two questions of great importance that I'd like to consider in closing. First, is spatial analysis—however pursued—simply a form of contextualization (when it comes to discussing the interpretation of human intellectual activity), or is it itself a form of interpretation? It is no doubt interesting, for example, to think about the geography of Kant's famous essay, "What Is Enlightenment?," as it has progressed across and created landscapes as varied as the Berlin Wednesday Society, or your average American college commencement speech. From this point of view, Kant can be used as a tracer for larger questions about the production of power, society, and indeed space itself. But what about the human activity of reading—or attempting to understand—Kant's ideas themselves? Does this form of analysis simply become another way to avoid thinking about the intellectual component of intellectual history, in favor of becoming social, political, or spatial historians, under another name?

It seems to me this question can be approached from two angles. The first is to say, yes, spatial analysis can of course be construed simply as a new backdrop for interpreting the history of thought as represented by a range of artifacts, including the complex philosophical systems that no doubt retain a great deal to tell us about how people have tried to grapple with the problems of existence, over time. Whether space can serve as a sharpening context in a Skinnerian or other sense—that is, whether it can help us sharpen our understanding of original meaning or impact—depends a lot on what aspect of the text we wish to understand. As Franco Moretti has recently remarked, "Geography is a useful tool, but it does not explain *everything*. For that we have astrology and 'Theory'"— and, we may add less sarcastically, other modes of interpretation, some intuitive, some abstract, through which we always produce understandings.[62]

It seems important, however, to remember that space is itself not simply a container for human action, but also an artifact of human existence: not simply a "context" for textual interpretation, but a mode of intellectual production deserving of interpretation in its own right. Though the fugitive worlds of geosophy—the worlds as known by peoples and communities of the past—are often hard to find (as poorly recorded in or even purposefully erased from historical records) and even harder to understand (as related to practices and ambitions now likewise obscure), they would seem to have tremendous philosophical importance to us today. Thus it may well be that spaces may need to join the list of complex artifacts, whose job it is for intellectual history to help recognize and interpret. (This has, indeed, happened in the realm of the history of cartography, but could well be extended beyond official and scientific settings.)[63]

Last there is the question of genre. Many of the projects currently under way in the realm of GIS have as their main final product the goal of producing open-ended resources that others can use to study and create history. For now, it seems, the working assumption seems to be that we are in an age of electronic interactive edition—that is, a new generation of historians is engaging in the kind of foundational work in creating scholarly resources that began, in the textual realm, with Gutenberg. The question, however, becomes whether, and at what stage, a map or visualization itself becomes the main genre for historical interpretation and narration. Will an interactive graphic of "Enlightenment" in space ever take the place of an essay about it? One thinks that not only will it, to a certain extent, it already has, if not inevitably and for all purposes. Even two-dimensional pictures seem to tell us a lot "at a glance," and animations are beginning to give them the narrative depth and chronological sequencing that has been the traditional advantage of text. So the question then becomes, what are the standards for visualizing intellectual history—in space or in any other terms—and how should such visual interpretation be evaluated? What are its signal advantages, and what are its signal dangers? Such questions arise naturally when thinking about the spatial dimension of intellectual history; but they also transcend it to be something the field as a whole needs to confront, as mapping continues to go global as a form of intellectual life.

Notes

1. For discussion of the AGS emblem, see Helena Michie and Ronald R. Thomas, "Introduction," to *Nineteenth-Century Geographies: The Transformation of Space from the Victorian Age to the American Century* (New Brunswick, NJ: Rutgers University Press, 2003), 5–6.

2. On recent rises in "spatial IQ"—as measured by standardized testing—and the plateauing of equivalent textual scores, see Nicholas G. Carr, *The Shallows: What the Internet Is Doing to Our Brains* (New York: Norton, 2010).

3. For the 2008 data on Google Earth, see Chikai Ohazama, "Truly Global," *Lat Long Blog*, February 11, 2008, http://google-latlong.blogspot.com/2008/02/truly-global.html (accessed July 14, 2013).

4. In the corporate and military spheres, of course, GIS (geographical information system) usage was already a boom industry by the early 1990s, a fact that encouraged similar reckonings within the field of geography: see John Pickles, "Representations in an Electronic Age: Geography, GIS and Democracy," in *Ground Truth: The Social Implications of Geographic Information Systems*, ed. Pickles (New York: Guilford Press, 1995), 1–30.

5. The phrase is Edward W. Soja's; I'll return to it below: Edward W. Soja, *Postmodern Geographies: The Reassertion of Space in Critical Social Theory* (London: Verso, 1989).

6. For recent histories of intellectual history, see Anthony Grafton, "The History of Ideas: Precept and Practice, 1950–2000 and Beyond," *Journal of the History of Ideas* 67, no. 1 (January 2006): 1–32; Donald R. Kelley, *The Descent of Ideas: The History of Intellectual History* (Burlington, VT: Ashgate, 2002). Although Donald Kelley's work situates this tradition in a much deeper perspective, in this essay I will work only from the academic formalization of this subdiscipline in the early twentieth century.

7. H. Minkowski, "Space and Time," in *The Principle of Relativity*, by A. Einstein et al., trans. W. Perrett and G. B. Jeffery (n.p.: Dover, 1923), 75.

8. Alfred Whitehead, *Process and Reality: An Essay in Cosmology* (New York: Macmillan, 1929), ix; H. Wildon Carr, *A Theory of Monads: Outlines of the Philosophy of the Principle of Relativity* (London: Macmillan, 1922), 8, 11–12. Whether this is a correct or useful reading of the physics of space-time, of course, was disputed then and since: see D'Arcy Wentworth Thompson, *On Growth and Form* (Cambridge: The University Press, 1942), 20; W. H. Newton Smith, "Space, Time and Space-time: A Philosopher's View," in *The Nature of Time*, ed. Raymond Flood and Michael Lockwood (Cambridge, MA: Basil Blackwell, 1986), 22–35.

9. For a general discussion, see Soja, *Postmodern Geographies*, 31–35. For touchstone critiques of the gap between space and social theory, see Michel Foucault, "Questions on Geography," in *Power/Knowledge: Selected Interviews and Other Writings, 1972–1977*, ed. Colin Gordon, trans. Colin Gordon (Brighton, UK: Harvester, 1980), 70; Henri Lefebvre, *The Production of Space*, trans. Donald Nicholson-Smith (Malden, MA: Blackwell, 1991); Anthony Giddens, *The Constitution of Society: Outline of the Theory of Structuration* (Berkeley: University of California

Press, 1984), 355, 363; Allan Pred, *Making Histories and Constructing Human Geographies: The Local Transformation of Practice, Power Relations, and Consciousness* (Boulder, CO: Westview, 1990), 1–2; Doreen Massey, "New Directions in Space," in *Social Relations and Spatial Structures*, ed. Derek Gregory and John Urry (London: Macmillan, 1985), 9–19.

10. Geography was undoubtedly a powerful social discourse in nineteenth-century life, routinely invoked to explain other phenomena (as in the national-areal constructions of nineteenth-century nationalism). The nineteenth century was also the founding era of innumerable geographical societies. See Helena Michie and Ronald R. Thomas, eds., *Nineteenth-Century Geographies: The Transformation of Space from the Victorian Age to the American Century* (New Brunswick, NJ: Rutgers University Press, 2003); J. B. Harley, "The Map and the Development of Cartography," in *The History of Cartography*, ed. J. B. Harley and David Woodward, vol. 1 (Chicago: University of Chicago Press, 1987), 14; Paul J. Cloke, Chris Philo, and David Sadler, *Approaching Human Geography: An Introduction to Contemporary Theoretical Debates* (New York: Guilford Press, 1991), 3–8; R. J Johnston and J. D. Sidaway, *Geography and Geographers: Anglo-American Human Geography since 1945*, 6th ed. (London: Arnold, 2004).

11. Pitirim Sorokin, *Social Mobility* (New York: Harper and Brothers, 1927), 3–4. Emphasis in the original.

12. In a preface to Sorokin's work, his colleague F. Stuart Chapin praised Sorokin for turning the page from physical distribution: "Present interest in the diffusion of culture has tended to withdraw attention from an equally important social process, namely, that of vertical social mobility." F. Stuart Chapin, "Editor's Introduction," to Sorokin, *Social Mobility*, viii. On the overdetermined locationism of nineteenth-century thought more broadly, see Michie and Thomas, "Introduction."

13. Sorokin, *Social Mobility*, ix, 133–215, 381–492. Emphasis in the original. Among the many channels for "vertical" social mobility in Sorokin's work—the army, the church, the family, professional organizations—physical movement through space is not ranked or thematized, beyond the opening acknowledgment that it is pervasive.

14. John Urry, *Sociology beyond Societies: Mobilities for the Twenty-First Century* (London: Routledge, 2000), 3.

15. For a thoughtful critique of this divorce between time and space, from the perspective of a historian, see Philip J. Ethington, "Placing the Past: 'Groundwork' for a Spatial Theory of History," *Rethinking History* 11, no. 4 (December 2007): 465–93.

16. Georg Simmel, "The Sociology of Space," in *Simmel on Culture: Selected Writings*, ed. David Frisby and Mike Featherstone (London: Sage, 1997), 160; Georg Simmel, "Bridge and Door," in ibid., 174; Georg Simmel, *Brücke und Tür: Essays des Philosophen zur Geschichte, Religion, Kunst und Gesellschaft*, ed. Michael Landmann (Stuttgart: K. F. Koehler, 1957). The phrase "miracle of the road" (from "Bridge and Door," 175) is cited as a key inspiration in Mimi Sheller and John Urry, "The New Mobilities Paradigm," *Environment and Planning A* 38, no. 2 (2006): 215.

17. Arthur O. Lovejoy, *The Great Chain of Being: A Study of the History of an Idea* (Cambridge, MA: Harvard University Press, 1936), 15.

18. For a useful discussion of the distinction between geometry and geography as it applies to cultural analysis, see Franco Moretti, *Graphs, Maps, Trees: Abstract*

Models for a Literary History (London: Verso, 2005), 54–56. As Antoine Lilti observes in this collection, this abstraction about how ideas actually circulate in the world was a focal point of social-historical critique of the history of ideas, in France and (through French history) abroad. Antoine Lilti, "Does Intellectual History Exist in France? The Chronicle of a Renaissance Foretold," this volume.

19. Daniel Mornet, *Les origines intellectuelles de la Révolution française, 1715–1787* (Lyon: La Manufacture, 1989).

20. Ibid., 23–26.

21. Lilti, "Intellectual History."

22. Using the phrase "the spatial turn" in a 2010 book, Soja comments that "the spatial turn is still in its early stages" (!), but here he has in mind a culture-wide "balancing" of the emphasis given to space and time, rather than specific academic study. Edward W. Soja, *Seeking Spatial Justice* (Minneapolis: University of Minnesota Press, 2010), 3.

23. On geography's slow return to respectability in the United States, see Arild Holt-Jensen, "Achievements of Spatial Science," in *Companion Encyclopedia of Geography: The Environment and Humankind*, ed. Ian Douglas, Richard Huggett, and Mike Robinson (London: Routledge, 1996), 820–23. On the expansion of geography in postwar Britain, see R. J. Johnston, "The Expansion and Fragmentation of Geography in Higher Education," in ibid., 794–817.

24. For a useful overview of these strands of human geography, see Johnston and Sidaway, *Geography and Geographers*, 111–300.

25. Gregory and Urry, "Introduction," to *Social Relations and Spatial Structures*, 3.

26. See Barney Warf and Santa Arias, "Introduction: The Reinsertion of Space in the Humanities and Social Sciences," in *The Spatial Turn: Interdisciplinary Perspectives*, ed. Barney Warf and Santa Arias, Routledge Studies in Human Geography (London: Routledge, 2009), 3; Lefebvre, *Production of Space*. For a full bibliography of David Harvey's works, see Noel Castree and Derek Gregory, eds., *David Harvey: A Critical Reader* (Malden, MA: Blackwell, 2006), 295–302. Prominent among his early works is David Harvey, *Social Justice and the City* (Baltimore: Johns Hopkins University Press, 1973).

27. In my ordering, I roughly follow that of Johnston and Sidaway, *Geography and Geographers*, inverting the position of humanistic and computational geography.

28. John K. Wright, "Terrae Incognitae: The Place of the Imagination in Geography," *Annals of the Association of American Geographers* 37, no. 1 (March 1947): 1–15. Wright's inspiration (albeit with some delay) of modern humanistic geography is noted in Johnston and Sidaway, *Geography and Geographers*, 190–91; Anne Buttimer, "Geography and Humanism in the Late Twentieth Century," in Douglas, Huggett, and Robinson, *Companion Encyclopedia of Geography*, 838–41. For future touchstones of "place"—a concept linked to experiential and hermeneutic modes of analysis probably best treated separately from "space" (because of the vast hermeneutic tradition within intellectual history)—see Yi-fu Tuan, *Space and Place: The Perspective of Experience* (Minneapolis: University of Minnesota Press, 1977); Edward S. Casey, *The Fate of Place: A Philosophical History* (Berkeley: University of California Press, 1997). For a

historian's view of the role of place in human geography, see Charles W. J. Withers, "Place and the 'Spatial Turn' in Geography and in History," *Journal of the History of Ideas* 70, no. 4 (2009): 637–58.

29. See Timothy W. Foresman, "GIS Early Years and the Threads of Evolution," in *The History of Geographic Information Systems: Perspectives from the Pioneers*, ed. Timothy W. Foresman (Upper Saddle River, NJ: Prentice Hall PTR, 1998), 4–5; Roger Tomlinson, "The Canada Geographic Information System," in ibid., 21–32.

30. On the controversies surrounding GIS, see Pickles, *Ground Truth*; Stan Openshaw, "A View on the GIS Crisis in Geography," in *Human Geography: An Essential Anthology*, ed. John Agnew, David N. Livingstone, and Alisdair Rogers (Malden, MA: Blackwell, 1996), 675–85.

31. Lefebvre, *Production of Space*, 1.

32. Lefebvre, *Production of Space*, 33–39.

33. For the conceptual scheme and examples just discussed, see David Harvey, "Space as Keyword," in Castree and Gregory, *David Harvey: A Critical Reader*, 271–84. Harvey developed his triadic conception of absolute, relative, and relational space in Harvey, *Social Justice*, 13–14. An extended discussion of "relational space"—whose reconciliation with materialism Harvey says is possible—may be found in David Harvey, *Justice, Nature and the Geography of Difference* (Cambridge, MA: Blackwell, 1996), 248–90.

34. Among recent books calling for renewed historical interest to space, see Anne Kelly Knowles, *Placing History: How Maps, Spatial Data, and GIS Are Changing Historical Scholarship* (Redlands, CA: ESRI Press, 2008); Charles W. J. Withers, *Placing the Enlightenment: Thinking Geographically about the Age of Reason* (Chicago: University of Chicago Press, 2007); David J. Bodenhamer, John Corrigan, and Trevor M. Harris, eds., *The Spatial Humanities: GIS and the Future of Humanities Scholarship* (Bloomington: Indiana University Press, 2010); Michael Dear et al., *GeoHumanities: Art, History, Text at the Edge of Place* (London: Routledge, 2011); Richard White, "What Is Spatial History?," n.d., http://www.stanford.edu/group/spatialhistory/media/images/publication/what%20is%20spatial%20history%20pub%20020110.pdf; Ethington, "Placing the Past"; David N. Livingstone, *Putting Science in Its Place: Geography of Scientific Knowledge* (Chicago: University of Chicago Press, 2003). A recent, what's-next book on history "after the linguistic turn" focuses on a sociological pragmatism in which space, when treated at all, is treated as a result of practice: *Practicing History: New Directions in Historical Writing after the Linguistic Turn (Rewriting Histories)*, ed. Gabrielle M. Spiegel (New York: Routledge, 2005).

35. Roger Chartier, "Intellectual History and the History of Mentalités: A Dual Re-evaluation," in Chartier, *Cultural History: Between Practices and Representations* (Cambridge: Polity, 1988), 27–37. See also Antoine Lilti's essay in this collection.

36. Robert Darnton, *The Kiss of Lamourette: Reflections in Cultural History* (New York: Norton, 1990), 221–22.

37. Lynn Hunt, "Introduction: History, Culture, and Text," in Hunt, ed., *The New Cultural History* (Berkeley: University of California Press, 1989), 3.

38. For a good discussion of the variety of elements that are sometimes confusingly grouped under the term "cultural history," see Bill Schwarz, "Cultural History," in *Encyclopedia of Historians and Historical Writing*, ed. Kelly Boyd, 2 vols. (London: Fitzroy Dearborn, 1999), 276–79.

39. Although I tend to see textual contextualism as more social than he implies, a similar reading of the broad "cultural sociology" of recent intellectual history is mounted by Jonathan I. Israel, *Enlightenment Contested: Philosophy, Modernity, and the Emancipation of Man, 1670–1752* (Oxford: Oxford University Press, 2006), 21–24.

40. See both Lucien Febvre's classic analysis of the spread of book printing, and the long tradition of the "history of the book" that has emerged from it: Lucien Febvre and Henri-Jean Martin, *The Coming of the Book: The Impact of Printing*, ed. Geoffrey Nowell-Smith and David Wootton, trans. David Gerard (London: NLB, 1976); Bill Bell, Phillip Bennett, and Jonquil Bevan, eds., *Across Boundaries: The Book in Culture and Commerce* (New Castle, DE: Oak Knoll Press, 2000).

41. Soja, *Postmodern Geographies*, 11, 23; Soja, *Seeking Spatial Justice*, 14–17.

42. Soja, *Postmodern Geographies*, 15–23; Soja, *Seeking Spatial Justice*, 13–20.

43. Harvey, *Justice, Nature*, 207.

44. Lefebvre, *Production of Space*, 47–51.

45. Ibid., 38.

46. Though the niggling nationalism of modern intellectual history (and the Enlightenment in its number) has been critiqued by many—including, most searingly, by Paul Gilroy in *The Black Atlantic: Modernity and Double Consciousness* (Cambridge, MA: Harvard University Press, 1993), 1–40—it should be said that the history of ideas (and Enlightenment historiography in particular) has always claimed to want to be transnational, crossing geographical and disciplinary boundaries freely: see Arthur O. Lovejoy, "Reflections on the History of Ideas," *Journal of the History of Ideas* 1, no. 1 (January 1940): 3–23; Peter Gay, *The Enlightenment, an Interpretation; The Rise of Modern Paganism*, 1st ed. (New York: Knopf, 1966).

47. Israel, *Enlightenment Contested*, 18–23.

48. Ibid., 24–26.

49. See ibid., 19–21. Within the main chapters of the book itself, chapter 5 would seem to be the one that most explicitly engages geographical matters. It argues that diasporic communities—specifically, Polish Socinians—played an important role in stimulating radical ideas about religious faith (and Christianity) at the end of the seventeenth century (ibid., 115–34, esp. 115–17). But the discussion of the making of this radical linkage does not go much further beyond that hypothesis, and its mechanisms are not explored. It seems fair to say that the goal of this text is not the study of how the spaces of controversy were made, but rather what ideas were articulated within these spaces.

50. Ethington, "Placing the Past," 465.

51. Ibid., 471. As will be discussed below, this idea is gaining currency among scholars interested in digital visualization: see Edward L. Ayers, "Turning toward Place, Space, and Time," in Bodenhamer, Corrigan, and Harris, *Spatial Humanities*, 10.

52. Withers, "Place and the 'Spatial Turn,'" 638–39; Withers, *Placing the Enlightenment*.

53. Lilti, "Intellectual History"; John Tresch, "Cosmologies Materialized: History of Science and History of Ideas," this volume.

54. White, "What Is Spatial History?," 3.

55. On the source base for the study of human movement in the early modern period (with specific reference to France), see Leslie Page Moch, *Moving Europeans: Migration in Western Europe since 1650*, 2nd ed. (Bloomington: Indiana University Press, 2003).

56. White, "What Is Spatial History?"; Withers, "Place and the 'Spatial Turn'"; Bodenhamer, Corrigan, and Harris, *Spatial Humanities*; Warf and Arias, *Spatial Turn*; Knowles, *Placing History*; Dear et al., *GeoHumanities*.

57. The project's overall website and ePistolarium web application may be found at http://ckcc.huygens.knaw.nl/.

58. See http://republicofletters.stanford.edu/ (accessed December 5, 2012). I thank Dan Edelstein, a primary investigator of the project, for meeting with me and discussing this work in November 2012.

59. Pickles, "Representations in an Electronic Age"; David J. Bodenhamer, "The Potential of Spatial Humanities," in Bodenhamer, Corrigan, and Harris, *Spatial Humanities*, 14–30.

60. I thank Dan Edelstein of the "Mapping the Republic of Letters Project" for pressing this point home to me (personal interview, Stanford, CA, November 2012).

61. White, "What Is Spatial History?," 5.

62. Moretti, *Graphs*, 53.

63. Mark S. Monmonier, *How to Lie with Maps* (Chicago: University of Chicago Press, 1991); J.B. Harley, *The New Nature of Maps: Essays in the History of Cartography*, ed. Paul Laxton (Baltimore: Johns Hopkins University Press, 2001); Valerie A. Kivelson, *Cartographies of Tsardom: The Land and Its Meanings in Seventeenth-Century Russia* (Ithaca, NY: Cornell University Press, 2006).

12

The International Turn in Intellectual History

David Armitage

... ideas are the most migratory things in the world.[1]
—(Arthur O. Lovejoy, 1940)

On croit souvent que la vie intellectuelle est spontanément internationale. Rien n'est plus faux.[2]
—(Pierre Bourdieu, 1990)

For most of the life span of the historical profession, in most parts of the world, historians were committed to methodological nationalism. Like most other social scientists, they assumed that self-identifying nations, organized politically into states, were the primary objects of historical study.[3] Their main tasks were accordingly to narrate how nation-states emerged, how they developed, and how they interacted with one another. Even those historians whose work deliberately crossed the borders of national histories worked along similar lines. For example, diplomatic historians used national archives to reconstruct relations among states. Historians of immigration tracked the arrival and assimilation of new peoples into existing states.[4] And imperial historians studied empires as the extensions of national histories, even though they generally maintained a strict separation between the histories of metropolitan states (mostly in Europe) and their colonies (mostly outside Europe). In all these fields, the matter of history concerned stability not mobility, what was fixed but not what was mixed.

Historians in all fields have more recently been moving toward studies they describe variously as international, transnational, comparative, and global. Their efforts have not been identical in scope, in subject matter, or in motivation, nor is there any consensus on how these non-national approaches to history should be distinguished from each other. International historians often take for granted the existence of a society of states but look beyond state boundaries to map inter-state relationships, from diplomacy and finance to migration and cultural exchanges. Transnational historians examine processes, movements, and institutions that overflow territorial boundaries: for example, the environment, organized crime, epidemics, corporations, religions, and international social movements. Comparative historians deal with distinct historical subjects—which are often, but not always, nationally defined—in conjunction with each, although not always on the basis of any actual historical connection between their objects of study. And global historians treat the history and prehistories of globalization, the histories of objects that have become universalized, and the links between subglobal arenas such as the Atlantic, Indian, and Pacific Oceans. The family resemblance that links these approaches is the desire to go above or beyond the histories of states defined by nations and of nations bounded by states. Taken together, these projects comprise the international turn in historical writing.[5]

This international turn represents perhaps the most transformative historiographical movement since the rise of social history in the 1960s and the linguistic turn of the 1970s.[6] Why it has taken place simultaneously across so many areas of historical work would be a good question for intellectual history. However, it poses a particular problem for intellectual historians, who have so far written little about the international turn. This absence of engagement can be attributed in part to the reigning materialism of many of the strains of history that comprise the international turn. Historians of capital, empire, and migration, alongside sociologists and archaeologists with global ambitions, have led debate on this movement and produced many of the major works of synthesis. For such historians, "Each age gets the thought it needs"—Buddhism, Christianity, Islam: it's all the same really.[7] To them, intellectual history has seemed immaterial in both senses of that term: a kind of history from the neck up, dealing with the insubstantial imaginings of disembodied beings from inner space. A major challenge for intellectual historians is how to combat this skepticism without succumbing to reductionism or dissolving the identity of their field. In this case, the best way to proceed is to return to the roots of intellectual history itself in the period before historiography had been adopted as a handmaiden of national states.

Intellectual history can justifiably claim to have been international history *avant la lettre*. As Donald Kelley has shown, the first practitioners of the history of ideas, from Thomas Stanley in mid-seventeenth-century England to Victor Cousin in post-Napoleonic France, produced works that were strikingly cosmopolitan in character and content. Their histories sprang from traditions of philosophical eclecticism stretching back to Diogenes Laertius but arose most immediately from early modern epistemological debates in which ideas were held to be independent of their origins, whether national or otherwise.[8] These early forms of the history of ideas were characteristic products of a Republic of Letters that was self-consciously supranational in its affiliations and the nature of its scholarly exchanges. The *Respublica literarum* "embraces the whole world and is composed of all nationalities, all social classes, all ages and both sexes," wrote one of its citizens, the French scholar and litterateur Bonaventure d'Argonne in 1699: "All languages, ancient as well as modern are spoken." Within a global community that extended from China to Peru, "ideas were colorless, ageless, raceless, genderless"—and, it might be added, placeless and stateless.[9]

Intellectual history was born international, and it remained so long after the rise of nationalism within and beyond the historical profession. The logic of territorial statehood marked it much less than other areas of historical inquiry, and it became an article of faith among historians of ideas that their objects of attention escaped national boundaries. For example, the "New History" pioneered in the late nineteenth-century United States by Frederick Jackson Turner and James Harvey Robinson questioned nationalist historiography at the moment of its birth and drew inspiration from those historical phenomena that evaded its clutches. As Turner noted in 1891, "Ideas, commodities even, refuse the bounds of a nation. . . . This is true especially of our modern world with its complex commerce and means of intellectual connection."[10] Half a century later, the founding father of the modern history of ideas, Arthur O. Lovejoy, might have been recalling Turner's words when he asserted in 1938, "Ideas are commodities which enter into interstate commerce." How those ideas were manufactured and how they traveled, who trafficked them and who consumed them, were not questions the classic historians of ideas thought to ask: that was a task they left to specialists in comparative literature, "understood to be the study of international intellectual relations."[11] Only with the rise of the social history of ideas and the history of the book would such material concerns inform the work of intellectual historians. This new strain of intellectual history also proclaimed its internationalism, as a history of *livres sans frontières* joined a history of ideas without borders.[12] "By their very nature, books refuse to be contained within any discipline," Robert Darnton argued in 1994: "They also refuse to respect national boundaries."[13]

Intellectual history's innate resistance to nationalism may have had the paradoxical effect of making it harder for the field to take an international turn in more recent years. Because intellectual historians have not needed to reject national categories or to embrace cosmopolitan alternatives to them, they might be methodologically underprepared for such a movement. Indeed, the international turn has lately come to intellectual history by the academic equivalent of technological leapfrogging, as the field shifts from the non-national to the supranational without ever having fully inhabited national frameworks.[14] This move entails facing up to some of the shortcomings of intellectual history as it has traditionally been practiced, especially its resistance to considering the spatial dimensions of context. It also demands greater insistence on the distinctive contributions intellectual history can make more generally to the broader international turn. Nonetheless, intellectual historians possess some of the best available tools for tracing the emergence of categories such as the international and the global, for tracking the circulation of ideas, and for tackling some of the challenges raised by the international turn, among them the dangers of idealism, classism, and presentism, and the challenges of redefining context. Intellectual history may therefore have as much to offer the international turn as the international turn has to offer to intellectual history.

A decade ago, I suggested that "a renaissance in the history of international thought" was beginning that might "open up new conversations between historians, political theorists, International Relations scholars and international lawyers."[15] That renaissance is now well under way and has produced the first fruits of intellectual history's international turn. This revival of the history of international thought marks the most recent of three phases of relations between intellectual history and international history: an age of engagement that lasted from roughly the end of the First World War until the 1950s; an age of estrangement running from the early 1960s to the mid-1990s; and an age of rapprochement that is still very much in progress.

In the initial age of engagement, historians of ideas were often methodologically cosmopolitan and politically internationalist in outlook, while historically minded students of international relations dealt openly in ideas rather than abstract models or theories. Thinkers otherwise as diverse as Hannah Arendt, Raymond Aron, Herbert Butterfield, Hans Morgenthau, Reinhold Niebuhr, Carl Schmitt, Kenneth Waltz, and Martin Wight drew upon shared historical canons even though they disagreed profoundly over such matters as the ethics of war and peace or the balance between national sovereignty and the authority of international institutions.[16]

During the succeeding age of estrangement, intellectual historians and international historians drew further apart. Disciplinary boundaries hardened and were more fiercely defended. The refinement of methodologies and the acceleration of professional specialization made conversations between fields less common. The separation between the domestic and the international sharpened. "Theory"—whether political or international—lost ground to positivist models, which excluded ideas and ethics from the realms of politics and international relations, particularly in the United States. In retrospect, the May 1954 Conference on International Politics convened in Washington, D.C., by the Rockefeller Foundation, in which Morgenthau, Niebuhr, and others participated, now looks like the high-water mark of an ethical approach to international affairs before the triumph of behavioralist social science in the United States.[17]

Over the next quarter century, intellectual historians moved ever further away from international historians as a resurgent social history pressed both fields to the margins of the historical profession, especially in the United States. What one clerk said to another clerk was as unfashionable as what one philosopher wrote about another philosopher. As Robert Darnton observed gloomily in a 1980 collection published on behalf of the American Historical Association, "A malaise is spreading among intellectual historians. . . . After a realignment of research during the last two decades, she now sits below the salt." In the same volume, Charles Maier offered a similarly downbeat assessment of international history: "The history of international relations . . . [has] little sense of collective enterprise, of being at the cutting edge of historical scholarship."[18]

As so often happens, intimations of obsolescence proved to be spurs to innovation. Within little more than a decade, the two fields had begun to converge again. The age of rapprochement beginning in the 1990s saw revivals in both intellectual history and international history alongside the increasing entanglement of the two fields. At least some scholars of international relations found themselves in a "post-positivist" phase marked by a renewed interest in theory, in the history of international affairs, and in the history of their own discipline. International historians became more interested in culture, ideology, and institutions, "champions of the international turn as well as vigorous proponents of intellectual and cultural history." At the same time, intellectual historians began to treat historically the norms and interactions between peoples, states, and other corporate bodies in the world beyond the domestic sphere under the rubric of the history of international thought.[19]

The term "international thought" was originally an invention of British publicists and litterateurs sympathetic to the League of Nations and nascent international institutions in the interwar years. Its original purpose had been to denote a usable past rather than to create a critical history.[20] It received support from equally committed internationalists across the Atlantic, notably the American international lawyer James Brown Scott, who created the earliest historical canon of works of international thought from Balthazar Ayala to Richard Zouche in the series sponsored by the Carnegie Endowment for International Peace, "Classics of International Law" (1911–1950).[21] The recent revival of the history of international thought has seen it emerge as a robust field in its own right, with a more expansive and less teleological canon of authors, problems, and movements, and not just as a subset of the history of political thought.[22] International thought now means less a body of authoritative doctrine to be deployed for present purposes than the past tense of international thinking as the activity of theoretical reflection upon international affairs.

A humanistic return to the sources of international thought revealed the distance between what thinkers like Hugo Grotius, Thomas Hobbes, and Immanuel Kant were doing—or, just as often, what they were *not* attempting to do—and the uses made of them within later disciplinary histories. Grotius could have had no intention of fathering international law. Hobbes was no "Hobbesian," at least as far as that term had been used as a term of art by students of international relations. And Kant was rather more than the theorist of the "democratic peace" to which he had been reduced by teleological internationalists since the early twentieth century.[23] For the twentieth century, there are historical studies of international thinkers of all stripes from Norman Angell and Hannah Arendt to Leonard Woolf and Alfred Zimmern, with an especially vigorous cottage industry devoted to the work of Carl Schmitt.[24] At the same time, self-critical disciplinary historians of international relations and international law have, for example, exposed how a "discourse of anarchy" contingently generated in the interwar years became a timeless truth for the later Realist school of international relations and have shown the complicity of idealistic international lawyers with imperial enterprises from the Belgian Congo to the Bay of Pigs.[25]

Intellectual historians have been well placed to assist skeptical international historians in questioning some of the basic building blocks of their discipline. For example, no date was more foundational for international relations than 1648 and the Peace of Westphalia. The demolition of the "myth of 1648" as the origins of a world of mutually recognizing, noninterfering sovereign states was a relatively straightforward process. It relied on a reading of the treaties of Münster and Osnabrück, the recognition that empires, federations, and other kinds of layered or divided sovereignty were more characteristic of political authority than any alleged "Westphalian" sovereignty, and attention to the world beyond northern Europe, to see how little respect was paid to the putative sovereignty of many of the world's peoples under the regime of empire.[26] The Westphalian myth had in turn underpinned a set of assumptions that defined modern international thought: that states, not individuals, were the primary actors in international affairs; that the spheres of the domestic and the foreign were distinct and separate; that positive law trumped natural law; that a hierarchical standard of civilization applied across the globe; and that the international realm was anarchical and hence governed by maxims of reason of state. These fundamental assumptions were neither uniform nor uncontested, but they did set the terms of debate for at least a century and a half.[27]

The intellectual history of the international still teems with possibilities for research. For example, what were the media for international thought, and how might they be understood using the methods of history of the book?[28] Starting in the late seventeenth century and continuing to the present, new and persistent genres of writing and publication, among them treaty collections, diplomatic manuals, and histories of international relations and of the law of nations, proliferated amid the clerical, scholarly, and humanistic cultures that intersected so often with transnational diplomatic and military communities. Further examination of such genres might help us to understand why Kant cast *Zum ewigen Frieden* (1795) in the form of a treaty, for instance.[29] What were the novel philosophical personae adopted by casuistical envoys, literary-minded administrators, and intellectuals in office in the burgeoning international institutions of the eighteenth century and beyond?[30] And how was international thought itself internationalized? To take just one example, the translation and circulation in Asia of a major vector of Henry Wheaton's *Elements of International Law* (1836) suggests that the assumptions underlying modern international thought were becoming increasingly transregional, if not yet fully global, by the middle of the nineteenth century.[31] In this sense, the receptivity of the world to the contagion of sovereignty that almost universally affected it still demands explanation, especially by attending to the domestic determinants and conditions of its reception and domestication.[32] Only then can we fully understand the energetic coproduction of the national and the international around the globe in the nineteenth and twentieth centuries.[33]

The internationalization of the international can also be approached through the intellectual history of international institutions. Proponents of the new international history have long urged their colleagues to "internationalize international history," not least by studying nonstate actors in the international realm: corporations, nongovernmental organizations, transnational social movements and bodies such as the World Health Organization or the United Nations.[34] This call has more recently generated new opportunities for archival intellectual histories of the Institut de Droit international, the Carnegie Endowment for International Peace, the League of Nations, UNESCO, and the European Union, to name only some of the most prominent. Some of this work has been internalist and celebratory, notably that generated through the United

Nations Intellectual History Project, but much of it has helped to expand the range of actors, archives, and institutions open to examination by intellectual historians.[35] One product of this expansion has been the new history of human rights, a field now in its second wave, as it has moved from its teleological phase of telling just-so stories into a more critical literature alert to context and to discontinuity.[36]

Other subjects of concern to intellectual historians—the history of economic thought; conceptions of war and government; public health; and the history of science—can all be researched in the archives of international institutions, companies, and corporations. In this regard, modern intellectual historians can learn from those early modernists who have followed historians of science in constructing intellectual histories of the English and Dutch trading companies in the seventeenth and eighteenth centuries.[37] The explosion of interest among political theorists and students of ethics in the international and global dimensions of their concerns has helped to accelerate all these developments, which took place amid an ever-growing public awareness of the transnational dimensions of human affairs captured by the catch-all term "globalization."[38] All these movements have in turn encouraged and reinforced internal tendencies within intellectual history to reconstruct arguments dealing with matters beyond the nation or the state that, collectively, I have called the international turn among intellectual historians.

Space is now the final frontier for intellectual history. The international turn has revived interest in conceptions of space by attending to arenas that were larger than nations, unconfined by the political boundaries of states, and connected by transnational linkages and circulations. Most of the world's population, for most of recorded history, lived not in nation-states but in empires, those far-flung, stratified polities that projected various kinds of universalism in order to suspend differences among populations without striving for uniformity between them. For a relatively brief period, between the early sixteenth and early twentieth centuries, some of those empires were the outgrowths of confidently national cultures, particularly in Europe and Asia, but most were prenational or supranational in composition. Oceanic spaces connected elements of these empires in the modern period, but maritime arenas such as the Mediterranean, the Indian Ocean, the Atlantic, and the Pacific also segmented sovereignties and became cockpits of inter-imperial rivalry.[39] In light of the long history of empire, the eternal world of states posited by modern conceptions of international relations seems fleeting, even marginal. Indeed, if by some estimates a world of true nation-states, detached from empire, emerged only with the zenith of decolonization, soon to be swept away by the wave of transnationalism that erupted after the end of the Cold War, then the heyday of the state lasted less than a generation, from about 1975 to 1989.[40] All history, before and after, was either prenational or postnational history.

By simultaneously uniting and dividing, empires spurred conceptual competition and facilitated the circulation of ideas among diasporic peoples and across commercial routes.[41] From such collisions and transmissions emerged "competing universalisms" of empire, religion, and political economy, for instance, as well as the expansive ideologies that countered or subsumed them, such as pan-Islamism, pan-Africanism, nationalism, anticolonialism, and other forms of "colored cosmopolitanism."[42] Most of these movements were invisible as long as history was viewed through nation-shaped spectacles. They returned to view only when older experiences of space—more extensive, more fluid, and less confined by territorial boundaries—again framed questions about the past.

The field is rife with spatial metaphors—of ideas as "migratory" and of books escaping the bounds of nations; of "horizons" of understanding and the public "sphere"; of "localism" and "provincialism" as determinants of ideas; and conceptions of hermeneutic "containment" and critical "movement," for example—but such figures of speech do not indicate any substantive engagement with questions of space and place. They are instead shorthand indications that ideas lack material determinants and that they need to be placed into contexts construed almost entirely as temporal and linguistic, not physical or spatial.[43] As John Randolph remarks in this volume, "The result is a kind of intellectual geometry—the positioning of ideas in abstract space— rather than intellectual geography."[44] Michel Foucault might have been speaking for intellectual historians when he declared in an interview: "Space was that which was dead, fixed, non-dialectical, immobile. On the other hand, time was rich, fertile, vibrant, dialectical."[45]

Space can be understood intensively as well as extensively. In this regard historians of science may have much to teach both international historians and intellectual historians. A "spatial turn" in the history of science put in doubt the universality of truth and insisted upon local knowledge: there could be no view from nowhere when every view sprang from somewhere. Ideas emerged from tightly defined spaces, from littoral beaches as well as laboratory benches, and from public drinking-houses as well as royal academies. When viewed microscopically in this way, the seamless web of abstract knowledge turned out to be a brittle mosaic of contingent concerns.[46] If one aim of this literature was to debunk the presumed universality of scientific reason, another was to show just how fragments of knowledge were accumulated and collected and how their credibility was secured. "We need to understand not only how knowledge is made in specific places but also how transactions occur between places": that is, how ideas travel, who transports them, what baggage they carry on their journeys, and how they become domesticated and naturalized upon arrival.[47]

This approach revealed the intricate mechanisms of information-gathering that made scientific knowledge both possible and plausible. Even the most physically isolated of thinkers like the landlocked Isaac Newton, who never saw the sea in his life, could become a global center of calculation because he commanded a worldwide web of correspondents from the Gulf of Tonkin to the Strait of Magellan.[48] Corporate bodies such as the Society of Jesus and the English and Dutch East India Companies facilitated big science, in the sense of the long-distance production of knowledge.[49] And later "webs of empire" dissolved distinctions between centers and peripheries as each alleged periphery earned a central place in accumulating imperial archives, testing hypotheses, and generating ideologies through intercolonial exchanges.[50] In these ways, extensively elaborated connections linked intensively cultivated locations to create new maps of knowledge and transnational canons through the transmission of ideas and information across continents and oceans.

These studies in what Pierre Bourdieu called the "science of international relations with regard to culture" offer more generally replicable models for intellectual history.[51] When conceptions of space expand, webs of significance ramify and networks of exchange proliferate to create novel contexts and unanticipated connections among them. Shifting patterns of sociability and correspondence, of the distribution of books and the spatial organization of knowledge—in rooms and buildings, streets and squares, cities and regions, countries and continents, empires and oceans—forced thinkers to reconceive the nature of their audiences, the potential impact of their arguments, and the extent of their spheres of action. In light of these considerations, to answer the question, "What was Enlightenment?," intellectual historians attuned to space must now ask, "*Where* was Enlightenment?," a question only fully answerable in a global context across the *longue durée*.[52]

Changing conceptions of space expanded the contexts for ideas and, with them, the very possibilities for thought. The most familiar example for European intellectual historians might be the broader contexts that transoceanic exploration and colonization generated for thinkers in early modern Europe, as intercultural encounters and the proliferation of empires around the Indian Ocean, the Atlantic world, and later the Pacific tested conceptions of nature, civilization, political community, property, religious diversity, and toleration, among other questions.[53] For instance, John Locke, a voracious reader of travel literature, confronted instances of diversity and belief and practice drawn from accounts of five continents;[54] Thomas Hobbes, a more modest consumer of

Americana, shaped his understanding of international relations by reference to ethnographic descriptions of the state of nature;[55] and David Hume's political economy owed much to his Atlantic connections.[56] As the "Great Map of Mankind" was unrolled (in Edmund Burke's resonant phrase), truly global possibilities for thought opened up for the generations of thinkers writing after the mid-eighteenth century—among them Diderot, Turgot, Smith, Kant, Herder, Burke, and Bentham—with consequences for their constructions of universalism and cosmopolitanism as well as for their conceptions of culture and difference.[57] Moving into the later nineteenth century, the compression of space by technology—above all, the steamship, the railway, and the telegraph—made new forms of political community imaginable over the expanses of empire and across the world. *Pace* Foucault, space was dynamic, not static. The contexts for thinking expanded to encompass the entire globe. Modern intellectual historians accordingly have to track ideas on ever-larger scales: continental, interregional, transoceanic, and ultimately planetary. As Heidegger, Schmitt, and Arendt were among the first to note in the mid-twentieth century, *outer* space may be the truly final frontier for intellectual history.[58]

So far, this account of the international turn in intellectual history has been overwhelmingly upbeat, a *tour d'horizon* of achievements sustained and promises yet to be fulfilled. But every silver lining has a cloud. In what ways could the international turn possibly be a turn for the worse? This movement has not yet entered the phase of well-earned self-criticism, nor has it attracted much sustained attention from outsiders. However, some charges have already been arrayed against it, among them reification, presentism, "classism," and changing conceptions of context.[59] None of these criticisms is peculiar to international intellectual history: all are familiar from debates on the history of ideas over at least the last half century. Yet they have all become sharper when intellectual history extends over greater expanses of space, as new forms of disjunction between ideas and novel analytical demands come to the fore.

Reification is a familiar charge, going back at least as far as the Cambridge School's criticisms of Lovejoy's history of ideas: what appear to be iterations of the same idea turn out to be distinct conceptions in need of disaggregation rather than assimilation into broader narratives over time or across space. For example, liberalism in Britain was not the same as liberalism in India: each developed within its own ecological niche, yet they did not emerge in ignorance of each other, but rather in dialogues mediated by local conditions of the reception, circulation, and hybridization of arguments.[60] After at least the mid-eighteenth century, the conditions of reception were transregional and increasingly global: Indian "liberals" in the early nineteenth century like

Rammohan Roy saw their own struggles against despotism as part of world-wide movements encompassing British and Portuguese colonies in Asia, the Spanish monarchy in the Atlantic world, and Britain itself. Texts carried ideas but always amid framing paratexts, and then into unpredictable contexts for their translation and reappropriation. These conditions generated dissimilitude out of similarity, but rarely to the extent of complete disjuncture and incomparability. With such caveats in mind, the danger of falling into reification may be overblown. With methodological assistance where necessary from, say, *Rezeptionsgeschichte*, the history of the book, and postcolonial theory, it should be possible to avoid the dangers of an older, less sophisticated, transhistorical history *of* ideas and replace it with a more methodologically robust transtemporal history *in* ideas.[61]

Presentism may offer a more serious danger for the international turn. "The whole enterprise [of international intellectual history] is itself presentist," Emma Rothschild has noted, "in the sense that the transnational turn is influenced, in evident respects, by the late twentieth and early twenty-first century public controversies over 'globalization.'"[62] Yet we can no more wish away current arguments than we can deny the presence of debates over cosmopolitan, universal, or global connections and conceptions in the past. It is a truism—and, like all truisms, by definition at least partly true—that our ever-changing present continually reveals aspects of the past that have been overlooked or underappreciated. In this case, as in other aspects of transnational history, two approaches are possible: "A first would suggest that connections did exist and were known to past actors, but have for some reason been forgotten or laid aside. The task of the historian would then be to rediscover these lost traces. A second view would instead posit that historians might act as electricians, connecting circuits by acts of imaginative reconstitution rather than simple restitution."[63] The first of these approaches—connective rather than comparative, reconstitutive rather than restitutive—might be preferable for most historians, but the second is also surely necessary for the creation of the requisite historical distance between past imperatives and current concerns. We surely delude ourselves if we imagine we do not see those concerns through a glass darkly. We will only be able to see them more clearly if we place them in long-range perspective.

"Classism"—the idea that "only the high, or the great, or the highly educated, have been the subject, in general, of histories of the individual mind, or the individual self"—is a familiar charge against intellectual history, rather than a failing peculiar to intellectual history with an international twist.[64] J. S. Mill, for one, had rebutted it as early as 1838 in his defense of Bentham and Coleridge:

> Speculative philosophy, which to the superficial appears a thing so
> remote from the business of life and the outward interests of men,
> is in reality the thing on earth which most influences them, and in
> the long run overbears every other influence save those which it
> must itself obey. The writers of whom we speak have never been
> read by the multitude; except for the more slight of their works, their
> readers have been few: but they have been the teachers of the
> teachers.[65]

In between the speculative philosophers and the great multitude are the
thinkers of what Rothschild has called "intermediate" or "medium thoughts,"
the reflections of those too undistinguished to be the subjects of individual
intellectual biography but too profuse in leaving their reflective traces to be
subsumed into any history of *mentalités*, especially, but not exclusively, those
engaged in public policy of various kinds.[66] Such people were often globetrot-
ters and go-betweens, members of the massive Asian, European, and African
migrations that crossed (and re-crossed) the Atlantic and Pacific Oceans and
the steppes, but also the intercultural agents who trafficked in local knowledge
and the creation of "global intelligence."[67] As historians reconstruct their forms
of intellection, and the histories of their ideas, we can expect to find even more
widespread evidence of forms of transnational thinking.[68]

The increasingly elastic definitions of context demanded by transnational
history should not deter intellectual historians. Some are beginning to ask
how precisely any idea can be understood "in context" if context is now defined
to encompass intercontinental communications, multilingual communities,
or the expansion of world systems.[69] Here again the opportunities may be
greater than the dangers. Canons of relevance must be defined, routes of
active (or at least plausible) transmission mapped, and scales of reference calibrated according to contemporaries' conceptions of the international or the
global; with such boundaries in place, it should be feasible to reconstruct
meaningful spatial contexts for the ideas we trace across borders and bounded
discursive communities.

Historicizing conceptions of space—of the national, the international, the
transnational, and the global—may in fact be the implied agenda for intellectual history after the international turn, just as historicizing conceptions of
time was a major project for intellectual history in the nineteenth and twentieth
centuries. This agenda leads inexorably to the question what it might mean for
intellectual history to take a global turn. Quite what a global intellectual history
would comprise, or even what its subject-matter will be, is still far from clear,
though vigorous debate has already begun.[70] Whether the global turn is just one

logical extension of the international turn or a distinct endeavor in its own right remains to be seen. With such widening horizons and enticing prospects, it surely cannot be premature to welcome both the international and the global as turns for the better in intellectual history, as they have been for historical writing *tout court*.

Notes

For their comments on earlier versions of this chapter, I am especially grateful to Alexander Bevilacqua, Philip Fileri, and Mira Siegelberg; to participants in the Radcliffe Exploratory Seminar at Harvard University; and to audiences in Helsinki, London, and Princeton.

1. Arthur O. Lovejoy, "Reflections on the History of Ideas," *Journal of the History of Ideas* 1 (1940): 4.

2. Pierre Bourdieu, "Les conditions sociales de la circulation internationale des idées," *Romanistische Zeitschrift für Literaturgeschichte/Cahiers d'Histoire des Littératures Romanes* 14 (1990): 2.

3. "A nation is a community of sentiment which would adequately manifest itself in a state of its own; hence, a nation is a community which normally tends to produce a state of its own": Max Weber, *From Max Weber: Essays in Sociology*, ed. H. H. Gerth and C. Wright Mills, new ed. (London: Routledge, 1991), 176.

4. Andreas Wimmer and Nina Glick Schiller, "Methodological Nationalism, the Social Sciences, and the Study of Migration: An Essay in Historical Epistemology," *International Migration Review* 37 (2003): 576–610.

5. Patricia Clavin, "Defining Transnationalism," *Contemporary European History* 14 (2005): 421–39; C. A. Bayly, Sven Beckert, Matthew Connelly, Isabel Hofmeyr, Wendy Kozol, and Patricia Seed, "*AHR* Conversation: On Transnational History," *American Historical Review* 111 (2006): 1441–64; Pierre-Yves Saunier, "Transnational," in *The Palgrave Dictionary of Transnational History*, ed. Akira Iriye and Pierre-Yves Saunier (Basingstoke: Palgrave Macmillan, 2009), 1047–55; Akira Iriye, *Global and Transnational History: The Past, Present, and Future* (Basingstoke: Palgrave Macmillan, 2013).

6. For a broader discussion of recent "turns" in historical writing, see Judith Surkis, Gary Wilder, James W. Cook, Durba Ghosh, Julia Adeney Thomas, and Nathan Perl-Rosenthal, "*AHR* Forum: Historiographic 'Turns' in Critical Perspective," *American Historical Review* 117 (2012): 698–813.

7. Ian Morris, *Why the West Rules—For Now: The Patterns of History, and What They Reveal about the Future* (London: Profile Books, 2010), 420, 476, 568, 621.

8. Donald R. Kelley, *The Descent of Ideas: The History of Intellectual History* (Aldershot: Ashgate, 2002), chaps. 1–2.

9. Bonaventure d'Argonne, quoted in Anthony Grafton, "A Sketch Map of a Lost Continent: The Republic of Letters," in Grafton, *Worlds Made by Words: Scholarship and Community in the Modern West* (Cambridge, MA: Harvard University Press, 2009), 9.

10. Frederick Jackson Turner, "The Significance of History" (1891), in Turner, *The Early Writings of Frederick Jackson Turner*, ed. Everett E. Edwards (Madison: University of Wisconsin Press, 1938), 57; Peter Novick, *That Noble Dream: The "Objectivity Question" and the American Historical Profession* (Cambridge: Cambridge University Press, 1988), 89–95.

11. Arthur O. Lovejoy, "The Historiography of Ideas" (1938), in Lovejoy, *Essays in the History of Ideas* (Baltimore: Johns Hopkins University Press, 1948), 3, 1.

12. Leslie Howsam and James Raven, "Introduction," to Howsam and Raven, eds., *Books between Europe and the Americas: Connections and Communities, 1620–1860* (Basingstoke: Palgrave Macmillan, 2011), 1.

13. Robert Darnton and Krassimira Daskalova, "Book History, the State of Play: An Interview with Robert Darnton," *SHARP News* 3, 3 (Summer 1994): 2.

14. Margrit Pernau, "Whither Conceptual History? From National to Entangled Histories," *Contributions to the History of Concepts* 7 (2012): 1–11.

15. David Armitage, "The Fifty Years' Rift: Intellectual History and International Relations," *Modern Intellectual History* 1 (2004): 108–9.

16. Brunello Vigezzi, *The British Committee on the Theory of International Politics (1954–1985): The Rediscovery of History* (Milan: Edizioni Unicopli, 2005).

17. Martin Wight, "Why Is There No International Theory?" (1959), in Herbert Butterfield and Martin Wight, eds., *Diplomatic Investigations: Essays in the Theory of International Politics* (London: Allen and Unwin, 1966), 17–34; Stanley Hoffman, "An American Social Science: International Relations," *Daedalus* 106 (1977): 41–60; Nicolas Guilhot, ed., *The Invention of International Relations Theory: Realism, the Rockefeller Foundation, and the 1954 Conference on Theory* (New York: Columbia University Press, 2011).

18. Robert Darnton, "Intellectual History and Cultural History," in *The Past before Us: Contemporary Historical Writing in the United States*, ed. Michael Kammen (Ithaca, NY: Cornell University Press, 1980), 327; Charles Maier, "Marking Time: The Historiography of International Relations," in ibid., 355.

19. Lucian M. Ashworth, "Interdisciplinarity and International Relations," *European Political Science* 8 (2009): 16–25; Duncan Bell, "Writing the World: Disciplinary History and Beyond," *International Affairs* 85 (2009): 3–22; Thomas W. Zeiler, "The Diplomatic History Bandwagon: A State of the Field," *Journal of American History* 95 (2009): 1053 (quoted).

20. John Galsworthy, *International Thought* (Cambridge: Heffers, 1923); F. Melian Stawell, *The Growth of International Thought* (London: Butterworth, 1929). On their immediate antecedents, see Casper Sylvest, *British Liberal Internationalism, 1880–1930: Making Progress?* (Manchester: Manchester University Press, 2009).

21. John Hepp, "James Brown Scott and the Rise of Public International Law," *Journal of the Gilded Age and Progressive Era* 7 (2008): 151–79; Benjamin Allen Coates, "Trans-Atlantic Advocates: American International Law and U.S. Foreign Relations, 1898–1919" (Ph.D. thesis, Columbia University, 2010), 101–5.

22. Edward Keene, *International Political Thought: A Historical Introduction* (Cambridge: Polity, 2005); Beate Jahn, ed., *Classical Theory in International Relations* (Cambridge: Cambridge University Press, 2006); Duncan Bell, ed., *Victorian Visions*

of Global Order: Empire and International Relations in Nineteenth-Century Political Thought (Cambridge: Cambridge University Press, 2007); Ian Hall and Lisa Hill, eds., *British International Thinkers from Hobbes to Namier* (Basingstoke: Palgrave Macmillan, 2009).

23. Richard Tuck, *The Rights of War and Peace: Political Thought and the International Order from Grotius to Kant* (Oxford: Oxford University Press, 1999); Martine Julia van Ittersum, *Profit and Principle: Hugo Grotius, Natural Rights Theories and the Rise of Dutch Power in the East Indies, 1595–1615* (Leiden: Brill, 2006); Noel Malcolm, "Hobbes's Theory of International Relations," in Malcolm, *Aspects of Hobbes* (Oxford: Oxford University Press, 2002), 432–56; Sankar Muthu, *Enlightenment against Empire* (Princeton, NJ: Princeton University Press, 2003); Eric S. Easley, *The War over Perpetual Peace: An Exploration into the History of a Foundational International Relations Text* (Basingstoke: Palgrave Macmillan, 2004); David Armitage, *Foundations of Modern International Thought* (Cambridge: Cambridge University Press, 2013).

24. David Long and Peter Wilson, eds., *Thinkers of the Twenty Years' Crisis: Inter-War Idealism Reassessed* (Oxford: Oxford University Press, 1995); Patricia Owens, *Between War and Politics: International Relations and the Thought of Hannah Arendt* (Oxford: Oxford University Press, 2007); Jeanne Morefield, *Covenants without Swords: Idealist Liberalism and the Spirit of Empire* (Princeton, NJ: Princeton University Press, 2005); Louiza Odysseos and Fabio Petito, eds., *The International Political Thought of Carl Schmitt: Terror, Liberal War and the Crisis of Global Order* (London: Routledge, 2007); William Hooker, *Carl Schmitt's International Thought: Order and Orientation* (Cambridge: Cambridge University Press, 2009); Stephen Legg, ed., *Spatiality, Sovereignty and Carl Schmitt: Geographies of the Nomos* (London: Routledge, 2011).

25. Brian Schmidt, *The Political Discourse of Anarchy: A Disciplinary History of International Relations* (Albany, NY: State University of New York Press, 1998); Martti Koskenniemi, *The Gentle Civilizer of Nations: The Rise and Fall of International Law, 1870–1960* (Cambridge: Cambridge University Press, 2001).

26. Andreas Osiander, "Sovereignty, International Relations, and the Westphalian Myth," *International Organization* 55 (2001): 251–87; Benno Teschke, *The Myth of 1648: Class, Geopolitics and the Making of Modern International Relations* (London: Verso, 2003); Benjamin Straumann, "The Peace of Westphalia as a Secular Constitution," *Constellations* 15 (2008): 173–88; Pärtel Piirimäe, "The Westphalian Myth of Sovereignty and the Idea of External Sovereignty," in *Sovereignty in Fragments: The Past, Present and Future of a Contested Concept*, ed. Hent Kalmo and Quentin Skinner (Cambridge: Cambridge University Press, 2010), 64–80.

27. Armitage, *Foundations of Modern International Thought*.

28. For a model study of the translation and circulation of economic texts along these lines, see Sophus Reinert, *Translating Empire: Emulation and the Origins of Political Economy* (Cambridge, MA: Harvard University Press, 2011).

29. For suggestive work in these directions, see Randall Lesaffer, ed., *Peace Treaties and International Law in European History: From the Late Middle Ages to World War One* (Cambridge: Cambridge University Press, 2004); Daniel Ménager,

Diplomatie et théologie à la Renaissance (Paris: Presses Universitaires de France, 2001); Ellen M. McClure, *Sunspots and the Sun King: Sovereignty and Mediation in Seventeenth-century France* (Urbana: University of Illinois Press, 2006); Timothy Hampton, *Fictions of Embassy: Literature and Diplomacy in Early Modern Europe* (Ithaca, NY: Cornell University Press, 2009).

30. Ian Hunter, "Vattel's Law of Nations: Diplomatic Casuistry for the Protestant Nation," *Grotiana* 31 (2010): 108–40.

31. Lydia H. Liu, *The Clash of Empires: The Invention of China in Modern World Making* (Cambridge, MA: Harvard University Press, 2004), 108–39; Liu, ed., *Tokens of Exchange: The Problem of Translation in Global Circulations* (Durham, NC: Duke University Press, 1999); Carol Gluck and Anne Lowenhaupt Tsing, eds., *Words in Motion: Toward a Global Lexicon* (Durham, NC: Duke University, Press, 2009).

32. David Armitage, *The Declaration of Independence: A Global History* (Cambridge, MA: Harvard University Press, 2007), 107–12; C. A. Bayly, "European Political Thought and the Wider World during the Nineteenth Century," in *The Cambridge History of Nineteenth-Century Political Thought*, ed. Gareth Stedman Jones and Gregory Claeys (Cambridge: Cambridge University Press, 2011), 835–63.

33. C. A. Bayly and Eugenio Biagini, eds., *Giuseppe Mazzini and the Globalization of Democratic Nationalism, 1830–1920* (Oxford: Oxford University Press for the British Academy, 2008); Maurizio Isabella, *Risorgimento in Exile: Italian Émigrés and the Liberal International in the Post-Napoleonic Era* (Oxford: Oxford University Press, 2009).

34. Akira Iriye, "Internationalizing International History," in *Rethinking American History in a Global Age*, ed. Thomas Bender (Berkeley: University of California Press, 2002), 47–62; Iriye, *Global Community: The Role of International Organizations in the Making of the Contemporary World* (Berkeley: University of California Press, 2002).

35. Koskenniemi, *The Gentle Civilizer of Nations*; Roger-Pol Droit, *L'Humanité toujours à construire: regard sur l'histoire intellectuelle de l'UNESCO, 1945–2005* (Paris: UNESCO, 2005); Glenda Sluga and Sunil Amrith, "New Histories of the United Nations," *Journal of World History* 19 (2008): 251–74; Emma Rothschild, "The Archives of Universal History," *Journal of World History* 19 (2008): 375–401; Mark Mazower, *Governing the World: The History of an Idea* (London: Allen Lane, 2012); Richard Jolly, Louis Emmerij, and Thomas G. Weiss, *UN Ideas That Changed the World* (Bloomington: Indiana University Press, 2009), and similar works from the United Nations Intellectual History Project.

36. For the first, see for example Elizabeth Borgwardt, *A New Deal for the World: America's Vision for Human Rights* (Cambridge, MA: Harvard University Press, 2005); Lynn Hunt, *Inventing Human Rights: A History* (New York: Norton, 2007); Jenny S. Martinez, *The Slave Trade and the Origins of International Humanitarian Law* (New York: Oxford University Press, 2012). For the second, Samuel Moyn, *The Last Utopia: Human Rights in History* (Cambridge, MA: Belknap Press of Harvard University Press, 2010); Stefan-Ludwig Hoffmann, ed., *Human Rights in the Twentieth Century* (Cambridge: Cambridge University Press, 2010); Akira Iriye, Petra Goedde, and William I. Hitchcock, eds., *The Human Rights Revolution: An International History* (Oxford: Oxford University Press, 2011).

37. Van Ittersum, *Profit and Principle*; Philip J. Stern, *The Company-State: Corporate Sovereignty and the Early Modern Foundations of the British Empire in India* (New York: Oxford University Press, 2011).

38. For an excellent primer, see Duncan Bell, ed., *Ethics and World Politics* (Oxford: Oxford University Press, 2010).

39. Lauren Benton, *Law and Colonial Cultures: Legal Regimes in World History, 1400–1900* (Cambridge: Cambridge University Press, 2002); Benton, *A Search for Sovereignty: Law and Geography in European Empires, 1400–1900* (Cambridge: Cambridge University Press, 2010).

40. Frederick Cooper, *Colonialism in Question: Theory, Knowledge, History* (Berkeley: University of California Press, 2005); Cooper and Jane Burbank, *Empires in World History: Power and the Politics of Difference* (Princeton, NJ: Princeton University Press, 2010).

41. On the intellectual history of empire, see especially David Armitage, ed., *Theories of Empire, 1450–1800* (Aldershot: Variorum, 1998); Ruth Ben-Ghiat, ed., *Gli imperi. Dall'antichità all'età contemporanea* (Bologna: Il Mulino, 2009); Sankar Muthu, ed., *Empire and Modern Political Thought* (Cambridge: Cambridge University Press, 2012).

42. Sugata Bose, *A Hundred Horizons: The Indian Ocean in the Age of Global Empire* (Cambridge, MA: Harvard University Press, 2006); Bose and Kris Manjapra, eds., *Cosmopolitan Thought Zones: South Asia and the Global Circulation of Ideas* (Basingstoke: Palgrave Macmillan, 2010); Cemil Aydin, *The Politics of Anti-Westernism in Asia: Visions of World Order in Pan-Islamic and Pan-Asian Thought* (New York: Columbia University Press, 2007); Erez Manela, *The Wilsonian Moment: Self-Determination and the International Origins of Anticolonial Nationalism* (New York: Oxford University Press, 2007); Nico Slate, *Colored Cosmopolitanism: The Shared Struggle for Freedom in the United States and India* (Cambridge, MA: Harvard University Press, 2011).

43. Peter Burke, "Context in Context," *Common Knowledge* 8 (2002): 152–77; Rita Felski and Herbert F. Tucker, eds., "Context?," *New Literary History* 42 (2011): vii–xii, 557–756; Peter E. Gordon, "Contextualism and Criticism in the History of Ideas," in this volume.

44. John Randolph, "The Space of Intellect and the Intellect of Space," in this volume.

45. "L'espace, c'est ce qui était mort, figé, non dialectique, immobile. En revanche, le temps, c'était riche, fécond, vivant, dialectique": "Questions à Michel Foucault sur la géographie," *Hérodote* 1 (1976): 78.

46. Adi Ophir and Steven Shapin, "The Place of Knowledge: A Methodological Survey," *Science in Context* 4 (1991): 3–21; Diarmid A. Finnegan, "The Spatial Turn: Geographical Approaches to the History of Science," *Journal of the History of Biology* 41 (2008): 369–88; Charles W. J. Withers, "Place and the 'Spatial Turn' in Geography and in History," *Journal of the History of Ideas* 70 (2009): 637–58. More generally see Jo Guldi, "What Is the Spatial Turn?": http://spatial.scholarslab.org/spatial-turn (accessed January 31, 2013).

47. Steven Shapin, "Placing the View from Nowhere: Historical and Sociological Problems in the Location of Science," *Transactions of the Institute of British Geographers,*

n.s., 23 (1998): 6–7 (quoted); John Tresch, "Cosmologies Materialized: History of Science and History of Ideas," in this volume.

48. Simon Schaffer, "Newton on the Beach: The Information Order of *Principia Mathematica*," *History of Science* 47 (2009): 243–76.

49. Steven J. Harris, "Long-Distance Corporations, Big Sciences, and the Geography of Knowledge," *Configurations* 6 (1998): 269–304; Harold J. Cook, *Matters of Exchange:* Commerce, Medicine, and Science in the Dutch Golden Age (New Haven, CT: Yale University Press, 2007); Luke Clossey, *Salvation and Globalization in the Early Jesuit Missions* (Cambridge: Cambridge University Press, 2008); Anna Winterbottom, "Producing and Using the *Historical Relation of Ceylon*: Robert Knox, the East India Company and the Royal Society," *British Journal for the History of Science* 42 (2009): 515–38.

50. Tony Ballantyne, *Orientalism and Race: Aryanism in the British Empire* (Basingstoke: Palgrave Macmillan, 2002), 1–17.

51. "Une science des relations internationales en matière de culture": Bourdieu, "Les conditions sociales de la circulation internationale des idées," 1.

52. Charles W. J. Withers, *Placing the Enlightenment: Thinking Geographically about the Age of Reason* (Chicago: University of Chicago Press, 2007); Withers and Robert Mayhew, "Geography: Space, Place and Intellectual History in the Eighteenth Century," *Journal for Eighteenth Century Studies* 34 (2011): 445–52; Caroline Winterer, "Where Is America in the Republic of Letters?," *Modern Intellectual History* 9 (2012): 597–623; Sebastian Conrad, "Enlightenment in Global History: A Historiographical Critique," *American Historical Review* 117 (2012): 999–1027.

53. Anthony Pagden, *The Fall of Natural Man: The American Indian and the Origins of Comparative Ethnology*, rev. ed. (Cambridge: Cambridge University Press, 1986); Annabel Brett, *Changes of State: Nature and the Limits of the City in Early Modern Natural Law* (Princeton, NJ: Princeton University Press, 2011); David Armitage and Alison Bashford, eds., *Pacific Histories: Ocean, Land, People* (Basingstoke: Palgrave Macmillan, 2014).

54. Daniel Carey, *Locke, Shaftesbury, and Hutcheson: Contesting Diversity in the Enlightenment and Beyond* (Cambridge: Cambridge University Press, 2006).

55. Srinivas Aravamudan, "Hobbes and America," in *The Postcolonial Enlightenment: Eighteenth-Century Colonialism and Postcolonial Theory*, ed. Daniel Carey and Lynn Festa (Oxford: Oxford University Press, 2009), 37–70; Pat Moloney, "Hobbes, Savagery, and International Anarchy," *American Political Science Review* 105 (2011): 189–204.

56. Emma Rothschild, "The Atlantic Worlds of David Hume," in *Soundings in Atlantic History: Latent Structures and Intellectual Currents, 1500–1830*, ed. Bernard Bailyn and Patricia L. Denault (Cambridge, MA: Harvard University Press, 2009), 405–48.

57. P. J. Marshall and Glyndwr Williams, *The Great Map of Mankind: British Perceptions of the World in the Age of Enlightenment* (London: Dent, 1982); Paul Cheney, *Revolutionary Commerce: Globalization and the French Monarchy* (Cambridge, MA: Harvard University Press, 2010); Muthu, *Enlightenment against Empire*; Jennifer Pitts, *A Turn to Empire: The Rise of Imperial Liberalism in Britain and France* (Princeton, NJ:

Princeton University Press, 2005); David Armitage, "Globalizing Jeremy Bentham," *History of Political Thought* 32 (2011): 63–82.

58. Duncan Bell, "Dissolving Distance: Technology, Space, and Empire in British Political Thought, c. 1770–1900," *Journal of Modern History* 77 (2005): 523–63; Michael Lang, "Mapping Globalization or Globalizing the Map: Heidegger and Planetary Discourse," *Genre: Forms of Discourse and Culture* 36 (2006): 239–50; Benjamin Lazier, "Earthrise; or, The Globalization of the World Picture," *American Historical Review* 116 (2011): 602–30.

59. Emma Rothschild, "Arcs of Ideas: International History and Intellectual History," in *Transnationale Geschichte: Themen, Tendenzen und Theorien,* ed. Gunilla Budde, Sebastian Conrad, and Oliver Janz (Göttingen: Vandenhoeck and Ruprecht, 2006), 217–26; Chris Goto-Jones, "The Kyoto School, the Cambridge School, and the History of the Political Philosophy in Wartime Japan," *Positions: East Asia Cultures Critique* 17 (2009): 13–42.

60. C. A. Bayly, *Recovering Liberties: Indian Thought in the Age of Liberalism and Empire* (Cambridge: Cambridge University Press, 2012).

61. David Armitage, "What's the Big Idea? Intellectual History and the *Longue Durée,*" *History of European Ideas* 38 (2012): 493–507; Armitage, *Civil War: A History in Ideas* (New York: Knopf, forthcoming).

62. Rothschild, "Arcs of Ideas," 221.

63. David Armitage and Sanjay Subrahmanyam, "The Age of Revolutions, *c.* 1760–1840: Global Causation, Connection, and Comparison," in *The Age of Revolutions in Global Context, c. 1760–1840,* ed. Armitage and Subrahmanyam (Basingstoke: Palgrave Macmillan, 2010), xxxi.

64. Rothschild, "Arcs of Ideas," 222. For implied rebuttals of this accusation, see, for example, Jonathan Rose, *The Intellectual Life of the British Working Classes,* 2nd ed. (New Haven, CT: Yale University Press, 2010); Christopher Hilliard, *To Exercise Our Talents: The Democratization of Writing in Britain* (Cambridge, MA: Harvard University Press, 2007).

65. J. S. Mill, "Bentham," *London and Westminster Review* 19 (August 1838): 467.

66. Emma Rothschild, "Language and Empire, *c.* 1800," *Historical Research* 78 (2005): 210; Rothschild, "Political Economy," in Stedman Jones and Claeys, *Cambridge History of Nineteenth-Century Political Thought,* 774–76.

67. Simon Schaffer, Lissa Roberts, Kapil Raj, and James Delbourgo, eds., *The Brokered World: Go-Betweens and Global Intelligence, 1780–1820* (Sagamore Beach, MA: Science History Publications, 2009).

68. Bose and Manjapra, *Cosmopolitan Thought Zones*; Emma Rothschild, *The Inner Life of Empires: An Eighteenth-Century History* (Princeton, NJ: Princeton University Press, 2011).

69. Goto-Jones, "The Kyoto School," 14 ("historical context does not appear to overlap with spatiocultural context").

70. Donald R. Kelley, Joseph Levine, Allan Megill, J. B. Schneewind, and Ulrich Johannes Schneider, "Intellectual History in a Global Age," *Journal of the History of Ideas* 66 (2005): 143–200; Andrew Sartori, *Bengal in Global Concept History:*

Culturalism in the Age of Capital (Chicago: University of Chicago Press, 2008); Antony Black, "Toward a Global History of Political Thought," in *Western Political Thought in Dialogue with Asia*, ed. Takashi Shōgimen and Cary J. Nederman (Lanham, MD: Lexington Books, 2009), 25–42; Samuel Moyn and Andrew Sartori, eds., *Global Intellectual History* (New York: Columbia University Press, 2013); Shruti Kapila, "Global Intellectual History and the Indian Political," in this volume.

13

Global Intellectual History and the Indian Political

Shruti Kapila

In the absence of a historically defined field of inquiry and conversation of the kind that European intellectual history or political and social theory have been conducting for nearly a century, the term "global intellectual history" signals a new debate. This is a conversation, however, that is increasingly intrusive and significant, though one without any established norms or consensual reference points. Nevertheless, a series of historical conjunctures has produced, if not the efficacy of the term "global intellectual history," then certainly the need for it. The first conjuncture relates to the pluralization, or perhaps the death, of Enlightenment Europe. The "postwar" serves as the Archimedean point in the life of the twentieth century in which the promises and goods of the Enlightenment, even if not directly challenged, seemed to be decomposing under their own weight.[1] It had become apparent that freedom and liberty did not lead necessarily to peace, but to a level of destruction that called into question the viability of the human subject (or "Man"), who had always been central to the project of the Enlightenment.[2] Encapsulating his own prodigious and influential project, Michel Foucault famously stated, "Man is an invention whose recent date, and whose nearing end perhaps, are easily shown by the archaeology of our thought."[3] In other words, the sacred subject of the Enlightenment and its countercurrents was not merely questioned but the modalities of epistemology and metaphysics that had effectively universalized man and his history were rendered increasingly parochial to a time past.

Second, and by contrast, the very goods of the Enlightenment that were supposedly freighted abroad over the previous century took on a life of their own well beyond Europe even in its most extensive sense. To adapt Dipesh Chakrabarty's metaphor, with Indian independence and decolonization across the globe, the "waiting-room of history" was violently burst open.[4] Chakrabarty's main concern in his work was the "temporal horizon" that had consigned the majority of humanity to a "not yet" state of readiness and one incapable of freedom and self-government. Consequently history was occupied by Europe while the rest of the world, so to speak, languished in its waiting room. Eschewing claims of "cultural relativism" or any redemptive potential in "nationalist, nativist, or atavistic" assertions, the project of "provincializing Europe" for Chakrabraty is to "problematize India" and to simultaneously "dismantle Europe." The critical role of history for subject-formation, or historicism, more generally is central to his project that encompasses Marx's *Capital* and the new culture of Indian intellectual sociability in a single volume. Instead of provincializing Europe to its own cultural and historical specificity, Chakrabarty's powerful intervention examines how the idea of "Europe" became the original habitus of modern ideas including "reason." He equally aimed to demonstrate how this had been "made to look obvious far beyond the ground where it originated." In these terms, the postcolonial intervention was neither anti-Enlightenment in any simple sense, nor concerned with the declaration of the death of Man, but a reflection on the coproduction by empire and Enlightenment of the normative import of Europe itself. In this reckoning then, it is neither particularly desirable nor easily possible to break away from normative categories, be they capital, the state, or history. Yet it is vital to signify the struggle inherent in wrestling with "categories whose global currency can no longer be taken for granted."[5]

Finally, there is no question that the scope of European intellectual history has recently been extended. Once more, the rubric of Empire, much as it did in the nineteenth century, has provided the vehicle for the outward freighting and trafficking of European ideas.[6] This large, growing, and impressive body of literature, however, has generally failed to note significant ruptures in the meaning, content, and use of "European ideas," which, in the very act of dislocation from Europe, were significantly transformed.[7] The alteration of ideas over time, especially for a historian of India, the transformative potential of place for ideas, remains significant. This does not necessarily mean that ideas—whether of liberty or democracy—were transformed by some "indigenous' tradition, or through the work of cultural nativism. Both the extension and the provincialization of Europe refer to a number of parallel interventions in scholarship. Whether or not these interventions belong to the same conversation, some broad methodological features can be identified. Yet it is highly improbable that these features will amount to or signal the emergence of "global intellectual history" in any homogenous sense.

In the last two decades a heady conversation with the nearly unrecognizable ghosts of Foucault and Edward Said centered postcoloniality primarily as a concern with knowledge and its coercive effects. In acrimonious disputes arising out of their work, others argued that "dialogue" and "exchange" had marked the European encounter with non-Europeans especially in the realm of knowledge and culture.[8] This set of debates nevertheless partook of parallel discussions in social and political theory that were increasingly becoming skeptical of "modular" approaches. By the end of the twentieth century, terms such as "modernity" and the "universal" were therefore increasingly viewed with deep skepticism. This skepticism related as much to questions of culture as it did to more traditional power relations.

In this context it is interesting to note that Indian historical writing took a very different trajectory from that of the history of political thought over this period. Both instrumental, "Namierite" interpretations of Indian nationalism and easily relocated class-based analyses were challenged. India emerged as a "culture" or "society" and latterly as a locus of the generative and transformative potential of political ideas. "Western" political thought was transfixed on the wreckage of the twentieth century's grand ideological projects—communism, fascism—and more recently liberal democracy's uneven relationship with late capitalism. India, on the other hand, emerged in the mid-twentieth century as a republic and democracy with an arguably flawed but vibrant agenda of social justice. Later, and perhaps paradoxically, its leaders forged a Faustian compact with neoliberalism. From the perspective of the present and in the shadow of financial and related "crises," the relationship of the political with the economic has been resurrected across the globe. In the Indian context, the mid-twentieth century moment of independence and Partition is instructive. The economic context was far from propitious for the flourishing of any ambitious political ideas, especially those of social justice and democracy that increasingly became central to the "idea" of independent India.[9] Yet the power of the imagination to institutionalize a democratic politics stands in direct contrast to the economic frailty of the Indian context. As the political theorist Uday Mehta has argued, the founding figures of India institutionalized what he describes as a form of "political absolutism."[10] The primacy of the political, as the second half of this essay will demonstrate, was, nevertheless, an outcome of ideological maneuvers that cannot be explained away by exigent and contingent historical and economic factors alone.

All this poses a challenge to grand historical narratives both of liberal democratic diffusion and national liberation. Parallel to this, "the global" in recent years has become the preferred rubric under which to investigate modernity, not as a Weberian project through which capitalist rationality came to replace "the dream societies of the East," but one in which jagged and uneven power relations across the globe were reflected in many divergent and often incommensurable political ideologies.[11] While it may be in the vein of the "too early to say" syndrome to cast historical judgment on the nature of the new economic order in India in relation to the political, it is nevertheless possible to state that any effort to universalize neoliberalism and its "crisis" is difficult.[12] Abstractions such as "capital" are not necessarily impeded in their universalistic claims via "culture" or difference alone, but rather as the instruction from India will exemplify, the imagination of the political had the power not only to create a new nation-state, but significantly to redistribute concepts such as democracy into a new historical trajectory, one that belies any derivative relationship with Europe or the universal.

Placing the Global

The opening of the twenty-first century has witnessed a number of scholarly interventions marking the reinvigoration of the claims of intellectual history and the history of ideas to be major drivers of historical change. More significantly, this has resurrected the question of the relationship of ideas themselves to the material and political world that was sidelined either by deep textuality or by the retreat to microhistory that marked earlier histories of ideas and European intellectual history. While the intellectual frontier of European political thought has been extended, by the same token, the related trajectory of postcolonial historiography that was fixated on issues of representation has relegated issues of identity to a secondary order compared with more fundamental questions of politics and economy.[13]

One emerging aspect of this new historiography has been an emphasis on the "exchange" of ideas across cultural or civilizational boundaries, a feature that was conspicuous by its absence in earlier, but equally ambitious, intellectual histories. The approach stressing "exchange," with its corollary of "dialogue," foregrounds forms of circulation and "networks" that facilitated such exchanges of ideas.[14] This is a method that resonates with current debates on the "global" career of science in the age of empires.[15]

The model of diffusion-derivation or the impact-response approaches of an earlier era have thus been jettisoned in favor of "circulation" and "exchange."

To say nothing of the reductive nature of the earlier, but dominant, impact-response method that privileged an active "core" (Europe) with a passive and recipient "periphery" (the rest of the world) to explain the expansive horizon of ideas ranging from science to modernization. There is nevertheless a shared assumption between the older and the newer but critical approach that privileges exchange across the global context. In other words, both of these methods take the global as the horizon of ideas—including those of empire, economy, and science—while eliding, avoiding, and circumventing questions of conflict. A shared strategy of avoidance, then, at best deems conflict a historical context often associated with colonialism, but rarely goes so far as to consider conflict as endemic to any interaction between diverse cultures or politically incommensurable relations of power. This strategy also fails to recognize conflict as constitutive of arguments over the meaning of concepts. Though not unique to India, argument, conflict, and debate over the meaning of a concept is productive of political discourse rather than a vehicle for its silent reception.[16]

While the global has gained ascendancy as the preferred rubric of insight, strikingly the term itself has invoked little historical-conceptual treatment.[17] It remains unclear, however, what the interpretative purchase of the term "global" may be. Is it a historical epoch marked by both the fruition and the critique of the "national"? Or is it the reinterpretation of modernization theory in which globalization can be identified as a historical process that is marked not so much by exchange as by homogenization and convergence?[18] Or, is it an entirely new arrangement in human affairs marked by "virtual capital" and deterritorialization?[19] In many of these approaches territory is transcended, and movement and mobility, whether of ideas or people, become dominant themes.

Much like their mid-twentieth-century counterparts, recent philosophical appraisals of the term "global," by contrast, deploy the term with a potential for pessimism in which the figure of the "human" and its destruction form the core consideration.[20] If the atomic bomb made it possible to think of the finitude of humanity and indeed the human as a category or species in relation to the global, then equally the events of September 11, 2001, have rearticulated a similar philosophical plaintiveness. Jean-Luc Nancy archly posits a distinction between the abstract totality of the global and "world-forming" processes marked by human endeavor.[21] This distinction as offered by Nancy between the world and the global is nevertheless useful inasmuch as the former is marked by the expansion of the human horizon, whether of capital or technology, while the latter is understood as something "abstract," as a "totality" and within this philosophical disposition, endowed with the capacity to destroy the world itself.

More often than not, the term "global" for the historian serves as a measure and a scale of space rather than an abstraction or a totality. Fundamentally, the term "global" in sociohistorical discussions is emerging as the extension of physical context, or more precisely as a spatial unit that acts as a receptacle of ideas.[22] The term "global" thus invites interpretative vigilance. Its insistent use seems as such to be a convenient, though not robust, circumvention of earlier terminology, such as "modernity" or the "universal" itself. Indeed, "the global," used unreflectively, runs the danger of reinscribing the very concepts it seeks to critique. This is especially the case when the term is deployed as a general heuristic device rather than as a critical description of interconnected debates or projects, whether in the realm of politics or the economy. This perspective on the spatial as a global measure is especially underscored in relation to the normative scale of the nation-state in the twentieth century.

A "global intellectual history" that may or may not gain currency has nevertheless identified the necessity of reopening the issue of the "national." The "national" in question refers both to the unit and telos of inquiry and to the nature of the intellectual and ideological work that was done in the name of nationalism. To that extent, global intellectual history may indeed be able to liberate and denationalize "area studies" and make them conversant with other disciplinary formations, whether of international relations or political theory. This is especially fruitful in critiquing political-spatial divisions of the world bound up with historiographical norms of the Cold War in which a new hierarchy of first, second, and the third world became salient.[23] Interestingly, this categorization also underplayed the significance and normative value of the nation-state, as "area studies" were molded along civilizational-linguistic and subcontinental lines by terms such as the "Middle East" or "South Asia."[24]

In the case of India, global intellectual history has been an instructive correction to a pervasive inwardness. Previously, the place of India in the humanities and social sciences was reduced to a discussion of its "society" or "culture." Its politics and historical change were largely explained in categories that repeatedly returned to caste and religion. Recent works, by contrast, have highlighted the power of ideas as an object of inquiry in their own right, but also as a driver of historical change. Neither resentment nor celebration should be our disposition, but rather the acknowledgment that, despite historical subordination to a European power, intellectual activity in the subcontinent produced creative political thinking on the future of an India about which little was previously known and everything was possible to imagine.[25] In other words, whether it was a Gandhi or an Ambedkar or a Nehru, what was at stake for these founding figures was not so much the parting of ways with Europe, but a parting with, and decoupling from history itself, the creation of a new world, a new moral vocabulary, and a new imaginary.

In his famous speech that formally announced Indian independence in the pitch darkness of midnight of August 15, 1947, Nehru named that moment a "tryst with destiny." Yet the import of the speech was geared to the future and declared the moment itself as an "opening" and an inauguration of History itself. Announcing India's sovereignty and freedom, Nehru remarked that the past was filled with a "sorrow" that remained, yet he still avowed, "Nevertheless the past is over . . . the turning point is past, and history begins anew for us, the history which we shall live and act and others will write about." This was not naive nationalist conceit, as Nehru, who was also a popular and best-selling historian, was mindful in situating India in world history and dubbed India's destiny and future a "responsibility" to "humanity" that generated "dreams" that were "for the world." Further, this world, much like the concept of "freedom," was indivisible in peace and disaster given that this "one world c[ould] no longer be split into isolated fragments."[26]

The question to be asked, especially for the deeply interconnected twentieth century, is not how ideas such as liberalism, democracy, communism, and social justice changed India, but, rather, how India radically reformulated these ideas and practices themselves and then projected them into the global arena. The shift in perspective is crucial and fundamental, for until very recently, Europe and America have remained the unchallenged and almost exclusive loci of intellectual history.

Modern India is the world's largest democracy, with linguistic and religious diversity and a highly politicized society, which plunged into republicanism, universal suffrage, and affirmative action and rewrote their scripts. Its methodological importance for political theory and intellectual history should be as great as, if not greater than, that of Euro-America. But how should something that might broadly be called global intellectual history be conducted? A number of case studies illustrate different approaches, which have been adopted by authors who, despite their differences, place India near the center of a global transaction of ideas.

Two metaphors have recently been used to inform "global intellectual history." The first refers to capital, exchange, and circulation. It has been argued that the rise of culture as a concept can only be understood in the context of the emergence of global capital. While not representing an entirely new perspective, Andrew Sartori's work nevertheless identifies circulation—whether of commodities, capital, or ideas—as the modality of the global.[27] Yet unlike commodities, political ideas elude ownership, and they can only have purchase once they have been settled in a particular place, as opposed to gaining in "value" via constant circulation. Their "worth" may dramatically fluctuate, and ideas may become incommensurable, since unlike commodities and currencies, ideas cannot be fixed. Ideas thus defy any easy and plausible pairing with "capital."

A second metaphor explains the global history of ideas in terms of paternity and hybridization, an analogy with plants. Akin to cross-pollination, dialogic approaches privilege diffusion. To take the iconic example of John Stuart Mill and liberty, it is striking that though ever-present in Indian intellectual debates of the nineteenth century, Mill and his concepts were entirely remade. In C. A. Bayly's new work, which examines the Indian career of the nineteenth-century global concept of liberalism, what emerges is neither the diffusion nor difference of concepts across time and space.[28] Instead, a form of betrayal of the original is what gave liberalism any claim to universality. As such, a transaction or exchange of ideas is marked not by hermeneutic dissonance alone but is further staked on the life and future of political projects. A form of betrayal then allowed liberalism to be situated within Indian "life worlds" and in the process became the foundational lineage of Indian democracy and the nation-state.

The Instruction of India for the Century and the Globe

If the global cannot be exhausted by its spatial unity or as a planetary receptacle for the movement of ideas, then the issue of temporality remains equally significant. The late eighteenth and nineteenth centuries and the imperial transaction of ideas are increasingly gaining the attention of intellectual historians. The "age of empires" undoubtedly created historical connections, asymmetries, and political vocabularies that transcended locality.[29]

However, what is of critical importance here is the appearance of the radically new and the conditions that make its acceptance possible and plausible. Those concepts and ideas that do not have a deep history but appear as powerful and inevitable or as the "event" require our attention. For instance, democracy and republicanism had no deep history in what is now the world's largest democracy, namely India. Neither of these concepts had been the principles of a long historical struggle as they had been in North America or France. Rather, they were unexpected and contingent outcomes of the freedom movement and nationalism.

Secondly, it is departure from History that will create the novelty of the field of global intellectual history and decisively distinguish it from a mere politically acceptable version of the "expansion of Europe." Finally, and relatedly, the twentieth century is particularly hospitable to such an approach. The question of the century is significant and offers a potential specification of the "global." The aim would not be to construe or describe the twentieth century as totalitarian, liberal, national, or communist, even though much of it can be understood in these terms. Following on from some recent appraisals, particularly that of Alain Badiou, the aim is to examine the century from its own subjective nature. In other words, what was the character or key trait of the century itself?

Badiou's ambitious project, which ultimately aims to philosophically reinterpret communism, nevertheless clarifies the conceptual stakes that made the century political, violent, and quite unlike any other temporal horizon. Three themes exemplified below in the case of India are pertinent. First, he positions the subject construed both as a "lack" and its "becoming" through an event, as central to the political. Secondly, he argues that unlike freedom or equality, "fraternity" becomes the "real manifestation of the new world." Finally, he argues that the century had "its own vision of historical time," which was part of what he terms the "subjective horizon."

The central characteristic of the twentieth century thus is that of a confrontation with History. This was indeed the Nietzschean century in which the past had to be confronted and annihilated in order to create a wholly new beginning. This radical commencement of the future had, by necessity, to be taken as discontinuous with the inherited past. This included notions of the subject both as the site of the political and as one that can "be sacrificed to a historical cause that exceeds him." In Badiou's words, "The century has borne a combative conception of existence. . . . Whatever its scale, private or planetary, every real situation is a scission, a confrontation, a war."[30]

At least for the twentieth century, whether in the case of the Iranian revolution, al-Qaeda, or even Chinese communism, historical genealogy and a relationship with circulating European ideas reflect only a small part of the story, yet the idea of war and confrontation remains central. Even for a universally accepted philosopher and critic of the last century, namely Hannah Arendt, the theme of a new beginning is central to considerations of the political, revolutionary or otherwise.[31] The task of a global intellectual history would be to place radical ruptures at the heart of its analysis. It was their discontinuity with the past and apprehension of the future with the appearance and acceptance of the "new" that determined the character of the century's political projects. Indeed, the nature of the "political" stands at the very center of a possible global intellectual history. These themes will be discussed in the remainder of the essay.

Indian political thought, especially as it emerged in and through the nationalist canon of the twentieth century, was primarily the domain of political practitioners whether be they leaders, reformers, jurists, or ideologues. In other words, be it Ambedkar or Nehru, they were all primarily preoccupied, to invert Marx's dictum, with changing the world rather than interpreting it. Their thought was consequentialist in nature and operated in a context that was by definition well "beyond the arm-chair." Perhaps this is precisely why it is only very recently and more than sixty years after the deliverance of the nation-state in South Asia that the field of "intellectual history" and the powerful words of these men have regained the attention of scholars. It is a historical fact that their words have had great impact, perhaps too much so. Unlike the case in Europe, the issue of "reception" and the reputation of political thinkers do not pose themselves as problems. On the contrary, it was their very effectiveness as political practitioners that obfuscated their role as political thinkers. Indeed, the burden falls on the intellectual historian to reconstruct these "politicians" as thinkers and their words as concepts that were central to the making of political thought in our global century.[32] Moreover, as historical actors, they operated in a world that was already and simultaneously imperial, national, and global.

The Eventuality of the Political and Its Ethical Echoes

The opening decade of the twentieth century in India witnessed a radical appraisal of questions of historical transformation involving violence and nonviolence, freedom and equality, and the form of the political and national subject. The primacy of the political in India was initially forged through the rewriting of liberalism and visions of national political economy in which "positive" intervention became salient.[33] As they became icons of an ideological revolution Gandhi and his genealogical predecessor Tilak forged a new vocabulary that broke with liberal considerations as they critiqued and circumvented dominant ideas of contract and self-interest as the basis of political life. This was achieved, over and above, by invoking the political in relation to its ethical articulation.[34]

Questions of enmity, violence and sacrifice, and a de-historicized but ethical understanding of the subject were made central and revised by these and other innovators in the short period of the first few decades of the twentieth century. To briefly summarize some of the new intellectual history of India, the aims of this historiography have been to reconstruct some of the foundational thinking on the political in twentieth-century India, placing ideas above historical contingency to explain the trajectory of some of the period's critical and ambitious changes, including freedom from colonization, partition, violence, and the founding of the world's largest democracy in a context marked by diversity.[35] The aim is to interpret the formation of the political and yet to denationalize nationalism. Equally, some of these works recover the persistence, though occlusion, of theological precepts in modern politics.[36]

The example of the interpretative life of the *Bhagavad-Gita*, an ur-text of modern Indian politics, brings the above into focus, broaching contemporary concerns of war, ethics, and the question of violence in political transformation.[37] In commenting upon the *Gita*, as they increasingly did from the nineteenth century on, India's literary and political leaders were participating in a transnational conversation, one that detached India from its own neighborhood to link it with a community of readers and writers in America and Europe. This was quite unlike the trajectory taken by Islamic texts with a similar colonial pedigree, for instance a juridical digest known as the *Hedaya* or even the Koran in its English translation, whose legitimacy depended upon recognition by an audience of Muslims outside India. For the *Gita*, and with it, the Hindu tradition, itself achieved a kind of territorial transcendence by forsaking the rest of Asia to join a debate with the West alone, given that the book attracted little attention in other parts of the world. This debate, moreover, broke with the exegetical tradition within which the text had previously been studied.

At the same time as it allowed Hinduism to become in some sense a "Western" religion, the *Gita* also permitted Indian political thought to part company with its European equivalent, particularly through the use that was made of the text to rethink politics in a novel language of "action without consequence." Indeed, it is remarkable how many of India's political and intellectual leaders of the last century and a half wrote detailed and extensive commentaries on the *Gita*, which they saw not simply in a romantic way as some authentic source of statecraft, but as a book that allowed them to reconsider the very nature of politics itself. In this sense the text plays the kind of role in Indian political thinking that Machiavelli's *The Prince* or Hobbes's *Leviathan* do for Europe, being like them a thoroughly modern work, and one that acted as a beginning rather than a vehicle of transition or appropriation.

As a text for colonial politics, the *Gita* permitted war to be placed at the center of debate in a national movement that would not, or could not, wage it against Britain. Rather than seeing the attention paid war in these discussions as a fantasy of imperialism's violent overthrow, what is interesting about it is the fact that the enemy who must be killed is always, as was the case with Arjuna in the original, a brother, friend, or teacher. At no point do these commentaries define the political opponent as alien, the problem being always the reverse, that he is familiar and far too intimate. As if this did not render the political relationship problematic enough, the text's modern interpreters rarely if ever named the colonial power as their enemy, not out of fear so much as because they were interested in generalizing what they thought was the political truth enunciated by the *Gita*—namely, the ethical implications of political enmity, into a theoretical one capable of universal application.

Questions of enmity and violence that have been central to modern Indian understandings of the political were unlike Western conceptions in this respect, in being detached from the state. An ideological innovator such as B. G. Tilak, the key nationalist figure prior to the arrival of Gandhi, was a thinker of the revolution who created a new and normative vocabulary of politics that made the question of violence possible and plausible. Tilak did so by directly confronting the possibility of the "event" of war and the ethics of killing. Tilak's commentary on the *Gita* was written at the same time as Gandhi's *Hind Swaraj*. Foundational of the twentieth-century political in India, these texts also mark out critical ideological distinctions. For Tilak, the political was staked on the question of the enemy and the ability to suspend ethical norms for the eruption of a new historical sequence. Violence in this instance was transformative of the political. Significantly, violence was not directed toward the "outsider" but was meaningful only when directed toward the familiar kin or the intimate. Thus, enmity was understood as fraternal in nature in which the conversion of the kinsman into the enemy became central. The powerful idea of "detached action" (*nishkaam karma*), enunciated by Krishna in the text, equipped Tilak with a conceptual repertoire with which he could create the political subject whose existence was entirely dependent on the event of violence. Consequently, the political emerged as the exception to the everyday, the former marked by violence and the latter by ethical norms, including nonviolence. As such, it is striking, and far from coincidental, that it was violence toward one's own, namely fratricide, that laid the conditions for and marked the moment of freedom and decolonization in the Indian subcontinent.[38]

While emblematic of and associated with violence and nonviolence, respectively, Tilak and Gandhi mounted a political language that lay beyond the claims and contract of the state and that emanated, above all, from the subject.[39] For Tilak this subject (whom he termed *stithiprajna*) was expounded as dehistoricist and detached and identity was marked by immutability and desireless action. Much as in Krishna's discourse to Arjuna, Tilak privileged the duty of action detached from its outcome and made central the ability to discriminate between the exception of the event and the normal unfolding of time. Founded and concluded within the limits of the event (in this instance, a fraternal war), such a subject beyond the event was rendered as a bundle of ethical and normative obligations to family, kin, and society. By extension, enmity was marked by the moment of war rather than as a primordial and/or repressed relationship of hatred, since in such a rendering, the end of war marked a return to fraternity and peace.[40]

The ethical "shores" of the political, to invert Jacques Rancière's formulation, nevertheless acquired its most extensive and consequentialist treatment in the global icon and "impossible Indian," Gandhi.[41] As Faisal Devji argues, Gandhi's conversion of the ethical into the political was founded on ideas of self-sacrifice in which the primacy of life itself was relegated to the duty to sacrifice interest and exhibit fearlessness toward death, thus marking out the political subject. By "separating dying from killing," Gandhi's nonviolence, as Devji expounds it, was at once "so ubiquitous and fundamental to social relations" and to human flourishing "as to have no history of its own." This separation and the virtue of death detached sovereignty from the state and deposited it into the individual.[42]

The privileging of the subject was produced through a visible set of techniques that ranged from celibacy to spinning, which operated at the level of the individual. As Gandhi often said, the essence of *Swaraj* (the nationalist term for self-rule) was self-transformation, and he provocatively argued that, were it possible under British rule, the question of imperial control over India would be an irrelevant one.[43] Analogously, Gandhi privileged the everyday as the sacred frame for such an ethical, if highly disciplinarian, subjectivity that unlike the revolutionary reckoning ushered in a "politics of patience."[44]

The event of the political for Gandhi was constitutive of the emergence and visibility of a central Gandhian precept, namely truth, or *satya*.[45] In other words, the highly visible movements—whether the Transvaal Campaign in 1901–1902 or the Salt Satyagraha of 1930—now stand for the indexicality of nonviolence in a century marked by violence and war. Here, however, the claim is that Gandhi took truth not as an act of speech or an aspect of conduct and cultivation. Rather, truth was a capacity, in its most ordinary enactment, of revelation. Truth was a visible form of the political in which all that was hidden came to the surface to display the ordering that made the practical world. Yet as a form of the political or as the visible, it could only be announced within a sequence of actions and events such as the Transvaal, Champaran, or salt *satyagrahas*. By deploying the technology of walking as political practice, as with the Salt Satyagraha, Gandhi converted it into political action equally available to one and all. The end of the walk was simple, culminating as it did in the making of salt. The making of this commodity, at once essential and prohibitively taxed, announced an essential, but true, paradox of power. This disruption of the abstract through the immediate centered Gandhi's political project. The insistence on truth or *satyagraha* was the interruption of the accepted or the consensual aspect of the real. Instead, in the simple act of breaking salt, under the banner of *satyagraha* (which translates as the insistence on truth), Gandhi made visible the oppression of abstraction. All these mobilizations sought to uncover or make visible the "real" nature of relations between Indians and whites, the cultivators and the planters, and the poor and the empire. It was the mirror image of the radical terrorists who, by their defined targets of assassination and bombings, identi-fied or made visible through the narcissism of violence the perpetrators of power who were oppressing the many. Truth was thus rendered as the opposite of violence.[46]

This radical politics of truth, while impossible to institutionalize, neverthe-less signaled the twentieth-century reevaluation of human experience. Despite his occasional gestures to Tolstoy, Ruskin, and Christ, Gandhi is difficult to place within any conventional genealogy of political ideas, despite the efforts of gener-ations of historians. Gandhi's own statement on "influences" is instructive. While not claiming to be "original" and having confessed to "have read much," Gandhi at the outset of *Hind Swaraj* states, "These views are mine. . . . They are mine because I hope to act according to them." Yet at the same time, it is not the direct historical influence of a particular thinker, but rather that Gandhi becomes comprehensible as a critic of the twentieth century when placed alongside a Nietzsche or a Foucault. Much like these thinkers, Gandhi was concerned with a post-Enlightenment and dehistoricist, if occasionally antihumanist, rendering of the human, but unlike them left a very different order of influence.

In resorting to everyday practices such as spinning or celibacy, Gandhi circumvented the political in the sense Carl Schmitt understood it in terms of the distinction between the friend and the foe. Yet at the same time, focusing on self-sacrifice and truth—the "moralization of politics," or what Chantal Mouffe calls the conduct of politics in the moral register—was not a case of merely obfuscating the friend/enemy antithesis.[47] Equally, it allowed for moral and political agonism, since Gandhi shared in the idea of the full recognition of the "Other."[48] Gandhi's assassination revealed the true nature of enmity and the secret life of Hindu nationalism. Significantly the ideological work of the full recognition but nonviolent solution of social antagonism/enmity became fun-damental to Indian democracy that was given an institutional life.

If and only *if* Gandhi is iconic of Indian freedom, then the final element in the modern political triad of liberty, fraternity, and equality was rewritten by the Indian constitution. The inexplicable arrival of democracy as an outcome of the freedom movement remains a contested question.[49] The radical and am-bitious project of a republican democracy that made equality its centerpiece was made possible only through the recognition and integration of the "social" into an aspect of the political via constitutionalism. It is argued that the found-ing of the constitution with the principle of India as a republic and a democ-racy institutionalized liberty, but held out freedom as a "distant prospect." The independent national state emerged, not as transcendent of interests or a dis-tant abstraction, but as all-powerful and interventionist. This, in contrast to

European and American examples, according to Uday Mehta, has produced a "form of political absolutism" in India.[50] Yet he critiques Hannah Arendt's "prophecy" that political power, which identifies political power with the "social," leads to terror, partly because that prophecy remains unfulfilled, but mainly because the "social" and its uplift became the "political" foundation of Indian democracy and its constitutionalism.[51] Such a project is associated above all with B. R. Ambedkar and his radical break with History.

The Political to Politics: Ambedkar and Agonistic Democracy

B. R. Ambedkar, the principal drafter of the Indian constitution, was a jurist who had broken away from many established trajectories. He was a *Dalit* (untouchable) who, despite the odds—considering that what separates Brahmins from untouchables is knowledge itself—obtained a Ph.D. from Columbia University. It is unclear why he chose Columbia, but significantly he did not follow the Indian elite's habit of going to Oxford or Cambridge. Whether or not he actively chose to study with John Dewey, both Dewey and Edwin Seligman were interlocutors in Ambedkar's intellectual life.[52] A radical critic of caste who famously renounced Hinduism for Buddhism, Ambedkar's entry into public life owed to his legal expertise. On his return to India from the London School of Economics in 1919, Ambedkar was appointed as the sole spokesman on the question of caste in imperial deliberations around electorates and representation. By the mid-1930s, the question of caste representation made public the hostility between Gandhi and Ambedkar. This departure, while signaling various ideological differences, can also be construed as a distinction between the present and the future of India's political life.

The key and acrimonious difference was that, while Gandhi accepted the recognition of Muslims for distinct legal and electoral representation, he refused the same recognition of difference for the low caste and the untouchables. Ambedkar, however, remained steadfast before and after his break with Gandhi and, in the end, was vindicated. In his first legal interventions in 1919, Ambedkar introduced the recognition of the "social" as an aspect of the political, a critical maneuver that would define India's democracy. Giving evidence to the Committee on Indian Franchise, he declared:

> The Congress has denied communal representation except in the case of Mohammedans [sic] and it also denied the extensive use of nomination, the only way then left open to the untouchables is to

fight in a general electorate. Now this is as it should be if all were
equally free to fight. . . . But it must never be forgotten that the
Congress is largely composed of men who are by design political
Radicals and social Tories. Their chant is that the social and the
political are two distinct things having no bearing on each other. To
them the social and the political are two suits and can be worn one at
a time as the season demands. Such a psychology has to be laughed
at because it is too interested to be seriously taken into consideration
either for acceptance or for rejection. As it pays to believe in it, it will
die a hard death.[53]

Thirty years after he first proclaimed it, the death of the separation of the
political from the social was delivered by the Indian Constitution. For Ambedkar, social inequality was made central to the idea of being a free Indian. The
instrumentality of citizenship as the form of contract between subject and the
state only occurred with the simultaneous recognition of the *Dalit* (the
oppressed) and social inequality. This entailed widespread reservation—a form
of affirmative action—for *Dalits* and "tribals" in all public institutions ranging
from education and employment to electoral representation and government.

If the political was constituted for Tilak as the exception to the everyday,
and if for Gandhi the everyday was the sacred time of political practice, then
Ambedkar's intervention on the political referred to the very object that both
Gandhi and Tilak had circumvented. The state and law became for Ambedkar's
project the critical site of the political. Ambedkar's paramount interest was in
the transition from the political in the Schmittian sense to "politics" and the
continuation of politics. In other words, in what ways could democracy ensure
the political, not as the exceptional event or as war with the specter of destruction hanging over it, but critically without erasing difference? The life of "political association" (a favored term of Ambedkar's) with distinct others and
unequals animates Ambedkar's political thought. Social conflict, which was
structural, historical, and based in caste, was recognized yet reconfigured as
institutionalized and perpetual competition. This is to say that conflict was
rendered nonviolent through caste-based affirmative action in all arenas of
public life, from education to employment to public office. Without aiming to
erase or transcend the categorical social difference between the *Dalit* and the
Brahmin, Ambedkar's project converted this inequality into a political relationship. The term "political association" allowed him to reject British and imperial
claims that India was but a conglomeration of "peoples" rather than a nation.
At the same time, it allowed him to accept and make legal the variegated nature
of India itself.

This had radical outcomes for the nature of democracy in India. For one, Amebdkar's view of democracy was premised on the renunciation of killing, but with the absolute recognition of adversaries. This politics, much like war, was decisionist in outcome in terms of victors and vanquished. For Ambedkar, enmity had to be tamed, though not denied, and converted into an adversarial politics. He did so by establishing legal and institutional practices that ranged from republicanism to affirmative action.[54]

Significantly, democracy was premised and staked upon making social strife part of the political and as a form of agonism. Ambedkar sought to institutionalize social strife and set it into a competitive framework through affirmative action.[55] Social agonism was elaborated through three critical maneuvers. In the first instance, the recognition of, and separation from, Muslim nationality, indeed the creation of Pakistan itself, was for Ambedkar the necessary precondition for the democratic agonism of the social.[56] Strikingly of all the leading nationalists, including Mohammad Ali Jinnah, the founder of Pakistan, Ambedkar mounted the clearest and the most elaborate discussion of Muslim nationality. This was deemed necessary as it had a direct relationship to the nature of democracy in India as he envisioned it. That is to say that it was only after the recognition of Muslim nationality that the case of the conversion of social antagonism in the form of caste in India could be institutionalized in a democratic form.

Throughout his long career, the underlying assumption of Ambedkar's project was that caste, unlike Muslim nationality, could not be territorially demarcated or provincialized.[57] If the social, as Uday Mehta rightly observes, is the foundation of the Indian constitution, then by extension it was precisely the inequity of caste that was generalizable into the national form.[58] The enduring legacy remains that the recognition of the *Dalit* premises the idea of a national subject. Political association for Ambedkar's influential project was entirely dependent upon the recognition of unequal differences.[59] Such a rethinking of social antagonism as political competition further stood apart from the competing ideology of the mid-twentieth century, namely communism, which sought to transcend social distinction. Moreover, and unlike fascism, which also gained short-lived popularity in Europe, and much like his political peers, Ambedkar's project did not externalize opposition as a means of undoing division but instead made it perpetually immanent.

Finally, Ambedkar, like Nehru, had recourse to European and global history. His examples ranged from the Roman republic and the League of Nations to American pragmatism. Yet the work of history for him was not to place India in a preexisting, evolving, and universal narrative. Instead, whether it was Rome or England, these examples were viewed and deployed as legal evidence and precedents to sever India's connection with those histories. This severance from history was made possible only by law. At stake, in the end, was a future that could only be founded through a rupture with the past.

The turn away from representation, culture, and identity has reopened the question of the political.[60] In the twenty-first century the global language of emancipation is democracy. According to various political theorists and philosophers, its very universality makes democracy meaningless, yet others have alerted us to the post-democratic present and to the tyranny of consensus.[61] By contrast and through the reinscription of foundational political precepts, India's ambitious ideological experiments that defy easy paternity exhort otherwise. An agonism that might nourish a democratic Europe, as several commentators and theorists demand, has not only been long-established, but has already presented its own problems in India. If global intellectual history is to become a coherent and viable field of scholarly debate, it will need to place rupture and departure at the center of its interests. It will therefore need to depart from conventional methodologies of European intellectual history, even when they are spatially expanded to an imperial and planetary dimension. Rather than derivation, influence, or exchange, which are dominant frames of reference for global intellectual history, India is instructive of the radical transformation of global ideas, whether of liberty, equality, and fraternity or what constitutes the political. To that extent, it is only the afterlife of Europe that will constitute something like global intellectual history, because "Europe" is now made elsewhere.

Notes

I am grateful to the editors, Sam Moyn and Darrin McMahon, as well as to Peter Gordon, Judith Surkis, and David Armitage for their comments at the Harvard workshop. I remain indebted to Chris Bayly, Faisal Devji, David Todd, and the Cambridge graduate students who have made the "Global Intellectual History" seminar for the last few years a vibrant forum for new ideas.

    1. Theodor W. Adorno and Max Horkheimer, *Dialectic of Enlightenment: Philosophical Fragments*, trans. John Cumming (1944; New York: Continuum, 1975); and Martin Jay, *The Dialectical Imagination: A History of the Frankfurt School and the Institute of Social Research, 1923–1950* (Berkeley: University of California Press, 1973).

    2. Jacques Derrida, "The Ends of Man," *Philosophy and Phenomenological Research* 30, no. 1 (1969): 31–57.

    3. Cited in ibid., 31.

    4. Dipesh Chakrabarty, *Provincializing Europe: Postcolonial Thought and Historical Difference* (Princeton, NJ: Princeton University Press, 2000).

5. Ibid., 8, 43, 45.

6. Sankar Muthu, *Enlightenment against Empire* (Princeton, NJ: Princeton University Press, 2003); Jennifer Pitts, *A Turn to Empire: The Rise of Imperial Liberalism in Britain and France* (Princeton, NJ: Princeton University Press, 2005); and Karuna Mantena, *Alibis of Empire: Henry Maine and the Ends of Liberal Imperialism* (Princeton, NJ: Princeton University Press, 2010).

7. Partha Chatterjee, *Nationalist Thought and the Colonial World: A Derivative Discourse?* (London: Zed, 1986); Ranajit Guha, *Dominance without Hegemony: History and Power in Colonial India* (Cambridge, MA: Harvard University Press, 1997); C. A. Bayly, *Origins of Nationality in South Asia: Patriotism and Ethical Government in the Making of Modern India* (Delhi: Oxford University Press, 1998); Sudipta Kaviraj, *The Imaginary Institution of India* (New York: Columbia University Press, 2010).

8. Mary Louis Pratt, *Imperial Eyes: Travel Writing and Transculturation* (London: Routledge, 1992); Bernard S. Cohn, *Colonialism and Its Forms of Knowledge* (Princeton, NJ: Princeton University Press, 1996); C. A. Bayly, *Empire and Information: Intelligence Gathering and Social Communication in India, 1780–1870* (Cambridge: Cambridge University Press, 1996); and Nicholas B. Dirks, *Castes of Mind: Colonialism and the Making of Modern India* (Princeton, NJ: Princeton University Press, 2001), have been the most influential.

9. Sunil Khilnani, *The Idea of India* (London: Hamish Hamilton, 1997).

10. Uday S. Mehta, "The Social Question and the Absolutism of Politics," *Seminar* 615 (2010): 23–27.

11. Frederick Cooper, *Colonialism in Question: Theory, Knowledge and History* (Berkeley: University of California Press, 2005).

12. Amartya Sen, *Development as Freedom* (Oxford: Oxford University Press, 1999), and for more contemporary issues, see Abhijit V. Banerjee and Esther Duflo, *Poor Economics: A Radical Rethinking of the Way to Fight Global Poverty* (New York: Public Affairs, 2011).

13. Aamir Mufti, *Enlightenment in the Colony: The Jewish Question and the Crisis of Postcolonial Culture* (Princeton, NJ: Princeton University Press, 2007); and Ritu Birla, *Stages of Capital: Law, Culture and Market Governance in Late Colonial India* (Durham, NC: Duke University Press, 2009).

14. Sugata Bose and Kris Manjapra, eds., *Cosmopolitan Thought Zones: South Asia and the Global Circulation of Ideas* (Basingstoke: Palgrave Macmillan, 2010).

15. Sujit Sivasundaram, ed., "Focus: Global Histories of Science," *Isis* 101, no. 1 (March 2010): 95–158.

16. Hannah Arendt, *On Revolution* (London: Penguin, 1963), and for an Indian culture of debate, Amartya Sen, *The Argumentative Indian: Writings on Indian History, Culture, and Identity* (London: Penguin, 2006).

17. But see Jean-Luc Nancy, *The Creation of the World or Globalization*, trans. from the French by François Raffoul and David Pettigrew (Albany: State University of New York Press, 2007).

18. C. A. Bayly, *The Birth of the Modern World, 1780–1914: Global Connections and Comparisons* (Malden, MA: Blackwell, 2004).

19. Arjun Appadurai, *Modernity at Large: Cultural Dimensions of Globalization* (Minneapolis: University of Minnesota Press, 1996).

20. "The world has lost its capacity to 'form a world.' . . . In the end, everything takes place as if the world affected and permeated itself with a death drive that soon would have nothing else to destroy but the world itself" (Nancy, *Creation*, 34). Also see Hannah Arendt, *The Origins of Totalitarianism* (London: Allen and Unwin, 1958), 267–302, and for a post–9/11 reflection, Faisal Devji, *The Terrorist in Search of Humanity: Militant Islam and Global Politics* (London: Hurst and Co. and Columbia University Press, 2008).

21. Nancy, *Creation*, 30–55.

22. But see Stephen Legg, ed., *Spatiality, Sovereignty and Carl Schmitt: Geographies of the Nomos* (London: Routledge, 2011).

23. Aijaz Ahmad, *In Theory: Classes, Nations, Literatures* (London: Verso, 1992), and Mark T. Berger, "After the Third World: History, Destiny and the Fate of Third Worldism," *Third World Quarterly* 25, no. 1 (2004): 9–39.

24. Nationalist narratives, for example, Bipan Chandra, *The Rise and Growth of Economic Nationalism in India: Economic Policies of Indian National Leadership, 1880–1905* (New Delhi: People's Publishing House, 1966), and officially sanctioned narratives, for example, Tara Chand, *History of the Freedom Movement in India*, 4 vols. (Delhi: Publications Division, Ministry of Information and Broadcasting, 1961–1972), were coterminous with the above.

25. Pratap Bhanu Mehta, *The Burden of Democracy* (Delhi: Penguin, 2003), and Khilnani, *Idea of India*.

26. Jawaharlal Nehru, *The Discovery of India* (London: Meridian, 1946) and *Glimpses of World History* (London: Drummond, 1939).

27. Andrew Sartori, *Bengal in Global Concept History: Culturalism in the Age of Capital* (Chicago: University of Chicago Press, 2008).

28. C. A. Bayly, *Recovering Liberties: Indian Thought in the Age of Liberalism and Empire* (New Delhi: Cambridge University Press, 2011).

29. Gabriel Paquette, *Enlightenment, Governance, and Reform in Spain and Its Empire, 1759–1808* (London: Palgrave, 2008); and David Todd, "A French Imperial Meridian, 1814–1870," *Past and Present*, no. 210 (February 2011): 155–86, for studies beyond the British Empire.

30. Alain Badiou, *The Century*, trans. Alberto Toscano (Cambridge: Polity, 2005), 98–110, 100, 37.

31. Arendt, *On Revolution*, 28–42.

32. Akeel Bilgrami, "Gandhi the Philosopher," *Economic and Political Weekly* 27 (2003): 4159–65.

33. Bayly, *Recovering Liberties*.

34. Shruti Kapila and Faisal Devji, eds., *Political Thought in Action: The Bhagavad Gita and Modern India* (New Delhi: Cambridge University Press, 2013); and Faisal Devji, *The Impossible Indian: Gandhi and the Temptations of Violence* (London: Hurst and Co. and Harvard University Press, 2012).

35. Shruti Kapila, ed., *An Intellectual History for India* (New Delhi: Cambridge University Press, 2010); Ramchandra Guha, ed., *Makers of Modern India* (London: Harvard University Press, 2011); Sunil Khilnani, ed., *Indian Political Thought* (forthcoming).

36. Paul W. Kahn, *Out of Eden: Adam and Eve and the Problem of Evil* (Princeton, NJ: Princeton University Press, 2007).

37. Faisal Devji and Ritu Birla, eds., "Itineraries of Self-Rule: Essays on the Centenary of Gandhi's *Hind Swaraj*," special issue of *Public Culture* 23, no. 2 (2011).

38. Shruti Kapila, "A History of Violence," in Kapila and Devji, *Political Thought*, 177–99.

39. It is equally striking that key political concepts of the twentieth century from Swadeshi (home-industry) to Swaraj (self-rule) owed their etymological root to the subject or self (*swa*) in Sanskrit. See Ajay Skaria, "Gandhi's Politics: Liberalism and the Question of the Ashram," *South Atlantic Quarterly* 101, no. 4 (2004): 955–86, and his "Living by Dying: Gandhi, *Satyagraha*, and the Warrior," in Anand Pandian and Daud Ali, eds., *Ethical Life in South Asia* (Bloomington: Indiana University Press, 2010). Parallel and overlapping discussions of *khudi* (self) as an ethical precept dominate the works of Muhammad Iqbal, often considered the ideological figurehead of modern Muslim nationality in South Asia. See Javed Majeed, *Muhammad Iqbal: Islam, Aesthetics and Postcolonialism* (New Delhi: Routledge, 2009).

40. B. G. Tilak, *Shrimad Bhagavadgita-Rahasya or Karma Yoga Shastra*, trans. B. S. Suthankar (Bombay: Bombay Vaibhav Press, 1935), 510–65 and 667–709.

41. Devji, *Impossible Indian*; compare Jacques Rancière, *On the Shores of Politics*, trans. Liz Heron (London: Verso, 1995).

42. Devji, *Impossible Indian*, 5–9.

43. Mohandas Gandhi, *Hind Swaraj*, ed. Anthony J. Parel (Cambridge: Cambridge University Press, 2005), 72–76.

44. Uday S. Mehta, "Patience, Inwardness, and Self-Knowledge in Gandhi's *Hind Swaraj*," *Public Culture* 23, no. 2 (2011): 417–29.

45. Shruti Kapila, "Gandhi before Mahatma: The Foundations of Political Truth," *Public Culture* 23, no. 2 (2011): 431–48.

46. Gandhi circumvented the dominant and available political languages of liberalism, historicism, and Marxism by focusing on sacrifice and the transformation of the self.

47. Chantal Mouffe, *On the Political* (Milton Park, Abingdon: Routledge, 2005).

48. Devji, *Impossible Indian*, 67–93.

49. Sumit Sarkar argues for the "decisive link between anti-colonial mass nationalism and the coming of democracy" and the radical ruptures of the debates of the Constituent Assembly that drafted the Indian constitution in the late 1940s. See his "Indian Democracy: The Historical Inheritance," in *The Success of India's Democracy*, ed. Atul Kohli (Cambridge: Cambridge University Press, 2001), 23–46.

50. Mehta, "The Social Question," 23–27.

51. Arendt, *On Revolution*, 59–114. Her central argument is that equality is made possible only under republicanism.

52. Arun P. Mukherjee, "B. R. Ambedkar, John Dewey, and the Meaning of Democracy," *New Literary History* 40, no. 2 (2009): 345–70.

53. B. R. Ambedkar, Evidence before the Southborough Committee on Franchise," January 27, 1919, para. 33 http://www.ambedkar.org/ambcd/07.%20Evidence%20 before%20the%20Southborough%20Committee.htm (accessed July 14, 2013).

54. David Held, *Models of Democracy*, 2nd ed. (Cambridge: Polity, 2003).

55. Christophe Jaffrelot, *India's Silent Revolution: The Rise of the Low Castes in North Indian Politics* (London: Hurst and Co., 2003).

56. B. R. Ambedkar, *Pakistan or the Partition of India: The Indian Political What's What!* (Bombay: Thacker and Co., 1946).

57. A position that became strident in the interwar period when Gandhi refused separate electorates for *Dalits*. Ambedkar prevailed only after Indian independence.

58. D. R. Nagaraj, *The Flaming Feet and Other Essays: The Dalit Movement in India* (Ranikhet: Permanent Black, 2010).

59. Rochana Bajpai, *Debating Difference: Group Rights and Liberal Democracy in India* (New Delhi: Oxford University Press, 2011).

60. Slavoj Žižek, *Welcome to the Desert of the Real! Five Essays on September 11 and Related Dates* (London: Verso, 2002), to cite the most popular.

61. Jacques Rancière, *Hatred of Democracy*, trans. Steve Corcoran (London: Verso, 2009); and Pierre Rosanvallon, *Democracy Past and Future*, ed. Samuel Moyn (New York: Columbia University Press, 2006).

14

Intellectual History and the Interdisciplinary Ideal

Warren Breckman

Interdisciplinarity is one of the most widespread values of the contemporary university. It is embraced as an ideal of a community of thought that transcends the tribal identities of the disciplines, a vision of integrated research and learning, geared not toward the preservation of academic turf but toward the real complexity of the world and its problems. If it is an ideal, it is also a reality, or at least partially. In addition to myriad instances of individual researchers finding common ground across disciplinary lines, people and resources cluster in interdisciplinary centers, institutes, and programs in the humanities, social sciences, natural sciences, and professional schools. As both an ideal of intellectual work and an institutional reality, interdisciplinarity taps impulses from "below" as well as "above": researchers spontaneously forge links and collaborations, even as administrators regard interdisciplinarity as a strategic tool toward many different ends. Interdisciplinarity provides an umbrella term that simultaneously unites a range of impulses, initiatives, interests, and practices, but at the same time, it may mask divergences and conflicts between different conceptions and implementations of the interdisciplinary ideal.

Intellectual historians sometimes feel themselves to be members of a marginal, if not alienated, subfield within their typical disciplinary home in history departments. Even as they may occasionally lament that condition, they will at least as often strike a self-congratulatory note by describing their activity as interdisciplinary. Indeed, a quick Internet search reveals a striking number of instances where intellectual history is declared to be "intrinsically" or "inherently" interdisciplinary. A repeated mantra either lulls us to sleep or its very repetition provokes questions. This essay will choose the latter over the former. In what way (or ways) is intellectual history interdisciplinary? What might we learn about the past and present state of this field by posing this question? What is revealed by the fact that intellectual history may just as often be described as a "subdiscipline" of history as an interdiscipline? How does intellectual history relate to the broader currents of interdisciplinarity that have swept through the modern university?

Two Interdisciplinarities

In the history of intellectual history in twentieth-century America, there were two moments of particularly clear reflection on its interdisciplinarity. The first centered on the emergence of the history of ideas and the founding of the *Journal of the History of Ideas* in the 1930s and early 1940s. Arthur Lovejoy first used the term "history of ideas" in 1919; in 1923, he formed the "History of Ideas Club" at Johns Hopkins University, where he was professor of philosophy. The club met monthly to discuss papers presented by members and guests. Regular participants came from philosophy, but also from literature, classics, history, history of medicine and science, and political science. Lovejoy's notion of a club that would embody an ideal of sociability and conversation across disciplines already pointed to the interdisciplinary commitment that formed a central part of his concept of the history of ideas. His most important work of intellectual history, *The Great Chain of Being*, opens with his most widely read definition of the history of ideas: "By the history of ideas I mean something at once more specific and less restricted than the history of philosophy. It is differentiated primarily by the character of the units with which it concerns itself."[1] These are the "unit-ideas," the enduring intellectual motifs and basic philosophical concepts that Lovejoy believed underlie the history of human thought. Using chemical metaphors, he described the historian of ideas as a kind of analytical chemist pursuing the basic elements that combine and recombine throughout the history of human intellectual endeavor. Critics like Leo Spitzer immediately attacked this "analytical" method, and there is no denying that Lovejoy's chemical metaphors suggested an arid and simplistic reductionism. In truth, though, he repeatedly emphasized that "nearly all of the great catchwords have been equivocal—or rather, multivocal," hence the need for careful study of the "role of semantic shifts, ambiguities, and confusions."[2] Moreover, he insisted that historians must consider the nonrational element, the "endemic assumptions," "unconscious mental habits," and "metaphysical pathos" that could create powerful attachments to certain ideas.

Lovejoy opened the first issue of the *Journal of the History of Ideas* with a programmatic essay laying out his vision for the journal. He intended it to counteract the tendency of modern scholarship toward narrow academic specialization. "A preconception, category, postulate, dialectical motive, pregnant metaphor or analogy, 'sacred word,' mood of thought, or explicit doctrine, which makes its first appearance upon the scene in one of the conventionally distinguished provinces of history . . . may, and frequently does, cross over into a dozen others."[3] To track these moving targets required an encyclopedic agenda and the cooperation of multiple disciplines. In its essence, the journal would replicate the ideal of the History of Ideas Club, with its interdisciplinary sociability and conversation. Yet, the history of ideas was not meant only as an adjunct to the various disciplines, nor even just the sum of an interdisciplinary inquiry. Rather, Lovejoy considered it a crowning form of historical knowledge. Hence, in a statement with an unmistakably idealistic tenor, he asserted that the "hero" of history is *homo sapiens*, so "the general task of intellectual historiography is to exhibit, so far as may be, the thinking animal engaged—sometimes fortunately, sometimes disastrously—in his most characteristic occupation."[4] The concept of interdisciplinarity emerging from this account pictures intellectual history as a bridge between the discrete disciplines; even more robustly, it imagines intellectual history as a kind of metadiscipline that studies the common core of all the disciplines.

Given the de facto fragility of this fledgling field within the humanities, one cannot but be struck by Lovejoy's bold imperialist claim. To be sure, there was resistance, for example from the literary historian René Wellek, who had already crossed swords with Lovejoy in a famous exchange over Romanticism. When Lovejoy suggested that "the ideas in serious reflective literature are, of course, in great part philosophical ideas in dilution," Wellek immediately attacked him for imposing external, philosophical standards on works of imagination, in short for not being interdisciplinary enough.[5] As well as opponents, there were also supporters, for Lovejoy's foundational gesture intersected with broader interdisciplinary impulses in American higher education. In the decades after World War I, concern about the fragmentation of knowledge as well as fear that Western civilization was falling apart fueled calls for a general education curriculum. Closely associated with the "Chicago Plan" conceived by the philosopher Mortimer Adler and the University of Chicago's long-serving president R. M. Hutchins, general education aimed, in Hutchins's words, to overcome "the disorder of specialization, vocationalism, and unqualified empiricism" by "framing a curriculum which educes the elements of our common human nature . . . a common stock of ideas and common methods of dealing with them."[6] After World War II, and with the advent of the Cold War, both

Adler and Hutchins carried this campaign to the national level, Hutchins as the head of the Ford Foundation, Adler as a popular philosophical writer, Columbia University professor, and editor of the fifty-four-volume *Great Books of the Western World*. Specific connections have been persuasively traced between Adler's idea of general education and Lovejoy's philosophical and historical conception.[7] Broadly speaking, the history of ideas and the champions of core curricula and canons found mutually reinforcing common ground in an ideal of interdisciplinarity based on the unity of Western culture, the values of liberty, and the ultimate oneness of the human mind. This context likely best explains why the *Journal of the History of Ideas* and the field it represented enjoyed a certain glamour in the twenty or so years after World War II.[8]

The constellation of forces that supported this form of liberal universalist interdisciplinarity came under attack in the 1960s and 1970s as more radical academics challenged the conceptual structures, canons, and disciplinary hierarchies of the American university. Interdisciplinarity went from being a tool of preservation to a tool for dismantling and reconstructing the academy. This critical reinvention of the interdisciplinary ideal drew on many different motives, from criticisms of the epistemological foundations and methodological premises of the disciplines to the desire to redraw the disciplines in ways that would open the gates to the excluded, including women, people of color, non-Westerners, or gays and lesbians. Some critics sought to expose the disciplines as bastions of authority and privilege. Inspired by Foucault, some would point to the double meaning of discipline to underscore the entanglements of knowledge organization and the disciplining institutions of modern society. "Discipline and Publish" might seem to be the academy's guiding ethos, judged from this perspective. Still others were motivated by critical theory, especially the antifoundationalist thought stemming from France in the 1960s, to charge the disciplines with masking the made-up, constructed nature of knowledge. Hence, deconstructionist Michael Ryan insisted that present disciplinary boundaries conceal the "relationality" of allegedly separate undertakings and prevent recognition that the disciplines are "nothing 'in themselves' and that they constitute each other as mutually interdependent determinations or differentiations of a complex system of heterogeneous forces." In a similar vein, S. P. Mohanty called for scholars to "suspend the process of this continuity, to question the self-evidence of meanings by invoking the radical—but determining—alterities that disrupt our . . . discourses of knowledge."[9] The radical critique of the disciplines generated a lot of heat and, at its upper register, the hope that enough heat might melt the disciplines into one. Though that notion had been largely repudiated by the 1990s, subsequent commentators could readily recall the utopianism, idealism, and even "quasireligious and quasicommunal imagery" that it could inspire.[10] Of course, the experimental spirit opened a period of interdisciplinary initiatives led by university administrations responsive, sometimes, perhaps, to faculty and student demands, but also eager to manage diversity on campus, maximize efficiency, tack on further criteria in hirings, weaken the autonomous power of faculty by regrouping resources and people outside the redoubts of the established disciplines, and enhance prestige by creating high-profile centers or by headhunting prominent senior academics ostensibly capable of integrating knowledge across the traditional disciplines. Clearly, this mix of interests and motives persists, although interdisciplinarity is hardly the dominant educational paradigm in the twenty-first century in light of evidence of the ongoing power of the disciplines.[11]

The widespread challenge to the disciplinary structures and hierarchies of the university in the wake of the 1960s formed the general backdrop for the second important moment of reflection upon intellectual history and interdisciplinarity, while the more specific circumstances were a feeling that the history of ideas was suffering an internal crisis of methods and rationale, even as the rise of social history posed an external threat to the allegedly elitist and idealist orientation of intellectual history. In this atmosphere, for example, the Renaissance intellectual historian William Bouwsma joined the chorus urging historians en masse to make an "anthropological turn." Based on that hoped-for convergence, he foresaw a great unification of the diverse fields of history, including the history of ideas, into the one great plot of the history of meaning.[12] More influentially, both Hayden White and Dominick LaCapra urged intellectual historians to open themselves up to the literary disciplines, to learn from them that even discursive texts may be read in terms of structure, narrative, rhetoric, and tropes that are not merely incidental but at least partly constitutive of meaning and argument. Lovejoy's interdisciplinary vision rested on a claim that behind surface differences, many disciplines share the same objects—unit-ideas—while LaCapra's and White's rested on the hope that method—in other words, critical theory, and more specifically, French structuralist and poststructuralist theory—might renovate the practices of intellectual history.

The critical and inventive currents within intellectual history epitomized by White and LaCapra were not insensitive to the radical implications of the critique of disciplinarity. Interestingly, in the landmark volume *Modern European Intellectual History: Reappraisals and New Perspectives*, edited by Dominick LaCapra and Steven L. Kaplan, the word "interdisciplinary" makes only one appearance, and then to describe struggles between, rather than unions of, disciplines.[13] Yet the spirit of radical interdisciplinarity breathes in various essays in the volume, for example, in Mark Poster's discussion of Foucault, whose effort to revise the nature of intellectual history was, according to Poster, motivated by its "cultural and ultimately political implications."[14] It is certainly a guiding impulse in LaCapra's own contribution, which acknowledges that a "territorial impera- tive" is at stake in questioning intellectual history. LaCapra rejects the desire to defend a "specious autonomy for intellectual history within historiography or within the disciplines in general," and instead he opts to describe the "subdisci- pline of intellectual history" as "in important respects transdisciplinary."[15]

At the end of the 1980s, LaCapra succinctly articulated the premises of the maximalist version of interdisciplinarity when he claimed of efforts to dismantle the old and give rise to new discursive and practical formations, that, "To be genuinely provocative, such a multigeneric or hybridized activity must address significant problems that are not coterminous with, and may even be poorly housed within, existing disciplines and departments—problems such as the very relations between knowledge and critical theory, history and criticism, or texts and contexts. In this sense the daunting task becomes one of rearticulating disciplines or even departments around problem areas in a displaced and refor- mulated frame of reference." Somewhat ruefully, LaCapra immediately noted that, "In this respect, it is fairly obvious, we are more advanced on the discur- sive level than on the institutional."[16]

Yet some disciplines were more ready than others to advance on both levels, perhaps none more so than English, which embraced theory and recre- ated itself as a form of cultural studies by gravitating toward new objects, methods, and heuristic models, even as its traditional literary objects and its conventional modes of analysis began to lose traction in the academy and in culture more broadly. Already by 1992, Stephen Greenblatt and Giles Gunn could speak of several decades of "methodological and interdisciplinary initia- tives" that had transformed literary studies: "deconstruction, cultural materi- alism, gender studies, new historicism."[17] Ten years later, a literary scholar could relate that a colleague told him that "he could no longer imagine teaching literature in any context other than cultural studies—that is, in a setting in which the literary text was at most an illustration of an ideological, historical, or theoretical theme, no different from any other cultural manifestation."[18]

Even as the historical discipline participated in the interdisciplinary reshuf- fling of knowledge in the 1970s and 1980s, it proved almost fully immune to the radical forces remaking literary studies largely by evacuating the discipline of its traditional objects. Indeed, Sarah Maza is right when she remarks that "the social sciences—political science, sociology, cultural anthropology—are generally considered 'safe' interdisciplines for a historian, while the main- stream of the profession reacts with suspicion to literary and other critical the- ories applied to history."[19] In fact, even intellectual historians remained largely unmoved by the allure of radical interdisciplinarity. Of course, intellectual historians could and did play an important role in challenging seemingly natural borders by contributing new histories of the various disciplines, including of History itself, histories that were no longer confirmational narratives offered from within the respective disciplines, but rather histories that emphasized contingent acts of inclusion and exclusion, collusions with authority, deployments of social status and cultural capital, and so on. Ironically, such critical histories performed more or less confident acts of historicization, so that even as they exposed the constructedness of the disciplines, they tended to reaffirm the power of history as a disciplinary practice. As for an interdisciplinarity inspired by literary theory, Donald Kelley, then editor of *Journal of the History of Ideas*, spoke for many intellectual historians when he warned against the "enticements of postmodern theories and the siren song of 'cultural criticism'" and called the wayward back to "their proper work and their own traditions— which are not as negligible nor as disposable as enthusiasts for recent theories assume."[20]

Intellectual History and the Taxonomies of Interdisciplinarity

Social scientists and other scholars exploring the phenomenon of interdisciplinary study have generated numerous taxonomies, with one of the most influential stemming from an international conference sponsored in part by the Organization for Economic Cooperation and Development in 1970. In the publication that followed in 1972, Guy Michaud opened by distinguishing interdisciplinarity from several other related concepts: discipline, multidisciplinarity, pluridisciplinarity, and transdisciplinarity. Interdisciplinary, Michaud defined as "an adjective describing the *interaction* among two or more different disciplines. This interaction may range from simple communication of ideas to the mutual integration of organizing *concepts, methodology, procedures, epistemology, terminology . . . and data*."[21] From there, taxonomies have gone on to parse interdisciplinarity into myriad forms. Close examination of these efforts would likely yield diminishing returns; but as one of the leading experts in interdisciplinary studies, Julie Klein Thompson, usefully diagrams, the taxonomies typically spread out along several lines of continua that signal degrees of integration, interaction, and collaboration: from partial integration to full integration; from "methodological" interdisciplinarity aimed at improving results to "theoretical" interdisciplinarity aimed at building comprehensive general views, epistemological forms, and conceptual frameworks; from "bridge building" to "restructuring"; from "instrumental" uses of interdisciplinarity in the name of problem-solving to "critical" interdisciplinarity that interrogates the structures of knowledge and education with the goal of transformation.[22] The moment one moves from social science to humanistic literature on inter- disciplinarity, the general refrain shifts to the impossibility of firm, fixed, pre- cise definitions and the lack of agreement among scholars as to what actually constitutes interdisciplinary work. Of course, in outlining continua, Klein is doing nothing other than acknowledging the complexity of claims, activities, and structures that have evolved around the idea of interdisciplinarity.

The difficulty of defining interdisciplinarity is greatly compounded the mo- ment one turns the lens upon the disciplines themselves. Much of the militant interdisciplinary rhetoric of 1960s, 1970s, and 1980s depended not only on vilifying the disciplines, but also on setting up the disciplines as monolithic foils, which hardened into rigid, thing-like entities after their initial birth in contingent circumstances. Disciplines lend themselves quite readily to general definition: the academy, writes Johan Heilbron, is organized into "structures of judgment and authority which are founded on a disciplinary division of labor. This division of labor is an institutional arrangement, inseparably consisting of cognitive and social structures, that is of fairly coherent sets of concepts, ques- tions, references, and methods, and a corresponding social order of acknowl- edged specialists in departments, committees, and professional associations."[23] Despite the precision of such initial definitions, the skeptical interrogation of the history and cognitive foundations of the disciplines has sensitized us to the complex makeup of the disciplines themselves. Commentators like Bruno Latour and Heilbron warn that the stabilities of disciplines are frequently over- stated and idealized.[24] Behind homogenizing labels are heterogeneous practices and intellectual traditions.

Considered in this way, the peripheries of disciplines may be less like clear boundaries than transition zones.[25] Even the image of periphery still suggests that the disciplines have readily identifiable cores, whereas some sociologists of science would urge us to think of a discipline as a "cluster of specialties." As Willy Østreng suggests, a discipline would thus be a "multidimensional net- work in which it is difficult to identify a pure core that is independent from other disciplines."[26] In a particularly compelling image, Irene Dölling and Sabine Hark imagine disciplines "less constituted around a core than orga- nized like knots in a weblike structure."[27] Perhaps the most useful way of assessing disciplines is once again to identify a number of intersecting conti- nua. Klein proposes several: from "restricted sciences" that are highly specific in subject and precision to "configurational sciences" such as social and life sciences; from "consensual" to "nonconsensual" fields; from "highly codified fields" like mathematics and the natural sciences to "less codified fields" such as the social sciences and especially the humanities; from "high-paradigm fields" such as physics and chemistry to "low-paradigm fields" such as sociology and political science.[28]

Proclamations that we inhabit a postdisciplinary world seem grossly inflated. Disciplines remain the core organizational principle of the modern university. They do most of the training, teaching, and hiring; they serve as gatekeepers, taskmasters, and, sometimes still, police. There remain in each and every discipline members who are quite confident that they know exactly what the essence of their discipline is. The power of disciplinarity is evident in the many instances where bold interdisciplinary initiatives eventually seem to be recolonized by a disciplinary logic.[29] Moreover, as numerous commentators remark, interdisciplinarity is a legible concept only because there are disciplines; a situation where there was only interdisciplinarity would render the word and concept meaningless. After all, the prefix "inter" carries an ambiguity, insofar as it simultaneously suggests relation *and* division. Still further, skills learned within disciplines remain crucial, though not exclusive preconditions for interdisciplinary work. "Disciplinary practice," writes Lynn Hunt, "with all its connotations of rigorous training, supervision of conduct, and potential for censure, forms the basis for learning between disciplines as well as within them." The best interdisciplinary work, she maintains, "produces its effects back in the various disciplines that it crosses rather than creating an altogether new and different interstitial space." Hunt, a historian not known to shy away from interdisciplinary ventures, insists that we should understand interdisciplinarity less as union, than as agon, with disciplinary identity—even with its negative connotations—serving as an important dimension in the ongoing "dialogue and negotiation of interdisciplinarity."[30]

Reflections such as Hunt's, dating from the mid-1990s, are indicative of the sober retreat from the more utopian versions of interdisciplinarity. Still, even with full acknowledgment of the ongoing power and even, in part, desirability of disciplines, it seems fair to say that the disciplines of the humanities and social sciences now exist self-consciously on a mobile continuum between strong and weak disciplinarity. Intellectual historians' frequent claim that theirs is an "intrinsically" or "inherently" interdisciplinary undertaking is thus in itself not a very revealing claim in an academic setting where almost any scholar might say the same of his or her scholarly practice. Clearly, in the first instance, intellectual history's claim for interdisciplinarity rests on the broad scope of its undertaking, spread as it is across the domains of human thought and culture. Its key (though not exclusive) set of "objects" is comprised of thinkers and their texts. These objects often transcend any disciplinary boundary, as LaCapra emphasized when he claimed that "no discipline has the imperial right of dominion over a Freud, Marx, Nietzsche, or Joyce."[31] Invert that remark, and one can also say with equal accuracy that the thought of a Freud, Marx, Nietzsche, or Joyce implicates a wide range of human concerns in the present, and those concerns have found multiple residences in the recognized disciplines.[32]

Lovejoy had already recognized this, but as we saw, he then went on to conceive interdisciplinarity as, in fact, metadisciplinarity, which meant that he expected to find one standard behind the diverse manifestations of a unit-idea tracked through the disciplines. By contrast, contemporary humanistic interdisciplinarity must be just as aware of the differences as the commonalities among the disciplines. Hence, to recognize that intellectual history shares sets of objects with various disciplines obligates the intellectual historian to acknowledge that those disciplines typically have different methods and, even more important, significantly different problems and goals. In certain cases, these differences can go so far that one scarcely recognizes the "object" that is ostensibly shared. "My Hegel is not your Hegel," is an unspoken thought that may well occur to both the intellectual historian and the philosopher halfway through a chat. Yet intellectual historians and philosophers, or political theorists, literary scholars, or social scientists can and do talk with each other. The best of these conversations occur when both sides have learned something of the other's language. Clearly, the degree to which one masters the other's field will determine whether the ensuing conversation is in pidgin or in Creole. Productive communication between disciplines also requires a sense—a sense going deeper, perhaps, than mere acquisition of some of the technical terms and precepts of the other—of what constitutes a "problem" for the other: Isaiah Berlin's comment that an intellectual historian will get nowhere if she does not understand what a philosophical problem is may be generalized to all the territories into which intellectual historians venture.

Of course, the need to learn something of another discipline's language, its evaluative strategies, and its goals is a prerequisite for any sort of interdisciplinary work. However, it might be that intellectual history faces a particularly interesting version of this challenge insofar as the "objects" it shares with other disciplines may be more than simply the objects of *study*. In many cases, these objects may also be constitutive elements in the self-understanding of the practitioner of that other discipline, as when a philosopher shapes her sense of the life of philosophy—its goals, problems, and prospects—through intense interaction with a past figure or set of figures who in another disciplinary setting might serve as more distanced objects of historical understanding. That different dynamic can make for two quite differently curved hermeneutical circles. Insofar as intellectual historians do not study only explicitly articulated ideas, but may also direct their attention to background conditions of intelligibility and more or less unarticulated assumptions that at their farthest remove form "mentalities," they may find themselves excavating what amounts to the *unconscious* of other disciplines. In either scenario, the fact that the intellectual historian studies objects that frequently are constitutive elements of another discipline's self-identity calls for particularly delicate and complicated negotiations that may not be demanded when, for example, a political historian and a political scientist discuss the best ways to think about the dynamics of electoral politics.

Again and again, the humanistic literature on interdisciplinarity emphasizes conversation. For the anthropologist Renato Rosaldo, who offers one of the best discussions of interdisciplinarity in the humanities, interdisciplinarity is not a division of labor, a view that would accord with the technocratic logic of bureaucrats and administrators, but rather it is a conversation. By this measure, Rosaldo writes, "My criterion for the outer boundaries of interdisciplinarity is the impossibility of significant dialogue."[33] Such dialogue thrives particularly well in interstitial spaces, like the informal seminar and the reading group (though, of course, the most common interstitial space of all is the scholar's private study, where the dialogue is interiorized as textual encounter). Intellectual history is clearly part of such a dialogue, but as an interlocutor and not as the space itself.

To say this is to qualify the "intrinsically" interdisciplinary nature of intellectual history. Measured by the continua discussed by Klein, intellectual history is a form of *weak* interdisciplinarity. It shares objects with a staggering array of disciplines; but even though it must be sensitive to the methods, problems, and, indeed, the *habitus* of those disciplines, it does not share them. Rather, it brings to bear on their objects its own set of interests in historical explanation and its own set of cognitive tools: various possible strategies of contextualization and, it must not be forgotten, techniques of narration, for after all, intellectual historians are, like other historically-minded scholars, interested in tracing and accounting for change over time.

If intellectual history has a weak interdisciplinarity, then conversely, it lacks some of the robust markers of disciplinary identity measured by the standards of institutional frameworks. With just a few exceptions in England and continental Europe, there are no departments of intellectual history, history of political thought, or history of ideas. Some initiatives, such as the International Society for Intellectual History, have tried to establish disciplinary committees and professional associations, but typically, the intellectual historian finds himself under the sway of the institutions, organizations, and standards of a larger discipline—in the American context, most frequently history. Yet intellectual historians in America have always stood in an eccentric relationship to what might be identified as core or classic concerns of their colleagues. If a historian like Lynn Hunt speaks with considerable confidence of carrying the fruits of her interdisciplinary forays back to her home discipline, the intellectual historian returns to a somewhat different place. If intellectual historians share their historical colleagues' concern with large social and political processes, they also share the interest of colleagues in fields like literary studies, philosophy, and art history in singular cultural objects that call for appropriate interpretive strategies. Where many historians would readily agree to the utility of intellectual history in contributing to the understanding of historical processes, the intellectual historian may see her inquiries leading just as much to an understanding of a certain set of cultural objects. This object-centered hermeneutical concern inevitably places intellectual historians at some distance from the disciplinary identity of historians, even as their concern with context and narrative creates a different imperative than is typically at the core of the object-centered disciplines.

Indeed, intellectual history may best be characterized as a scholarly practice where weak interdisciplinarity intersects with weak disciplinarity. This may not sound like a particularly uplifting characterization, but it is meant as such. After all, the weakness here does not refer to the quality or value of the work, but rather to its lack of firm location within the present epistemological and institutional organization of the disciplines. Far from being a detriment, it is perhaps one of intellectual history's greatest strengths that it does not know for certain where it stands. Judith Butler has asked of her own style of border-crossing theoretical work in relation to the philosophical discipline, "Could it be that not knowing for sure what should and should not be acknowledged as philosophy has itself a certain philosophical value?"[34] The same may be asked of intellectual history, though Butler's productive uncertainty extends more broadly to what should and should not be acknowledged as belonging to a range of different disciplines, history included.

Perhaps a more uplifting way to express this involves moving away from a metaphor of *non-place* to one of *place* by invoking David Downes's description of criminology as a "rendezvous discipline." As with Downes's understanding of his own discipline, intellectual history is a discipline where other disciplines meet, and its liveliness and potential intellectual interest emerge from its position at a busy intersection of a wide range of scholars and scholarship from other disciplines.[35] What presides over this intersection is not exclusively disciplinary history, for, in fact, the various disciplines generate their own forms of historical reflexivity, but rather, historical-mindedness as a temperament and historical explanation as an imperative of understanding. This historical-mindedness generates fertile overlaps in interests and opens toward contacts that remain within the bounds of significant dialogue, even as they do not fully override the specificity of discrete disciplinary concerns, which ultimately preserve the ambiguity of union and division entailed in the modifier *inter*-disciplinary.

Two Cheers for Eclecticism

While almost every contemporary academic heralds interdisciplinarity in one form or another, its virtues are shadowed by a fear of dilettantism. According to such worries, true interdisciplinary work, done well, must take seriously the methods and means of the other. Not to do so threatens eclecticism. "There is and will continue to be a vast difference between trendy eclecticism and the hard work of a well-practiced interdisciplinarity," writes historian Joan Landes of a worry that crops up frequently in the literature. Landes concedes almost immediately that "not everything that passes for eclecticism is unhealthy, and we may risk more by completely sanctioning eclecticism than letting it proceed."[36] Still, the "inherently" interdisciplinary nature of intellectual history—particularly if it is accurately characterized as a *weak* form of interdisciplinarity—would seem to make concerns about eclecticism particularly warranted, although one might hope that the potential fruitfulness of intellectual history's eclecticism would earn it the kind of liberal allowance granted by Landes. Yet, beyond a set of generalized anxieties that any and all interdisciplinary undertaking may produce what Neil Smelser denounces as "watered-down, eclectic accounts," the current situation of intellectual history raises more specific questions about eclecticism that need to be addressed.[37]

Returning a final time to Dominick LaCapra's influential essay from the early 1980s, the vehicle of his interdisciplinarity is theory. Theoretical arguments, he tells us, are particularly urgent in times of transition.[38] Just a few years later, he wrote that "we seem to be in a kind of lull—a not unprecedented epigonal position of 'no longer and not yet.'"[39] The period of transition had, evidently, not yet ended. At the same time, by the end of the 1980s, many were speaking of the *end* of theory; by the close of the 1990s, it had become a commonplace to say that ours is a *post-theoretical* age.[40] Intellectual history never completed a transition to the full and robust future envisioned by LaCapra. But it would be foolish to deny the profound impact of the theoretical debates of the 1980s, even if their glowing passions are now fading embers. Intellectual historians are now sensitized to the epistemological issues of the linguistic turn, even if its most extreme claims for the death of the author, the subject as language-effect, and so on have given way to a more moderate awareness that the search for language's referential truth must be balanced against the density of language itself, the attempt to understand authorial intention weighed against the power of discourse to precede and exceed the intended meaning of any speaker. Moreover, the boundaries of inquiry have been reshuffled to a large extent; very few intellectual historians would maintain that the objects of their study exist outside of innumerable exchanges with political, social, and cultural objects and vectors of force. The basic postulate that there is no pristine realm of thought is a given. If theoretical debates helped move intellectual history to its present situation, no particular theoretical perspective or specific methodology dominates current practice. Even if intellectual historians accepts that empirical research can never be divorced from theoretical self-consciousness, in the present situation, questions of theory and method seem more bound to the exigencies of specific research projects than to antagonistically formulated epistemologies or social ontologies.

At the opening of the twenty-first century, intellectual historians are in a period of eclecticism. Such a declaration must immediately confront deep-rooted and age-old charges that eclecticism is watered-down and complacent. Eclecticism as a stated principle has typically been met with criticism, if not outright contempt. Blaise Pascal lamented the muddle of Montaigne's eclectic thought; the socialist Pierre Leroux denounced Victor Cousin's *Eclecticisme* as a "bastard philosophy"; and recently, Joan Scott has declared herself "Against Eclecticism." The criticism is usually either epistemological confusion or political quietism. Is it possible to envision a more critically robust concept of eclecticism? This is not the place to launch into a full-scale answer to that question, but let me register a few points for eclecticism.

To begin with, consider the history of intellectual history Donald Kelley has outlined in his magisterial *Descent of Ideas*. Kelley shows that some form of self-conscious historicization is as old as the activity of formal thought itself; but he argues specifically that the practice of the history of ideas really begins to emerge in early modern polyhistorians and eclectic philosophers and then in eclectics like Victor Cousin.[41] The eclectic impulse carried into twentieth-century practices, where the acknowledged impurity of the objects of intellectual historical inquiry seems to make it impossible to rely on one methodological framework or insist upon a sharply defined philosophical position. Intellectual historians' commitment to some form of contextualism reinforces the call for an eclectic sensibility. Contextualization is a deceptively straightforward mandate that conceals a range of possible approaches, a complexity that already suggests a certain need for eclecticism. Yet, indispensable as contextualism is to the intellectual historian, it is not the only valuable analytic tool; nor is contextualism the monopoly of any one methodology. Here, Peter Burke is on firm ground when he suggests that contexualism is less a methodology than a perspective, or, we might say, a kind of *habitus* or attitude. As Burke writes, "It is obviously paradoxical to speak about a "contextual method" for studying one text, object, or situation after another, regardless of differences or circumstances."[42]

An eclectic attitude is necessary for making any headway whatsoever on the question of the evident gap between historicist contextualism and contemporary normative theorizing in the disciplines with which intellectual history has so much intercourse. Let me address this matter in a field where it is acutely posed, the history of political thought. In the syllabus of errors with which Quentin Skinner launched an extremely influential new approach to the study of the history of political thought in the late 1960s, presentism was a cardinal sin. Skinner and his followers evolved around a strict attempt to understand past political texts only in relation to their time and the controversies and languages that shaped authorial intentions. More recently, however, Skinner has adjusted his position and insisted that the history of political thought can contribute to contemporary critical theory. He claims of the contextualist study of political ideas that it "offers us an additional means of reflecting on what we believe, and thus of strengthening our present beliefs by way of testing them against alternative possibilities."[43] In a sharp rebuke to Skinner, philosopher Robert Lamb has argued that "there is no necessary connection between thinking about history or politics contextually on the one hand and thinking critically in the way Skinner, [Kari] Palonen and [James] Tully would like us to." Lamb goes on to insist that "the relationship between contextualism and the sorts of political claims Skinner wishes to make is at best a contingent one."[44] But if this relationship is contingent, then it stands to reason that the *non-relationship* of contextualism and critical thinking is also contingent. In the end, much hangs on Lamb's insistence on using the phrase "necessary connection." Why is it that so many philosophers have believed that *necessary* connections are their proper bailiwick, while *contingent* connections are somehow of a lower order? Why believe that politics or the critical vocabulary we employ to describe politics might be answerable to a logician's demand for *necessary* connections? The connection between historical understanding and contemporary critique can never be *necessary* or *unitary*. Like all things political, it must be argued.

What of the age-old charge of eclectic complacency? In her essay "Against Eclecticism," Joan Scott sees the scaling down of conflict and fundamental debate in the aftermath of the age of theory as a symptom of an onset of quietism and conservatism. Our present eclectic moment, she argues, resembles the period of the French Restoration, when Victor Cousin's tepid eclecticism became the official ideology of the *juste milieu*. Yet the historical analogy seems only partly right. If contemporary conservative forces have latched onto eclecticism to *neutralize* debate, then the kind of rigorous, relentless interrogation that she celebrates in Jacques Derrida prompts its own form of eclecticism. After all, eclecticism has deep roots in the skeptical tradition. We should recall this connection to skepticism, even if we also acknowledge that it is indeed a fine line separating eclecticism from syncretism, what Donald Kelley calls the "eclectic search for truth" from the "syncretistic desire for peace."[45]

As Pierre Force reminds us in a superb discussion of Montaigne and eclecticism, historians of ancient thought distinguish between Pyrrhonian skepticism and Academic skepticism: Pyrrhonian skepticism practiced the "suspension of judgment in order to achieve a state of indifference that brought inner tranquility," whereas the Academic skeptic combined "suspension of judgment with an inquisitive ('zetetic') posture. The duty of the Academic Skeptic (as described for instance in Cicero's *Academica*) was to keep searching for truth even while knowing that truth was probably out of reach. In addition, the Academic Skeptic would exercise *libertas philosophandi* by picking and choosing among various philosophical schools and embracing some opinions on a provisional basis if they seemed more plausible."[46] The Skeptic practiced philosophy by examining the thought of other, non-Skeptical philosophers. As Force suggests, this was a "serious and reasoned form of eclecticism." It was neither facile nor complacent.[47]

Such a sensibility does not lead one to believe that all positions are equally valid, nor that all positions are commensurable. But it does reject the belief that one true method exists or awaits our discovery. Measured against this standard, Victor Cousin's officially approved "Eclecticism" might be seen less as the embodiment of the eclectic spirit than its perversion. Likewise, whatever the accuracy of Joan Scott's portrayal of a present-day eclecticism aimed at establishing a new *juste milieu*, then the deconstructionist's willingness to interrogate each and every foundational claim must surely point us to a serious and reasoned skepticism toward the hegemonic claims of each and every system, school, or intellectual master. Ultimately, as Pierre Force argues of Montaigne, the value of the eclectic is that she is ready to speak freely and openly to everyone. If this is the true value of the eclectic, then eclecticism is not a threat, but a prerequisite to the ideal of interdisciplinary conversation in the humanities. Intellectual history takes its important place in that conversation not because it is intrinsically interdisciplinary, but because, as a rendezvous discipline, at the intersection of weak interdisciplinarity and weak disciplinarity, it is the eclectic discipline par excellence.

Notes

1. Arthur Lovejoy, *The Great Chain of Being: A Study of the History of an Idea* (Cambridge, MA: Harvard University Press, 1936), 3.

2. Arthur Lovejoy, *Essays in the History of Ideas* (Baltimore: Johns Hopkins Press, 1948), xii–xiii.

3. Arthur Lovejoy, "Reflections on the History of Ideas," *Journal of the History of Ideas* 1, no. 1 (January 1940): 4.

4. Ibid., 8.

5. See Gerald Graff, *Professing Literature: An Institutional History* (Chicago: University of Chicago Press, 1987), 185. Wellek's misgivings find an echo in a recent article by Leo Catana. Catana argues that Lovejoy's concept of "unit-ideas" represents a thinly veiled continuation of the emphasis of nineteenth-century historians of philosophy upon "principles" and "systems." Hence, he writes, "Lovejoy's notion of interdisciplinarity reinforces the ahistorical assumption endorsed by nineteenth-century historians of philosophy, where unit-ideas, the replacement of principles, now constitute the deductive starting point for the content of various disciplines." See Catana, "Lovejoy's Readings of Bruno; or, How Nineteenth-Century History of Philosophy Was 'Transformed' into the History of Ideas," *Journal of the History of Ideas* 71, no. 1 (January 2010): 91–112.

6. Hutchins, cited in Graff, *Professing Literature*, 164–65.

7. See Tim Lacy, "The Lovejovian Roots of Adler's Philosophy of History: Authority, Democracy, Irony, and Paradox in Britannica's *Great Books of the Western World*," *Journal of the History of Ideas* 71, no. 1 (January 2010): 113–37.

8. For a colorful evocation of that period, see Anthony Grafton, "The History of Ideas: Precept and Practice, 1950–2000 and Beyond," *Journal of the History of Ideas* 67, no. 1 (January 2006): 1–2.

9. Ryan and Mohanty are cited in Stanley Fish, "Being Interdisciplinary Is So Very Hard to Do," in *There's No Such Thing as Free Speech, and It's a Good Thing, Too* (New York: Oxford University Press, 1994), 232–33.

10. See Neil J. Smelser, "Interdisciplinarity in Theory and Practice," in *The Dialogical Turn: New Roles for Sociology in the Postdisciplinary Age: Essays in Honor of Donald N. Levine*, ed. Charles Camic and Hans Joas (Lanham, MD: Rowman and Littlefield, 2004), 52; and Tanya Augsburg and Stuart Henry, eds., *The Politics of Interdisciplinary Studies: Essays on Transformations in American Undergraduate Programs* (Jefferson, NC: McFarland, 2009), 228.

11. Ethan Kleinberg, "Interdisciplinary Studies at a Crossroads," *Liberal Education* 94, no. 1 (2008): 6. Where Kleinberg sees the ubiquity of the interdisciplinary ideal, others see rollbacks of specific programs. Consider, for example, the essays in Augsburg and Henry, *Politics of Interdisciplinary Studies*.

12. William Bouwsma, "Intellectual History in the 1980s: From History of Ideas to History of Meaning," *Journal of Interdisciplinary History* 12, no. 2 (Autumn 1981): 279–91.

13. See Roger Chartier, "Intellectual History or Sociocultural History? The French Trajectories," *Modern European Intellectual History: Reappraisals and New Perspectives*, ed.

Dominick LaCapra and Steven L. Kaplan (Ithaca, NY: Cornell University Press, 1982), 15. The volume is now available in digital form, making it possible to conduct this word search.

14. Mark Poster, "The Future According to Foucault: *The Archaeology of Knowledge* and Intellectual History," in LaCapra and Kaplan, *Modern European Intellectual History*, 141.

15. Dominick LaCapra, "Rethinking Intellectual History and Reading Texts," in LaCapra and Kaplan, *Modern European Intellectual History*, 48. First published in *History and Theory* in 1980, LaCapra's essay was also reprinted in LaCapra, *Rethinking Intellectual History: Texts Contexts Language* (Ithaca, NY: Cornell University Press, 1983).

16. Dominick LaCapra, "On the Line: Between History and Criticism," *Profession* 89 (1989): 5.

17. Stephen Greenblatt and Giles B. Gunn, "Introduction," to *Redrawing the Boundaries: The Transformation of English and American Literary Studies* (New York: Modern Language Association of America, 1992), 1.

18. David F. Bell, "A Moratorium on Suspicion?," *PMLA* 117 (2002): 487.

19. Sarah Maza, "Interdisciplinarity: (Why) Is It Still an Issue?," in *Interdisciplinarity; Qu'est-ce que les Lumières?; La reconnaissance au dix-huitième siècle (Studies on Voltaire and the Eighteenth Century)* (Oxford: Voltaire Foundation, 2006): 12, 8.

20. Donald R. Kelley, "What Is Happening to the History of Ideas?," *Journal of the History of Ideas* 51, no. 1 (January–March 1990): 24–25.

21. Guy Michaud, "Introduction," in *Interdisciplinarity: Problems of Teaching and Research in Universities* (Paris: Organization for Economic Cooperation and Development, 1972), 23–26.

22. Julie Thompson Klein, "A Taxonomy of Interdisciplinarity," in *The Oxford Handbook of Interdisciplinarity*, ed. Robert Frodeman et al. (New York: Oxford University Press, 2010), 15–30.

23. Johan Heilbron, "A Regime of Disciplines: Toward a Historical Sociology of Disciplinary Knowledge," in Camic and Joas, *The Dialogical Turn*, 23.

24. Bruno Latour, *Pandora's Hope: Essays on the Reality of Science Studies* (Cambridge: Cambridge University Press, 1999), 296; Heilbron, "Regime of Disciplines," 34–36.

25. Willy Østreng, *Science without Boundaries: Interdisciplinarity in Research, Society, and Politics* (Lanham, MD: University Press of America, 2010), 21.

26. Ibid., 22.

27. Irene Dölling and Sabine Hark, "She Who Speaks Shadows Speaks Truth: Transdisciplinarity in Women's and Gender Studies," *Signs* 25, no. 4 (2000): 1196.

28. Julie Thompson Klein, *Interdisciplinarity: History, Theory, and Practice* (Detroit: Bloodaxe Books, 1990), 104.

29. See, for example, Cindi Katz's lament for Women's Studies, "Disciplining Interdisciplinarity," *Feminist Studies* 27, no. 2 (Summer 2001): 519–25. More broadly, this is the argument of a brilliant and characteristically polemical piece by Fish, "Being Interdisciplinary Is So Very Hard to Do."

30. Lynn Hunt, "The Virtues of Disciplinarity," *Eighteenth-Century Studies* 28, no. 1 (Autumn 1994): 1–7.

31. LaCapra, "Rethinking Intellectual History and Reading Texts," 77.

32. In making this point, I have benefited from a forthcoming interview, Allan Megill and Xupeng Zhang, "Questions on Intellectual History and Its Neighbours," *Rethinking History* 17, no. 3 (2013).

33. Renato Rosaldo, "Reflections on Interdisciplinarity," in *Schools of Thought: Twenty-Five Years of Interpretive Social Science*, ed. Joan W. Scott and Debra Keates (Princeton, NJ: Princeton University Press, 2001), 69.

34. Judith Butler, "Can the 'Other' of Philosophy Speak?," in Scott and Keates, *Schools of Thought*, 53.

35. In a private communication, Downes has confirmed that this formulation originated with him, but he only used it in oral presentation. For one discussion, see Jock Young, "In Praise of Dangerous Thoughts," *Punishment and Society* 5, no. 1 (2003): 97.

36. Joan B. Landes, "Trespassing: Notes from the Boundaries," in *The Interdisciplinary Century: Tensions and Convergences in Eighteenth-Century Art, History, and Literature (Studies on Voltaire and the Eighteenth Century)*, ed. Julia V. Douthwaite and Mary Vidal (Oxford: Voltaire Foundation, 2005): 123.

37. Smelser, "Interdisciplinarity in Theory and Practice," 55.

38. LaCapra, "Rethinking Intellectual History and Reading Texts," 82.

39. Dominick LaCapra, "On the Line," *Profession* 89 (1989): 9.

40. See, for example, Martin McQuillan et al., *Post-Theory: New Directions in Criticism* (Edinburgh: Edinburgh University Press, 1999). I have tried to address some of the issues entailed in the "end" of theory in "Times of Theory: On Writing the History of French Theory," *Journal of the History of Ideas* 71, no. 3 (July 2010): 339–61.

41. Donald R. Kelley, *The Descent of Ideas: The History of Intellectual History* (Aldershot: Ashgate, 2002).

42. Peter Burke, "Context in Context," *Common Knowledge* 8, no. 1 (2002): 173.

43. Quentin Skinner, *Visions of Politics*, vol. 1, *Regarding Method* (Cambridge: Cambridge University Press, 2002), 126–27.

44. Robert Lamb, "Recent Developments in the Thought of Quentin Skinner and the Ambitions of Contextualism," *Journal of the Philosophy of History* 3 (2009): 263–64.

45. Kelley, *Descent of Ideas*, 52.

46. Pierre Force, "Montaigne and the Coherence of Eclecticism," *Journal of the History of Ideas* 70, no. 4 (October 2009): 527.

47. Ibid., 532.

Index

Note: Page numbers in *italics* indicate illustrations.